Jakob Nielsen

Designing Web Usability

New Riders

New Riders Publishing, Indianapolis, Indiana USA

Designing Web Usability: The Practice of Simplicity

© 2000 by New Riders Publishing

International Standard Book Number: 1-56205-810-X

Library of Congress Catalog Card Number: 99-63014

Printed in the United States of America

First Printing: December 1999

03 02 01 00   7 6 5

Interpretation of the printing code: The rightmost double-digit number is the year of the book's printing; the rightmost single-digit number is the number of the book's printing.

Trademarks

Warning and Disclaimer

Publisher
David Dwyer

Associate Publisher
Brad Koch

Executive Editor
Steve Weiss

Development Editor
Jennifer Eberhardt

Indexer
Lisa Stumpf

Reviewers
Michael Chanover
Perry Hewitt

Proofreaders
Bob LaRoche
Linda Seifert

Cover Design
James Tung,
Eric Baker Design
Associates, NY

Interior Design
Elizabeth Keyes

Interior Layout
Kim Scott,
Bumpy Design
www.bumpy.com

Contents at a Glance

Table of Contents

About the Author

Jakob Nielsen, Ph.D. is a User Advocate specializing in web usability and a principal of Nielsen Norman Group (www.nngroup. com), which he co-founded with Dr. Donald A. Norman, former vice president of Apple Research. Until 1998, Dr. Nielsen was a Sun Microsystems Distinguished Engineer and led that company's web usability efforts starting with the original design of SunWeb in early 1994. His previous affiliations include the IBM User Interface Institute, Bell Communications Research, and the Technical University of Denmark. Nielsen is the author and editor of 8 other books and more than 75 research papers on usability engineering, user interface design, and hypertext. He is also a frequent keynote presenter at industry conferences. Nielsen is the founder of the "discount usability engineering" movement for fast and simple ways of improving user interfaces. Nielsen's Alertbox column about web usability has been published on the Internet since 1995 (www.useit.com/alertbox) and currently has about 100,000 readers. He is also the usability columnist for Ziff-Davis Network's *DevHead* and a web design critic for *Internet World* magazine. He holds 46 U.S. patents, mainly on ways to make the Internet easier to use. Dr. Nielsen's website is at www.useit.com: It's text-only and pretty fast.

Author's Acknowledgments

I would like to thank the following for help in writing this book or in my web projects over the years: Franz Aman, Claire Amundsen, Rick Brennan, Bruce Browne, Marsh Chamberlain, Kreta Chandler, Debra Coelho, Steve Davis, Kathy Dickinson, Susan Doel, Meghan Ede, Karin Ellison, Susan Farrell, B.J. Fogg, Jonathan Fox, Michael Fuller, Don Gentner, Steve Gibson, Bob Glass, Rich Gold, Dana Greer, Chris Haaga, Melody Kean Haller, Martin Hardee, Perry Hewitt, Mark Hurst, Luice Hwang, Keith Instone, Matthew Johan, Chris Johnson, Hannah Kain, Wendy Kellogg, Erika Kindlund, Teresa Lau, Rick Levine, Judy Lindberg, Noel Lopez, Michael "Mac" McCarthy, Andrea Mankoski, Peter Merholz, Carl Meske, Rolf Molich, John Morkes, Jim Newton, Donald Norman, Larry Page, Judy Potzler, Bill Prouty, Darcy Provo, Janice Rohn, Victoria Ryan, Darrell Sano, Eric Schmidt, Hassan Schroeder, Hasmig Seropian, Will Snow, Jared Spool, David L. Stewart, Rory Swensen, John Tang, Bruce "Tog" Tognazzini, Nirav Tolia, Jeanie Treichel, Elizabeth Waymire, Ron Wilbur, and Debra Winters.

Also, even though I didn't work on many web projects with them, much of my thinking has been influenced by John M. Carroll, Susan Dumais, Dennis Egan, George Furnas, John Gould, Jim Hollan, Thomas K. Landauer, Mary Beth Rosson, Ben Shneiderman, Dennis Wixon, and Patricia Wright.

Jakob Nielsen

Publisher's Acknowledgements

We'd like to thank Jakob Nielsen, an extraordinary man, for his patience with an, at times, impatient publisher. Thanks also to Hannah Kain for her patience with the publisher as we asked her for an ever-increasing amount of Jakob's time near the end of this project. Thank you both for allowing us into your home and into your lives during the completion of this book.

Kudos as well to Kim Scott for an extraordinary job of turning the vision of a well-designed book into a reality. And special thanks to Jennifer Eberhardt.

A Message from New Riders

Jakob Nielsen is one of the busiest speakers and commentators in the world of high-tech because of his message and the eloquence with which he delivers it. His message is simple—at least on the surface—and is accessible to anyone who will listen (and multitudes do each year): Put USABILITY first. Practice SIMPLICITY.

The challenges and complexities to the 'put usability first' philosophy of design can begin when ideation turns to planning, and planning turns to implementation. The challenges never stop, and Jakob helps you to understand them and enable yourself to make the continual adjustments necessary to survive and prosper in the 'user-first' world of the Web.

The best thing about this book, along with what you'll learn about yourself and others who use the Web (and how to improve the usefulness of your website immeasurably), is that *Designing Web Usability* is flat-out one of the best reads you'll encounter—in technology publishing or elsewhere. Jakob has a gift for communication that enables him to wrap his vision in a lucid, compelling discourse that appeals to academics and lay people, web designers and web users. *Designing Web Usability* holds this broad appeal because Jakob's message makes so much sense, while being masterfully communicated on so many levels.

Who said you can't have fun while expanding your horizons?

New Riders is honored to have worked with Jakob Nielsen over the past two years as he's written and refined *Designing Web Usability: The Practice of Simplicity*. We believe it's been well worth the wait. Let us know what you think…

How to Contact Us

As the reader of this book, *you* are our most important critic and commentator. We value your opinion and want to know what we're doing right, what we could do better, in what areas you'd like to see us publish, and any other words of wisdom you're willing to pass our way.

As the Executive Editor for the Graphics team at New Riders, I welcome your comments. You can fax, email, or write me directly to let me know what you did or didn't like about this book—as well as what we can do to make our books better.

Please note that I cannot help you with technical problems related to the topic of this book, and that due to the high volume of mail I receive, I might not be able to reply to every message.

When you write, please be sure to include this book's title, ISBN, and author, as well as your name and phone or fax number. I will carefully review your comments and share them with the authors and editors who worked on the book.

For any issues directly related to this or other titles:

Email: steve.weiss@newriders.com

Mail: Steve Weiss
          Executive Editor
          Professional Graphics & Design Publishing
          New Riders Publishing
          201 West 103rd Street
          Indianapolis, IN 46290 USA

Visit Our Website: www.newriders.com

On our website you'll find information about our other books, the authors we partner with, book updates and file downloads, promotions, discussion boards for online interaction with other users and with technology experts, and a calendar of trade shows and other professional events with which we'll be involved. We hope to see you around.

Email Us from Our Website

Go to www.newriders.com and click on the Contact link if you

- Have comments or questions about this book
- Have a book proposal or are otherwise interested in writing with New Riders
- Would like us to send you one of our author kits
- Are an expert in a computer topic or technology and are interested in being a reviewer or technical editor
- Want to find a distributor for our titles in your area
- Are an educator/instructor who wishes to preview New Riders books for classroom use.

Call Us or Fax Us

You can reach us toll-free at (800) 571-5840 + 9 + 3567. Ask for New Riders. If outside the USA, please call 1-317-581-3500. Ask for New Riders.

You can fax us at 317-581-4663, Attention: New Riders.

Preface

"Enough, already, Jakob. Isn't it self-defeating to publish on dead trees when you are writing about the Web?"

I am sure that a lot of readers will be asking this question, so let me answer it up front.

I am a usability expert, so my choice of medium is governed by what is most usable for a given communications goal and not by what is most in fashion at any given time. Of course, the Web is a great communications medium (that's why I am writing about it), and it is well suited for shorter documents with many links (I have many such pages on my website, www.useit.com). The Web is *not* good for very long documents that need to present a steadily progressing argument.

If you really want to learn about a topic, it is still better to do so by reading a coherent, in-depth treatment of the topic written from a single perspective than to bounce among multiple shorter ideas and different perspectives. In other words, a book is still better than the Web for the goal I want to achieve: to get readers to understand the usability perspective of web design.

Three conditions would have to happen for me to give up writing books:

- Computer screens must improve to the point where reading from screens is as fast and as pleasant as reading from paper. I am confident that this will happen around the year 2002 for high-end computers and 2007 for mainstream computers, because such screens have already been demonstrated in the lab.
- Web browsing user interfaces must improve enough that it is as easy to navigate the Web as it is to leaf through the pages of a book. I am more skeptical on this count because browser vendors currently seem to invest more efforts on useless multimedia and advertising schemes than on helping users navigate; but even so, we might get useful browsers by the year 2003.
- Readers and writers must both adjust to non-linear information spaces, that is, how to *write* in ways that utilize hypertext and how to *read* without the safety of mind that comes from making no decisions beyond turning the page. Nothing but time and plenty of experience and exposure to well-crafted hypertexts will make this change happen. Unfortunately, there is a chicken-and-egg problem in that well-crafted hypertexts will not happen until good writers have become skilled in writing hypertext. I expect good hypertext writing to happen in greater quantities as the Web matures, around the year 2001, and the emphasis

A printed book allows the benefit of sidebars and other two-dimensional layouts that are not available on a web page, which is still essentially a one-dimensional scroll—just like the Egyptians knew and loved. In a book it is possible to place illustrations and captions in ways that supplement the text better than can be done on the Web. I can't take credit for the page design in this book, but I hope you find it useful.

irrevocably changes from dazzling people with the novelty of a new medium to satisfying user needs. Maybe four years later, in the year 2005, the majority of users will have gained sufficient experience in dealing with hypertext.

Comparing these three bullets leads to the conclusion that hardware technology is the constraining factor and that we have to wait until approximately the year 2007 for books to go away and be fully replaced with online information. Legacy publishers be warned: This *will* happen.

Guide to This Book

The book you are reading now is the first of two books on the subject of web usability. I chose to publish two books for two reasons. First, a book does no good if nobody reads it, and I have seen fat volumes sit on the shelf and gather dust too frequently to want to write one myself. A two-inch-thick tome on how to make Excel draw pie charts intimidates people from ever opening the book. They may feel good about owning such detailed wisdom, but they will not *read* it. Two relatively slim volumes stand a much better chance of being read than a single fat one.

Second, it may not be necessary for all readers to read both books because the different books focus on different aspects of web usability. Having more narrowly focused volumes makes the book more affordable for students and others who only need some of the information. No need to pay extra for a huge publication, half of which you don't need.

These two books attack the problem of usable web design from two angles. This first one is about the "what" of good websites, and the second book is about the "how." Everybody always wants to know the solution right away, so that's what I have concentrated on here. This book explains what is known about the properties of easy-to-use websites. Short preview: Relish simplicity, and focus on the users' goals rather than glitzy design.

This first chapter covers the main areas of web design: page design, content design, and the design of the overall site architecture. The subsequent chapters cover special issues that supplement the general basics with specific findings for intranets, users with disabilities, and international users. Finally, this volume ends with a view toward the future of the Internet and new developments on the Web.

The second book will cover the "how" of web usability and explain the methodologies that were used to derive the findings that are presented here in the first book. The impatient reader who just wants to know the facts can read this one. If you design sites that follow the rules I lay out here, your sites will definitely be among the easiest to use on the Internet. But to design really great sites requires additional insights that are specific to your project and your customers and their needs. There is no way around collecting additional usability data in your own project. How to do so will be explained in the second book.

Jakob Nielsen
Mountain View, California

1 Introduction: Why Web Usability?

Usability rules the Web. Simply stated, if the customer can't find a product, then he or she will not buy it.

The Web is the ultimate customer-empowering environment. He or she who clicks the mouse gets to decide *everything*. It is so easy to go elsewhere; all the competitors in the world are but a mouseclick away.

With about 10 million sites on the Web in January 2000 (and about 25 million by the end of the year and a hundred million by 2002), users have more choices than ever. Why should they waste their time on anything that is confusing, slow, or that doesn't satisfy their needs?

Why, indeed?

As a result of this overwhelming choice and the ease of going elsewhere, web users exhibit a remarkable impatience and insistence on instant gratification. If they can't figure out how to use a website in a minute or so, they conclude that it won't be worth their time. And they leave.

Usability has assumed a much greater importance in the Internet economy than it has in the past.

Usability has assumed a much greater importance in the Internet economy than it has in the past. In traditional physical product development, customers did not get to experience the usability of the product until *after* they had already bought and paid for it. Say, for example, you buy a VCR and discover that it's difficult to set the clock and that you cannot figure out how to program the taping of your favorite shows. Tough luck—the manufacturer is laughing all the way to the bank.

The software industry has slightly more motivation than the physical product industry to improve usability. For software, users typically have access to a support center they can call when experiencing problems. Such support calls are very expensive to handle (estimates range from $30 to $100 per call, depending on the complexity of the software), and more than half of the calls are due to poor usability. Unfortunately, the cost of running the support center is usually charged to a different account than the cost of improving usability, so the individual development managers are not overly motivated to ship great user interfaces. Shipping on time is what pays the big bonuses; saving money on the support department's budget next year doesn't.

The Web reverses the picture. Now, users experience the usability of a site *before* they have committed to using it and *before* they have spent any money on potential purchases.

The equation is simple:

- In product design and software design, customers pay first and experience usability later.

- On the Web, users experience usability first and pay later.

Very clear why usability is more important for web design.

Art Versus Engineering

There are essentially two basic approaches to design: the artistic ideal of expressing yourself and the engineering ideal of solving a problem for a customer. This book is firmly on the side of engineering. While I acknowledge that there is a need for art, fun, and a general good time on the Web, I believe that the main goal of most web projects should be to make it easy for customers to perform useful tasks.

I describe a very systematic approach to web design, with a sequence of methods anybody can use to discover users' needs and any difficulties they may be having using the site. Treating a web project as a software development project will make it easier to meet schedules and to ensure the quality of the site. In particular, pervasive application of usability engineering methodology throughout your web project will lead to continuous improvement of the site, both with respect to the initial design and subsequent redesigns.

You will find many rules, principles, guidelines, and methods in this book. They all derive from experience of what actually works when real users try to perform real tasks on the Web. Ever since the early years of the Web, I have observed hundreds of users using hundreds of websites—plus, of course, hundreds of other users using many different types of online information systems and hypertext designs since the early 1980s.

I do not claim that every last one of my teachings has to be followed slavishly to the letter in every project. The skilled professional knows when to follow the rules and when to bend a rule or even break it. You must know the rules in the first place before you can consider whether it might improve a specific project to deviate from some of them. Also, a fundamental guiding principle for rule-breaking is that you only do so when you have a really good reason to do so.

The Competitive Bar Is High

On the Web, your competition is not limited to the other companies in your industry. With all the other millions of sites out there, you are in competition for the users' time and attention, and web users get their expectations for great usability from the very best of all these other sites. The thinking goes, "If I can get this great service when buying a $5 paperback book, why can't I get good online service when I spend thousands of dollars with you?" Very good question, by the way.

The engineering approach has one major benefit: When you are in doubt about whether to choose one design or another, you can pose an empirical question that can be resolved by gathering real data from your customers. Can people find information faster with design A or design B? Do users rate design A or design B best on a standard customer-satisfaction questionnaire? Pick the one that gets the highest scores and not the one you personally like the best.

Of course, the scientific method can only take you so far. There is still a need for inspiration and creativity in design. A simple usability engineering method that anybody can follow can tell you that users have problems navigating your site or that everybody overlooks the search button on your home page. Taking these results and coming up with a better navigation scheme or a better look or placement of the search button is not simply a matter of following a series of easy steps. You also need some design inspiration to strike. However, remember that innovation is 10 percent inspiration and 90 percent perspiration. The way you get *appropriate* design ideas (and not just ideas for cool designs that nobody can use) is to watch users and see what they like, what they find easy, and where they stumble. The way to get good design ideas is quite often to follow usability engineering methodology and steep yourself in user reactions and data.

Web usability changes less rapidly than web technology, so the methods and concepts you will learn from this book will be useful to you for many years, even if the implementation of your design will change quite a lot. Many of the principles I present in this book stem from research by myself and others into hypertext and other interactive presentation systems. I, personally, did my first hypertext project in 1984, but others have been at it since the 1960s. Many of these results have withstood the test of time. When methodologies and results from the mid–1980s continue to be useful in the late 1990s, there is every reason to believe that they will continue to hold into the 21st century.

About the Examples

The book has many screenshots of real web designs, and the examples and comments refer to the sites the way they were the day of my visit. Because I have been collecting examples and screenshots for several years, many of these sites will have changed—one would hope that most of them have improved—by the time you read this book. If you go to one of the sites depicted in this book and find that it has changed, that will not invalidate my example. The reason to give examples is not to criticize or praise specific sites, companies, or designers. All designs have their good and not-so-good parts, and sometimes I point out a good part of a bad site or a bad part of a good site. The examples are used to illustrate my general web design principles and methodologies because it is hard to understand abstract theory without concrete examples.

A Call for Action

If you read this book and put it away, I will have failed. Of course, if you put it away without even reading it, I will have *utterly* failed, but I trust that the book is sufficiently appealing that you will at least glance through it before consigning it to permanent storage on your bookshelf.

The goal of this book is to change your behavior. I am an evangelist at heart, and I want you to be able to provide better service to your users after you have read my book. There are so many actionable steps that can be taken to make life less miserable for web users. This book is full of specific methods that can be used at almost every stage of a web project to dramatically enhance the user experience. There is no excuse for not using some of these methods because many of them are extremely cheap. There is also no excuse for not planning to include some usability methods in your next web design project because many of them are extremely easy to learn.

After you have read this book, *you are ready to take* **action**. Your very next design project can employ usability methods, and only if you do so will you gain any improvements in your site. Reading about usability doesn't make your site better; only *doing* something about it will help. Remember, you can do it. Anybody can do it. But most web designers blatantly ignore usability and design for their own pleasure (or worse, the boss's pleasure) instead of trying to satisfy user needs. This is good news for you because this book is your secret weapon to making your site better than 90 percent of the Internet—all because 90 percent of the designers don't know (or don't bother to use) the simple techniques I will teach you.

What This Book Is Not

This is not a book about HTML or how to draw an icon or other web implementation technology. There are many good books that will teach you how to implement websites, so I am not even going to try. In any case, it's much too tough a job to write books about something that changes as rapidly as web implementation details.

You are probably going to have to buy two books (booksellers will love this part): this book to tell you *what* to do with your site and an implementation book to tell you *how* to put that design on the Net. I recommend reading the two books in the order I just indicated. You should read my book first because you should start your web project by finding out what your customers want and good ways of designing a site that works for them. It is dangerous to read books about technology, coding, layout, or illustration techniques first, because most people can't keep themselves from hacking up a few pages as soon as they know how. And these pages and sites usually turn out to be useless if they are built from an understanding of HTML or Adobe Photoshop without a corresponding understanding of web design and user needs.

This is also not a book about Internet business strategy as such, even though there are several strategic considerations discussed throughout. There is no way I can tell you how to run your business on the Internet. One has to know the specifics of each industry and each company to do so.

The book does, however, focus on one big-picture strategic idea: Place your customers' needs at the center of your web strategy. The remaining strategies will differ from company to company, but I can guarantee that any company that makes its site easy to use will have a major advantage over its competitors, no matter what industry it's in.

Why Everybody Designs Websites Incorrectly

This book is based on observations of usability tests with about 400 users from a wide variety of backgrounds and using a large number of different websites over the last six years. I have also drawn on lessons from the 10 years I worked on usability, online information systems, and hypertext during the dark ages before the Web.

Since I started designing for the Web in 1994, I have made many mistakes. In the beginning I thought these mistakes were simply due to my own limitations (you always tend to blame yourself). I have continued to see most other companies make the same mistakes I made in 1994 and 1995, so I have come to conclude that these problems are inevitable in a company's first web project unless proactive and explicit action is taken to avoid them. One of the main goals of this book is to help others avoid making

Jakob Nielsen: Designing Web Usability

these mistakes again and again. After all, those who do not know history are doomed to repeat it. But if you know, you can do better.

Fundamental errors are common on all levels of web design:

- Business model: treating the Web as a Marcom brochure instead of a fundamental shift that will change the way we conduct business in the network economy.
- Project management: managing a web project as if it were a traditional corporate project. This leads to an internally focused design with an inconsistent user interface. Instead, a website should be managed as a single customer-interface project.
- Information architecture: structuring the site to mirror the way the company is structured. Instead, the site should be structured to mirror the users' tasks and their views of the information space.
- Page design: creating pages that look gorgeous and that evoke positive feelings when demo'd inside the company. Internal demos do not suffer the response-time delays that are the main determinant of web usability; similarly, a demo does not expose the difficulties a novice user will have in finding and understanding the various page elements. Instead, design for an optimal user experience under realistic circumstances, even if your demos will be less "cool."
- Content authoring: writing in the same linear style as you've always written. Instead, force yourself to write in the new style that is optimized for online readers who frequently scan text and who need very short pages with secondary information relegated to supporting pages.
- Linking strategy: treating your own site as the only one that matters, without proper links to other sites and without well-designed entry-points for others to link to. Many companies don't even use proper links when they mention their own site in their own advertising. Instead, remember that hypertext is the foundation of the Web and that no site is an island.

In every one of these cases, the natural way people go about doing web projects based on their non-web experience turns out to be wrong. The Web is a new medium and requires a new approach, as explained in this book.

2 Page Design

Page design is the most immediately visible part of web design. With current browser technology, users are looking at a single page at a time (or, at most, two or three pages if they have a large screen with multiple windows open). This chapter concerns the usability of the surface appearance of a website: What's on the individual pages?

Site design, however, is often more important for usability because users are never going to even get close to the correct pages unless the site is structured according to user needs and contains a navigation scheme that allows people to find what they want. These site design issues are discussed in a later chapter, as is the design of the actual content that goes inside each page.

Screen Real Estate

Web pages should be dominated by content of interest to the user. Unfortunately, we see many sites that spend more screen space on navigation than they do on the information that supposedly caused the user to visit in the first place. Navigation is a necessary evil that is not a goal in itself and should be minimized.

For an interesting exercise, try blocking out the main regions in a web page and count the proportion of pixels used for various purposes. My examples in these images include space used by the browser and operating system. Even though web designers usually cannot influence this space, the users don't care. All users know is that they paid for a certain number of pixels on their monitor and only 20 and 14 percent, respectively, of these pixels are being used to display the content they want.

As with all layout, whitespace is not necessarily useless, and it would be a mistake to design overly compact pages. Whitespace can guide the eye and help users understand the grouping of information. If you have the choice between separating two segments of content by a heavy line or by some whitespace, it will often look better to use the whitespace solution, which will typically also download faster.

(Facing page)   When visiting MapQuest, most of the screen space ends up being used for distracting machinery that is extraneous to the content the user came for. Of the 480,000 precious pixels on an 800×600 display, only 20% are used for the content of interest to the user (indicated in green on the map). Additionally, 31% of the pixels are used for operating system and browser controls (blue), 23% are used for site navigation (yellow), and 10% are used for advertising (red). The remaining 16% of the pixels go unused (white) because the coding of this page does not allow it to reformat to fit the window.

Jakob Nielsen: Designing Web Usability

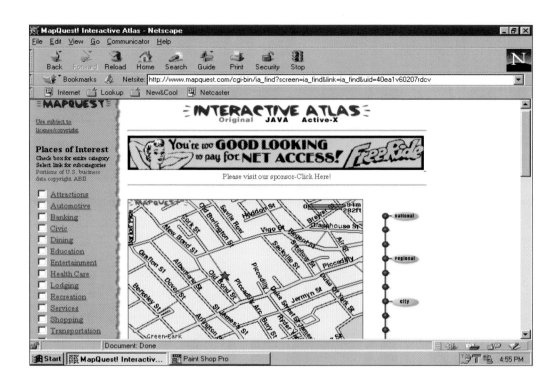

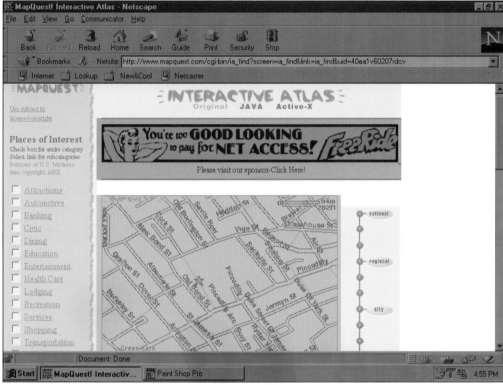

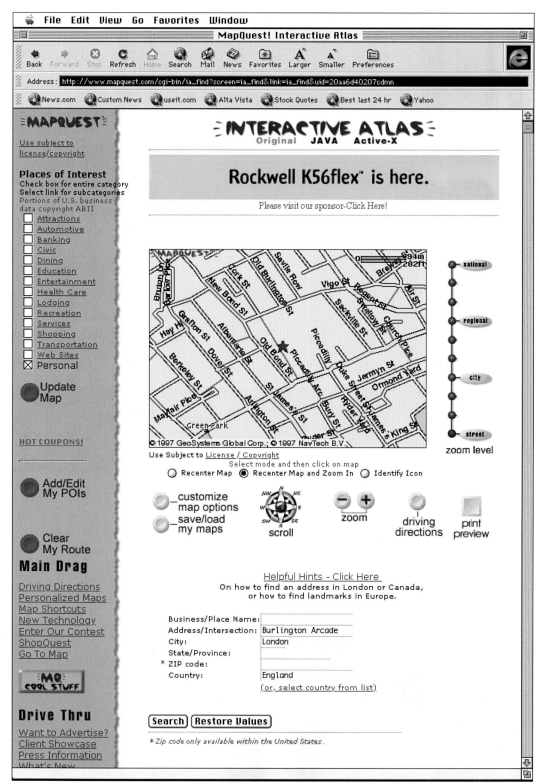

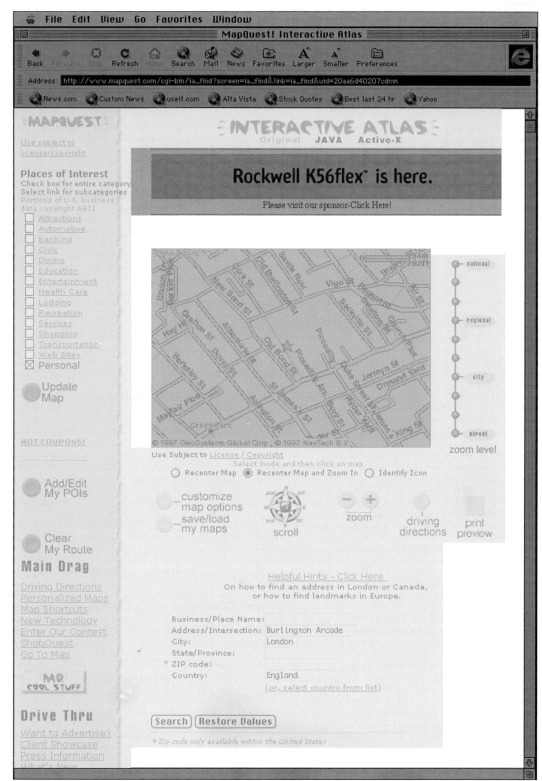

www.mapquest.com

(Previous pages) **Displaying MapQuest** on a bigger screen results in an equally bad utilization of the pixels. Of a 700×1024 pixel area, only 14% is used for content (indicated in green on the map). A more acceptable, but still heavy, 16% is used for operating system and browser controls (blue), a dominating 51% is used for site navigation (yellow), and a reasonable 6% is used for advertising. The remaining 13% of the pixels go unused (white).

(Facing page) **The previous screenshots** of MapQuest were taken in 1997. After I had shown these pages in lectures all over the world for two years, I hoped that the site might have been redesigned. Indeed it has been, but not substantially for the better—with respect to focus on the user's content. In 1999, 15% of the pixels were used for content out of the 642×1014 pixels used by the current page design and Internet Explorer 5.

The new design introduces a new type of advertising pollution in the form of special buttons to add map listings for selected companies. It is fairly useless for anybody who travels to London (my example) to have a feature map the location of the nearest Denny's or Fairfield Inn. Some of the new features are useful, such as the capability of Quick Maps to get the location of an airport (although it would have been better to make Heathrow the default airport when displaying a map of an address in London).

I do not consider whitespace wasted when it is part of content design or navigation design, but the examples here show that there is also some amount of whitespace that is not present due to any design considerations; instead, it simply shows up because the page does not adjust itself to fit the available window. Some amount of wasted space is inevitable in most designs because it is almost impossible to make a page that will be shown as a perfect rectangle within the user's browser under all circumstances. Some holes will usually be left over.

As a rule of thumb, content should account for at least half of a page's design, and preferably closer to 80 percent. Navigation should be kept below 20 percent of the space for destination pages, although navigation options may account for much higher proportions of home pages and intermediate navigation pages. From a usability perspective, it would be best to eliminate advertising; if you do need to run ads, you should consider them part of the page overhead together with the navigation options, meaning that the navigation design will have to be reduced in weight.

A general principle for all user interface design is to go through all of your design elements and remove them one at a time. If the design works as well without a certain design element, kill it. Simplicity always wins over complexity, especially on the Web where every five bytes saved is a millisecond less download time.

On the Web it is impossible to predict what size monitor the user will have and what size window will be used to display a page. In the future detailed content negotiation between browsers and servers will result in more intelligent deployment of pages that are optimized for the characteristics of the specific monitor on which they are going to be displayed. For example, images will be made smaller if they are going to appear on a small monitor. Also, a style sheet with a tighter layout may be sent when a small monitor is used, and a more expansive style sheet might be sent when a large display area is available. For now, these predictions for adaptable content remain a hope for the future, and it is necessary to use a single page design to work with all the different display devices.

Jakob Nielsen: Designing Web Usability

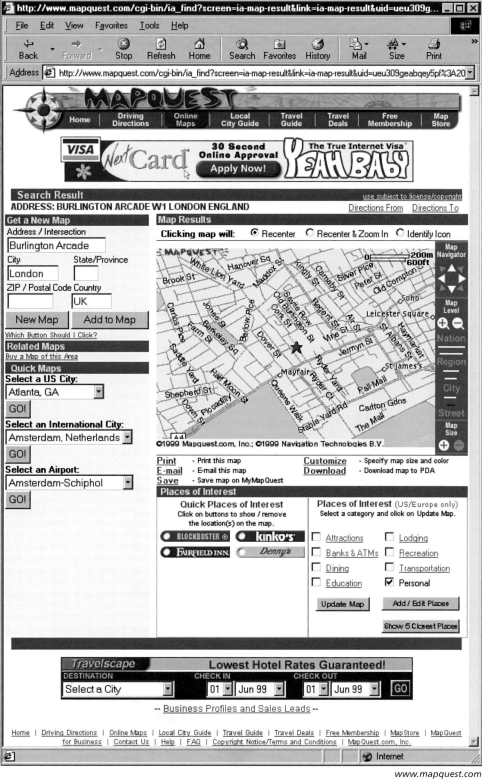

www.mapquest.com

February 1997 design.

(Above) Avoiding wasteful amounts of whitespace should not lead to extremely dense layouts like the February 1997 version of Pathfinder's home page. This claustrophobic design looks like the America Online welcome screen on steroids.

www.pathfinder.com

June 1997 design.

www.pathfinder.com

Suggested redesign.

(Facing page, bottom)   The June 1997 version of the home page feels much less stressful, although it is still somewhat confusing and over- whelming. The lines separating the feature headlines do not seem nec- essary; as an experiment, I tried to delete the lines and move the headlines closer to the magazine logos to more clearly denote which magazine goes with which story. The revised design (above) uses whitespace rather than lines and seems less cluttered.

Cross-Platform Design

In traditional GUI design, you control every pixel on the screen: As you lay out a dialog box, you can rest assured that it will look *exactly* the same on the user's screen. You know what system you are designing for, you know what fonts it has installed, you know how large the screen typi- cally will be, and you have the system vendor's style guide to tell you the rules for combining the interaction wid- gets. You can even gray out menu options that are not applicable in the current state, and you can display a modal dialog box that takes over the computer until the user has answered the question.

On the Web, however, the user fundamentally controls his or her navigation through the pages. Users can take paths that were never intended by the designer. They can, for example, jump straight into the guts of a site from a search engine, without ever going through the site's home page. Users can also control their own bookmark menu and can use it to create a customized interface for a site.

Web designers need to accommodate and support user- controlled navigation. Sometimes, you can force users through set paths and prevent them from linking to cer- tain pages, but sites that do so feel harsh and dominating. It is better to design for freedom of movement and, for

www.quote.com

Being overly specific in the use of fonts on the Web is extremely dangerous. This page used a typeface that was not available on the machine I used to access the site, so much of the text displayed incorrectly. Often, it is best not to specify fonts at all, but rather simply to accept the default font because you know that will work all the time. Alternatively, when you do want a certain font, make sure to list several alternatives to maximize the probability that one of the fonts will in fact be available on the user's machine.

example, put a logo (linked to the home page) on every page to provide context and navigation for users who have gone straight to an internal page.

One final difference between the two interfaces is organizational and historical, rather than technical. With GUIs we had the luxury of an initial phase of slow research and development at leading companies staffed with responsible user interface experts like the many researchers at Xerox PARC and Bruce Tognazzini at Apple. As a result, bad ideas were rejected and good ideas were codified into guidelines before any GUIs were inflicted upon the average computer user. In contrast, the Web is developing as we speak, and experiments happen on the open Internet with us all as test subjects (not in a videotaped usability lab).

Where Are Users Coming From?

On the Web many of the assumptions that are true for GUI design fall apart. Users may be accessing the Web through traditional computers, but they could just as easily be using a pen-based, hand-held device, a Nokia cell phone, or even their car as an Internet device. In traditional design the difference in screen area between a laptop and a high-end workstation is a factor of six. On the Web we currently need to accommodate a factor of 100 in screen area between hand-helds and workstations, and a factor of 1,000 in bandwidth between modems and T3 connections.

Most web pages work well only on a 17-inch monitor running at a resolution of at least 1024×768 pixels. Anything less and many layouts become cramped, and users have to scroll to see all the parts of the page they need. It should not be this way. We can all wish for users to get decent monitors, but for the next several years, it is a fact that we have to design pages that will work on small screens.

The following table shows the distribution of screen sizes used to access the Internet in 1997 and 1999. The striking conclusion is that two years have made almost no difference to the dominance of small screens. Although there were not quite as many very small screens in 1999, their numbers may start growing again in 2000 as information appliances become popular.

Distribution of Monitor Size in 1997 and 1999[*]

Screen Size	Horus and GVU 1997	StatMarket 1999
Very small (640×480 or less)	22%	13%
Small (800×600)	47%	55%
Medium (1024×768)	25%	25%
Large (1280×1024 or larger)[**]	6%	2%

[*]The 1997 data is averaged across results from 5,000 users accessing www.horus.com and for more than 11,000 respondents to the GVU survey. The 1999 data is from www.statmarket.com.

[**]Screens with 1600×1200 pixels and larger will become more widely used starting in the year 2000.

Any given web design will look different on this variety of devices. Clearly, WYSIWYG is dead. Instead of attempting to re-create exactly the same visual appearance for all users, designers must specify pages in terms that enable browsers to optimize the display for each individual user's circumstances. Designing an abstract user interface specification that is instantiated differently for each platform is much harder than it sounds. The basic principles of HTML can take the designer a long way toward the ideal, but not all the way there. It is recommended to separate meaning and presentation, and to use style sheets to specify presentation, but doing so works better for informational content than for interaction.

The Car as a Web Browser

Mercedes-Benz has designed a concept car with full Internet connectivity. The prototype Mercedes E420 comes with three flat-panel displays: one for the driver and two for the passengers. The Internet connection in a car must be wireless, so bandwidth will be severely limited, especially if shared between three users. Passengers may browse the Web in much the same way as computer users, except that they'll use touch screens as their input device instead of a keyboard and a mouse. Because the driver needs to be looking at the road and not at a screen, it's possible to browse the Web through speech input and output. Also, the car itself can become an input device by transmitting its location to the server, and some simplified output could be projected on the windshield, turning it into a heads-up display.

Resolution-Independent Design

Because there is no way of knowing how large a screen your users have, you should design for all screen resolutions—in other words, resolution-independent pages that adapt to whatever size screen they are displayed on. The main principle for resolution-independent design is to never use a fixed pixel-width for any tables, frames, or other design elements (except possibly for thin stripes down the side of the page). Instead of using fixed sizes, you should specify layouts as percentages of the available space.

Remember also that users have different preferences with respect to font size, so ensure that your designs work well with both larger and smaller fonts than your personal preferences. People may use different fonts because of a visual disability, or they may simply have a high-resolution screen on which small font sizes are too tiny to be readable.

Graphic elements should also be designed with different resolutions in mind. In particular, icons must continue to work when they are displayed at 100 dpi resolution or better. The higher the resolution, the smaller any given graphic will be displayed, so to continue to be readable, any text that is embedded in the graphic must use a relatively large font size. In general, it is recommended not to include any text in graphics because doing so slows down transmission and makes for more work to translate the user interface into foreign languages.

Color Depth Getting Deeper

In 1997 slightly less than half of the users were restricted to 256 colors, and slightly more than half of the users were capable of displaying thousands or millions of colors. Two years later, in 1999, only 11% of the users were restricted to a color palette of 256 colors, while 89% of users could view thousands of colors or more. Thus, the need to design for an extremely limited number of colors may not be with us for much longer. At the same time, the expected growth of portable consumer devices with web access will lead to increased requirements for web graphics to work on grayscale displays.

Why have we seen this great progress in color depth and yet so little progress in monitor size? Because color depth mainly follows Moore's Law: It gets cheaper to have more capable video cards as computer power increases and memory prices drop. In contrast, monitors are physical beasts that are still much too expensive if you want a big one.

In many ways a printer can be seen as a special kind of display; it has high resolution but is not as wide as most monitors. Because of these differences, web pages that are not resolution-independent will often not work well as printouts. Online reading is the main use of web pages, and as discussed in the section on printing, it is best to provide a separate print version for any long documents— although we still know that users frequently print out web pages directly from the browser. Pages that are designed to display in a fixed width will look horrible when printed; either they come out as a thin stripe wasting loads of

A particularly nasty resolution-dependent page from Pepsi. No matter how large a window the user has, it is still necessary to scroll the listing because it doesn't resize to fill up the available space.

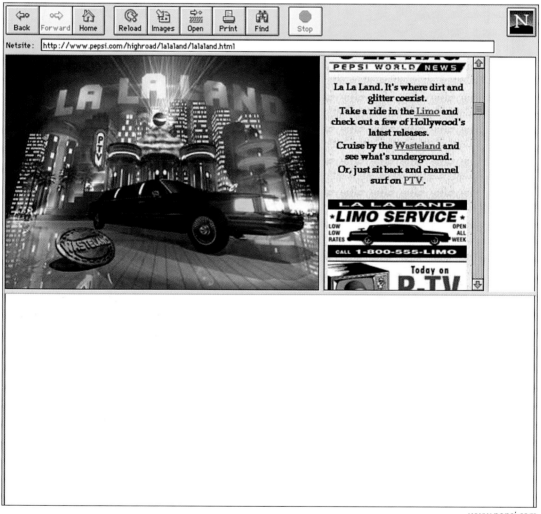

www.pepsi.com

paper, or they are cut off because they are too wide for the printer. A typical 600-pixel-wide layout that works on most normal computer monitors (although not on WebTV and small-screen devices) will be 8.3 inches wide when printed at the standard resolution of 72 pixels to the inch. Because printers need between one-quarter and one-half inch of margin, the printable area on an 8.5×11 sheet is between 7.5 and 8.0 inches wide, meaning that at least 0.3 inch of the page will be cut off. Users printing on A4 paper will lose an even larger part of the page.

Using Non-Standard Content

The Web is constantly changing, and I can safely predict that within a few weeks of the time you read this chapter, some new web technology is going to be launched, and you will be tempted to use it to jazz up your site. Don't do it.

The first time I saw the Bohemialab page in Internet Explorer, I thought that Microsoft deviously had introduced code to eliminate links to its rival, but the truth is simpler and less sinister: Bohemialab had specified that the page background should be white and that hypertext links should be white (why they did this, I don't know). The specific HTML code for the link to Netscape has the following non-standard way of specifying yet another font color:

```
<A HREF="http://www.netscape.com/comprod/mirror/index.html"
TARGET="blank"><FONT COLOR="000000">Netscape 3.0
</FONT COLOR></A>
```

This code can be interpreted in two ways:

- The <FONT> tag is supposed to change the color of the body text, so make body text black (but of course, link text should be rendered in the specified link color).
- The <FONT> tag acts differently inside an <A> tag than it would elsewhere, so don't use it to change the color of body text (keep it the previous color) but do change the color of the link text.

Two lessons from this failure: Avoid non-standard codes if possible and, if not, at least use reasonable defaults that will work even if your hacks don't.

b o h e m i a

note

With the exception of

the portfolio sections,

this site is not

graphically intense.

However, much of its

functionality relies

on features supported by

Netscape 3.0 or above.

We strongly suggest you

download this browser

if you haven't already

done so.

Netscape

b o h e m i a

note

With the exception of

the portfolio sections,

this site is not

graphically intense.

However, much of its

functionality relies

on features supported by

or above.

We strongly suggest you

download this browser

if you haven't already

done so.

Explorer

www.bohemialab.com

Installation Inertia

In the early years of the Web, users would upgrade to new browser versions at a speed of about two percent per week. In other words, every week, two percent of the users would go to the leading browser vendor's site and download the newest version. At two percent upgrading weekly, 50 weeks (essentially, one full year) would be needed to move all the users to the new version, but because new versions were being released more often than once per year, users were constantly behind.

I predict that version transitions will happen much more slowly in the future. First, the pressure to upgrade is getting weaker because many site designers now understand the need to be backwards-compatible and not require that their visitors use the latest beta releases. Second, the desire to upgrade is weakening because the older browsers are reasonably good and the usability differential between versions is less. In the early years of the Web, there were huge benefits in upgrading to a newer browser, but recent browser upgrades do not seem to have had the same level of innovative benefits. Third, and most important, the user population has changed from a pioneering group of enthusiasts to a more mainstream mass of early adopters. In the early years of the Web, people went online to *be* online, and collecting new browser releases became a goal in itself and a way to prove to your friends that you were on the cutting edge. Today, people go online for the sake of the content and in order to get their work done. As long as their old browser works perfectly well, they will not go to the trouble of seeking out a new version, downloading it, and installing it. As shown by the figure on the next page, the upgrade speed was about one percent per week in 1998 and 1999.

When Is It Safe to Upgrade?

The only format you can use with complete confidence is the original HTML 1.0 specification. Anything beyond that will be beyond the capabilities of some of your visitors.

Do not let any beta-phase web technology anywhere near your site unless you are the inventor or have other reasons for wanting to promote the specific technology. Beta software is likely to crash, and crashes distract users from the

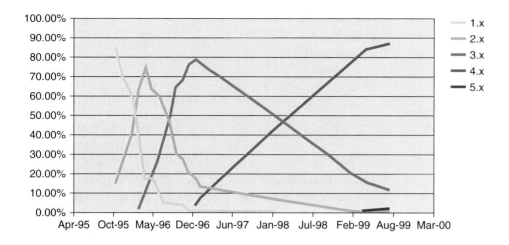

| | | | | | | | | | | | 1.x |
| 2.x |
| 3.x |
| 4.x |
| 5.x |

Apr-95 Oct-95 May-96 Dec-96 Jun-97 Jan-98 Jul-98 Feb-99 Aug-99 Mar-00

The relative proportion of Netscape users using the different versions of the browser over time. Data from www.interse.com (1995–1997) and www.statmarket.com (1998–1999). The remarkable conclusion from the figure is that the change from version 1 to version 2 happened with almost exactly the same speed as the transition from version 2 to version 3: Both curves have a slope of about 2 percent per week. The more recent version transition from 3 to 4 happened at half that speed: only 1 percent per week. The transition from 4 to 5 may be even slower than that.

purpose of your site, which hopefully is to offer some real value and not simply dazzle them with your command of bleeding-edge technology.

I recommend holding off on using any new web technology on your site until one or two years after it is officially introduced in a non-beta version. Things that should be avoided the first year include new versions of HTML or other specs, plug-ins or other software components, new data formats, and any browser-specific features. There are three reasons to be conservative in embracing web innovations:

- With an upgrade speed of about one percent per week, it will be a year before the majority of users will even be able to access your fancy use of the new technology— and two years before everybody has it.

- Even after a new technology moves from beta status to official FCS (first customer shipment), it will probably still have some bugs that will need to be ironed out in subsequent dot releases.

- A lot of trial-and-error is involved in determining the best ways of using a new web technology to communicate with users. The first sites to use a new feature usually do so in ways that harm users more than help them. Only after collecting experience and usability test results from a wide variety of designs that employ a new technology do we have any hope of applying it in a manner that adds value to a site.

Jakob Nielsen: Designing Web Usability

Let somebody else make the mistakes and concentrate your own efforts on giving your users valuable content that helps them do things they want to do. By avoiding the latest—and possibly greatest—you ensure yourself against the very distinct possibility that the latest turned out to be a dud that never caught on.

The main exceptions to the rule of holding off for a year include web consultants who want to demonstrate their prowess with advanced technology and sites that want to do something that can be done much better with a new feature. In either case I advise some amount of caution: Consultants should make sure that they are not simply putting rope that will be used to hang them on their own site (because prospective customers find their use of the new feature to be frivolous). A site that "needs" a new gizmo to provide certain user benefits might, after some reflection, find that the simpler ways would provide almost the same benefits to a much larger number of users.

If you decide to break my one-year waiting period for whatever reason, however, you should make sure to provide your content in an alternative format for the sake of those users who have not yet upgraded and, therefore, cannot use the new feature.

Helpful Super-Users

Many people get their web browser installed by a friend or colleague who is a "super-user." Most companies and many families include a few individuals who enjoy technology for its own sake, even though their real job has nothing to do with computers. These tinkerers often become super-users who know all the bells and whistles of modern fatware applications and who make it their business to get a hold of the newest releases as soon as possible. (I once interviewed a super-user who said that she liked learning one new application every week just to stay in shape with her computer skills.)

When a super-user installs a web browser for a normal user, the normal user will have no knowledge about how the web browser was downloaded or how to upgrade it. Therefore, the user will happily keep using the browser long after the release of a newer version. Even users who installed their own browsers will often operate under the rule "if it ain't broke, don't fix it." The result of these two phenomena is a heavy installation inertia, where people keep using whatever browser version they already have installed. Most major websites still get hits from Netscape version 2.

After a year, you do not need to create dual versions of your pages (with and without the new feature), because you can assume that most people will have upgraded. But there is a two-year rule that still needs to be followed: For the first two years after the official launch of a new web technology, you will need to test whether any use of this new feature degrades gracefully for people with older browsers. It is acceptable if users with old browsers don't get all the benefits from your use of fancy features, but it is not acceptable if your site breaks or looks jumbled in an old browser.

Separating Meaning and Presentation

The original design of the Web and its underlying data format, HTML, were based on encoding the *meaning* of information and not its *presentation*.

For example, a section heading should be encoded as a level-2 heading (<H2>), meaning that it is the highest level of subheading below the level-1 heading that's the heading for the entire page. This encoding style was chosen by Tim Berners-Lee because he wanted the Web to be a universal information system. Thus, he could not know what computer equipment the various users would have (some might have high-resolution color screens and others might be blind and use a voice-only interface), and it was necessary to keep the details of the rendering of the information out of the file itself. The exact way pages would be shown (or read) to the user would be determined by the user's own equipment.

The notion of encoding the meaning of documents, known as *semantic encoding*, was temporarily lost when some browser vendors introduced proprietary tags to encode the exact rendering of the information. Many web designers, for example, have been trained to use presentation-based text encodings such as "18 pixels tall bold Garamond" instead of using the semantic encoding of a level-2 heading. The benefit of presentation-based encoding is that the page may display in a close approximation to the intended design if the user has a combination of hardware and software that is similar to that used by the designer. Thus, more sophisticated layouts became possible.

Jakob Nielsen: Designing Web Usability

However, presentation-based design works only as long as it is possible to predict the user's hardware, software, and preferences. This was reasonably easy in the early years of the Web:

- In 1991 and 1992, most users had text-only access.
- In 1993 and 1994, most users got Mosaic.
- In 1995 and 1996, most users moved to Netscape.

But starting in 1997, the notion of a canonical browser used by everybody had been abandoned, except for intranets that standardized on a single vendor. On the open Internet, there was no longer a single software platform that dominated to the exclusion of all others.

It is true that Internet Explorer has been increasing in market share from 1997 to 1999. But I predict that IE will never reach the same market dominance as that enjoyed by line-mode, Mosaic, and Netscape from 1991 to 1996. In the future, a wide variety of information appliances will become popular, each with its own characteristics. It is extremely unlikely that a single browser would provide the optimal user interface under widely varying conditions—from a small screen-phone to a flat-panel virtual magazine, for example.

Non-traditional computers, such as WebTV, and personal digital assistants, such as the Palm Pilot, will become much

Platform Transition

The first two transitions in web platform dominance happened quickly. The transition from line-mode to Mosaic in 1993 was almost instantaneous. No data is available, but my guess from what I remember about those heady days is that the upgrade speed was about 30 percent per month, meaning that 30 percent of users moved to Mosaic the first month. The web community was small and tight, and we all exchanged information with each other by email and Usenet, so everybody knew almost instantly when something better came out.

The transition from Mosaic to Netscape at the end of 1994 and the beginning of 1995 was also fast, at maybe 25 percent per month.

Netscape gained about 80 percent market share in only a few months.

The transition to Internet Explorer and the continued transition to a multi-platform Web are happening much more slowly. A best-fit regression line to the most credible market research reports shows that Netscape lost market share at about 1.2 percent per month from 1997 to 1999. The two main reasons for the slower transitions are that the user community is more dispersed (therefore, less likely to move in unison) and that the software changes are less dramatic than the initial change from text-based interaction to a GUI.

(Following pages) Edward Traxler designed a site that shows the differences among the various browsers. The figures show the same page displayed in Netscape 3.01, Netscape 4.01, and Internet Explorer 3.01. Not only are the graphics aligned differently, but there are also differences in type spacing and line breaks. All three browsers were given a 618-pixels-wide window, but because Netscape 4 uses a wider window border, it has a much shorter line length. As an example, the horizontal rules are 574 pixels wide in Netscape 3, 559 pixels wide in Netscape 4, and 583 pixels wide in Internet Explorer 3. Finally, it seems that Netscape 4 is less forgiving in rendering &lt without the ending semicolon (the normal way to encode a "<" character in HTML is <).

more prevalent. These devices have display capabilities extremely different from the traditional computer (typically, a much smaller screen) and, thus, cannot display web pages well that have been coded for a specific presentation that looks good on a standard monitor. The use of semantic encoding enables the device to optimize the display to its capabilities.

Speech-based browsers are going to happen soon. Enhanced accessibility for users with disabilities (especially visually impaired users) is one reason for speech browsing. Sighted users also find themselves in hands-busy, eyes-busy situations (such as driving a car) where they could access web-based information if it were read out loud. It is obvious that speech interfaces to the Web will be much better if semantic encoding is used so that the system can understand the structure of the page. Knowing which parts of the text constitute headlines, for example, would enable a speech system to read a summary to the user, who could then easily choose what sections to have read in full.

A final reason for reverting to semantic encoding instead of presentation encoding is the increased diversity in software used to access the Web. If one compares screenshots of the same page in different browsers (or even the "same" browser in different versions or running on different platforms), it is very clear that the resulting presentations differ substantially. As different browser vendors gain market share and as all of the vendors release ever more versions of their browsers, there will be so many versions that it will become impossible to test pages for all of them if page designers insist on tweaking display appearance. You never know what will come next, and because "Data Lives Forever," your only hope of page survival is to follow the standard.

Instead of embedding appearance-specifications in the content, a better solution is to separate content and display-specific instructions. Information relating to the presentation of the information should be kept in a separate style sheet file that is linked to a content file that contains only semantic markup. Style sheets are a new development on the Web and not yet widely used, but they are the only solution to getting nice presentation with ever-increasing numbers of browsers and display devices. For example, a page could link to three different style sheets: one for

First try: This is how the original coding started. The graphics are placed in two rows; each row containing one data cell. The individual graphics are seperated by line breaks to make the code easier to read.

```
<TABLE>
<TR><TD>
<IMG SRC="Graphics/Header/G1.gif" WIDTH=103 HEIGHT=21 BORDER=0 ALT="G1">
<IMG SRC="Graphics/Header/G2.gif" WIDTH=103 HEIGHT=21 BORDER=0 ALT="G2">
</TD></TR>
<TR><TD>
<IMG SRC="Graphics/Header/G3.gif" WIDTH=103 HEIGHT=21 BORDER=0 ALT="G3">
<IMG SRC="Graphics/Header/G4.gif" WIDTH=103 HEIGHT=21 BORDER=0 ALT="G4">
</TD></TR>
</TABLE>
```

Graphic 1 *Graphic 2*
Graphic 3 *Graphic 4*

IE: Shows a gap between the rows, but adjacent graphics line up without any gap between them
NN: Shows a gap between the rows and between adjacent graphics. Kind of neat as you can see all of the bits and pieces that make up the whole.

Second Try: Same code as above but set HSPACE=0 and VSPACE=0

Graphic 1 *Graphic 2*
Graphic 3 *Graphic 4*

IE and NN: Nada. Nothing. No change.

Third Try: It was suggested align top might work .. so ...

Graphic 1 *Graphic 2*
Graphic 3 *Graphic 4*

IE: Nada. Nothing. No change.
NN: Well .. the gap between the rows is smaller ...

Fourth Try: OK. Take out all references to align="top", VSPACE and HSPACE. Take Ruth's advice and remove all spacing and line breaks. I will use only one table row (<TR>) and use the break tag (<BR>) to seperate everything into two rows.

Graphic 1Graphic 2
Graphic 3Graphic 4

IE: Shazam!! Well, that fixed IE.
NN: OK. Got rid of the spacing between adjacent graphics. There is still a gap between the two rows ... but it is the smallest yet.

Fifth Try: Got to try it ... using Align="Top" made the gap between the rows smaller... so did the last try. So next .. combine them. I'll add back Align="Top" to the code above.

Graphic 1Graphic 2
Graphic 3Graphic 4

IE: Nada. Nothing. No change, still good.
NN: Sounds of shouting and hand clapping. Now, if I can only figure out how to NOT have to code everything on one line....

www.thegrid.net/edtrax

Netscape 3.01

First try: This is how the original coding started. The graphics are placed in two rows; each row containing one data cell. The individual graphics are seperated by line breaks to make the code easier to read.

```
<TABLE>
<TR><TD>
<IMG SRC="Graphics/Header/G1.gif" WIDTH=103 HEIGHT=21 BORDER=0 ALT="G1">
<IMG SRC="Graphics/Header/G2.gif" WIDTH=103 HEIGHT=21 BORDER=0 ALT="G2">
</TD></TR>
<TR><TD>
<IMG SRC="Graphics/Header/G3.gif" WIDTH=103 HEIGHT=21 BORDER=0 ALT="G3">
<IMG SRC="Graphics/Header/G4.gif" WIDTH=103 HEIGHT=21 BORDER=0 ALT="G4">
</TD></TR>
</TABLE>
```

*Graphic 1**Graphic 2*
*Graphic 3**Graphic 4*

IE: Shows a gap between the rows, but adjacent graphics line up without any gap between them
NN: Shows a gap between the rows and between adjacent graphics. Kind of neat as you can see all of the bits and pieces that make up the whole.

Second Try: Same code as above but set HSPACE=0 and VSPACE=0
*Graphic 1**Graphic 2*
*Graphic 3**Graphic 4*

IE and NN: Nada. Nothing. No change.

Third Try: It was suggested align top might work .. so ...
*Graphic 1**Graphic 2*
*Graphic 3**Graphic 4*

IE: Nada. Nothing. No change.
NN: Well .. the gap between the rows is smaller ...

Fourth Try: OK. Take out all references to align="top", VSPACE and HSPACE. Take Ruth's advice and remove all spacing and line breaks. I will use only one table row (<TR>) and use the break tag (<BR>) to seperate everything into two rows.
*Graphic 1**Graphic 2*
*Graphic 3**Graphic 4*

IE: Shazam!! Well, that fixed IE.
NN: OK. Got rid of the spacing between adjacent graphics. There is still a gap between the two rows ... but it is the smallest yet.

Fifth Try: Got to try it ... using Align="Top" made the gap between the rows smaller... so did the last try. So next .. combine them. I'll add back Align="Top" to the code above.
*Graphic 1**Graphic 2*
*Graphic 3**Graphic 4*

IE: Nada. Nothing. No change, still good.
NN: Sounds of shouting and hand clapping. Now, if I can only figure out how to NOT have to code everything on one line....

Internet Explorer 3.01

www.thegrid.net/edtrax

First try: This is how the original coding started. The graphics are placed in two rows; each row containing one data cell. The individual graphics are seperated by line breaks to make the code easier to read.

```
&ltTABLE>
&ltTR>&ltTD>
&ltIMG SRC="Graphics/Header/G1.gif" WIDTH=103 HEIGHT=21 BORDER=0 ALT="G1">
&ltIMG SRC="Graphics/Header/G2.gif" WIDTH=103 HEIGHT=21 BORDER=0 ALT="G2">
</TD></TR>
&ltTR>&ltTD>
&ltIMG SRC="Graphics/Header/G3.gif" WIDTH=103 HEIGHT=21 BORDER=0 ALT="G3">
&ltIMG SRC="Graphics/Header/G4.gif" WIDTH=103 HEIGHT=21 BORDER=0 ALT="G4">
</TD></TR>
</TABLE>
```

Graphic 1 *Graphic 2*
Graphic 3 *Graphic 4*

IE: Shows a gap between the rows, but adjacent graphics line up without any gap between them
NN: Shows a gap between the rows and between adjacent graphics. Kind of neat as you can see all of the bits and pieces that make up the whole.

Second Try: Same code as above but set HSPACE=0 and VSPACE=0

Graphic 1 *Graphic 2*
Graphic 3 *Graphic 4*

IE and NN: Nada. Nothing. No change.

Third Try: It was suggested align top might work .. so ...

Graphic 1 *Graphic 2*
Graphic 3 *Graphic 4*

IE: Nada. Nothing. No change.
NN: Well .. the gap between the rows is smaller ...

Fourth Try: OK. Take out all references to align="top", VSPACE and HSPACE. Take Ruth's advice and remove all spacing and line breaks. I will use only one table row (&ltTR>) and use the break tag (&ltBR>) to seperate everything into two rows.

*Graphic 1**Graphic 2*
*Graphic 3**Graphic 4*

IE: Shazam!! Well, that fixed IE.
NN: OK. Got rid of the spacing between adjacent graphics. There is still a gap between the two rows ... but it is the smallest yet.

Fifth Try: Got to try it ... using Align="Top" made the gap between the rows smaller... so did the last try. So next .. combine them. I'll add back Align="Top" to the code above.

*Graphic 1**Graphic 2*
*Graphic 3**Graphic 4*

IE: Nada. Nothing. No change, still good.
NN: Sounds of shouting and hand clapping. Now, if I can only figure out how to NOT have to code everything on one line....

www.thegrid.net/edtrax

Netscape 4.01

desktop computers, one for small-screen devices, and one for television sets. Currently, browsers do not have the smarts to automatically select the best style sheet, but such a feature should come in a few years. If your design separates meaning and presentation, it will be better suited to take advantage of such future opportunities for optimized display.

Response Times

Every web usability study I have conducted since 1994 has shown the same thing: Users beg us to speed up page downloads. In the beginning my reaction was along the lines of "Let's just give them better design, and they will be *happy* to wait for it." I have since become a reformed sinner believing that fast response times are the most important design criterion for web pages; even *my* skull isn't thick enough to withstand consistent user pleas year after year.

Research on a wide variety of hypertext systems has shown that users need response times of less than one second when moving from one page to another if they are to navigate freely through an information space. Traditional human factors research into response times also shows the need for response times faster than one second. Studies done at IBM in the 1970s and 1980s, for example, found that mainframe users were more productive when the time between pressing a function key and getting the requested screen was less than one second.

Unfortunately, we will not be getting subsecond response times on the Web any time soon, so we know that users are going to continue to be hurt by slow downloads. Currently, the minimum goal for response times should therefore be to get pages to users in no more than 10 seconds, because that's the limit of people's ability to keep their attention focused while waiting.

The basic advice regarding response times has been about the same since Robert B. Miller presented a classic paper on the topic at the Fall Joint Computer Conference in 1968:

- One tenth of a second (0.1) is about the limit for having the user feel that the system is reacting instantaneously, meaning that no special feedback is

Before the advent of the web, people used to say that

- Hardware lives a few years, and then you upgrade to a faster computer.

- Software lives for decades. Even when you get a faster computer, you want to keep running your old software.

   Thus, many companies still depend on software that was written 20 or more years ago, when people thought that the year 2000 was so far away that it was acceptable to encode dates without recording the century (7/4/75, for example). Also, even when software is upgraded, much of the old code lives on in the new version (MS Word users still suffer from bad design decisions made in the 1980s before Microsoft got a usability lab).

- Data lives forever. Once you record, say, a customer's address, you want to keep that information even when you get so tired of your old hardware and software that you implement an entirely new solution from scratch.

The same is true on the Web. Hardware definitely lives dangerously; any successful site will need to upgrade servers several times a year. And we all know how browsers and other software are in a constant state of flux.

Web data (mainly in the form of pages) should live much longer than web hardware and software. Even though most users go to the newer pages, older pages will still be of interest to some users. For example, Sun still has customers using almost every product that was ever shipped, so information about these old products is still of interest. Even the sales pages will be of interest to any third-party customer who might be thinking about buying old equipment from a company that has moved to fresh machines. And it is in their best interest to support these third-party customers even if they don't make a cent from them buying used equipment. They may take out a service contract, and they will certainly become prime prospects for buying their own upgrades at a later date.

Consider, as another example, a user who is thinking about seeing the 1946 Humphrey Bogart film *The Big Sleep*. Sure, he or she can find a modern review in, say, *Cinemania*, but wouldn't it be more interesting to see what *The New York Times* wrote about the film back in 1946? Certainly, film students would want to know how the film was received under the circumstances for which it was produced. This example shows that the *Times* would have a better website if it had 50-year-old pages online.

The conclusion is clear: Pages designed today may well be used many years from now, so designers are advised to mark up the information as close to the standard as possible. Also, try to create information with persistent value as far as possible. In theory, you *could* always go back and fix up old pages (just as people *had* to hire expensive consultants to solve the Year 2000 problem in their software because they didn't think far enough ahead originally), but it will be expensive and the likely outcome is that the old pages get discarded—and with them, the opportunities from providing customers with added benefits.

necessary except to display the result. This would be the response time limit for any applets that allow users to move, zoom, or otherwise manipulate screen elements in real time.

- One second (1.0) is about the limit for the user's flow of thought to remain uninterrupted, even though the user will notice the delay. Normally, no special feedback is necessary during delays of more than 0.1 but less than 1.0 second, but the user does lose the feeling of operating directly on the data. Getting a new page within a second means that the user arrived at the page without undue delay.

- Ten seconds (10.0) is about the limit for keeping the user's attention focused on the dialogue. For longer delays, users turn to other tasks while waiting for the computer to finish. Getting a new page within 10 seconds, while annoying, at least means that the user can stay focused on navigating the site.

Normally, response times should be as fast as possible, but keep in mind that it is possible for the computer to react so fast that the user cannot keep up. For example, a scrolling list may move so fast that the user cannot stop it in time for the desired element to remain within the available window.

Predictable Response Times

In addition to speed, low variability is also important for response time usability. Unfortunately, web response times are usually highly variable, which is one reason users are so upset about the slowness of the Web. The satisfaction of users depends on their expectations as well as the actual response time performance. If the same action sometimes happens fast and sometimes is slow, users won't know what to expect and, therefore, cannot adjust their behavior to optimize their use of the system. If people assume that an action will be fast, they will be disappointed if it is slow; on the other hand, if they *expect* it to be slow, they will be more tolerant of exactly the same delay. This phenomenon is one of the reasons response time variability should be kept to a minimum. If the same action always takes the same time, users will learn what to expect. Anything you can do to stabilize your response times will result in a usability improvement.

For example, you can help users predict the response time in downloading large pages or multimedia files by indicating the size of the download next to the link. As a rule of thumb, sizes should be given for files that will take more than 10 seconds to download at the prevalent bandwidth available to most users. If most of your users have analog modems, you will need to warn them of the download size for anything beyond 50 kilobytes.

In the future, I expect browsers to be integrated with proxy services that keep track of the bandwidth and quality of service that has historically been delivered by the various sites on the Web. By using this information, the browser can change the appearance of links depending on the expected service; a link to a site that is often off the Internet or that usually delivers slow throughput may be rendered in faded colors, for example. This information will help users form expectations before they click, and will thus enhance the overall usability of the Web.

The problem, however, is that the user's experienced response time is determined by the weakest link in the chain from server to browser:

- The throughput of the server. Ought not to be a problem because the cost of hardware is the smallest part of developing a website, but popular sites often get surprised by rapidly increasing traffic and do not upgrade their machines fast enough.
- The server's connection to the Internet. Many sites try to save on their connection and put off upgrading from, say, a T1 to a T3 even when their current connection is saturated.
- The Internet itself. Although the Net is continually being upgraded, it still has bottlenecks, especially for cross-continent connections and for use during peak hours.
- The user's connection to the Internet. As discussed, connection speeds are extremely low for the majority of users and will stay that way for several years.
- The rendering speed of the user's browser and computer. Rarely a big problem, although complex tables can take significant time to lay out on low-end machines.

Each of these many steps introduces its own delay in getting a web page from the server to the user. Unfortunately,

Server Response Time

The growth in web-based applications, e-commerce, and personalization often means that each page view must be computed on the fly. As a result, the experienced delay in loading the page is determined not simply by the download delay (bad as it is) but also by the server performance. Sometimes, building a page also involves connections to back-end mainframes or database servers, slowing down the process even further.

Users, however, don't care why response times are slow. All they know is that the site doesn't offer good service. Slow response times often translate directly into a reduced level of trust, and they always cause a loss of traffic as users take their business elsewhere. To avoid this, invest in a fast server and get a performance expert to review your system architecture and code quality to optimize response times.

In 1999 I measured the download time for the home pages of 20 major websites. Half of the sites were the 10 most widely used sites on the Internet, and the other half were the sites of the 10 largest companies in the United States. Corporate home pages downloaded at a snail's pace, taking 19 seconds on average, whereas the popular sites' home pages took an average of eight seconds to download.

This simple survey showed that the sites that get the most traffic are more than twice as fast as the sites built by big, famous companies from the old economy. I would argue that the causality goes as follows: It is *because* the good half of the sites in my study are fast that they get so much traffic.

(Facing Page) Much of the design of this page from C|net is achieved by combining colored table cells with interesting fonts. The page does not require the download of a lot of graphics. In principle, the only graphics needed would be the site logo and the photo of the columnist. In practice, the "personalities" header is still a graphic due to the small dots and the beveled look. The headline "making a speedier CNET" is pure text in a colored cell, and a similar treatment could have been used for "personalities."

the delays are cumulative, meaning that we are not going to get snappy response times simply by improving a single link in the chain. When you upgrade from a modem to an ISDN line, you typically get twice as good web performance and not the five times improvement implied by the bit rates.

Speedy Downloads, Speedy Connections

Considering the fundamental facts in both human factors and computer networking, there is only one conclusion: Web pages must be designed with speed in mind. In fact, speed must be the overriding design criterion. To keep page sizes small, graphics should be kept to a minimum, and multimedia effects should be used only when they truly add to the user's understanding of the information. Remove graphic; increase traffic. It's that simple.

Conservative use of graphics does not imply boring pages. Much can be done with colored table cells and creative (but restrained) use of different fonts. In particular, style sheets can be used to improve page design without incurring a download penalty.

When it's necessary to use graphics, however, try using multiple occurrences of the same image instead of using different images; subsequent instances of the same image file will render quickly because the image will be in the user's local cache. Within a single page, image reuse will typically be relevant for smaller, decorative images such as buttons, arrows, and icons. In fact, frequent reuse of a small visual vocabulary will not only speed up download times but will also tie your entire site together visually.

Across pages, you can sometimes reuse larger images such as a product photo or a process diagram. When a large image is reused, it should retain its meaning from page to page, because users will often recognize the image. If you want to communicate two different concepts, you probably need to use two different images, even if download time will suffer.

ARUP Laboratories is a medical reference laboratory. ARUP's clients include hospitals, physicians, and companies interested in occupational testing. Rory Swensen, ARUP's web administrator, reports that www.arup-lab.com was designed to have almost no graphics in order to speed download times.

When the site opened, customers were invited to comment on the site in a feedback form. Of 201 comments, 45 praised the fast speed and only one customer complained that the site was *"not very visually stimulating."* Among the 45 comments on the download times was a hospital director who said, *"I like that the pages are not too fancy and therefore do not take too long to download,"* and a laboratory director who said, *"Well organized and easy to use. Loads quickly without large numbers of graphics."* Considering that the feedback form was completely free-form and did not ask specifically about any particular design issues, it is remarkable how many users commented on the speed. People do like fast service, which unfortunately is rare enough on the Internet to be noticeable.

Of course, customer feedback forms do tend to collect a biased sample of users because the majority of users don't bother providing feedback. However, experience from most sites is that people tend to be more motivated to comment when they are missing something or are otherwise annoyed about some aspect of the site; people rarely comment on things that just work. But having the positive comments outnumber the negative by a factor of 45-to-1 does support the finding that the users much preferred the site to be fast rather than fancy.

c|net

CNET.COM
home

Join now FREE!

MENU
NEWS.COM
Radio

BROWSERS!

REVIEWS
Hot List
Just In
All comparisons
CD-ROM central
Best of the Web

FEATURES
Techno
How to
Digital life
Events

GAMECENTER

personalities   Christopher Barr

Christopher **Barr** on the Web

making a speedier CNET
(5/12/97)

Publishing on the Web is not only about developing great-looking Web sites with killer content. It's also about the user experience. After all, what good is great content if it takes too long to get to it?

That's why at CNET, in addition to delivering new content on a daily--or even an hourly--basis, we're also working to deliver that information as quickly as possible. Fast downloads are especially important if you're dogged by the bandwidth blues. If your connection to the Net is 28.8 kbps or slower, then you're one of the bandwidth-deprived. And at CNET, to paraphrase a certain politician, we feel your pain. We keep you in mind and always consider what it's like to be continually blasted with Web sites cluttered with too many graphics or built around complicated table structures that keep you waiting as your browser assembles the pages. We take the speed factor very seriously.

www.cnet.com

Understanding Page Size

The concept of "page size" is defined as the sum of the file sizes for all the elements that make up a page, including the defining HTML file as well as all embedded objects (e.g., image files with GIF and JPG pictures). Fortunately, it is possible to get away with page designs that have larger page sizes as long as the HTML file is small and is coded to reduce the browser's rendering time.

You Need Your Own T1 Line

Under the optimistic assumption that Internet latency can be kept to half a second (0.5), a user will need to download a web page in half a second in order to achieve the one-second response time required for optimal hypertext usability. Many web pages are about 100 kilobytes in size and can be downloaded in half a second only if the user has full use of a T1 line at 1.5 Mbps. This simple calculation shows that anything slower than a T1 will result in usability problems when browsing the Web.

In addition to fast downloads, it's essential to have fast Internet connections. Slow 14.4 Kbps modems have been history since early 1999, but the proportion of users who connect at modem-speeds is staying about the same. The only thing that happened from 1995 to 1999 was that slow modems were replaced by the faster 56 Kbps models.

The following table shows the maximum allowable page size needed to achieve desired response times for various connection speeds. The numbers assume half a second in latency, which is faster than most web connections these days. For many realistic purposes, page sizes really need to be even smaller than indicated in the table.

	One-Second (1.0) Response Time	Ten-Seconds (10.0) Response Time
Modem	2 KB	34 KB
ISDN	8 KB	150 KB
T1	100 KB	2 MB

The one-second response-time limit is required for users to feel that they are moving freely through the information space. Staying below the 10-second limit is required for users to keep their attention on the task. Although many intranets run on Ethernets that are at least seven times faster than a T1 line, I still advise that most intranet designs need to remain less than 100 kilobytes per page because it is rare that users get the full theoretical throughput of the network. The main exception would be access to mission-critical applets that are truly useful to the user's job and which do not need to be downloaded on every page, but rather, only when the user starts a new task.

The need to keep page sizes below 34 KB for modem users is confirmed by a case study from www.provenedge.com. Proven Edge Inc. serves small businesses, so it is reasonable to assume that most of its users are accessing the site through analog modems. The webmaster, Claire Amundsen, reports that pages that were 32–33 KB in size had a 7–10 percent bailout rate (the proportion of users who don't wait for the full download).

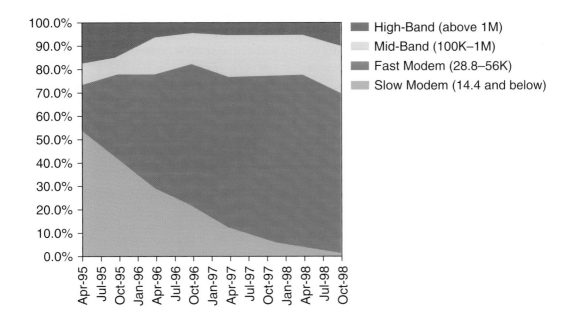

100.0%
90.0%
80.0%
70.0%
60.0%
50.0%
40.0%
30.0%
20.0%
10.0%
0.0%

Apr-95 Jul-95 Oct-95 Jan-96 Apr-96 Jul-96 Oct-96 Jan-97 Apr-97 Jul-97 Oct-97 Jan-98 Apr-98 Jul-98 Oct-98

■ High-Band (above 1M)
░ Mid-Band (100K–1M)
■ Fast Modem (28.8–56K)
▒ Slow Modem (14.4 and below)

The distribution of users connecting to the Internet at various speeds. Slow modems are 14.4 or below, fast modems are 28.8–56 Kbps, mid-band includes ISDN and leased lines, and high-band is T1 or faster. Unfortunately, this survey stopped in 1998, but I think it's reasonable to project the lines out a few years and predict that modem speeds will dominate in 2000 and 2001. (Data from the Georgia Institute of Technology surveys of web users.)

The original design of www.provenedge.com had a limit on page size at 40 K, but those pages that did reach the 40 K limit recorded a 25–30 percent bailout rate. Not knowing whether the bailout rate was a result of page size or the difference in information on the various pages, Amundsen went forward with some significant reduction of the graphics on the "fat" pages. File size of the graphics was the *only* thing changed. After the change, the pages that used to have a 25–30 percent bailout rate fell right in line with the others, at 7–10 percent.

Even though the page size limits in the table may seem strict, there is no doubt that sites pay a severe penalty in loss of users when they go beyond the recommendations. In the Proven Edge example, readership went up by about 25 percent when fat pages were put in line with the recommended maximum.

A practical tip: Links to a directory should include the final slash in the URL when embedded in web pages. (The slash should be left out when writing the URL for human consumption.) For example, the link to my list of Alertbox columns should be written as http://www.useit.com/alertbox in a (printed) magazine article but coded as http://www.useit.com/alertbox/ for the hypertext anchor in the online version of the article. The reason to include the slash in online links is to avoid a redirect when the server would have told the browser that the link refers to a directory and not a file. Adding trailing slashes to HREFs when appropriate reduces latency by a small but noticeable amount, so you may as well do it.

Glimpsing the First Screenful

The most important issue in response time is when the user gets to see a screenful of useful information. It matters less if it takes longer to load the full page and all its illustrations if the user can start acting on some information quickly. Guidelines for fast initial loading include the following:

- The top of the page should be meaningful even when no images have been downloaded (that is, more text and less images).

- Use ALT text attributes for images so that users can understand what they are about before they are rendered. Most browsers show the ALT text in the space reserved for an image as long as the picture has not been downloaded. (See Chapter 6 for more info on ALT attributes.)

- The browser must draw the top of the page quickly. However, it can do so only if it has all the information it will need for layout. Be sure to include WIDTH and HEIGHT attributes on all images and table columns.

- Complex tables often take a long time to render, so to cut down on the complexity of your tables, split the information into several tables. In particular, the top table should be simple and fast to render.

Taking Advantage of HTTP Keep-Alive

The original version of the HyperText Transfer Protocol (HTTP) was not efficient for downloading complex pages with many embedded images and applets. The protocol was optimized for the simple pages used in the early years of the Web. The main problem, however, was that HTTP would open a new TCP/IP connection to the server for every "hit," even when all the hits were to the component objects for a single page. Thus, every additional icon or colored bullet on the page would incur the overhead of having the browser contact the server and open a new connection; for small image files, the time needed to establish the connection would often be much longer than the time needed to transfer the actual bits.

Version 1.1 of the HTTP protocol introduced the notion of keep-alive connections, meaning that when both the browser and server use HTTP 1.1 (or newer), a single connection will be kept open as long as additional objects remain to be downloaded. Saving the overhead of establishing a new connection for every "hit" cuts latency dramatically. The experienced response time to load a page often drops to about half by using keep-alive. Therefore, it is highly recommended to upgrade your web server to software that supports keep-alive.

Linking

Links are the most important part of hypertext: They connect the pages and allow users to go to new and exciting places on the Web. There are three main forms of links:

- Structural navigation links. These links outline the structure of the information space and allow users to go to other parts of the space. Typical examples are home page buttons and links to a set of pages that are subordinate to the current page.
- Associative links within the content of the page. These links are usually underlined words (although they can also be imagemaps) and point to pages with more information about the anchor text.
- See Also lists of additional references. These links are provided to help users find what they want if the current page isn't the right one. Considering the difficulty of navigating the Web, users are often saved by a well-chosen set of See Also links.

(Following pages) Note how the AnchorDesk home page works equally well whether the user waits for the graphics to load or not. Almost the entire page definition is contained in a reasonably short HTML file so that the page can display immediately. The only page elements that don't work in the initial display are the buttons in the left column, but this is mainly due to bad browser design (the browser should be smart enough to use a smaller font to display the ALT text when the available area is too small to contain the text in the default font).

Back Issues
Companies
Products
TalkBack
Forums
Don't GoThere
Get MAD!
Home
Help?

Get the
AnchorDesk
Email
Alert
FREE!

Learn
online

Free Email!
hotmail.

get
PointCast free

PREVIOUS
ISSUE

Your source for tech intelligence

BERST ALERT

The Bad Guys Behind the Internet Brownout

Last week's Internet brownout wasn't a random glitch. It was the latest screwup by Network Solutions, Inc., which has kidnapped an essential part of the Internet as part of a get-rich-quick scheme. The company claims it owns the rights to the Internet's domain naming database (the "phone directory" for Web sites). *My take*: We need to run these bad boys out of town before they ruin it for all of us. Full Story

THIS JUST IN
How to Win the Web: The Quickest Way to Get More Visitors to Your Site

If search engines aren't part of your traffic-building solution, they are part of your problem. Web specialist Annette Hamilton reveals why updating your search engine lists should be your #1 priority this week. And she explains how to do it fast. Full Story

WIN!
Win a Free 6.4GB Hard Drive

Stop singing the no-more-room-on-my-hard-drive blues! Enter the new *PC Computing* sweepstakes and win the perfect solution: a 6.4GB Medalist hard drive. Full Story

HOT PRODUCTS
Get the Latest on Hot New Products

Want to set up a Web storefront fast? *ZD Internet Magazine* reviewers say LiveStore is best. And find out why *PC Magazine* reviewers named GoldMine the top contact manager for the THIRD year. Details on these and more hot products at the Web site, including IBM's Java tool and a top-notch Web site manager for Macintosh. Full Story

MONDAY JUL 21, 1997

ZDNN

On the ZDNN Radar Screen Today

Top stories from top ZDNN news editor Patrick Houston:

Happy days are here again! You don't have to be an investor to be gladdened by the financial results being reported by high-tech companies. Big question: How much longer can these good times roll? Answer: Quite a while, thanks to the global market.

Whacked out week un-wires Web. Backhoes, black-outs and bizarre human behavior made last week Web-less for some. Maybe it's time for an international treaty—not to control or censor the Web but just to administer it.

Ready? Get SET ... now wait a little longer. MasterCard and VISA unveil their schedule for rolling out SET, the security scheme for conducting credit card transactions over the Net. But SET isn't here quite yet. Full Story

PICK OF THE DAY
Road Warriors Worst Worry Solved

Nothing worse than being on the road and having your laptop battery give up. And it doesn't have to happen if you

www.zdnet.com

(Image)

Oracle 8 is here.

ZDNet AnchorDesk

Preview

(Image)

Here to Join

(Image)

Learn onl

FREE Em

Get Point

BERST ALERT

The Bad Guys Behind the Internet Brownout

Jesse Berst

Last week's Internet brownout wasn't a random glitch. It was the latest screwup by Network Solutions, Inc., which has kidnapped an essential part of the Internet as part of a get-rich-quick scheme. The company claims it owns the rights to the Internet's domain naming database (the "phone directory" for Web sites). *My take*: We need to run these bad boys out of town before they ruin it for all of us. Full Story

THIS JUST IN

How to Win the Web: The Quickest Way to Get More Visitors to Your Site

If search engines aren't part of your traffic-building solution, they are part of your problem. Web specialist Annette Hamilton reveals why updating your search engine lists should be your #1 priority this week. And she explains how to do it fast. Full Story

WIN!

Win a Free 6.4GB Hard Drive

Stop singing the no-more-room-on-my-hard-drive blues! Enter the new *PC Computing* sweepstakes and win the perfect solution: a 6.4GB Medalist hard drive. Full Story

HOT PRODUCTS

Get the Latest on Hot New Products

Want to set up a Web storefront fast? *ZD Internet Magazine* reviewers say LiveStore is best. And find out why *PC Magazine* reviewers named GoldMine the top contact manager for the THIRD year. Details on these and more hot products at the Web site, including IBM's Java tool and a top-notch Web site manager for Macintosh. Full Story

MONDAY JUL 21, 1997

ZDNN

On the ZDNN Radar Screen Today

Top stories from top ZDNN news editor Patrick Houston:

Happy days are here again! You don't have to be an investor to be gladdened by the financial results being reported by high-tech companies. Big question: How much longer can these good times roll? Answer: Quite a while, thanks to the global market.

Whacked out week un-wires Web. Backhoes, black-outs and bizarre human behavior made last week Web-less for some. Maybe it's time for an international treaty—not to control or censor the Web but just to administer it.

Ready? Get SET ... now wait a little longer. MasterCard and VISA unveil their schedule for rolling out SET, the security scheme for conducting credit card transactions over the Net. But SET isn't here quite yet. Full Story

PICK OF THE DAY
Road Warriors Worst Worry Solved

Nothing worse than being on the road and having your laptop battery give up. And it doesn't have to happen if you

www.zdnet.com

NEWS.COM
front page

Join now FREE!

MENU
Front Door
The Net
Computing
Intranets
Business
CNET Radio
Perspectives
Newsmakers
Rumor Mill

NEWS OPTIONS
One Week View
Desktop News
News Alerts
Custom News
Advanced Search
Push

click here. ▼

Novell.

Click Here.

advertisement

RESOURCES
Subscribe
Member Services
Contact Us
Help

CNET SERVICES
CNET.COM
BUILDER.COM

The Net

◁ back to

Netscape, Excite do foreign news

By Jeff Pelline
July 17, 1997, 8 a.m. PT

update Netscape Communications (NSCP) and Excite (XCIT) have announced an alliance under which the search engine company will produce a new navigational service providing international information.

Dubbed International Netscape Guide by Excite, it will be offered for Japan and Germany in the third quarter and for France and United Kingdom in the fourth quarter. Netscape struck a similar partnership with Yahoo for the domestic market in March, creating a site that went live in April.

For Netscape, the deal is a chance to generate revenues from its valuable Web site real estate--among the most traveled on the Internet--without producing content. For Excite, it is a chance to become a more global brand and create new advertising revenues.

Excite will be responsible for the programming, production, operations, and ad sales of the service. Financial terms were not disclosed, but sources said it involved a revenue split.

The international guide will offer local news, information, and entertainment. It will replace the international version of Netscape's Destination page.

The guide will be organized into a channel format focused around topics. They initially will include business and finance, computers and the Internet, fun and games, automotive and motoring, shopping, sport, travel, news, and weather.

related news stories

* Yahoo Netscape guide goes live April 29, 1997
* Search engines turn on to TV April 21, 1997
* Yahoo, Netscape strike deal March 18, 1997

FREE newsletter

enter email

[Subscribe]

Latest Headlines
display on desktop

The Net
• Pac Bell in DSL market trial
• Netscape fixes Communicator bug
• Database problem at InterNIC
• Netscape, Excite do foreign news

Computing
• RCA launches NC for the home
• Panda uses 500-MHz Alpha chip
• BeOS hits the stands
• Next generation of Mac clones
• Intel to cut chip prices up to 50%

Intranets
• First U.S. SET trials under way
• CA ascends to big leagues
• IBM, Gemplus team on smart cards
• E-commerce blitz by Oracle

Business
• Apple stock up 10% on earnings report
• Sun profits could climb 25%
• Will Sybase revenues follow profits up?
• Gates profits from strong earnings hopes
• Microsoft to hire 3,600 this year
• Cyrix shrinks losses, misses mark
• Iomega execs head for Software AG

www.cnet.com

Link Descriptions

Hypertext links are anchored in the text that the user clicks on to follow the link. These anchors should not be overly long because users scan pages for the links to see what they can do on any given page. The links serve a function somewhat similar to callouts in printed magazines: They give the user's eyes something to rest on while scanning through an article. If too many words are used for a link, the user cannot pick up its meaning by scanning. Only the most important information-carrying terms should be made into hypertext links.

The oldest web design rule is to avoid using "Click Here" as the anchor text for a hypertext link. There are two reasons for this rule. First, only mouse-using visitors do in fact click, whereas disabled users or users with a touch-screen or other alternative device don't click. Second, the words "Click" and "Here" are hardly information-carrying and, as such, should not be used as a design element that attracts the user's attention. Instead of saying

> For background information on the blue-nosed honey-bee, click here.

It is better to say

> We have additional background information about the blue-nosed honeybee.

Underlining the words that matter is important, but even better would be to include text that provides a short summary of what kind of additional information is available.

Although the actual hypertext anchor should be no more than two to four words long, it is strongly recommended to include additional (non-anchor) verbiage that explains the link. The Web is so slow that users cannot be expected to follow all links simply to learn what they are about. The departure page must include sufficient information to enable users to decide what link to follow next. In particular, links that seem overly similar need to be differentiated with supplementary text so that users can determine which one has the information they need.

(Facing page) News.com provides a list of related articles at the end of each story, encouraging users to give the service more page views. Readers who are interested in this story—indicated by the fact that they linked to this particular story from the front page—are prime candidates for related stories and are therefore given links to related stories they may have missed. My main complaint about this design is that it would be better to place the related links in the upper part of the page where they would be seen by users who do not finish reading to the end of the story. The column with "latest headlines" is much less useful in the context of this page than the related stories: Users can always get the latest headlines from the front page, and they probably came from there anyway.

STOP THE PRESSES!

Newspaper New Media News & Analysis

1997 Archive of "Stop the Presses!"

By Steve Outing

07/09/97- NetMedia Brings U.K. Internet Press Into Focus

07/07/97- Alternative Press' Answer to NCN

07/02/97- Reader Usability Wisdom From a Web Guru

06/30/97- Newspaper's Web Bios Rile Privacy-Concerned Reporters

06/27/97- New Century Chooses HTML E-mail as First 'Push' Service

06/25/97- We See the Problem; What Are the Solutions?

06/23/97- Newspaper Print Editions Fail to Promote Their Own Web Sites

06/20/97- Hollinger Web Network Covers Chicago Region, North to South

06/18/97- What Matters Isn't the Technology

06/16/97- NY Regional Web Ad Program Goes After TV Revenues

06/13/97- Summer Reading for Interactive Media Aficionados

06/11/97- Prom Baby Web Coverage: A Study in Contrasts

06/06/97- A New Web News Presentation That Looks Old

06/04/97- Tornado Web Forum Provides Public With a Voice

06/02/97- Canada Shuts Down Media Polls, But Not Internet

05/30/97- Online-Original Content Finds Its Way to Print

05/28/97- Does Your Site Contribute to Data Smog?

05/23/97- Post Licenses CitySearch Technology Rather Than Fight It

www.mediainfo.com

Links to "more of the same" are one of the easiest ways of increasing the use of your site. Whenever a user has read a page and linked it, that user should be given the opportunity to see other pages in the same series or by the same author whenever possible. A regular column, such as Steve Outing's "Stop The Presses!" or Jane Weaver's "Click•thru," is an obvious source of "more of the same links." Unfortunately, "Click•thru" does not have a link to earlier articles in the series, so users are left to hunt for them on their own—something only the most determined users will do. What a wasted linking opportunity.

MSNBC   ON AIR   PERSONAL   FIND   Hand

COVER PAGE   HIGHLIGHTS   FRONT PAGE   NEXT   Click here for more info.

COMMERCE

WORLD   COMMERCE   SPORTS   SCITECH   LIFE   OPINION   WEATHER   LOCAL   INDEX

The Web makes a perfect pitch

New ads from IBM, AT&T, FedEx sell the Net more than any product

By Jane Weaver
MSNBC

Click **.thru**

MSNBC
Jane Weaver
🔊 In AT&T's 'Rubber Eyes' commercial, frustrated entrepreneurs open up a virtual store.

A young furniture designer discovers "a doorway to the world" in an ad for Federal Express. Two female pals overcome initial obstacles to start their own business on the Web in an AT&T ad. A start-up company realizes that electronic commerce means more than dancing logos in a spot for IBM Internet Solutions.

This trio of TV ads from three of the world's largest companies pitch the Internet as the great equalizer, the next generation in the American dream. And while most such ads strain to link their business with the Net, these ads work because their messages tap into a growing awareness that small businesses truly are the Web's big growth market.

In fact, industry studies find that the Internet is becoming the fastest-growing channel for small business to create demand for their products.

It's not always clear what products these ads are pushing — except for the FedEx spot, the corporate logos are flashed only at the end. But the executions are well-written and stylish enough that the underlying message of the Internet as a tool for entrepreneurial empowerment shines through.

At a time when anxiety over corporate downsizing has even filtered down to the funny pages (the comic strip "Cathy" is currently coping with office cutbacks), it's appealing to think that anyone with a computer and an Internet connection can open a storefront to the world.

SHOPKEEPERS ON THE WEB

AT&T

"Rubber Eyes," a spot for AT&T Business Markets Division, is a testament to entrepreneurial inspiration: two women stumble on an idea for unbreakable sun glasses while vacationing in a tropical paradise. The infectious reggae classic, "I Can See Clearly Now," is a perfect musical commentary as they encounter various obstacles: snooty store owners who refuse to stock their creations, an outrageous real estate market and an overburdened catalog business. How can they launch their dream company? Via the Web.

"Soon we were open for business everywhere," says one of the characters. "Before we knew it, we were selling shades to everyone under the sun."

Eric Keshin, executive vice president at AT&T's ad agency, McCann-Erickson of New York, says the creative team realized that "just getting started is one of the economic challenges of small businesses."

In the ad, the Web is the storefront — forget the costs of real estate and counter clerks. "It's more than an information resource, it's actually a place to do business," Keshin says.

www.msn.com

www.onlineinsider.com

This is one of the least informative hypertext links I have seen. Seidman writes a great column, but the link to "current issue" is virtually useless to regular readers. What is the current issue about? Is it a topic I want to spend time on? Has the issue been updated since the last time I was here? The unchanging link to "current issue" answers none of these common user questions. A very simple redesign could keep the graphic buttons, if desired, but would supplement them with a short textual summary of the current column and its publication date (and possibly a direct link to the most-recent previous column, thereby bypassing the need to download an entire list for users who missed a column).

RESOURCES

Subscribe

Member Services

Contact Us

Help

CNET SERVICES

CNET.COM

BUILDER.COM

BROWSERS.COM

GAMECENTER.COM

SEARCH.COM

DOWNLOAD.COM

SHAREWARE.COM

ACTIVEX.COM

MEDIADOME

MARKETPLACE

CNET Store

How to advertise

update Work meant to increase Net capacity causes a three-hour slowdown this morning, especially for those trying to connect to and from West Coast Web sites.
July 11, 4:30 p.m. PT in The Net

Hitachi plays the blues on DVD
Hitachi will reportedly use blue laser technology to triple the data capacity of DVD-ROMs and DVD-RAMs by the year 2001.
July 11, 12:15 p.m. PT in Computing

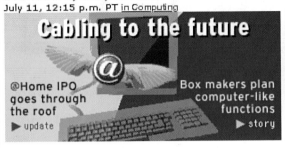

Cabling to the future

@Home IPO goes through the roof
▶ update

Box makers plan computer-like functions
▶ story

UPDATE ▶ story

Bug may be worse than thought

JavaScript hole exposes information

more news from around the web

Is technology rendering conversation obsolete?
Computer Currents Interactive

Netscape stalks the enterprise
Computerworld

Surfing up the '60s
Netly News

Dennis Rodman and AOL: What do they have in common? They're both rude
Inc. Online

Gamers face new charges
PC Magazine

It's Pretty Good, new . . . and free
Internet News

A critical shortage of programmers has prompted a worldwide labor hunt
Business Week

short takes

The House Commerce Committee Subcommittee on Telecommunications, Trade, and Consumer Protection will begin hearings July 11 on the Internet Tax Freedom Act, which would ban state and local taxes that target the Internet. The goals of the legislation have been endorsed by the White House, although it has not specifically endorsed the act itself.

Microsoft said that a "broad investigation" of New York and New Jersey computer swap meetings has led to the identification of 12 vendors allegedly involved in the illegal distribution of Microsoft software, according to a Reuters report. Microsoft said it filed lawsuits in U.S. District Court for the Eastern District of New York against five companies and reached settlements with seven others.

www.cnet.com

At the bottom of its home page, News.com provides a carefully selected list of the best current stories on other sites. This list is one of the most valuable features on News.com and a major reason to use the service. Note in this example, how some of the link descriptions are poorly chosen. How are users going to assess whether they have any interest in following a link called "Surfing up the '60s"? I believe that News.com simply picks the heading from the destination page to use as a link, but slightly more editorial value-add would be useful in the form of text that was explicitly written to be a good link.

Link Titles

Internet Explorer 4.0 and newer browsers have the capability to pop up a short explanation of a link before the user selects it. Such explanations can give users a preview of where the link will lead and improve their navigation.

Bad links are less likely to be followed, and users will waste less time going down the garden path if they know what they will get before they go there. When users do decide to follow a link after reading what it is, they will be faster at understanding the destination page upon arrival: Disorientation is reduced.

The link explanation is called a *link title*, and it's extremely easy to encode. For example, the HTML code for making my name into an anchor could be

```
<A HREF="http://www.useit.com/jakob/" TITLE="Author biography">Jakob Nielsen</A>
```

If you rested your cursor on this link in a browser, the words "Author biography" would pop up after about a second.

Having the title "Author biography" pop up when users are thinking about what might be linked from my name gives them an indication of the type of information they can expect from following the link. Among other things, it makes it clear that the link is not a "mailto" link that will spawn an email message.

Guidelines for Link Titles

The goal of the link title is to help users predict what will happen if they follow a link. Appropriate information to include in a link title can be:

- Name of the site the link will lead to (if different from the current site)
- Name of the subsite the link will lead to (if staying within the current site but moving to a different part of the site)
- Added details about the kind of information to be found on the destination page, as well as how it relates to the anchor text and to the context of the current page

---

Use Link Titles Without Waiting

Normally, I advise against using new web technologies that cannot be seen by all users. In most cases, using anything new is asking for trouble and will alienate users with older browsers.

Link titles are an exception to the need to wait. First, their use does not hurt users with browsers that don't display link titles (assuming you follow the guideline to keep the link anchor understandable when the link title is not displayed). Second, a browser that does not understand link titles will simply skip them. Because the title is not a new tag or otherwise intended to influence the layout of the page, the page will look exactly the same whether or not the browser does anything with the link titles. The only downside is that link titles will add approximately one tenth of a second (0.1) to the download time for a typical web page over a modem connection. This is admittedly a penalty, but worth paying because of the increased navigation usability for those users who do get to see the link titles.

Jakob Nielsen: Designing Web Usability

Value-Added Web Services

Websites will realize that they do not need to do everything themselves. The Web is built on linking, and the Internet is ... well ... a network. These technologies are a perfect match for **letting other sites handle services that you don't want to do** yourself. Two examples that are already in place are outsourcing the acceptance of credit card payments and having a discussion forum hosted on another site. Currently, most large websites install their own search engines, but it would be easier to handle search through a link to an external search engine that was maintained by search experts but could still be configured to display the search

> C|net article on discussion groups (and outsourcing of same)

As another example, all corporate websites need to give visitors directions to headquarters and other company facilities. There is no need for every site to design its own maps since there are sites that specialize in mapping services. Instead, give directions through an appropriate link to a preferred mapping service. Many of these services even provide customized directions from the individual user's starting point to the desired destination. The mapping service would be paid in whatever way it otherwise got paid. Currently, this means advertising, but in the future a micropayment might ensure enhanced maps (paid by the user or by the referring site, as appropriate for the circumstances).

Unfortunately, links to many Web services currently require authors to reverse-engineer the URLs used by the destination sites. Very few sites make it easy for third parties to link to them in programmatic ways to generate desired pages. Since most websites should be interested in getting new customers referred, I encourage them to use **simple linking schemes according to a protocol** that is published on the site. Once specified, such linking schemes must not be changed since that would cause the referring site's services to fail, causing bad will for everybody.

In the future, increased use of XML will allow far more intelligent data interchange between sites and thus for more advanced value-added Web services.

www.useit.com

Windows

Value-Added Web Services

Websites will realize that they do not need to do everything themselves. The Web is built on linking, and the Internet is ... well ... a network. These technologies are a perfect match for **letting other sites handle services that you don't want to do** yourself. Two examples that are already in place are outsourcing the acceptance of credit card payments and having a discussion forum hosted on another site. Currently, most large websites install their own search engines, but it would be easier to handle search through a link to an external search engine that was maintained by search experts but could still be configured to display the search results on pages

> C|net article on discussion groups (and outsourcing of same)

As another example, all corporate websites need to give visitors directions to headquarters and other company facilities. There is no need for every site to design its own maps since there are sites that specialize in mapping services. Instead, give directions through an appropriate link to a preferred mapping service. Many of these services even provide customized directions from the individual user's starting point to the desired destination. The mapping service would be paid in whatever way it otherwise got paid. Currently, this means advertising, but in the future a micropayment might ensure enhanced maps (paid by the user or by the referring site, as appropriate for the circumstances).

Unfortunately, links to many Web services currently require authors to reverse-engineer the URLs used by the destination sites. Very few sites make it easy for third parties to link to them in programmatic ways to generate desired pages. Since most websites should be interested in getting new customers referred, I encourage them to use **simple linking schemes according to a protocol** that is published on the site. Once specified, such linking schemes must not be changed since that would cause the referring site's services to fail, causing bad will for everybody.

In the future, increased use of XML will allow far more intelligent data interchange between sites and thus for more advanced value-added Web services.

www.useit.com

Macintosh

Note how the same link title looks different in Windows than on the Macintosh. In general, you should not assume that a link title would have a certain appearance or that it will word-wrap in a certain way. Simply provide plain text that describes the destination of the link.

(Facing page, top) Razorfish uses the same color for all links, whether the user has visited them or not. This makes it difficult for users to navigate the site because they have no clues as to which options they have tried and which remain to be explored. As an example, a user who does not know whether information about another company is found under clients, case studies, or partners may not remember which of these options were tried at an earlier time (assuming that the user spends some time navigating the area below each of the choices before returning to the home page).

(Facing page, bottom) Even when different colors are used for visited and unvisited links, users may not be able to tell which color is used for which kind of link. At least The Blue Dot uses vague derivatives of the default link colors, but I have seen sites that have yellow and green links. Which is which?

- Warnings about possible problems at the other end of the link (for example, "user registration required" when linking to *The New York Times*)

Link titles should be less than 80 characters, and rarely should they ever exceed 60 characters. Shorter link titles are better.

Also, you don't have to add link titles for all links. If it's obvious from the link anchor and its surrounding context where the link will lead, then a link title will reduce usability by being one more thing users have to look at. A link title is superfluous if it simply repeats the same text as is already shown in the anchor.

Do not assume that the link title will look the same for all users. Indeed, auditory browsers will read the text aloud and not display it visually. Different browsers will display link titles in extremely different ways, as shown in the figure.

And, finally, note that link titles do not eliminate the need to make the link anchor and its surrounding text understandable without seeing the link title. Users should not have to point to a link to understand what it means; the link title should be reserved for supplementary information. Also, for many years to come, some users will have browsers that do not display link titles.

Coloring Your Links

Most web browsers use two different colors to display links: Links to pages that the user has not seen before are typically displayed in blue, whereas links to pages that the user did see earlier are displayed in purple or red. It is critical for web usability to retain this color coding in your link colors. Although it is unnecessary to use exactly the same shade of blue as the browser default, unvisited links must unmistakably be blue and visited links must unmistakably be reddish or purple.

When non-standard link colors are used, users lose the ability to clearly see which parts of the site they have already visited and which parts remain to be explored.

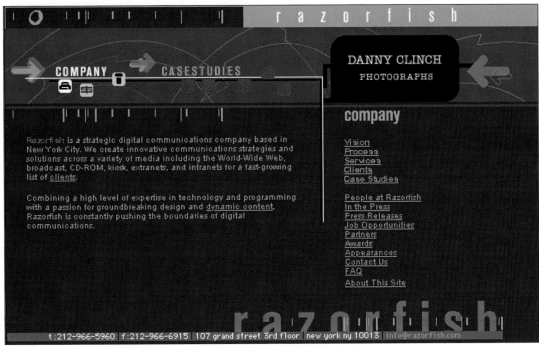

www.razorfish.com

www.thebluedot.com

The user's sense of structure and location in the site is significantly weakened, and navigational usability suffers as a result. Some users will waste time selecting the same option repeatedly; other users will give up prematurely, thinking they have explored all options when in fact they have not; and some users will not be able to get back to a section they read and found useful because it is not differentiated in the list.

In a study of a large number of websites, Jared Spool and colleagues from User Interface Engineering found a correlation of $r=0.4$ between using standard link colors and user task success. (A correlation of 0.4 means that standard link colors explained about 16 percent of the variability in a user's ability to do things on the sites and that all other factors combined to explain the remaining 84 percent. In other words, link colors are definitely not the most important issue in web usability, but they do matter.)

Link Expectations

Always use the same URL to refer to a given page. If one link uses one URL and another link uses a different URL, the browser will not know that both links lead to the same page. So, even if the user has followed the first link, the second one will be displayed as an unvisited link—certainly confusing to users when the link color clearly indicates they haven't seen a page that they in fact have seen. Users are never going to learn the structure of a site that commits this design sin.

The Physiology of Blue

If we were designing the Web all over today, few skilled user interface designers would pick blue as the color for unvisited links. Blue text is slightly harder to read than text in other colors such as black or red (assuming white backgrounds) because the human eye has fewer receptors for blue wavelengths. Despite this physiological fact, I still recommend using blue as the default link color. The reason is that users have grown accustomed to blue being the link color, so they have zero delay in figuring out how to work with a page if it uses blue for unvisited links. They just go: blue, boom, click. The few milliseconds lost from reading a few words more slowly because they appear in blue are more than made up for with the several seconds saved in cognitive overhead pondering a non-standard set of page colors and with the several minutes saved from improved navigation when users *know* what links they have visited before.

nybg events and calendar

July 1997 Calendar of Events

Spring 1997
Summer 1997
Autumn 1997
Winter/Holidays 1997-1998

The Enid A. Haupt Conservatory
A World of Plants
Opened May 3, 1997

Photographer: Alan Rokach

[NYBG | About | Gardens | Education | Research | Events | Plant Info | Shop]

www.nybg.org

Note how the use of standard link colors makes it trivial for users to see at a glance which of the links on this New York Botanical Gardens page they have already followed. On this site, users only go down the garden path when they want to.

A hypertext link fundamentally has two ends: the departure page and the destination page. Links should follow two principles to increase their usability relative to their two ends:

- The rhetoric of departure. Clearly explain to users why they should leave their current context and what value they will get at the other end of the link.
- The rhetoric of arrival. Clearly have the arrival page situate users in the new context and provide them with value relative to their point of origin.

Outbound Links

Some web designers avoid links to external sites under the theory that you want to keep users at your own site and not present them with opportunities to escape. I do not like this approach to linking because it contradicts the basic nature of the Web: Users are in control of their own destiny. Get over it. You don't own them. And besides, there is no way to truly trap a user because it's always possible to escape by using a bookmark or by typing in a fresh URL.

Some sites provide warning clues that you're about to leave the site, as is the case with Microsoft's Sitebuilder, but I don't recommend this. With this site in particular,

Peoplelinks

When the name of a person is made into a link, I recommend having it go to a biography page about that person. In the interest of fast downloads, the personal page should have a relatively small, traditional portrait photo (possibly linked to additional larger and/or more varied photos of the person in various settings). The personal page should also briefly describe the person's background with appropriate links to more detailed information. If the person is the author of a regular column or other topical contributions to the site, it is reasonable to have a link to a full list of all pages written by that person on the site. A list of all the person's writings may also be linked from the page.

Finally, the personal page should list all those contact mechanisms that the person is willing to make publicly available. If at all possible, this should include an email address made into a mailto: link that automatically launches an email program with an appropriately pread-dressed message.

I recommend against making a person's name into a link to email that person. Doing so violates expectations on the Web because a link normally takes you to information *about* the thing you clicked to rather than making you communicate *with* the thing. Also, it is jarring to click on a normal hypertext link and be transferred into an email application.

Opening up new browser windows is like the vacuum cleaner sales person who starts a visit by emptying an ashtray on the customer's carpet. Don't pollute my screen with any more windows, thanks (particularly because current operating systems have miserable window management). If I want a new window, I'll open it myself!

Designers open new browser windows on the theory that it keeps users on their site. But even disregarding the user-hostile message implied in taking over the user's machine, the strategy is self-defeating because it disables the Back button, which is the normal way users return to previous sites. Users often don't notice that a new window has opened, especially if they are using a small monitor where the windows are maximized to fill the screen. So, a user who tries to return to the origin will be confused by a grayed-out Back button.

Entering

Accessories

We've launched a new browser for this shopping experience.

CONTINUE

www.gateway2000.com

I have three problems. First, because the glyphs are not Internet standards, users may not always understand what they mean. Second, learnability is made particularly hard because of the need to differentiate three classes of links rather than two; in particular, I think many users will not understand why some of the Microsoft-internal links are marked and others are not. Third, the glyphs make external links appear more prominent than internal links; the eye is drawn to the multi-colored glyphs, which distract from reading. One thing I do like on this page is how the list of Further Reading references has been nicely categorized with subheadings that facilitate scanning.

Improving the site design would be easy enough. The first idea is simply to have the pointer change color whenever it's over an outgoing link. This idea could be extended to using different colors depending on whether the new site had been previously visited by the user. It would also be possible to change the pointer shape depending on the quality rating of the site from a reputation server—by adding Michelin-like stars under the hand, for example.

SiteBuilder network

more or hess

Robert Hess

Made for Each Other? Making Your Site Browser Compatible

Posted June 2, 1997   To be archived July 2, 1997

I often find myself talking with people about the new features coming in the next version of Internet Explorer, or available from Windows NT Server, for serving up Web pages. After I've showed them the cool new features, and described how they might be used in a Web document, people usually get anxious to try a new feature on their own sites.

Then *the* question always comes up:

"How do I get this to work on the browsers currently available?"

I just look at them with a blank stare. If you could do this with a current browser, it wouldn't be a *new* feature, now would it? It always amazes me how, on one hand, Web developers clamor for some special, whizzy feature that they think would really improve their Web site, yet they want it to work on every browser their audience might be using.

Creating a "generic" but representative site is a pretty good exercise to check the quality of your message and information.

It can't be ignored that compatibility, however frustrating for Web designers and browser developers, is an important issue that needs to be considered carefully. It can also be a very, very difficult problem to solve. At some point in your Web design, you will have no choice but to alienate some faction of your potential audience, either by adding a feature they can't see, or by making a site so simple looking that surfers seeking "entertainment" will ignore it.

There are several ways to create a Web site that provides an appropriate level of compatibility from platform to platform, and browser to browser. Let's take a look at a few different approaches; perhaps one will be appropriate for your projects.

Start simple

Create a Web site focused on the "Lowest-Common-Denominator" approach. This means the site doesn't use any fancy HTML, or rely on embedded applets, or client-side scripting. It's just information, simply presented but well structured. Actually, creating a "generic" but representative site is a pretty good exercise to check the quality of your message and information. Far too many sites rely so heavily on special effects and fancy graphics that their creators don't realize how little real information they provide.

Once you have set up an HTML 2.0 version of your pages, then you can start adding some visual features that allow newer browsers to utilize some of their functionality. This can easily be done in a compatible manner with things such as the <FONT> element, for affecting the color and typeface of the text, and the <TABLE> element, for helping fine-tune the layout of the page. And, of course, there is always the <IMG> element, but remember that some surfers still use

---

more:
 from the archives

Robert Hess is an evangelist in Microsoft's Developer Relations Group. Fortunately for all of us, his opinions are his own and do not necessarily reflect the positions of Microsoft.

Further Reading:

Simple HTML
Authoring for Multiple Platforms

How can I use inline images without alienating my users **MS⊛→**

Cascading Style Sheets
Style Sheets: A Brief Overview for Designers

W3C: Cascading Style Sheets **MS⊛→**

Client-side scripting
W3C: Client Side Scripting **MS⊛→**

Microsoft JScript Web site **⊛→**

Microsoft VBScript Web site **⊛→**

Browser sniffing
JavaScript example **MS⊛→**

---

www.msn.com

Microsoft's SiteBuilder subsite classifies links into three groups that are given different visual treatment: Links within SiteBuilder are shown without further ado, links to other parts of Microsoft are shown with an "outbound link" glyph, and links to external sites are shown with a "leaving MS" glyph.

Site**Builder**
n e t w o r k

more or hess

Robert Hess

Made for Each Other? Making Your Site Browser Compatible

Posted June 2, 1997   To be archived July 2, 1997

I often find myself talking with people about the new features coming in the next version of Internet Explorer, or available from Windows NT Server, for serving up Web pages. After I've showed them the cool new features, and described how they might be used in a Web document, people usually get anxious to try a new feature on their own sites.

Robert Hess *is an evangelist in Microsoft's Developer Relations Group. Fortunately for all of us, his opinions are his own and do not necessarily reflect the positions of Microsoft.*

Then *the* question always comes up:

"How do I get this to work on the browsers currently available?"

I just look at them with a blank stare. If you could do this with a current browser, it wouldn't be a *new* feature, now would it? It always amazes me how, on one hand, Web developers clamor for some special, whizzy feature that they think would really improve their Web site, yet they want it to work on every browser their audience might be using.

Further Reading:

Simple HTML
Authoring for Multiple Platforms

How can I use inline images without alienating my users

Cascading Style Sheets
Style Sheets: A Brief Overview for Designers

W3C: Cascading Style Sheets

Client-side scripting
W3C: Client Side Scripting

Microsoft JScript Web site

Microsoft VBScript Web s

Browser sniff
JavaScript example

Creating a "generic" but representative site is a pretty good exercise to check the quality of your message and information.

It can't be ignored that compatibility, however frustrating for Web designers and browser developers, is an important issue that needs to be considered carefully. It can also be a very, very difficult problem to solve. At some point in your Web design, you will have no choice but to alienate some faction of your potential audience, either by adding a feature they can't see, or by making a site so simple looking that surfers seeking "entertainment" will ignore it.

There are several ways to create a Web site that provides an appropriate level of compatibility from platform to platform, and browser to browser. Let's take a look at a few different approaches; perhaps one will be appropriate for your projects.

Start simple

Create a Web site focused on the "Lowest-Common-Denominator" approach. This means the site doesn't use any fancy HTML, or rely on embedded applets, or client-side scripting. It's just information, simply presented but well structured. Actually, creating a "generic" but representative site is a pretty good exercise to check the quality of your message and information. Far too many sites rely so heavily on special effects and fancy graphics that their creators don't realize how little real information they provide.

Browser Detection (➡Newbies Net Guide)
http://www.newbies-netguide.com/web_pa~1/ndetect.html

.0 version of your pages, then you can start allow newer browsers to utilize some of their functionality. This can easily be done in a compatible manner with things such as the <FONT> element, for affecting the color and typeface of the text, and the <TABLE> element, for helping fine-tune the layout of the page. And, of course, there is always the <IMG> element, but remember that some surfers still use

www.msn.com

This hypothetical example shows two ways in which a browser could inform users that they are leaving a site, thus doing away with the special "outgoing link" glyphs. One way is to simply have the pointer change shape or color when it is over an outgoing link, or you could show a pop-up menu with additional information about the link.

A second option would be to show a pop-up with additional information about the link. In the example image on page 69, I am showing the title of the destination page (retrieved from a proxy server) as well as the name of the remote site (possibly retrieved from a site definition or from the title of the home page). The arrow pointing to the site name can change color depending on whether the user has been to any pages on that site before. As shown by these two simple examples, web browsers have a long way to go with respect to supporting users' navigation behavior. Too bad the main vendors spend their efforts on useless multimedia features instead.

The most fundamental reason to include outbound links on your site is that they form a value-added part of your content that comes very cheaply. At any given point, it is the web designer's duty to give users the best links to the most valuable destinations that will be of the most use to the users. Whatever value the user derives from the external site will partly rub off on your site because you guided the user to that site. If users feel that they get good results out of going to your site, they will return again and again. The links turn into content and become a reason all by themselves for users to like your site and use it.

By carefully selecting good external sites to link to, you leverage the work done by millions of content creators around the world. In principle, of course, the users could find these external destinations on their own and go there without stopping by your site. In practice, however, it is so hard to track down useful information on the Internet that users are going to love you for your links.

Outbound links should be picked judiciously. It is better to link a small number of highly relevant external pages than to link to all possible alternative sites on the Web. As in many aspects of design, more is less: The more sites you list, the less users are able to concentrate their attention on the valuable ones. Users typically have time to explore only about 10 percent of the links they encounter. Some users do want completeness and the option to survey a large body of related information; and to serve these users, it is a good idea to include a link to a good supersite for your topic. A *supersite* is a site that attempts to index, classify, and comment on as many other sites in a given area as possible.

(Facing page) Short annotations like the ones provided by The Mining Company can significantly enhance a set of outbound links. Instead of saying, "here's a bunch of stuff for you to check out (as if you had time)," the annotated list allows the user to estimate right here and now which of the different links are worth pursuing.

Jakob Nielsen: Designing Web Usability

Internet Solutions   click here

 Desktop Publishing

Aa   Sunday, July 06, 1997

Interest Areas ▼
Sub-Sections ▼
Related Sites ▼
▼ *navigate this site*

▪ **welcome**
  new feature
  previous features
  best of the net
  resource list
  feedback
  guide bio

▶ *search this site*

welcome

your guide
jacci howard
bear

Net Finds

Get a Drawing/Paint Program
Andy Evans has some nice descriptions of Vector, Raster, and 3D programs -- on the first stop of his exploration of **how to create great graphics**. The entire site is a delightful feast for the eyes full of fun, whimsical animated graphics.

The future of print by Christopher Guly
Changes in the way we print may have a profound effect on SOHO business owners. Read what one printer manufacturer has to say in this article from Toronto Computes!

Be Succinct! (Writing for the Web)
I should probably re-read this one every week! Jakob Nielsen describes the three main guidelines for writing for the Web. Whether you write original material for Web publishing or are transferring print documents to the Web, heed these tips.

Summertime Papers from Idea Art
From watermelons to sunflowers, browse this collection of fun summer designs in paper and envelopes from Idea Art.

Trademark Checklist
This checklist from the International Trademark Association (INTA) is a valuable tool for desktop publishers. It is an alphabetized list of thousands of trademarks and service marks showing to what they apply and how to spell them correctly.

Restore those faded photos
Polaroid's new software utility, Before & After, already has a tips page. Learn how to improve an old black and white photo.

www.miningco.com

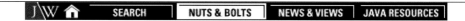

Resources

- Download this article and the complete source code as a gzipped tar file
  /javaworld/jw-08-1997/images/step/jw-08-step.tar.gz
- Download this article and the complete source code as a zip file
  /javaworld/jw-08-1997/images/step/jw-08-step.zip
- Download the latest BDK from JavaSoft's JavaBeans Web site
  http://splash.javasoft.com/beans/
- The JavaBeans specification
  http://splash.javasoft.com/beans/spec.html
- The "Glasgow" JavaBeans specification
  http://splash.javasoft.com/beans/glasgow.html
- Late-breaking advice for the JavaBeans developer from the *JavaBeans Advisor*
  http://splash.javasoft.com/beans/Advisor.html
- Online training from the Java Developer Connection
  http://developer.javasoft.com/developer/onlineTraining/
- Read *Intermediate & Advanced Java Programming Material* by Richard G. Baldwin
  http://www.phrantic.com/scoop/Java000.htm

Previous Step by Step articles

- "Chart your way to custom graph components" -- Learn to build a graph framework and custom graph components.
- " Scale an application from two to three tiers with JDBC" -- Learn how we can use JDBC to convert our Forum server application into a middleware layer.
- "Moving to JDK 1.1: Using the delegation event model to create custom AWT components" -- Learn how a move to JDK 1.1 affects the way you create custom components.
- "Creating custom components" -- Learn how easy it is to create specialized components, reuse them, and keep your application-level code cleaner with internal event handling.
- "Write your own threaded discussion forum: Part 2" -- Learn how to implement a simple communications protocol to get a forum discussion group up and running.
- "Write your own threaded discussion forum: Part 1" -- Use a forum to make your Web site more interactive, provide customer support, and more.
- "Stepping through a site navigator applet" -- Enhance your Web site with a convenient, hierarchical interface.
- "Stepping through an image map applet" -- Spice up any Web site with this reusable Java code.

If you have problems with this magazine, contact webmaster@javaworld.com
URL: http://www.javaworld.com/javaworld/jw-08-1997/jw-08-step.html
Last modified: Monday, July 14, 1997

www.javaworld.com

At the end of most articles, JavaWorld has a section of recommended resources that are of relevance to readers with an interest in the article. Because only readers who do care about the subject matter of an article will ever make it to the end, this placement is ideal for cross-references to rather heavy external sources. Users frequently find such see-also references valuable and use them as a way to get more in-depth information than can be provided in a single article. Unfortunately, the page design guides the user's eyes to the URLs for the resources because the URLs have been made into hypertext links, with the resulting color and underlining. It is fairly hard to scan the compact list of resources to pick out the ones of most interest to a given reader.

Resources

- Download <u>this article and the complete source code</u> as a **gzipped tar** file
  /javaworld/jw-08-1997/images/step/jw-08-step.tar.gz
- Download <u>this article and the complete source code</u> as a **zip** file
  /javaworld/jw-08-1997/images/step/jw-08-step.zip
- Download the <u>latest BDK</u> from JavaSoft's JavaBeans Web site
  http://splash.javasoft.com/beans/
- The <u>JavaBeans specification</u>
  http://splash.javasoft.com/beans/spec.html
- The <u>"Glasgow" JavaBeans</u> specification
  http://splash.javasoft.com/beans/glasgow.html
- Late-breaking advice for the JavaBeans developer from the *JavaBeans Advisor*
  http://splash.javasoft.com/beans/Advisor.html
- Online training from the <u>Java Developer Connection</u>
  http://developer.javasoft.com/developer/onlineTraining/
- Read *Intermediate & Advanced Java Programming Material* by Richard G. Baldwin
  http://www.phrantic.com/scoop/Java000.htm

Previous Step by Step articles

- "<u>Chart your way to custom graph components</u>" -- Learn to build a graph framework and custom graph components.
- "<u>Scale an application from two to three tiers with JDBC</u>" -- Learn how we can use JDBC to convert our Forum server application into a middleware layer.
- "<u>Moving to JDK 1.1: Using the delegation event model to create custom AWT components</u>" -- Learn how a move to JDK 1.1 affects the way you create custom components.
- "<u>Creating custom components</u>" -- Learn how easy it is to create specialized components, reuse them, and keep your application-level code cleaner with internal event handling.
- "<u>Write your own threaded discussion forum: Part 2</u>" -- Learn how to implement a simple communications protocol to get a forum discussion group up and running.
- "<u>Write your own threaded discussion forum: Part 1</u>" -- Use a forum to make your Web site more interactive, provide customer support, and more.
- "<u>Stepping through a site navigator applet</u>" -- Enhance your Web site with a convenient, hierarchical interface.
- "<u>Stepping through an image map applet</u>" -- Spice up any Web site with this reusable Java code.

If you have problems with this magazine, contact webmaster@javaworld.com
URL: http://www.javaworld.com/javaworld/jw-08-1997/jw-08-step.html
Last modified: Monday, July 14, 1997

www.javaworld.com

Here, I've done a light redesign job on the JavaWorld resource list. Because the URLs are the least important part of the list, they have been rendered in smaller type and with a less prominent color. Because the link automatically takes you to the URL, it's not always necessary to include the address in text format. One reason you may want to include the URL is when the URL adds credibility to the link. For example, if you're linking to a site about car repair, ford.com might be a more authoritative link than say, fredshappysite.com. By moving the hypertext links to the natural-language descriptions of the links, the user's eyes are guided to the information that is of most importance in deciding what links to follow. Scannability is further enhanced by not highlighting the entire line but instead highlighting only the most prominent words that describe the destination. As a final small detail, the only difference between the first two links is whether the source code is in .tar format or .zip format, so additional emphasis has been added to the format explanation to help users quickly understand why there are two links.

Incoming Links

Incoming links can be one of the most valuable means of generating traffic for your site. When others link to you, they provide you with free publicity and with an endorsement (remember that the author of the external page presumably followed my advice to be extremely selective in providing outgoing links). You should, therefore, be grateful for incoming links and do your best to support them. Some sites have formal affiliates programs that actually pay for inbound links.

The simplest way of enabling incoming links is to have permanent URLs for each of your pages. Whenever users see a URL for one of your pages, they should be able to copy it over as a hypertext link on their own pages in the knowledge that the link will keep working indefinitely. If you do have pages that will "disappear" on a certain date, say so; your linkers will not be disappointed.

Sometimes, a page may have a temporary URL as well as a permanent one. For example, the "current" version of a column may be a virtual URL that at any time resolves to the specific page that is then the current column. If so, both URLs should be made available to incoming links because some authors may want to link to the concept of the current column whereas others may want to link to specific columns about specific topics. See also the section on URL design in Chapter 4, "Site Design."

The best way of encouraging incoming links is simply to have content so great that others will *want* to link to it. Additionally, linking is facilitated when your pages are focused on specific issues to the extent that other authors can use them as references for specific information they want their readers to know about. An author is less likely to select a page as a destination for a link if it mixes too many different topics together; after all, the page would violate the rhetoric of arrival for that author's readers who would not understand why they had been pointed at the page.

(Facing page)   At the bottom of every page, Encarta Online includes a feature so that the user can generate a valid link to that page. This feature is necessary because the URL used to arrive at the page may have been generated by a search server and will not work in the future. It would obviously be preferable to use simple URLs that would keep working without this extra step, but given that users link to temporary URLs in various parts of the service, it is a great feature to allow users to easily discover a permanent URL. Services with background information should encourage as many users as possible to link to it. Generating a link to the page results in the following code

```
<A HREF=http://encarta.msn.com
/concise/default.asp?vs=x97&la=n
a&ty=1&vo=1B&ti=0330d000>
```

I assume that the "vs=x97" part of the URL implies linking to the 1997 edition. If so, it is probably a mistake to include this parameter in the link. Normally, it is better to link to the most recent version of the article instead of sticking with the 1997 edition forever.

Jakob Nielsen: Designing Web Usability

Guided fitness tour begins in **04** seconds.
NetGuide

| About Encarta | Find Article | Encarta Help | Microsoft **Encarta Concise Encyclopedia** |

Geography: Countries

Tonga

Tonga, country in the southern Pacific Ocean, southeast of Fiji and northeast of New Zealand. Tonga is the only remaining Polynesian monarchy. Its total land area is about 750 sq km (about 290 sq mi). Nuku'alofa is the capital and largest town.

Land and People

Tonga consists of more than 150 islands. The eastern islands are coral formations, while well-vegetated islands of volcanic origin lie in the west. The climate is tropical with high humidity.

The population is 105,600 (1995 estimate), with about two-thirds living on Tongatapu, the largest island. More than 99 percent of the people are Polynesians. Almost everyone is Christian; most are Methodists. Tonga's literacy rate, nearly 100 percent, is among the highest in the Pacific.

Economy and Government

Agriculture and fishing are the chief economic activities in Tonga, and about half the population works at the subsistence level. Because of a shortage of land, many Tongans seek employment overseas. Trade deficits are offset by tourism, money sent by Tongans working abroad, and foreign aid. The national currency is the *pa'anga* (1.27 pa'anga equal U.S.$1; 1995).

Tonga is a constitutional monarchy. King Taufa'ahou Tupou IV is the head of state, and the prime minister serves as head of government. The parliament consists of an 11-member cabinet, nine representatives elected by Tonga's 33 nobles, and nine representatives elected by the people. Elections are held every three years.

History

Tonga's first inhabitants probably arrived from Fiji about 3500 years ago. In 1616 Dutch explorers visited, and British explorer Captain James Cook made three visits between 1773 and 1777. Methodist missionaries arrived in the 1820s and converted the islanders to Christianity. George Tupou I founded the monarchy in 1875. In 1900 Tonga became a British Protected State, and in 1970 it achieved independence. The Pro-Democracy Movement, organized in 1992, faced strong opposition from the monarchy and the government.

Click here to generate a link to this page

How to Contact Us

Other Microsoft Products

Best experienced with

Microsoft
Internet
Explorer
FREE

Click here to start

encarta.msn.com

Linking to Subscriptions and Registrations

You may as well kiss incoming links good-bye as a source of new users if you require subscriptions or user registration. There is no way authors will link to a page if their users will have to sign up for a hefty subscription payment before being allowed in to read the page. Even user registration is enough of an impediment to user navigation to cut down on incoming links; a user who follows a link only to be dumped at a registration screen instead of a content page is not going to be happy.

You may as well kiss incoming links good-bye as a source of new users if you require subscriptions or user registration.

If your site does require subscription payments or user registration, then I recommend that you make certain pages at special URLs available for free linking—that is, any users who arrive at those URLs are let in without being harassed by a login screen. If you select your free pages to be representative of your service and of interest to remote authors, then you will likely be able to attract many referred users, some of whom will turn into permanent customers. You do have to communicate the "freely linkable" status of the selected pages, however, and establish an easy mechanism for authors to discover the URL they can use for their links.

Even though subscriptions and user registration are serious impediments to incoming links, I don't view micropayments in the same way. When micropayments become popular in a few years, users will be charged a few cents for certain pages through a mechanism that is as transparent as the current billing for telephone calls; it just happens, and the charge appears on your monthly statement without any user intervention or special authorization. Authors obviously need to consider the price of a page before they make a link to it, and an author will be more likely to link to a free page than to a microcharging page if the pages are of equal value. But a charge of a few cents should not deter anybody from linking to a good page. If the link isn't worth a few cents, then it should never be included in the first place.

Jakob Nielsen: Designing Web Usability

Advertising Links

Advertising is a special case of incoming links because you control the links yourself if you pay for the ad. I strongly recommend linking directly to payoff pages that follow up on the message in your ad instead of linking directly to your homepage.

Web advertising studies have found that about 20 to 30 percent of web users who click on a banner ad only to find out that they've been connected to a corporate home page hit the Back button almost immediately. The only surprise to me was that the percentage was not even larger. After all, if you dump users at your home page, you're leaving it to their own web-survival skills to ever find any valuable information that relates to the reason they clicked on the ad in the first place. Considering how hard it is to navigate most websites, this is a bad idea.

Some web marketers link their advertising banners to their home page because they want to entice potential customers to explore their site. Well, you can want this as much as you like, but users are not that motivated to struggle with your site. Your site is not the center of their universe. Web users are fleeting, and they want information now—not five clicks from now. If, and only if, the destination page provides interesting information related to the ad that attracted the user, may they reward your site with an extended visit.

As for the advertisement banner itself, it should be designed as a hypertext link. That is, it should have an excellent rhetoric of departure to give users expectations of the content they will meet at the other end and answers as to why they should bother traversing the link. Too many ads simply scream "Look at me!" with annoying animations, and yet they don't provide any link-following motivation beyond the incessant command to "Click Here."

infoseek®

Infoseek Home

You searched for **DVD manufacturing**

Sites 1 - 10 of 339,429

WHY BUY DVD? 10 reasons here.

Click Here for 10 Reasons Why You Should Buy DVD!

• **news center**

Desktop PCs From Gateway 2000 Are Latest to Select Mpact DVD

• **smart info**
People & Business
Stocks/Companies
Street Maps
Shareware/Chat
Desk Reference
Infoseek Investor

company capsules:

Simpson Manufacturing Co., Inc.

Lindsay Manufacturing Co.

Hunt Manufacturing Co.

KIT Manufacturing Company

Related Topics
CD-ROM
CD-ROM vendors

[   ] [**seek**] Tips

◉ Search **only** these results   ○ Search **the whole Web**

Sites 1 - 10 of 339,429   Hide Summaries   next 10

The Technology Of DVD
New DVD Analysis Equipment - One Manufacturer's View As the specification for DVD unfolds, so do new developments, considerations and requirements for test equipment. By Mark ...
100% http://www.kipinet.com/tdb/tdb_jul96/feat_dvdinspect.html (Size 5.6K)

Nimbus Begins DVD Production; Company is First Independent CD Manufacturer
to Offer DVD Manufacturing Nimbus Begins DVD Production; Company is First Independent CD Manufacturer to Offer DVD Manufacturing Source: PR Newswire CHARLOTTESVILLE, Va., Sept. 13 ...
100% http://www.digitaltheater.com/news/archive/sep145.html (Size 4.5K)

ALOM Technologies
ALOM Technologies offer disk/CD-ROM/DVD replication, assembly, logistics management, warehousing and fulfillment
100% http://www.alom.com/ (Size 2.8K)

www.infoseek.com

One great idea is for Infoseek to run a DVD ad that displays whenever the user searches Infoseek for "DVD manufacturing." Users who search for keywords related to the topic of an ad will often be very motivated to follow the link. This advertisement is particularly motivating because it promises a specific payoff (much better than a general "click here to visit us" banner).

Unfortunately, the link destination is a generic Convergence Point home page that does not list "10 reasons to buy DVD" as promised in the ad. Internet users are very cynical; and once you break a promise, they are going to assume that your site is worthless and they'll not investigate any further. The Back button beckons...

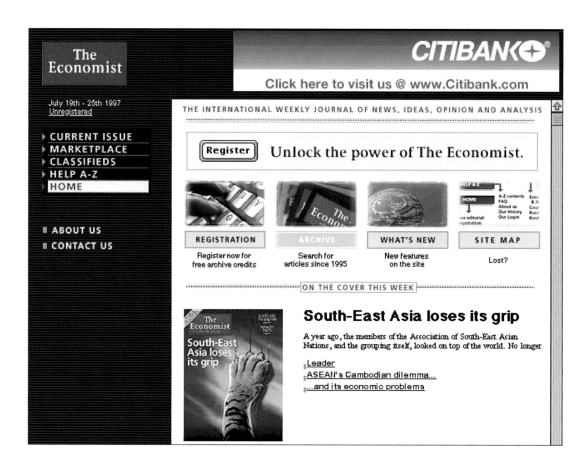

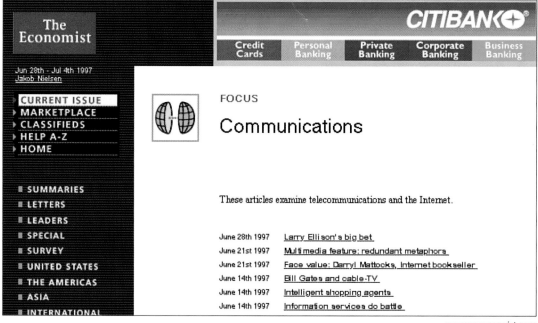

(Facing page)   Compare these two Citibank banner ads, which ran on *The Economist*'s site. Which one might have the power to divert you from reading interesting stories about the world economy? The general "visit us" ad only helps users who cannot guess that Citibank might have secured www.citibank.com as the domain for its site. The ad with the five colored buttons provides a better idea of some of the services the user will find. Also, the user can go to the general home page by clicking on the Citibank logo or go directly to a page about a specific service by clicking on its individual button.

Style Sheets

Cascading style sheets (CSS) are one of the greatest hopes for recapturing the Web's ideal of the separation of presentation and content. The Web is the ultimate cross-platform system, and your content will be presented on such a huge variety of devices that pages should specify the meaning of the information and leave presentation details to a merger (or "cascade") of site-specified style sheets and the user's preferences. If the introduction of WebTV broke your pages, you will appreciate the ability to introduce new page designs by creating a single style sheet file rather than by modifying thousands of content pages.

Use a single style sheet for all the pages on your site (or possibly a few coordinated ones if you have pages with very different needs: technical documentation versus marketing pages, for example). One of the main benefits of style sheets is to ensure visual continuity as the user navigates your site. Legacy publications have long known the value of basing print products on a single typeface: No matter where you turn in a magazine or a newspaper, the text and basic layout will look the same. Websites will gain the same brand cohesiveness when all the pages on a site link to the same style sheet.

There are two ways of implementing style sheets:

- An embedded style sheet is included simply as part of the web page in the form of extra lines of code.
- A linked style sheet is kept in a separate file, and each web page that wants to use that style has a hypertext link in its header that points to the style sheet.

Always use linked style sheets instead of embedded styles. Only by referencing an external file will you get the maintenance benefits of being able to update the look of your entire site with a single change. Also, by pulling style definitions out of your pages, you make them smaller and faster to download. If you use a single style sheet for your entire site, that file will be a single download once and for all.

Standardizing Design Through Style Sheets

For each site, all the style sheets should be designed by a single, central design group. There are two reasons for this. First, centralized design is the only way to ensure a consistent style and reap one of the main benefits of style sheets. Second, the majority of web content creators will not be capable of designing or writing good style sheets. Experience with word processors that support style sheets indicates that most authors mangle their style sheets terribly. Understanding the effect of style is relatively easy in traditional desktop publishing because it is a WYSIWYG environment with a single, canonical output form. But the Web is not WYSIWYG because of the variability in supported platforms. Furthermore, web style sheets are cascading, meaning that the site's style sheet is merged with the user's style sheet to create the ultimate presentation. These differences make it important that web style sheets are designed by specialists who understand the many ways in which the result may look different from what is on their screens.

WYSIWYG

Before the advent of graphical user interfaces, it was common for word processing to be done by mixing cryptic formatting codes in with the text. For example, boldfaced text might be indicated by a .bf code. A user editing the file would not see the word in **bold**, but would see the word preceded by .bf and followed by .nbf. The user would not see the intended formatting of the document until it was printed. This user interface led to many wasted printouts as users discovered that they were using the wrong formatting codes.

Graphical user interfaces introduced WYSIWYG editing, where "What You See Is What You Get." In other words, the document would appear the same way on-screen as it would appear when printed on paper, so users didn't need to print the document simply to debug the formatting. A great advance in usability.

On the Web, we have to give up WYSIWYG because pages will look noticeably different on various devices: A big monitor has about one hundred times as many pixels as a handheld device, and a fast T3 line transports data a thousand times faster than a modem. Indeed, looking different is a feature, not a bug, because an optimal user experience requires adjustments to the characteristics of each device. The more specialized or low-end the device, the stricter the requirements for web content to morph into something suited for the platform. The only way to make this happen is for designers to give up full control and let the presentation of their pages be determined by an interplay of page specifications and the preference settings and other characteristics of the client device: cascading style sheets.

To successfully introduce style sheets into your organization, you must fund an active evangelism program to teach your content creators how to use the centrally defined style sheet. Do not assume that people understand the concept of style and how to apply it simply because they are familiar with a word-processing program that incorporates style sheets. Research shows that most users make horrible mistakes in using word-processing style sheets, partly because the main word processors have particularly bad style sheet usability and partly because style is hard. Your style sheet should come with a small manual that explains the different styles, as well as when and how to use them. You'll need plenty of examples, including both raw HTML code (cutting-and-pasting examples is the main way people use documentation) and screenshots of the appearance of correctly coded pages in several mainstream browsers on several different platforms. The screenshots should be made into clickable imagemaps, allowing users to click on an effect they want to achieve and get to the documentation for the appropriate styles. In particular, if multiple styles have similar appearance, many mistakes can be avoided by explaining the differences and when to use which style.

Despite my preference for linked style sheets and central design, individual page authors should be allowed to create additional embedded styles for their own pages when necessary. Authors should be encouraged to do so only when absolutely necessary, but there will always be cases where a certain style is needed that is not supplied in the central style sheet. If many pages need the same effect, it should be added to the site's global style sheet, but it would be bad to inflate the one linked style sheet with styles that are needed only once. Single-page styles should be embedded rather than linked; the page should continue to link in the global style sheet and then override it with local, embedded styles as necessary. Doing so has the benefit of allowing future changes to the central style sheet to propagate to the modified page to the greatest extent possible.

Style Sheet Examples for Intranets

On an intranet, you are often able to avoid the added complexity of catering to a variety of browsers and platforms. If you have standardized on a single browser and on a single platform, your style sheet manual obviously needs to include only screenshots of pages rendered in the recommended configuration. Even so, you should still include shots of pages rendered in different sizes of windows (unless your organization has standardized the use of small monitors, you will find that users size their browsers differently).

However, intranets may have a variety of centrally supported style sheets due to the different needs of the different kinds of information in different departments. Your style sheet manual should clearly list all the available style sheets and explain when to use which style (richly illustrated with examples of typical content).

Making Sure Style Sheets Work

Pages must continue to work when style sheets are disabled by the end user or by the end user's browser. For example, do not use tricks where the same words are repeated multiple times with small offsets to create shadow effects; without the intended style, the text turns into gibberish. Retaining a decent presentation without the style sheet is mandatory to support users with older browsers, visually impaired users, and users who need to disable the style feature in their browser (either because of bugs or because your style conflicts too much with their preferences). Fortunately, it is easy to check conformance with this rule: Simply disable style sheets in your browser and reload the page.

Additionally, there are several other guidelines to keep in mind when working with style sheets:

- Do not use more than two fonts (plus possibly a third for special text like computer code). Remember the lesson from the early days of desktop publishing: Using a lot of fonts simply because you *can* will result in a ransom-note look. Typically, you can use one typeface for body text and another, bolder face for headings. Note that it's fine (indeed, recommended) to use a long list of alternative fonts in the style sheet specification for a given class of text. The user's browser will pick the first available font in the list and use it throughout your pages, meaning that the user will see a single font, making the site feel typographically unified. It is important that lists of font names have the fonts listed in the same order because the browser picks the first one it finds available.

- Do not use absolute font sizes. Instead, specify all text relative to the base font size defined by the user's preference setting. For example, large text could be defined as "200%", meaning that it would be set as 24 points if the user preferred 12 points for body text, but 20 points if the user prefers 10 points for body text. Whether people prefer large or small fonts depends on a variety of factors, including the size and resolution of their monitors, their eyesight, and whether they're looking at the page on their own or showing it to others. It's more than somewhat annoying to visit a website where the text is too small for comfortable reading, but

Although the Web Consortium's CSS logo button is nice, I recommend that you restrain yourself and do not plaster it all over your site. In particular, do not put it on the home page. Users do not care how you implement your site (except if they follow an "about this site" link, in which case it would be great to put a CSS button on the "About" page). A firm rule for home page design is "more is less": the *more* buttons and options you put on the home page, the *less* users are capable of quickly finding the information they need. (Because of this rule I am puzzled by the many home pages that feature download buttons for various browser vendors. Why anyone would reduce the usability of his or her own site in order to give another company free advertising is beyond me.)

Jakob Nielsen: Designing Web Usability

it is *extremely* annoying to click on the "make text bigger" button and have nothing happen because the font sizes were defined as an absolute number of points.

- CSS allows style sheets to specify that certain settings should override those in other levels of the cascade. This is done by adding an **!important** attribute to the specification. Do not use this feature. It is hard to imagine cases where you would be justified in ignoring the user's preferences if the user felt strongly enough to use his or her own **!important** rating, so **!important** should be reserved only for user style sheets and never for use in the website's style sheet.

- If you have multiple style sheets, make sure to use the same CLASS names for the same concept in all of the style sheets. Content creators who use two or more style sheets will be confused if different CLASSes are used for the same thing or if one style sheet has a CLASS that is missing in the other style sheet even though the concept applied in both cases. If, for example, you have a CLASS for the name of the author of a document, then all of your style sheets should have this CLASS, even though it may be defined to render differently, as appropriate for the different kinds of documents.

Frames

My main recommendation with respect to frames is

Frames: Just Say No

People who really know what they are doing can sometimes use frames to good effect, although even experienced designers are advised to use frames as sparingly as possible.

Part of the genius of Tim Berners-Lee's original design of the Web was a total unification of several concepts in a single idea, the page:

- The user's view of the information on the screen
- The unit of navigation, or what you get when you click a link or activate a navigation action such as a bookmark

<NOFRAMES>

If you insist on using frames despite my advice to the contrary, then at least provide a non-framed version for the many users who prefer to avoid frames. In particular, alternative content can be provided in a <NOFRAMES> section that will be shown to users who have frames turned off or who use a browser that doesn't support frames.

Unfortunately, most designers don't bother designing two versions of their pages and reserve <NOFRAMES> for a "helpful" link to the download site for a frames-supporting browser version. Sarcasm-impaired readers should note that I put the word "helpful" in quotes. Users are not going to be motivated to download a 10 MB browser just to see your pages, so a download link is useless.

- A textual address used to retrieve information over the Net (the URL)
- The storage of the information on the server and the author's editing unit, except when using embedded objects such as image files, which do require the author to manage multiple files for a page

In fact, these four concepts have been unified so well that you may not even think of them as being separate—great proof that the original design of the Web works as intended. Fundamentally, the Web is based on having the page as the atomic unit of information, and the notion of the page permeates all aspects of the Web. The simplicity of the original Web contributed to its ease of use and its rapid uptake.

Frames break the unified model of the Web and introduce a new way of looking at data that has not been well integrated into the other aspects of the Web. With frames, the user's view of information on the screen is now determined by a sequence of navigation actions rather than a single navigation action.

Navigation doesn't work with frames because the unit of navigation is different from the unit of view. If users create a bookmark in their browser, they may not get the same view back when they follow the bookmark at a later date, because the bookmark doesn't include a representation of the state of the frames on the page.

Even worse, URLs stop working. The addressing information shown at the top of the browser no longer constitutes a complete specification of the information shown in the window. If an author copies the URL in order to include it as a hypertext anchor in one of his or her own pages, then that anchor will not lead readers to the desired view but will instead lead them to the initial state of the frameset. Similarly, if a user decides to send an email message to a friend with the recommendation to check out a page, then copying the URL from the browser will not work if frames are used because the URL points to the frameset and not to the current view (with the information of interest to the friend). Given that social filtering is one of the most powerful mechanisms for information discovery on the Internet, it is an utter disaster to disable the URL as an addressing mechanism.

Jakob Nielsen: Designing Web Usability

The way most designers use frames assumes that the user has a standard computer with a reasonably large display. The following figure shows a typical example of a framed page that looks decent on a large screen but is close to useless on a PDA's small screen. Frames presumptuously reserve a part of the user's screen space for information that the designer deems to be of special importance. Sometimes, of course, the designer may be right, but usually it is impossible to predict what users will need and what is the best trade-off for their specific screen size. Commonly, frames are used to keep navigation bars permanently visible, but as the figure shows, users with small screens will prefer to use all of their space for content. A single scrolling pane without frames allows for more flexibility in accommodating different users.

In addition to these fundamental problems, there are also several minor problems with the current implementation of frames. These problems will disappear over the next few years, but for now they remain a reason to minimize use of frames. Additional reasons to avoid frames include the following:

- Many browsers cannot print framed pages appropriately. Of course, current browsers don't print *anything* really well, but at least regular pages normally print in full. With frames, it is common to have the Print command result in the printing of a single frame. Printing the full page is difficult with scrolling frames—should only the visible part of the frame be printed or should the content be allowed to expand and take up more room than it does on the screen?

- The original release of HTML was simple enough that many people learned it without any problems. Frames are another matter, though. Newsgroups like comp.infosystems.www.authoring.html are filled with questions from web authors who desperately need to know why their frames don't work as intended. Frames are so hard to learn that many page authors write buggy code when they try to use them.

- Search engines have trouble with frames because they don't know what composites of frames to include as navigation units in their index.

Borderless Frames

Most uses of frames can be improved by making the frame borders invisible. Users should not need to know how the design is implemented. Using borderless frames has two main advantages: There are more pixels left over for the content, and there is one less interface element for users to ponder.

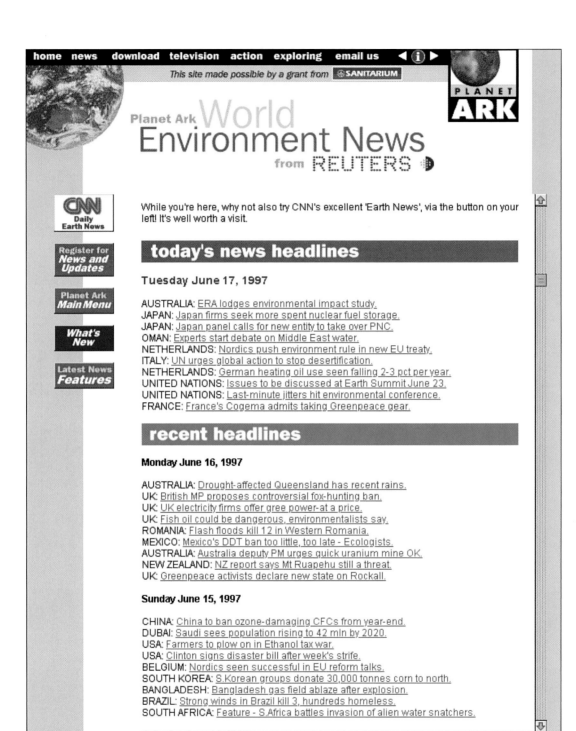

home   news   download   television   action   exploring   email us   ◄ ⓘ ►

This site made possible by a grant from ⊕SANITARIUM

PLANET
ARK

Planet Ark World
Environment News
from REUTERS ◖

CNN
Daily
Earth News

Register for
**News and
Updates**

Planet Ark
Main Menu

**What's
New**

Latest News
Features

While you're here, why not also try CNN's excellent 'Earth News', via the button on your left! It's well worth a visit.

today's news headlines

Tuesday June 17, 1997

AUSTRALIA: <u>ERA lodges environmental impact study.</u>
JAPAN: <u>Japan firms seek more spent nuclear fuel storage.</u>
JAPAN: <u>Japan panel calls for new entity to take over PNC.</u>
OMAN: <u>Experts start debate on Middle East water.</u>
NETHERLANDS: <u>Nordics push environment rule in new EU treaty.</u>
ITALY: <u>UN urges global action to stop desertification.</u>
NETHERLANDS: <u>German heating oil use seen falling 2-3 pct per year.</u>
UNITED NATIONS: <u>Issues to be discussed at Earth Summit June 23.</u>
UNITED NATIONS: <u>Last-minute jitters hit environmental conference.</u>
FRANCE: <u>France's Cogema admits taking Greenpeace gear.</u>

recent headlines

Monday June 16, 1997

AUSTRALIA: <u>Drought-affected Queensland has recent rains.</u>
UK: <u>British MP proposes controversial fox-hunting ban.</u>
UK: <u>UK electricity firms offer gree power-at a price.</u>
UK: <u>Fish oil could be dangerous, environmentalists say.</u>
ROMANIA: <u>Flash floods kill 12 in Western Romania.</u>
MEXICO: <u>Mexico's DDT ban too little, too late - Ecologists.</u>
AUSTRALIA: <u>Australia deputy PM urges quick uranium mine OK.</u>
NEW ZEALAND: <u>NZ report says Mt Ruapehu still a threat.</u>
UK: <u>Greenpeace activists declare new state on Rockall.</u>

Sunday June 15, 1997

CHINA: <u>China to ban ozone-damaging CFCs from year-end.</u>
DUBAI: <u>Saudi sees population rising to 42 mln by 2020.</u>
USA: <u>Farmers to plow on in Ethanol tax war.</u>
USA: <u>Clinton signs disaster bill after week's strife.</u>
BELGIUM: <u>Nordics seen successful in EU reform talks.</u>
SOUTH KOREA: <u>S.Korean groups donate 30,000 tonnes corn to north.</u>
BANGLADESH: <u>Bangladesh gas field ablaze after explosion.</u>
BRAZIL: <u>Strong winds in Brazil kill 3, hundreds homeless.</u>
SOUTH AFRICA: <u>Feature - S.Africa battles invasion of alien water snatchers.</u>

www.planetark.org

The frames look decent on a large computer monitor. The scrollbars are a little tacky, but there might be some benefit from being able to scroll through the list of stories while still keeping the site navigation bar and buttons visible at all times.

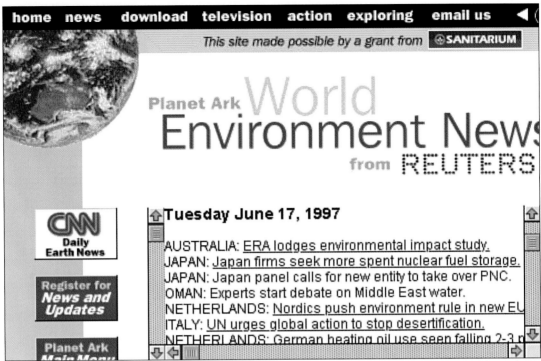

This site made possible by a grant from ⊕SANITARIUM

Planet Ark World
Environment News
from REUTERS

CNN
Daily
Earth News

Register for
News and
Updates

Planet Ark
Main Menu

Tuesday June 17, 1997

AUSTRALIA: ERA lodges environmental impact study.
JAPAN: Japan firms seek more spent nuclear fuel storage.
JAPAN: Japan panel calls for new entity to take over PNC.
OMAN: Experts start debate on Middle East water.
NETHERLANDS: Nordics push environment rule in new EU
ITALY: UN urges global action to stop desertification.
NETHERLANDS: German heating oil use seen falling 2-3 r

www.planetark.com

When the same site is visited by a user with a small 480-by-320-pixel display as one might find on an information appliance, the picture literally changes dramatically and the site's usability drops through the floor. Now, only 25 percent of the display is used to show the list of stories, and the remaining 75 percent are taken up by site decorations of little interest to the user. The smaller the display, the more critical it is to maximize the number of precious pixels devoted to useful information.

When using TotalNews, the actual articles come from other websites that are displayed within a frameset from TotalNews. Here, the user has requested baseball news, which comes from *USA Today*. Unless users are very sophisticated in deconstructing web design, they may not realize which part of the window comes from which site. Also, because of the improper way URLs are handled in frames, the browser window indicates that the user is visiting TotalNews, even if most of the screen is dominated by content from *USA Today*.

Frames as Copyright Violation

In my opinion, it is a copyright violation to display the contents of another website within your own frames. The exception would be limited use for critical purposes, which should be allowed under the fair-use clause. Because I am not a lawyer and because Internet law is in constant flux, you are advised to contact an intellectual property attorney for specific advice if you plan a design that makes substantive use of framing others' content.

The reason I believe it violates copyright to frame other sites is because the browser continues to display your own URL, leading users to believe that they are seeing your content. Displaying your navigation frames around the remote site will confirm this belief for your users.

- Some browsers make it difficult to bookmark frames.
- Many websites that offer users a choice between regular and framed versions have found that most users prefer frames–free designs.

Is It Ever OK to Use Frames?

The main issue in using frames is to ensure that URLs keep working. To do so, all hypertext links must have a TARGET="_top" attribute in their anchor tag (e.g., <A HREF=foo.html TARGET="_top">). Adding the _top target attribute makes the browser clear out all the frames and replace the entire window with a new frameset. The destination frameset may well have many frames that are identical to the ones in the departure frameset and will be cached in the browser, but by forcing a complete reload in principle, the browser gets a new URL for the destination. This means that navigation actions, such as bookmarking, work again and that the URL is available for other people to link to.

The only exception from the need to use a TARGET="_top" attribute is when frames are used as a shortcut for scrolling within a single page. For example, a long directory or other alphabetical listing could have a frame on top that lists the letters of the alphabet. Clicking one of these letters would cause the listing to scroll within another frame while keeping the user on the same page and thus not destroying navigation.

Frames are also useful for "meta-pages" that comment on other pages. For example, a web design style guide may need to mix discussions of design principles with live examples of entire pages that follow (or break) the rules. In these cases, the embedded page should be treated as an embedded image (even though it is implemented as an independent page) and the "main" information that users will want to bookmark should be the content of the commenting frame.

HTML version 4.0 introduced a new type of frames called *inline frames*. These frames nest as part of their host page and do not interfere with the user's navigation. As far as the user is concerned, the basic page model is maintained when using inline frames; it just so happens that, behind the scenes, part of the page is filled in with content from a different file that scrolls independently of the main content. Inline frames are wonderful for containing navigation bars or columns because the content can be made non-scrollable and only needs to be downloaded once. Thus, I strongly recommend making the frames into inline frames if you decide you need frames for your pages.

Credibility

"The Web is the Great Equalizer" as one of my test users once said. Anybody can put up a site, and increasingly, anybody does. As a result, users don't quite know what to make of information retrieved from the Web. It can be the deep truth, or it can be the ramblings of a nut. There is no easy way of telling whether a website is reliable. In the physical world, you typically know that certain sources like *The New York Times* are reliable, and you know that if you walk into a Toyota dealership, they will have the specifications of the latest Camry as released by Toyota headquarters.

One of the main goals of great web design is to establish your credibility as a professionally run operation. Do not fill your pages with amateur junk like heavy backgrounds or animated "send me more mail," continuously folding letter icons. Polished graphic design probably has relatively little impact on usability in the sense that users will be able to find the information equally fast even if the graphics are a little rough and not fully color-coordinated. But there is no doubt that the visual appearance is literally the first thing the user sees upon entering a site, and good-looking visuals are a major opportunity for establishing credibility.

In the future, I expect that credibility will be partly established through a reputation manager, that is, an Internet service that collects ratings from other users who tell it how satisfied they have been with pages and other products and services they have received from each of the sites on the Web. The reputation manager will be a sort of ultimate *Consumer Reports* for the network computing age.

Jakob Nielsen: Designing Web Usability

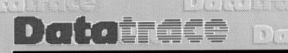

Information Services

...your source for land, mortage and title search information.

At Datatrace we service counties in the surrounding areas of our offices located in Tampa, Florida; Ft. Lauderdale, Florida; Mt. Clemens, Michigan; and Cleveland, Ohio.

Our headquarters are based in Richmond, Virginia.

These are the services we offer here at Datatrace.

- What Datatrace is about.
- Automated Title Search System
- Ownership Encumbrance Reports
- Asset Encumbrance Reports
- 1099S Services
- Check out career opportunities with Datatrace.

E-mail **Datatrace Information Services.**

Copyright 1996-97 Datatrace Information Services Company Inc.

www.datatrace.com

---

thank you

Thank you for participating in our survey. Please enter your email address so we can choose our Pilot and t-shirt winners (note: if you are not one of the lucky winners we won't use or store your email address).

email address: _____

[return to NEWS front door]

Again, we appreciate your taking the time to make NEWS.COM a better service.

Copyright © 1997 CNET, Inc. All rights reserved. Mail questions to survey@news.com.

www.cnet.com

Printing

Most of the users I have interviewed say that they print out a good deal of information from the Web. In principle, the Web ought to have made the need to print out information for archival purposes obsolete, but bitter experience has taught users that they cannot rely on retrieving information if they need it at a later date. Sometimes, the remote server will be down, sometimes the webmaster has removed the page, and sometimes the users are simply not able to find the page a second time. Printouts are also preferable if the user has a paper-based filing system with folders or binders for all the information relating to a certain project.

Because it is so unpleasant and slow to read large amounts of text from computer screens, users also often print out long documents to read offline. Additionally, users sometimes print out web pages to give to others to read, perhaps as handouts in meetings or seminars. Better computer screens may eventually reduce the need for printouts, but for the next several years, we must expect many users to continue to want to print out web-based information.

The implication for web design is to provide printable versions of any long documents. Web browsers are slowly improving their print functionality, but one cannot rely on browser companies to produce well-crafted printouts because their main interest is online information. For example, most browsers use the same typeface and font size for online viewing and printing, even though it is known to all typography specialists that the two media require different typefaces. Also, the layout of a document will typically be different: Single-column layouts make for easier scrolling in online viewing whereas two-column layouts are preferred for letter-sized paper.

My recommendation is to generate two versions of all long web documents. One version should be optimized for online viewing by being chunked appropriately into many files using plenty of hypertext links and a screen-oriented style sheet. Another version should keep the entire document in one file with a layout that is optimized for printing.

You must limit any PostScript pages to a printable area that will fit on both A4 sheets and 8.5"×11" sheets.

Currently, users will need to download the printable version manually, but hopefully browsers will soon start to implement the recommended standard for specifying alternative document versions. One such alternative is indeed the printable version, and it will not hurt to include the appropriate HTML in the HEAD part of documents with printable versions. The code reads as follows:

```
<LINK REL="alternate" MEDIA="print" HREF="mydoc.ps"
TYPE="application/postscript">
```

Older browsers will simply ignore any specifications of printable alternatives, but future browsers will recognize this code as indicating that any print command should be performed on the alternate file and not on the displayed version of the page.

The printable file should probably be in formats like PostScript or PDF. It is extremely important to denote any such files as being for printouts only, and always be sure to supplement them with links to the same content in HTML for online viewing by users who want to browse or search a small part of the document.

PostScript files should never be read online. PostScript viewers are fine for checking the nature of a document in order to determine whether it's worth printing, but users should not be tricked into the painful experience of actually spending an extended period of time with online PostScript. PostScript and PDF are page description languages that specify exactly how the text should look when printed. Such descriptions do not have the flexibility or cross-platform capabilities necessary for online viewing and interaction. For example, a two-column layout in PDF will look perfect when printed but will be almost impossible to read on a screen that is smaller than the sheet of paper for which the page was intended.

I repeat: Do not torment your users by making important documents available in PostScript form only. Always link to an HTML version for online reading.

Any file that is intended for printing must be able to accommodate the two most common international page formats: A4 and 8.5"×11" (U.S. Letter). To do so, the width of the page must fit on an A4 sheet, and the height of the page must fit on an 8.5"×11" sheet because A4 is the narrowest format and 8.5"×11" is the shortest format. It is recommended to leave a margin of at least half an inch (13 mm) for all four sides of the page to ensure that it will print on all printers and to facilitate photocopying. With half-inch margins, the printable area is 7 ¼" (18.5 cm) wide by 10" (25.4 cm) tall; with one-inch margins (preferred), the printable area would be 6 ¼" (15.9 cm) by 9" (22.9 cm).

Conclusion

Simplicity should be the goal of page design. Users are rarely on a site to enjoy the design; instead, they prefer to focus on the content (which I will discuss in the next chapter). It is also important to ensure that page designs work across a wide range of platforms and that they can be accessed by people who use old technology.

I recommend making sure that all pages work on two-year-old browsers and two-year-old versions of all plug-ins and other software. Also, make sure that the page design works on small monitors and has acceptable response times when using analog modems.

Some people may say that these limitations impose undue hardship on designers and that only 10 percent of the users actually employ old software and low-end hardware. This may be true, but it is usually a bad business decision to turn away 10 percent of your customer base at the door.

3 Content Design

Ultimately, users visit your website for its content. Everything else is just the backdrop. The design is there to allow people access to the content. The old analogy is somebody who goes to see a theater performance: When they leave the theater, you want them to be discussing how great the *play* was and not how great the costumes were.

Of course, good costume design contributes greatly to making the performance enjoyable and to bringing the author's and director's visions to the stage. But in the end, the play is the important thing.

Usability studies indicate a fierce content focus on the part of users. When they get to a new page, they look immediately in the main content area of the page and scan it for headlines and other indications of what the page is about. Only later, if they decide that the content is not of interest to them, will they scan the navigation area of the page for ideas of where else to go.

Content is number one.

Writing for the Web

It's the rare case indeed when a book about the Web discusses writing guidelines, which is why I will take the opportunity here. When writing for the Web, you're not only affecting the content, you're affecting the core user

The Value of an Editor

What is the impact of violating the guidelines for writing the headline for a news item on an intranet home page? For a company with 10,000 employees, the cost of a single poorly written headline on the intranet home page is almost $5,000. Considerably more than the cost of having a good home page editor rewrite the headline before it goes up.

I have based the preceding estimate on the following assumptions:

- All employees spend five seconds more than necessary pondering the headline because it is not sufficiently communicative.

- The poorly written headline causes 10 percent of employees to click on the headline even though the story is useless to them.

- People spend on average 30 seconds reading the story before they decide to back out because it's useless.

- The company has 10,000 employees using the intranet.

- The value of an employee's time is $50/hour. (Note that the value of an employee's time should be much more than his or her salary, and account not only for benefits and overhead but also for contributions to the company's bottom line. Therefore, a person who makes $25/hour usually ends up costing the company $50/hour, which is the relevant number for figuring out the cost of lost time.)

This little example also shows the basic principles for performing cost-benefit analyses of usability issues. You estimate the various ways in which the design causes people to lose time (or to avoid purchases, if you are discussing an e-commerce design) and multiply that by the percentage of users encountering the problem, as well as the total number of users and the value of their time (or purchases, in the case of e-commerce).

experience because users look at the text and the head-lines first. Although it's important to be grammatically correct, it's also important to present the content in a manner that draws in readers.

The three main guidelines for writing for the Web include the following:

- Be succinct. Write no more than 50 percent of the text you would have used to cover the same material in a print publication.
- Write for scannability. Don't require users to read long continuous blocks of text; instead, use short paragraphs, subheadings, and bulleted lists.
- Use hypertext to split up long information into multiple pages.

A fourth guideline is more of a process or management rule: Hire web editors. Good content requires a dedicated staff that knows how to write for the Web and how to massage content contributions into the format required by your design standards.

Keep Your Texts Short

Research has shown that reading from computer screens is about 25 percent slower than reading from paper. Even users who don't know about this human-factors research usually say that they feel unpleasant when reading online text. As a result, people don't want to read a lot of text from computer screens. Therefore, you should write 50

Web Attitude

Although web text should be short, it should not be without personality. Usability studies show that users appreciate some amount of humor and attitude in web pages. Note that "attitude" does not mean screaming or whining at readers, or treating them to a punkish diatribe. What's respected is the presence of a clear voice, perspective, and personality in the exposition. Angry young writers write for each other; most of the web audience tunes them out.

Users have a distinct dislike for anything they deem marketing fluff. The Web is a rather "cool" medium that encourages the use of facts with links to back-up datasheets and detailed numbers. You cannot get away with the superficial hyperbole that may work in television commercials or magazine advertising. When users see pages that have lots of blather in place of facts, they instantly discount the site's credibility.

The correct amount of attitude in a web page is: Not too much, not too little.

HOME   JOBS   NEWS   FIND   FEEDBACK

a **career**
with baxter

GO TO >

Patients & Donors
Medical Professionals
Customers
Corporate & Investor Info

Welcome

WELCOME

WHY CHOOSE
BAXTER?

WHAT'S
AVAILABLE?

  detailed search

  recently added
  positions

  return visitor
  log-in

RECRUITING
EVENTS

INTERNSHIPS

FINANCIAL
DEVELOPMENT
PROGRAM

HUMAN
RESOURCES
DEVELOPMENT
PROGRAM

CAREER SITE
FEEDBACK

Hello. I'd like to personally welcome you to Baxter's career site. We've developed this site in response to the many requests we've received for career-related information.

Baxter employs approximately 41,000 people in approximately 100 countries -- a diverse employee population that shares the company's vision to improve the quality of life for people worldwide. We are strongly committed to our employees, professionally and personally, as you'll see in the pages that follow.

Mike Tucker
Sr. Vice President
Human Resources

I invite you to check out our site. We've taken great care to provide you with a valuable tool that allows you to manage your career search with Baxter. We offer a unique feature -- an on-line résumé form that allows you to maintain your résumé or curriculum vitae on our system for up to one year. You may update your record at any time, and link it to employment opportunities as they become available. Our database is updated weekly. Search it and communicate your interest directly to our staffing representatives.

I hope you visit our site often. If you have comments or questions, please feel free to share them with us using the "career site feedback" link. Thank you for your interest in Baxter.

Baxter is an Equal Opportunity Employer

www.baxter.com

Starting a web page with the headline "Welcome" should be a warning signal. Users never want to read such happy, but useless, messages. Above is a page created for people who are looking for jobs. And guess what? User testing shows that job seekers immediately click on the button for available jobs without ever reading the welcome message.

percent less text—not just 25 percent less—because it's not only a matter of reading speed but also a matter of feeling good. We also know that users don't like to scroll: one more reason to keep pages short.

The screen readability problem will be solved in the future because screens with 300 dpi resolution have been invented and have been found to have readability as good as paper. Such high-resolution screens are currently too expensive (high-end monitors in commercial use have about 110 dpi), but they will be available for top-of-the-line computers around the year 2002 and in common use five years after that.

Copy Editing

At a minimum, all web pages should be run through a spelling checker. Misspelled words are an embarrassment and may slow down users or be confusing. Many errors will not be caught by current spelling-checking and grammar-checking technology, so it is also recommended to proofread pages carefully for grammatical mistakes and for words that may be in a dictionary—affect and effect—but are not the ones intended by the author.

Always run a spelling checker on your pages. Typos have a tendency to pop up where they are most embarrassing, as in DisCopyLabs' assurance that they pay "the strictiest attention to detail." Of course, a spelling checker won't catch mistakes like that shown in the second paragraph, which should read "and to shape" (instead of "and the shape"), or the misuse of the hyphen in the last line of the bullet item.

Turnkey Services

-Consider us your partner in product manufacturing-

Our customers consider us the manufacturing arm of their business. When you rely on DisCopyLabs as your partner, you can be free of the costly, complicated burden of manufacturing and distribution. You won't need to make a major investment in facilities, systems, staff and training. You won't need to pour your precious resources into every manufacturing detail.

Turnkey means we assume all manufacturing responsibility from beginning to end, competently and cost effectively. We work closely with our customers to identify their needs and the shape a comprehensive program, which may include the following:

- Project Management We will oversee your project through every phase from concept to completion, working closely with key people, paying the strictiest attention to detail and fulfilling our commmitment to quality- at no additional cost to you.

www.discopylabs.com

High-end web organizations should go beyond proofreading, however, and employ professional copy editors to go over the text of their pages. Not only can a copy editor correct many mistakes that are overlooked by automated checks, but they can also improve cases of bad or sloppy language. Most importantly, copy editors have a knack for tightening up writing. Many people—myself certainly included—have a tendency to love their own words and use rather many of them to elaborate on their position. Even for printed materials, a good copy editor can prune language to turn long-winded expositions into concise and tightly argued gems. For the Web, the copy editor's hunting instinct should be unleashed, and he or she should be even more ruthless than normal in tracking down and eliminating extraneous words.

Scannability

Because it is so painful to read text on computer screens and because the online experience seems to foster some amount of impatience, users tend not to read streams of text fully. Instead, users scan text and pick out keywords, sentences, and paragraphs of interest while skipping over those parts of the text they care less about.

In a study by John Morkes and myself, we found that 79 percent of our test users always scanned any new page they came across; only very few users would read word-by-word.

The following table shows five different ways of writing the same web content for a site about tourism in Nebraska (see facing page). John Morkes and I tested the usability of all five sites, and the table shows how much better each variation was compared with the original text, which served as the control condition in the study.

Skimming instead of reading is a fact of the Web, and it's been confirmed by countless usability studies. Those who write for the Web must acknowledge this fact and write for scannability:

- Structure articles with two, or even three, levels of headlines (a general page heading plus subheads—and sub-subheads when appropriate). Nested headings also facilitate access for visually impaired users with screen readers.

Site Version	Sample Paragraph	Usability Improvement (Relative to the Control Condition)
Promotional writing (control condition) Uses the "market-ese" found on many commercial websites	Nebraska is filled with internationally recognized attractions that draw large crowds of people every year, without fail. In 1996, some of the most popular places were Fort Robinson State Park (355,000 visitors), Scotts Bluff National Monument (132,166), Arbor Lodge State Historical Park & Museum (100,000), Carhenge (86,598), Stuhr Museum of the Prairie Pioneer (60,002), and Buffalo Bill Ranch State Historical Park (28,446).	**0% better** (this was the control condition)
Concise text About half the word count as the control condition	In 1996, six of the best-attended attractions in Nebraska were Fort Robinson State Park, Scotts Bluff National Monument, Arbor Lodge State Historical Park & Museum, Carhenge, Stuhr Museum of the Prairie Pioneer, and Buffalo Bill Ranch State Historical Park.	**58% better**
Scannable layout Uses the same text as the control condition in a layout that facilitated scanning	Nebraska is filled with internationally recognized attractions that draw large crowds of people every year, without fail. In 1996, some of the most popular places were: • Fort Robinson State Park (355,000 visitors) • Scotts Bluff National Monument (132,166) • Arbor Lodge State Historical Park & Museum (100,000) • Carhenge (86,598) • Stuhr Museum of the Prairie Pioneer (60,002) • Buffalo Bill Ranch State Historical Park (28,446)	**47% better**
Objective language Uses neutral rather than subjective, boastful, or exaggerated language (otherwise, the same as the control condition)	Nebraska has several attractions. In 1996, some of the most-visited places were Fort Robinson State Park (355,000 visitors), Scotts Bluff National Monument (132,166), Arbor Lodge State Historical Park & Museum (100,000), Carhenge (86,598), Stuhr Museum of the Prairie Pioneer (60,002), and Buffalo Bill Ranch State Historical Park (28,446).	**27% better**
Combined version Uses all three improvements in writing style: concise text, scannable layout, and objective language	In 1996, six of the most-visited places in Nebraska were: • Fort Robinson State Park • Scotts Bluff National Monument • Arbor Lodge State Historical Park & Museum • Carhenge • Stuhr Museum of the Prairie Pioneer • Buffalo Bill Ranch State Historical Park	**124% better**

- Use meaningful rather than "cute" headings. Reading a heading should tell the user what the page or section is about because it is too unpleasant to be forced to read the body text. For example, *USA Today* had a headline in the printed newspaper reading "Twosome tells wired world what's news" Cute, but worthless as a web headline. Luckily, its website rewrote the headline to read "Bringing news to the wired world." Better, though not perfect. My preference would have been something like "Editing news for Web portals' home pages."
- Bulleted lists and similar design elements should be used to break the flow of uniform text blocks.
- Use highlighting and emphasis to make important words catch the user's eye. Colored text can also be used for emphasis, and hypertext anchors stand out by virtue of being blue and underlined. Any highlighting or background colors must be chosen to look distinct from the link colors; otherwise, users will be confused and will try to click on the highlighted words in the belief that they are links.

Why Users Scan

More research is needed to truly know why 79 percent of web users scan rather than read, but here are four plausible reasons:

- Reading from computer screens is tiring for the eyes and about 25 percent slower than reading from paper. No wonder people attempt to minimize the number of words they read. To the extent this reason explains user behavior, users should read more when, in five years, those high-resolution, high-scanrate monitors are available.
- The Web is a user-driven medium where users feel that they have to move around and click on things. One test user said, "If I have to sit here and read the whole article, then I'm not productive." People want to feel that they are active when they are on the Web.
- Each page has to compete with hundreds of millions of other pages for the users' attention. Users don't know whether this page is the one they need or whether some other page would be better. And they are not willing to commit to the investment of reading the page in the hopes that it will be worthwhile. Most pages are in fact not worth the users' time, so experience encourages them to rely on information foraging. Instead of spending a lot of time on a single page, users move between many pages and try to pick the most tasty segments of each.
- Modern life is hectic and people simply don't have time to work too hard for their information. As one test user said, "If this [long page with blocks of text] happened to me at work, where I get 70 emails and 50 voicemails a day, then that would be the end of it. If it doesn't come right out at me, I'm going to give up on it."

Jakob Nielsen: Designing Web Usability

Hertz

RATES & RESERVATIONS

WORLDWIDE LOCATIONS

FLEET GUIDE

POLICIES & PROCEDURES

SPECIAL OFFERS

PARTNERSHIPS

HERTZ COMPANIES

TRAVEL AGENTS

HOME

United States Products

How Protected <u>Are</u> You?

Hertz wants you to know the facts. The Hertz representative will provide you with information on our optional protection services at the counter.

Making sure you travel with peace of mind is one of our main concerns. For this reason, in the U.S. Hertz offers these optional services: <u>Loss Damage Waiver</u> will protect you against loss and damage to the Hertz car, Liability Insurance Supplement provides supplement liability protection and <u>Personal Accident Insurance</u> and <u>Personal Effects Coverage</u> offers medical benefits, accidental death benefits, and protection for your personal belongings. Ask your Hertz Representative for more information about these services.

Credit Card Coverage

If you have an accident with a Hertz car and you've declined the Hertz Optional Loss Damage Waiver (LDW) Protection because you thought your credit card insurance covered you, consider these facts:

- Some cards only reimburse you for your deductible after your own insurance pays.

www.hertz.com

Any web users who see this page will think that Hertz offers three types of insurance: loss damage waiver, personal accident insurance, and personal effects coverage. People simply pick up the colored text and don't read the blocks of body text. Anybody who had enough time on his or her hands to read word-by-word would discover that Hertz has a fourth type of insurance: liability insurance supplement. But very few people will do so. Also note that the page headline violates the principle of plainspoken description of the page contents. It would have been better to use a headline such as "Optional Insurance Coverage" and to reduce the relative size of the line stating that the information applies to United States Products. Finally, it would have been smart not to illustrate United States Products with a photo of the Sydney Opera House.

(Facing page)   The goal of a product category page like this is to allow users to avoid looking at some of the products. Some marketers might be horrified at this statement, but if you assume that users have the time to read about all the details of all your products, you will be sorely disappointed. A site that doesn't help users narrow their attention on a few relevant products will be seen as confusing and not sufficiently helpful. Rather than spending hours wading through irrelevant products, many users will give up and take their money elsewhere. The combined link and headline for each product is its product number. This is fine for people who know the product line intimately and know that they want, say, a ThinkPad 570 but not a 390.

For less knowledgeable users, the product numbers are useless; they have to rely on the sub-category headers in the colored bars as well as the abbreviated product descriptions next to each photo. The sub-category headers are reasonably descriptive, although it is not clear what the difference between "Ultraportable" and "Mini-Notebook" is. Which of the two is the smallest? Which should I buy for my needs? Similarly, what's the difference between "All-in-One Value" and "Personal Computing"?

The usability of this page would improve if the sub-categories were clarified and ordered according to some understandable principle: For example, the products could be sorted with the smallest on top and progressively larger machines sorted below. The user's final hope—the product descriptions—are also useless (in addition to being in so small a font size as to be extremely difficult to read). Once you know that the 240 is a mini-notebook, you don't learn any more from being told that it is "The mini-notebook with full-sized convenience." Or, what's the difference between "Extreme performance mobile computing" and "The ideal balance of performance and portability"?

Jakob Nielsen: Designing Web Usability

Search [ ] [Go]

**Notebooks
and PC Companions**

ThinkPad

Overview
How to buy
Support
News & Awards
Accessories
   & upgrades
Library
Software
Mobile resource center
Spec sheets

Assistant
Year 2000

Worldwide

United States
1-888-411-1WEB

click here
for more
details

ThinkPad
A better place to think

Ways to Buy
Buy from an online dealer | Buy online from IBM
intel inside pentium II

Performance

   ThinkPad 770
Extreme performance mobile computing
Visual Tour

   ThinkPad 600
The ideal balance of performance and portability
Visual Tour

Ultraportable

   ThinkPad 570
The next generation of the ultraportable
Visual Tour

All-in-One Value

   ThinkPad 390
Affordable, all-in-one notebooks
Visual Tour

Mini-Notebook

   ThinkPad 240
The mini-notebook with full-sized convenience
Visual Tour

Personal Computing   Small Business Computing

   ThinkPad i Series 1400
Ingenious notebooks for mobile individuals
Visual Tour

   ThinkPad i Series 1500
Customized solutions for small business
New
Visual Tour

Find a dealer

Register your IBM product

What's New:
▶ Compute Now, Pay Later!
▶ Beware of 'chain letters' promising free IBM PCs
▶ Government Solutions
▶ PC Data Vaulting
▶ CASH BACK on selected Mobile products

Related Links:
▶ Small Business Center
▶ IBM PC Lifecycle Care program
▶ IBM & Microsoft Windows NT
▶ Microsoft Windows NT for Small Business

Privacy | Legal | Contact

www.pc.ibm.com

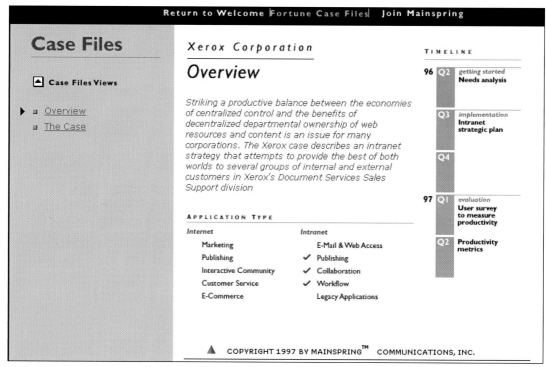

Case Files

Case Files Views

▶ Overview
The Case

Xerox Corporation

Overview

Striking a productive balance between the economies of centralized control and the benefits of decentralized departmental ownership of web resources and content is an issue for many corporations. The Xerox case describes an intranet strategy that attempts to provide the best of both worlds to several groups of internal and external customers in Xerox's Document Services Sales Support division

APPLICATION TYPE

Internet	Intranet
Marketing	E-Mail & Web Access
Publishing	✔ Publishing
Interactive Community	✔ Collaboration
Customer Service	✔ Workflow
E-Commerce	Legacy Applications

TIMELINE

96 Q2 *getting started*
Needs analysis

Q3 *implementation*
Intranet strategic plan

Q4

97 Q1 *evaluation*
User survey to measure productivity

Q2 Productivity metrics

▲ COPYRIGHT 1997 BY MAINSPRING™ COMMUNICATIONS, INC.

www.mainspring.com

Simple diagrams like the timeline on this Mainspring page enhance scannability; they provide a resting place for the user's eyes while moving over the page. Diagrams as clean as this one can quickly outline an information flow and get the structure of an argument across to the user. Users often want to click diagrams to get more information about a specific element, so ideally, the diagram should be linked to different subpages for each element.

Plain Language

Because web users don't take the time to read through a lot of material, it is important to start each page with the conclusion. Present the most important material up front, using the so-called inverted pyramid principle. Users should be able to tell in a glance what the page is about and what it can do for them.

Often, users who are scanning text will read only the first sentence of each paragraph. This suggests that topic sentences are important, as is the *"one idea per paragraph"* rule. If you cover multiple topics in a single paragraph, many users will never get to see the second idea if the first one does not stop their eye as they scan the page. Also, use simple sentence structures. Convoluted writing and complex words are even harder to understand online.

The use of metaphors should also be limited, particularly in headings. Users might take you literally.

Humor should be used with great caution on the Web. Because users scan the text, they may not realize when you are being humorous or sarcastic, and they may take statements at face value. Also, users are so goal-driven that they often prefer "just the facts, thanks" without having to

One of the worst error messages seen on the Web. Except, of course, for the many errors that don't even generate an error message but instead simply leave the user hanging or result in a blank screen. Error messages should always be written in plain and user-centered language, and they should not expose the system's dirty laundry. The one redeeming aspect of this page is the suggestion for what to do. Error messages should always be constructive and help users overcome the problem instead of simply pointing out that there is trouble.

Southwest Airlines Ticketless Reservations

What Happened?
Sched server socket read timeout
What You Need To Do...
Wait a few seconds and try again.

Return to Previous Page

www.southwest.com

spend extra time on material that doesn't help them get in and out as fast as possible. At the same time, users also often feel that websites take themselves too seriously and are somewhat of a drag to use. So a light touch of humor can work, if done carefully. Avoid puns, however, because they won't work for international users who may not be overly familiar with your language.

Page Chunking

Make text short without sacrificing depth of content by splitting the information into multiple nodes connected by hypertext links. Each page can be brief and yet the full hyperspace can contain much more information than would be feasible in a printed article. Long and detailed background information can be relegated to secondary pages; similarly, information of interest to a minority of readers can be made available through a link without penalizing those readers who don't want it.

Hypertext should not be used to segment a long linear story into multiple pages. Having to download several segments slows reading and makes printing more difficult. Proper hypertext structure is not a single flow "continued on page 2"; instead, split the information into coherent chunks that each focus on a certain topic. The guiding principle should be to allow readers to select those topics they care about and only download those pages. In other words, the hypertext structure should be based on an audience analysis.

Additionally, each hypertext page should be written according to the "inverted pyramid" principle that is commonly taught in journalism schools. Start with a short conclusion so that users can get the gist of the page even if they don't read all of it; then, gradually add detail. The guiding principle should be that the reader can stop at any time and still have read the most important pieces of information.

In the usability studies I did of early web users in 1994 and 1995, few users ever scrolled. Maybe 10 percent or so of the users would scroll beyond the information that was visible in the window when the page came up. The only exception from this finding was users who had arrived at a destination page with an article that they found interesting or important to their work. People *would* scroll as they

(Facing page) **This page shows an overly long article (guilty as charged), which has been split into two parts. At the end of part 1, a small link called "Continued" points to part 2. This link is not optimized for the Web because there is no way for the user to know what to expect at the other end. A better treatment would have provided a brief, one-line preview of the content of part 2 to motivate the reader to continue. The best design would have involved a rewrite to focus the text on one self-contained argument for the first page and then used hyperlinks to point to secondary arguments or in-depth examples. Also note in this page how the pull-quotes add visual interest to the design and help users scan the page to pick out the parts of the story that may interest them.**

Jakob Nielsen: Designing Web Usability

Perspectives

◁ back to

Data phones: The way it should be

May 15, 1997
by Jakob Nielsen

A recent NEWS.COM story reported that data phones have not sold well so far. The executives quoted seemed mystified. By all accounts, their so-called data phones--usually cellular phones with built-in data options like paging, faxing and email--should be a hit. Still, they're not doing all that well. I think I know why: It's the interface.

I do believe in the integration of telephony and computing, but data phones will not take off as long as they are designed from the wrong conceptual model. So far, all these devices have been designed as telephones with a   data add-on. They'd probably be more usable, and more successful, if they were designed as computers with voice capabilities added on.

DATA PHONES ARE BEING DESIGNED FROM THE **WRONG** CONCEPTUAL **MODEL.**

The difference lies in the user interface. Telephone user interfaces are horrible, which is why nobody can figure out how to use services like call waiting, much less how to forward a call to another extension in the office. Computer interfaces aren't perfect, but the usability and the design of multiple features is better done based on computer thinking. Users need an integrated interface rather than one that is half-telephone and half-kludge.

This is not to say that Windows CE is the solution: It is not appropriate to take a user interface that was optimized for large-screen desktop devices and use it for small-screen handhelds. The smaller the device, the more strict the requirements to optimize the interface for its specific characteristics.

Some people claim that the telephone is an example of perfect usability that should be emulated by software designers. After all, it's easy: you pick up the handset, punch in the number, and you are connected.

If only it were that easy in the real world. Of the three steps, only picking up the handset is truly easy. Turning on the device and "logging in" to your account are both accomplished by the simple action of picking up the handset. There is no "boot time," and the dial tone is always there. Computers (and in particular the Web) can definitely learn something from   the up-time requirements of the phone system. The Internet should supply users with "Web tone" at the same level of reliability as the telephone supplies dial tone.

USERS NEED AN INTEGRATED INTERFACE, RATHER THAN ONE THAT IS HALF-TELEPHONE, HALF-KLUDGE.

But, let's debunk the myth that punching in a number is an easy-to-use user interface that should be emulated. First, these numbers are actually hard to learn and remember. Quick, what's the number of your dentist?

Second, they are hard to type, and there is no forgiveness if you miss a digit. You have only one choice: hang up and start over. To make a long distance call from a typical office in the United States requires the user to type in 12 digits: This is cumbersome and takes a long time. International calls are even harder.

Continued

Back Issues
Companies
Products
TalkBack
Forums
Don't Go There
Get MAD!
Home
Help?

Get the
AnchorDesk
Email
Alert
FREE!

get
PointCast free

JESSE BERST'S
AnchorDesk
Your source for tech intelligence

NEXT
STORY

Berst Alert

MONDAY, JULY 21, 1997

The Bad Guys Behind the Internet Brownout

Jesse Berst, Editorial Director
ZDNet AnchorDesk

They don't wear black hats. But they may be as close to bad guys as we have on the Internet.

Last week, human error triggered one of the worst Internet outages in years. An employee of Network Solutions, Inc. (NSI) accidentally sent bad information to the Internet's major routers. As one Internet security expert told the *Wall Street Journal*: "Imagine if all the phone books disappeared and directory assistance didn't work."

It was a scary reminder how dependent we all are on NSI, the company that administers domain names (Web site addresses). A growing group of protesters claims NSI is putting the Internet at risk out of greed.

That's right, a single organization (NSI) controls the addressing system for the entire Internet. It's a badly run company that has made a series of stupid mistakes in the past few months. Canceling domain names by mistake. Failing to collect millions of dollars in fees. Last week's fiasco. It goes on. Even worse, the company is trying to go public. In their greed to become instant millionaires, NSI executives are making selfish claims. Dangerous claims.

Like claiming ownership of the domains ".com," ".org" and ".net," which they were supposed to be running in the public trust. As a result, protests and legal actions have sprung up all over the Internet. An alternative naming service call AlterNIC actually rerouted NSI's Web site last week in a mild form of cyber terrorism. Another rival, PGMedia, filed a lawsuit this spring. The Justice Department has initiated an investigation into NSI's claim that it deserves monopoly control over domain names. And a presidential task force is looking into the issue.

EMAIL THIS STORY TO A FRIEND

READ TALKBACKS

INTERNET LINKS:
ZDNet AnchorDesk Forums:
Should NSI Be Replaced?

Internet:
Network Solutions White Paper

Internet:
AlterNIC Protest Page

Internet:
PGMedia Legal Page

ZDNN:
Net Survives a Bad Week

ZDNN:
Jul 17 '97: Net Snafus a Real Hoedown

ZDNN:
Jul 17 '97: Webmasters Limit Impact of InterNIC Snafu

DISCUSSION GROUPS:
AnchorDesk Forums
COMPANIES:
Network Solutions Inc.
TOPICS:
Internet

www.anchordesk.com

(Facing page)   AnchorDesk has a nearly exemplary use of hypertext. The home page has one-paragraph summaries of each story with a link to a longer article like the one shown here. Actually, the home page has two levels of detail about each story: a short headline, followed by the one-paragraph summary. The article pages typically contain relatively short treatments of each topic, more or less fitting in a single screen on a large monitor. These short articles then have extensive hypertext links to much longer articles elsewhere on the ZDnet site and other parts of the Web. On this page, also note a unique feature of AnchorDesk: the "email this story to a friend" button. Pressing this button takes the user to a new page with fields to enter the friend's email address and a short comment. The article is automatically forwarded by AnchorDesk's server, together with a small explanation about how to subscribe to future story alerts.

scanned such long articles. On navigation pages, however, the rule definitely was that users would choose from among the visible options.

More recent studies have partly confirmed this finding, although more users have started scrolling. I would still say that some users are reluctant to scroll navigation pages, but it is no longer as pronounced. My guess is that the prevalence of badly designed, long pages on the Web has inured most users to some amount of scrolling.

Even if they would be willing to scroll, many users will make their selection from whatever options are visible "above the fold" if they see one that looks promising. The two main conclusions from this finding are to make pages relatively short and to make sure that the most important links will be visible on most common monitors without any scrolling.

Scrolling navigation pages are bad for users because they make it impossible to see all the available options at the same time. There will always be parts of a scrolling page that are invisible, so users will have to make their choice of their next action without being able to directly compare everything. Increasing the user's memory load is always bad for usability and increases the risk of errors.

Destination pages that mainly present content and have few navigation options are less harmed by scrolling than navigation pages. After a user has reached a destination page, studies show that he or she will scroll through a few screenfuls if the first screen seems promising. Users will almost never scroll through *very* long pages, though. As I mentioned earlier, web texts need to be short.

Limit Use of Within-Page Links

HTML provides a special type of link to scrolls within the current page. *Within-page links* may seem a solution to the problem of long scrolling pages, but they have their own usability problems and should be avoided as much as possible.

The worst usability problem of within-page linking is that users expect links to take them to a *different* page. Users often don't realize that they have jumped in place, as it were, so the within-page links can cause much confusion, especially when the user clicks the Back button and still stays on the same page.

The original design of *Slate* magazine in June 1996 was 2,154 pixels tall, requiring a typical small-screen user to scroll through four windowfuls (this page). After two months, *Slate* partly recanted and changed to a 1,516-pixels-tall home page (facing page). Finally, in February 1997, *Slate* produced its first usable home page at a height of 793 pixels (page 118). This latter home page is fully visible on a medium-sized screen and allows even small-screen users to see all of the most important links without scrolling because all of the main stories are within the top 550 pixels of the page.

Unfortunately, in 1999 the design reverted to an overly long scrolling model (1,450 pixels tall), as shown on the facing page. Admittedly, the bottom 215 pixels contained a standard MSN navigation footer that would be ignored by most *Slate* readers, so the actual height of the 1999 *Slate* home page was considered to be 1,235 pixels.

Note, of course, that the pixel counts in this caption refer to the size of the page on my computer with the fonts I have installed. The exact numbers will definitely be different on other configurations. The issue is not the precise number of pixels but whether small- and medium-screen users have any hope of using the site.

Original design: 2,154 pixels tall.

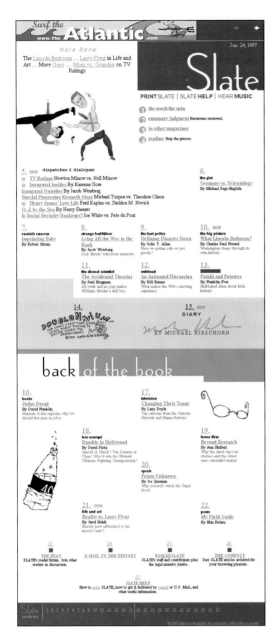

Early redesign: 1,516 pixels tall.

www.slate.com

1999 redesign: 1,450 pixels tall.

Feb. 19, 1997

Slate

PRINTSLATE | SLATEHELP | Contents by: PAGE NUMBER DATE |

BACK OF THE BOOK

www.slate.com

Most usable design (1997): 793 pixels tall.

An unpalatable example of shovel-ware from *Time* magazine. This page is 1,577 pixels tall and requires a small-screen user to scroll through three to four windowfuls, and yet it is only one of 12 pages in the total article. Great example of why repurposing doesn't work.

The Gates Operating System

JANUARY 13, 1997 VOL. 149 NO. 2   6 of 12

IN SEARCH OF THE REAL BILL GATES

It's a rainy night, and Gates is bombing around in his dark blue Lexus. He loves fast cars. When Microsoft was based in Albuquerque, New Mexico, in its early years, he bought a Porsche 911 and used to race it in the desert; Paul Allen had to bail him out of jail after one midnight escapade. He got three speeding tickets—two from the same cop who was trailing him—just on the drive from Albuquerque the weekend he moved Microsoft to Seattle. Later he bought a Porsche 930 Turbo he called the "rocket," then a Mercedes, a Jaguar XJ6, a $60,000 Carrera Cabriolet 964, a $380,000 Porsche 959 that ended up impounded in a customs shed because it couldn't meet import emission standards, and a Ferrari 348 that became known as the "dune buggy" after he spun it into the sand.

Despite this record, Gates is not wearing a seat belt. (A dilemma: Is it too uncool to use mine?) He rarely looks at you when he talks, which is disconcerting, but he does so when he's driving, which is doubly disconcerting. (I buckle up. As his mother and others have learned, it's not always prudent to compete.) He turns into a dark drive with a chain-link fence that slides open as the Lexus approaches. It's nearing midnight, and the security guard looks a bit startled.

Gates' home of the future has been under construction for more than four years, and is not expected to be completed until this summer. Built into a bluff fronting Lake Washington, it has 40,000 sq. ft. of space and will cost about $40 million. Looming against the night sky are three connected pavilions of glass and recycled Douglas fir beams, looking a bit like a corporate conference center masquerading as a resort.

Gates swings into a vaulted 30-car garage carved into the hillside. In the corner, like a museum piece, sits his parents' red Mustang convertible that he drove as a kid. "The first pavilion is mainly for public entertaining," he says as he picks his way past construction debris down four levels of stairs. Despite the hour, three technicians are working in the ground-floor reception hall, with its view of the Olympic Mountains across Lake Washington, adjusting two dozen 40-in. monitors that will form a flat-screen display covering an entire wall. "When you visit, you'll get an electronic pin encoded with your preferences," he explains. "As you wander toward any room, your favorite pictures will appear along with the music you like or a TV show or movie you're watching. The system will learn from your choices, and it will remember the music or pictures from your previous visits so you can choose to have them again or have similar but new ones. We'll have to have hierarchy guidelines, for when more than one person goes to a room." Like Gates himself, it's all very fascinating, fun and a little intimidating.

Moving into the center pavilion, Gates shows off what will be the library. A mammoth carved wooden dome hangs just above the floor, waiting to be raised into the cupola. (I wonder: Does this grand chamber dispel my fear that he will relegate print to museum status? Or inadvertently confirm it?) He has hired a New York rare-books dealer to stock the library for him. His current reading is eclectic. "On a recent trip to Italy," he says, "I took the new Stalin biography, a book about Hewlett-Packard, Seven Summits [a mountaineering book by Dick Bass and the late Disney president Frank Wells] and a Wallace Stegner novel." He's also a fan of Philip Roth's, John Irving's, Ernest J. Gaines' and David Halberstam's, but his all-time favorite novels are the schoolboy standards The Catcher in the Rye, The Great Gatsby and A Separate Peace. A nearby room will be filled by an enormous trampoline; at the office he sometimes surprises colleagues by joyfully leaping to touch the ceiling, and he finds bouncing on a trampoline as conducive to concentration as rocking.

The only completed part of the house is the indoor pool under the family quarters. A sleek lap pool reflecting images from a wall snakes through glass into an outdoor Japanese bath area. The security guard reappears and warns, "Be careful of what you do in there, since the boats on the lake can see inside." As the door to the pool room closes, Gates doubles over in laughter. Does he come in here often at night? "Sometimes with Melinda," he says.

We wander out to the deck, and the wind slams the door shut. It's locked. Gates tries to call the guard, but he's disappeared to a distant part of the estate. So he leads the way past bulldozers into trenches that will someday become an estuary and stocked trout stream. At the moment, however, it's a quagmire that proves impassable. Remarkably, Gates is able to avoid looking sheepish. After a few more minutes of shouting, he attracts the guard's attention.

Gates chose the austere and natural architectural style before he got married, but Melinda is now putting her own imprint on it. "The exposed concrete is going to have to go," he says, expressing some concern about how the architect might take this.

TIME

The Gates Operating System

INVENTION REBELLION CUPID FRIENDS FOES POSSESSIONS MUSE VISION COVER

Bill Sr. and Mary Gates

STEVE FIREBAUGH

Rebellion

Filial Disobedience

Already at war with his mother, Mary, by sixth grade, Gates was sent to a psychologist. She would call him up to dinner from his basement bedroom and he wouldn't respond. "What are you doing?" she once demanded over the intercom. "I'm thinking," he shouted back."You're thinking?" "Yes, Mom, I'm thinking," he said fiercely. "Have you ever tried thinking?"

The counselor's conclusion for Mary: "You're going to lose. You better just adjust to it, because there's no use trying to beat him."

Aptitude v. Attitude

"In ninth grade," Gates says, "I came up with a new form of rebellion. I hadn't been getting good grades, but I decided to get all A's without taking a book home. I didn't go to math class because I knew enough and had read ahead. I placed within the top 10 people in the nation on an aptitude exam. That established my independence and taught me I didn't need to rebel anymore."

Harvard Dropout

"Bill lived down the hall from me at Harvard sophomore year," says classmate Steve Ballmer. "He'd play poker until six in the morning, then I'd run into him at breakfast and discuss applied mathematics." In 1975, Gates quit Harvard to start the company he first called Micro-Soft with Paul Allen.

Steve Ballmer in Redmond, Washington
DAVID BURNETT-CONTACT

www.pathfinder.com

The *Time* editors must have realized that simply pouring the text from the printed magazine into a set of HTML pages would not make for great web content. To their credit, they also provided an alternative set of pages with chunked content, as well as links to multimedia content that takes advantage of the unique capabilities of the computer medium. I would have preferred links to more text content also. It would have been possible to take larger chunks of the original article and make them into subsidiary destinations for links that would be followed by readers with a special interest in one or more of the issues being briefly discussed here.

120   Jakob Nielsen: Designing Web Usability

The Gates Operating System

INVENTION REBELLION CUPID FRIENDS FOES POSSESSIONS MUSE VISION COVER

Napoleon Bonaparte

CORBIS-BETTMAN

Muse

Role Model

Having read about Napoleon's military strategies in junior high, Gates devised a computer version of Risk, a favorite board game in which the goal is world domination.

real audio
Gates on what he would do if not in the software business. Audio courtesy of CNN: Larry King Live, August 21, 1995

Anti-Hero

The photo of Henry Ford in Gates' office serves to remind the Microsoft magnate about the dangers of success. As Gates sees it, Ford slipped up by allowing Alfred Sloan's GM to seize leadership of the auto industry in 1927.

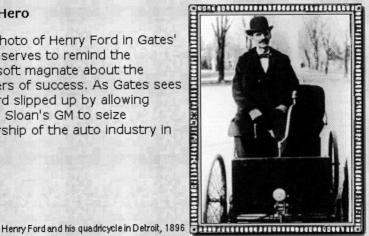

Henry Ford and his quadricycle in Detroit, 1896

HENRY FORD MUSEUM-REUTERS

www.pathfinder.com

3: Content Design   121

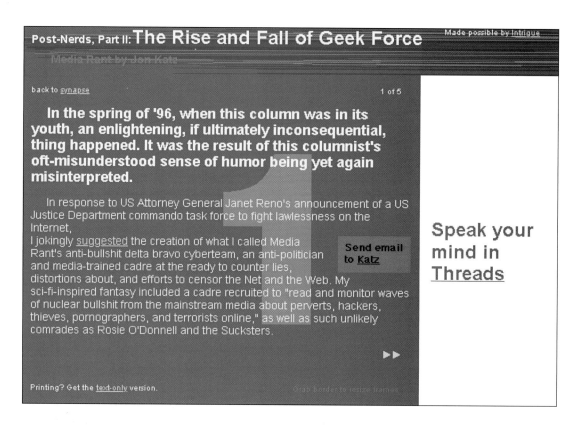

Made possible by Intrigue

Media Rant by Jon Katz

back to synapse

In the spring of '96, when this column was in its youth, an enlightening, if ultimately inconsequential, thing happened. It was the result of this columnist's oft-misunderstood sense of humor being yet again misinterpreted.

In response to US Attorney General Janet Reno's announcement of a US Justice Department commando task force to fight lawlessness on the Internet, I jokingly suggested the creation of what I called Media Rant's anti-bullshit delta bravo cyberteam, an anti-politician and media-trained cadre at the ready to counter lies, distortions about, and efforts to censor the Net and the Web. My sci-fi-inspired fantasy included a cadre recruited to "read and monitor waves of nuclear bullshit from the mainstream media about perverts, hackers, thieves, pornographers, and terrorists online," as well as such unlikely comrades as Rosie O'Donnell and the Sucksters.

Send email to Katz

Speak your mind in Threads

▶▶

Printing? Get the text-only version.

Grab border to resize frames

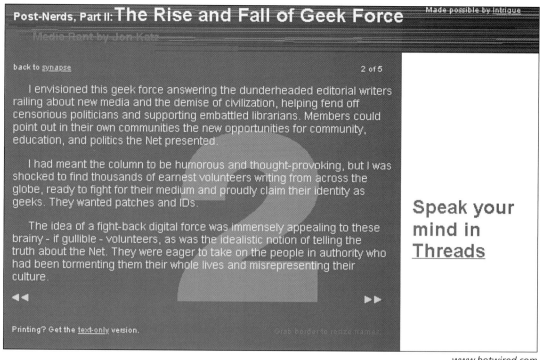

Made possible by Intrigue

Media Rant by Jon Katz

back to synapse

I envisioned this geek force answering the dunderheaded editorial writers railing about new media and the demise of civilization, helping fend off censorious politicians and supporting embattled librarians. Members could point out in their own communities the new opportunities for community, education, and politics the Net presented.

I had meant the column to be humorous and thought-provoking, but I was shocked to find thousands of earnest volunteers writing from across the globe, ready to fight for their medium and proudly claim their identity as geeks. They wanted patches and IDs.

The idea of a fight-back digital force was immensely appealing to these brainy - if gullible - volunteers, as was the idealistic notion of telling the truth about the Net. They were eager to take on the people in authority who had been tormenting them their whole lives and misrepresenting their culture.

Speak your mind in Threads

◀◀   ▶▶

Printing? Get the text-only version.

Grab border to resize frames

www.hotwired.com

Page Titles

Writing for the Web is often writing to be found. Users love search engines, both to navigate within a site and to discover resources on the open Internet. For people using a search, your website exists only in the form of the page title that is shown on the search results page.

In HTML, every page has a title that is specified in the header section of the page. It is important to specify good page titles because the titles are often used as the main reference to the pages. Page titles are also used in many navigation menus such as bookmark lists and history lists. Many of these important uses of page titles are taken out of context, so it is important that the title have enough words to stand on its own and be meaningful when read in a menu or a search listing. On the other hand, overly long titles slow down users, so it is best to aim at titles between two to six words. Home pages can even have a single word as their title (for example, "Excite").

A page title is microcontent and needs to be a pearl of clarity. You get 40 to 60 characters to explain what people will find on your page. Unless the title makes it absolutely clear what the page is about, users will never open it.

Different pages need different titles. It is most unpleasant to visit, say, seven pages with the same title and then try to go back to a specific page from the history list. Also, of course, bookmarking more than one page from such a site is a guaranteed usability problem because the bookmarks/favorites menu will contain several identical entries with different results.

A final point is to optimize titles for quick scanning. This implies moving information-carrying terms toward the beginning of the title and preferably starting with a word that will match the user's needs when scanning a menu or listing of titles. A classic mistake is to use a title such as "Welcome to MyCompany." It would be much better to call the page "MyCompany." To further facilitate scanning, eliminate the articles *A*, *An*, and *The* from the beginning of the title. Doing so is particularly important because some title listings are alphabetized. Titles do not need to be grammatical sentences; they need to be more in the nature of billboard slogans.

(Facing page) If you have a long article, then the best advice is to rewrite it and make it shorter, or to chunk it into smaller hypertext pages. If you do need to keep a linear structure for some reason, it is better to give in and show the entire article on one page. Even though users don't like to scroll, they like even less to have to wait for the next page to download while they are in the middle of reading a story. This example from HotWired shows what not to do, which is give people little snippets of the story, one page at a time. These pages are marked with a proud "1" and "2" as if users should care. If it's a linear unit, don't add navigational overhead to make users worry about page counts. It would have been more useful to have a link to the previous article about "post-nerds."

Writing Headlines

If you create listings of other people's content, it is almost always best to rewrite their headlines.

The requirements for online headlines are extremely different from printed headlines because they are used differently. The two main differences in headline use are:

- Online headlines are often displayed out of context: as part of a list of articles, in a search engine hitlist, or in a browser's bookmark menu or other navigation aid. Some of these situations are *very* out of context. Search engine hits can relate to any random topic, so users don't get the benefit of applying background understanding to the interpretation of the headline.

- Even when a headline is displayed with related content, the difficulty of reading online and the reduced amount of information that can be seen in a glance make it harder for users to learn enough from the surrounding data. In print, a headline is tightly associated with photos, decks, subheads, and the full body of the article, all of which can be interpreted in a single glance. Online, a much smaller amount of information will be visible in the window, and even that information is harder and more unpleasant to read, so people often don't do so. While scanning the list of stories on a home page or press release page, users often look only at the highlighted headlines and skip most of the summaries.

Because of these differences, the headline text has to stand on its own and make sense when the rest of the content is unavailable. Sure, users can click on the headline to get the full article, but they are too busy to do so for every single headline they see on the Web. I predict that users will soon be so deluged with email that they will delete messages unseen if the subject line doesn't make sense to them.

If you create listings of other people's content, it is almost always best to rewrite their headlines. Very few people currently understand the art of writing online microcontent that works when placed elsewhere on the Web. Thus, to serve your users better, you have to do the work yourself.

The main guidelines for writing headlines for the Web are:

- Clearly explain what the article is about in terms that relate to the user. Microcontent should be an ultra-short abstract of its associated macrocontent.

- Write in plain language: no puns, and no "cute" or "clever" headlines.

- Avoid teasers that try to entice people to click to find out what the story is about. Users have been burned too often to wait for a page to download unless they have clear expectations of what they will get. In print, curiosity can get people to turn the page or start reading an article. Online, it's simply too painful for people to do so.

- Skip leading articles such as *A*, *An*, and *The* in email subjects and page titles (but do include them in headlines that are embedded within a page). Shorter microcontent is more scannable, and because lists are often alphabetized, you don't want your content to be listed under "T" in a confused mess with many other pages starting with "The."

- Make the first word an important, information-carrying one, which will result in better positioning in alphabetized lists and facilitate scanning. For example, start with the name of the company, person, or concept discussed in an article.

- Do not start all page titles with the same word. They will be hard to differentiate when scanning a list. Move common markers toward the end of the line.

Legibility

All else—design, speed, content—fails when users can't read the text. There are a few basic rules that should be followed by all websites to ensure legibility:

- Use colors with high contrast between the text and the background. Optimal legibility requires black text on a white background (so-called positive text). White text on a black background (negative text) is almost as good. Although the contrast ratio is the same as for positive text, the inverted color scheme throws people off a little and slows their reading slightly. Legibility suffers much more for color schemes that make the text any lighter than pure black, especially if the background is made any darker than pure white. The worst are color schemes like pink text on green background: too little contrast to begin with and impossible to read for red-green colorblind users.

(Facing page) Low-contrast text is hard to read, especially when it is also tiny and rendered in italics like the main explanation on this page. It is a nice feature to be able to restrict the search to dealers who carry a specific product, but the system should have indicated a human-readable *name* of the product in addition to its model number. Computers are good at numbers. People are not.

- Use either plain-color backgrounds or extremely subtle background patterns. Background graphics interfere with the eye's capability to resolve the lines in the characters and recognize word shapes.
- Use big enough fonts that people can read the text, even if they don't have perfect vision. Tiny font sizes should be relegated to footnotes and legal disclaimers that few people are expected to read.
- Make the text stand still. Moving, blinking, or zooming text is much harder to read than static words.

Almost all text should be left-justified. By having a steady starting point for the eye to start scanning, the user can read much faster than when faced with centered or right-justified text. Of course, it is acceptable to center or right-justify a few lines for effect, but one should not do so for blocks of text. Similarly, lists are much easier to scan when the first word of each element is left-aligned along the same line.

Because of the low resolution of current computer screens, small text is more readable in sans-serif typefaces such as Verdana. There are simply not enough pixels available to resolve the fine detail needed for the serifs in a 10-point typeface. At the same time, most people prefer reading serif type (as used for most of the text in this book, including the text you are reading now), so we are left with something of a paradox. Legibility should win for any text that is *really* small (say, 9 points or less). Such small text needs to be in a sans-serif typeface (like that shown in the image captions for this book). Bigger text can use a serif face if it suits the site's typography better.

A FINAL LEGIBILITY GUIDELINE IS TO AVOID THE USE OF ALL CAPS FOR TEXT. USERS READ TEXT LIKE THIS PARAGRAPH ABOUT 10 PER-CENT SLOWER THAN THEY READ TEXT IN MIXED CASES, BECAUSE IT IS HARDER FOR THE EYE TO RECOGNIZE THE SHAPE OF WORDS AND CHARACTERS IN THE MORE UNIFORM AND BLOCKY APPEARANCE CAUSED BY UPPERCASE TEXT. DON'T DO IT.

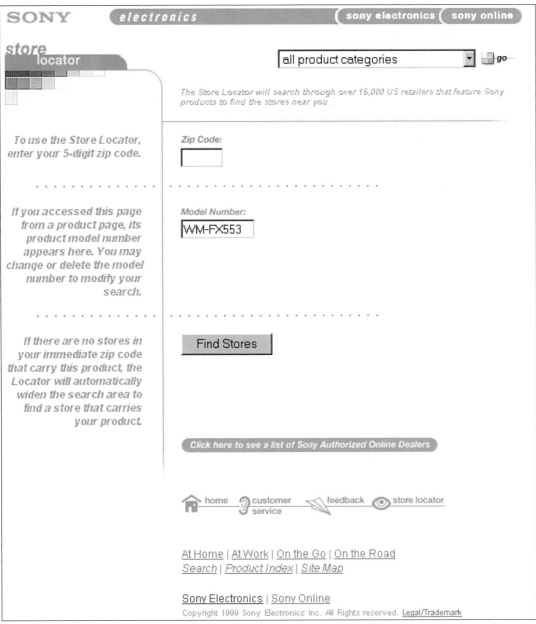

SONY   *electronics*   (sony electronics (sony online)

store
    locator

all product categories   [▼] 🔲go

The Store Locator will search through over 15,000 US retailers that feature Sony products to find the stores near you.

To use the Store Locator, enter your 5-digit zip code.

Zip Code:

[   ]

If you accessed this page from a product page, its product model number appears here. You may change or delete the model number to modify your search.

Model Number:

[WM-FX553   ]

If there are no stores in your immediate zip code that carry this product, the Locator will automatically widen the search area to find a store that carries your product.

[Find Stores]

(Click here to see a list of Sony Authorized Online Dealers)

🏠 home   ☎ customer service   ✈ feedback   👁 store locator

At Home | At Work | On the Go | On the Road
Search | Product Index | Site Map

Sony Electronics | Sony Online
Copyright 1999 Sony Electronics Inc. All Rights reserved. Legal/Trademark

www.sel.sony.com

www.hotwired.com

Do not use busy background patterns like this one from HotWired. Reading from computer screens is slow enough without interfering with the user's ability to recognize words and characters at a glance. Backgrounds should preferably be avoided or be a single color that has high contrast with the chosen text color. If you cannot restrain yourself from using a textured background, at least use a subtle texture instead of one that hits the user over the head and is more prominent than the content.

Online Documentation

It is always preferable to design user interfaces that are so easy to learn that nobody will ever need the documentation, and it should be considered a design defeat to ever say that, "Well, the users will just have to read about this on the help pages." In most cases, Internet users are so impatient that they won't be willing to read any documentation. It's just not acceptable for websites to come with manuals.

Even so, users sometimes do have to refer to help information. And because intranet users will be using the same pages repeatedly, they may in fact be willing to spend some time learning how to do so most effectively. Sophisticated or complex interactions may also require manuals or online help.

Because extranet users are chosen from your established business partners, they have some motivation to learn how to best use your extranet design. With respect to user motivation and willingness to learn, extranets are closer to intranets than to the open Internet where users surf freely and do not want to spend any time learning about individual websites because there are so many. Extranet designs can encompass slightly more complex applications where users may need to refer to help pages or even to printed manuals or cheat sheets that are mailed to those business partners who are allowed access to the extranet. Of course, any information contained in printed materials should also be available online because many users will discard the paper docs or will not be able to find them when needed.

Although some web applications may include online help and documentation, it is important to remember Nielsen's First Law of Computer Manuals:

People don't read documentation voluntarily.

In fact, the only time users touch the manual is when they are in trouble and cannot use the system. For most websites, such a situation would mean that the user was out of the site, never to return. For high-value web applications and on intranets or extranets, users might be motivated to follow a hyperlink to a help page and read the bare minimum necessary to complete the task.

Page Screenshots

Screenshots of a site are often used in documentation, press releases, and many other contexts. It is usually best to crop such screenshots such that the browser does not show. You want to focus the reader's attention on the page design and not on whatever browser version you happened to be using when snapping the screenshot.

If you do allow the browser to remain in a screenshot or if there are other elements of the screen that show the URL of the page in question, it is important to make sure that this URL is the same as that seen by users. This means that you should make screenshots from the production version of the site and not from your internal staging server or development machine. If an internal URL is showing anywhere in the screenshot, you can fix the problem in a graphics editor.

FEELING TRAPPED INSIDE YOUR OLD CAR?

ESCAPE HERE.

Search [the Web▼] **and Display the Results** [in Standard Form▼] [Submit]

Tip: To find good food in Chicago try: **pizza "deep dish" +Chicago**

Find files this fast on your PC!

ALTAVISTA TODAY

Hot job openings: join AltaVista!

FREE: Download the best, AltaVista Firewall 97, free for 30 days!

HOT: Spain's Telefonica to run an AltaVista Search Mirror Site for Iberia, Latin America.

COOL: Partners - May OnSite Summits: Greenbelt, MD, USA, 13-15th; Berg, Germany 21st-23rd.

DILBERT: Are you smarter than your boss? Prove it! Play The Dilbert Trivia Game & win signed Dilbert art & other cool stuff!

VISIT THESE SITES POWERED BY ALTAVISTA

Yahoo · CNET's SEARCH.COM · 100hot Websites · LôôkSmart · InfoSpace's Directories · BlueWindow · LawCrawler · PeekABoo · WorldPages · Internet Sleuth · TechWeb · Carrefour.net International · THE ANGLE · Netcreations · WhoWhere · Bigfoot · Webreference.com · Austronaut · 123Link · The Mining Company · Netway Austria · Samara Zimbabwe

ALTAVISTA: USING ALTAVISTA SEARCH SOFTWARE ON DIGITAL UNIX, DIGITAL ALPHA AND DIGITAL STORAGEWORKS

AltaVista gives you access to the largest Web index: 31 million pages found on 627,000 servers (1,158,000 host names), and four million articles from 14,000 Usenet news groups. It is accessed over 31 million times per weekday.

Surprise . Legal . FAQ . Add URL . Feedback . Help . Text-Only
AltaVista Software . Buy THE Book! . Advertising Info
Mirror Sites: Australia . Northern Europe

www.altavista.com

AltaVista's search page employs "just-in-time help" immediately below the text entry field to give users a tip about its search syntax. Despite the cluttered appearance of the page, users are likely to notice the tip if they are interested in learning about advanced searches because of the placement of the tip right at the spot where the user is looking when he or she feels the need to know about search syntax.

The wording of this tip is too cute for my taste and is likely to confuse more than it will help. In general, it is advisable to use serious examples rather than frivolous examples to help users understand how to apply the example to their own problem. Another problem with this design is that the help button is placed far away from the search tip. It would have been better to have a hyperlink stating something like "more search tips" right next to the tip. Because of the many other design elements on this page, many users will not see the help button, and they will not understand that they could have gotten more help than what is contained in the tip.

Writing documentation is a special skill, and I recommend that you hire a professional technical writer to craft help pages, online documentation, and any printed instructions. Larger projects should have the technical writer on the team from the beginning because the planning of the documentation should be integrated with all stages of the design. Smaller projects may outsource documentation to a contractor.

The basic rules for online documentation are as follows:

- Because users turn to the documentation only when they have specific problems, it is essential to make the documentation pages searchable.
- Online documentation should have an abundance of examples: Users find it much easier to follow examples and modify them to their own circumstances than to determine what to do from a generalized description.
- Instructions should be task-oriented and emphasize how to *do* things step-by-step. Much less space should be used for background information because users skip that anyway.
- Despite the preceding rule, it is a good idea to provide a short conceptual model of the system, often including a diagram that explains how the different parts work together.
- Hypertext links should be used to link any difficult concepts or system-oriented terms to a glossary.
- As always on the Web: Be brief.

I cannot stress enough the need for examples. Every user we have ever interviewed about computer documentation has requested more examples.

Multimedia

Multimedia is gaining popularity on the Web with several technologies to support use of animation, video, and audio to supplement the traditional media of text and images. These new media provide more design options but also require design discipline. Unconstrained use of multimedia results in user interfaces that confuse users and make it harder for them to understand the information. Not every web page needs to bombard the user with the equivalent of Times Square in impressions and movement.

Auto-Installing Plug-Ins

It is tempting to think that the plug-in problem has been solved by the ability to automatically have the browser download and install any necessary software. This is not so. The download delay is still with us, and users don't like their browsing being interrupted by having to wait for an unexpected download. Also, there is always the risk of crashing the user's computer whenever you download and install new software. If your site is responsible for a crash, then you can forget about ever seeing that user again.

(Facing page)   The Hunterian Museum at www.gla.ac.uk/Museum provides several interesting video clips connected to an exhibition about the Romans in Scotland. Note how each video link is annotated with an indication of its length to allow users to estimate the download time. I would probably have added the file length in megabytes (the Roman Dress video is 2.1 MB and took me 11 minutes to download on a trans-Atlantic link). The thumbnails of scenes from the videos help users determine whether they have an interest in any given video. Chris Johnson from the University of Glasgow studied 12- to 13-year-old children by using various versions of the museum's website and asked their opinion of the download times. Their modal reply was "unsatisfactory" when using a page that simply listed titles of the available videos (e.g., "wearing a suit of Roman armor" and "Roman clothes"), but the response changed to "very satisfactory" when using pages such as the one shown here, which also provided them with preview information for each video. Thus, even with exactly the same response times, users liked the site better when they were given better support for selecting those videos they would find interesting. The Web is so slow that you cannot simply let people explore without a guide to the obstacles ahead.

Client-Side Multimedia

The design of client-side multimedia has two additional response-time limits to consider:

- The feeling of directly manipulating objects on the screen requires one-tenth-of-a-second (0.1) response time. Thus, the time from when the user types a key on the keyboard or moves the mouse until the desired effect happens has to be faster than one-tenth of a second if the goal is to let the user control a screen object (for example, rotate a 3D figure or get pop-ups while moving over an imagemap).

- If users do not need to feel a direct physical connection between their actions and the changes on the screen, then response times of about one second (1.0) become acceptable. Any slower response, and the user starts feeling that he or she is waiting for the computer instead of operating freely on the data. So, for example, jumping to a new page or recalculating a spreadsheet should happen within one second. When response times surpass one second, users start changing their behavior to a more restricted use of the system (for example, they won't try out as many options or go to as many pages).

Jakob Nielsen: Designing Web Usability

Hunterian Museum   University of Glasgow

Have a look at a couple of these video clips and answer the following questions.

- 1. What do Romans soldiers call their shields?
- 2. Where do Romans get their clothes?
- 3. What do Romans use, to wash, instead of soap and water?
- 4. Between which two towns in Scotland does the Antonine wall stretch?

All you have to do is select the hypertext link. The clip running time is shown beside each clip title. Each video takes some time to 'load', the download time is displayed at the bottom of the screen. You can stop a movie loading by selecting the 'stop' button on the Netscape toolbar. Select another if you wish.

 ### Hands On Workshop

Join Cumbernauld Primary school pupils as they dress up as Roman soldiers, senators and slaves on a visit to the museum.

(clip length 22 secs)

 ### Roman Armour

See for yourself the armour of a Roman soldier and why it was so effective. Also includes his shield and sword.

(clip length 50 secs)

 ### Roman Dress

A Roman dress has an interesting design. See what this is and how the Roman ladies used a broach.

(clip length 34 secs)

Response Time

Many multimedia elements are big and take a long time to download with the horribly low bandwidth available to most users. Therefore, it is recommended that the file format and size be indicated in parentheses after the link whenever you point to a file that would take more than 10 seconds to download with the bandwidth available to most of your users. If you don't know what bandwidth your visitors are using, you should do a survey to find out because this information is important for many other page design issues. At this time, most home users have at most 56 Kbps, meaning that files larger than 50 KB need a size warning. Business users often have higher bandwidth, but you should probably still mark files larger than 200 KB. Also, be sure to state the running time of the clip, as well as the file format if you are using any type of non–standard format.

Before users decide to invest in a long multimedia download, it is necessary for them to understand what they will be getting. They won't click on something just because it's available; there is too much stuff on the Web these days.

Instead, provide previews of all multimedia objects on plain HTML pages. In the case of videos, it is often a good idea to include one or two still photos. Also, for both audio and video, write a short summary of what the user will get to hear or see.

Images and Photographs

The amount of graphics on web pages should be minimized because of the horribly long download times they require. Gratuitous graphics simply have to go, including all instances of text rendered as images (with the exception of captions that are so closely integrated within a business graphic that they need to be part of the image file itself).

Even so, users do want to see photos of the products they are buying because they can't otherwise touch and feel them. On a biography page, it is also best to include a photo of the person or text that focuses on an individual. There are also cases where the old saying "An image is worth a thousand words" is so fitting that it overcomes the corollary "An image takes two thousand words worth of download time."

The way to resolve the tension between these two design guidelines is to take advantage of the hypertext features of the Web. Higher-level pages should minimize the number of illustrations because the user has not yet indicated a concrete interest in an individual object that needs to be depicted. Then, as the user follows links to more specific pages, you can add more images. A top-level product page should usually have a small photo of the product but should still be mostly text and tables. If the user is *really* interested in the product, he or she will follow links from the product page to additional photos. Such photos should be large enough to show sufficient detail to support a purchase decision.

Image Reduction

The traditional way to produce small versions of images is to create thumbnails in a graphics program by using its resize command.

Unfortunately, scaling reduces the image so much that pictures with extensive detail wash out and become too crowded to be meaningful. Cropping preserves those details that are within the new viewport, but at the cost of losing the context of the image as a whole. My recommendation is to use a combination of cropping and scaling, resulting in a technique I call *relevance-enhanced image reduction*. For example, to get a thumbnail that is 10 percent of the original image, first crop the image to 32 percent of the original size and then scale the result to 32 percent. The final image will be $0.32 \times 0.32 = 0.1$ of the original.

(Following page) **The main product photo of the Walkman is about right, although it would be best to supplement it with a link to a large close-up shot of the product—possibly even from several angles, including a better look at the headset. The long column of thumbnails is worthless as a way of pointing users to additional models; you can't tell the differences between these products by looking at these tiny images. To add insult to injury, you can't even see the names or prices of the alternative products without having to sweep your mouse down the column. By only showing one price at a time, comparisons are made even harder, and users have to waste time moving the mouse around: Mine-sweeping doesn't belong in web design. Two additional problems with this page are the use of a low-contrast color for the main product description and the emphasis on market-ese instead of a useful summary of what customers this product is intended for.**

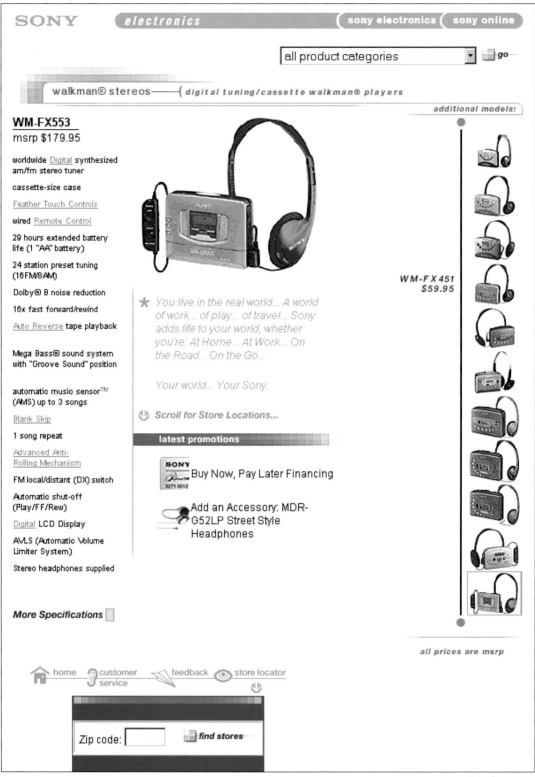

SONY

electronics

sony electronics | sony online

all product categories ▾ 🔲 go

walkman® stereos —— (*digital tuning/cassette walkman® players*

additional models:

WM-FX553
msrp $179.95

worldwide Digital synthesized am/fm stereo tuner

cassette-size case

Feather Touch Controls

wired Remote Control

29 hours extended battery life (1 "AA" battery)

24 station preset tuning (16FM/8AM)

Dolby® B noise reduction

16x fast forward/rewind

Auto Reverse tape playback

Mega Bass® sound system with "Groove Sound" position

automatic music sensor™ (AMS) up to 3 songs

Blank Skip

1 song repeat

Advanced Anti-Rolling Mechanism

FM local/distant (DX) switch

Automatic shut-off (Play/FF/Rew)

Digital LCD Display

AVLS (Automatic Volume Limiter System)

Stereo headphones supplied

More Specifications 📄

WM-FX451
$59.95

✱ *You live in the real world... A world of work... of play... of travel... Sony adds life to your world, whether you're: At Home... At Work... On the Road... On the Go...*

Your world... Your Sony.

🔄 ***Scroll for Store Locations...***

latest promotions

SONY 🔲 Buy Now, Pay Later Financing

Add an Accessory: MDR-G52LP Street Style Headphones

all prices are msrp

🏠 home   customer service   feedback   👁 store locator

Zip code: [   ]   🔲 *find stores*

The Starfire Desk-Sized Computer

Mail, calendar, family pictures

Video-conference windows

Information space

Documents

Mouse

Still some paper-based work being done ...

www.asktog.com

Two illustrations I designed in February 1995 for a website for Bruce Tognazzini's film "Starfire," which he directed for Sun Microsystems. Both illustrations are based on the same still from the film. The first photo is used on the home page and is only 13 KB as a JPEG (although the original site in 1995 used a 90 KB large GIF version of the photo because Mosaic didn't understand JPEGs). The small image is linked to the larger, annotated photo (241 KB). My user tests showed that people invariably click on the annotations in an attempt to get further information about the various elements in the photo.

Sometimes, a full-size image is too large to be included in the primary web page. Here, a still from Sun's "Starfire" film.

The two traditional approaches to making images smaller are cropping (left) and scaling (right). Unfortunately, cropping leads to loss of context, especially as the images get cropped very tightly, and scaling leads to loss of detail, making it hard to see what the image depicts.

Relevance-enhanced image reduction results in images that preserve both context and detail, even at very small sizes. In these examples, half of the reduction has been achieved by cropping the image (while keeping the center of the action in the center of the resulting viewport), and the other half has been achieved by scaling.

Jakob Nielsen: Designing Web Usability

My first attempt at making a comic-strip representation of a clip from Sun's "Starfire" film. This design does not work because it requires scrolling to see the entire scene and because the still images are too large, and therefore, download too slowly. In usability testing, I also found that users did not really want to read detailed plot summaries as those provided here. We know that people don't want to read long texts on the Web. And, of course, this also applies for the textual elements of multimedia designs. Duh!

Meeting of the Board of Directors

Click here for the *soundtrack* that goes with these film stills.

After Julie's multimedia presentation to the Board of Directors, her rival, Mike, springs a surprise on her. He claims that Julie's car will not sell well since a previous attempt at a similar car failed. You cannot launch a sportscar in the spring.

Faced with this surprise, Julie uses her laptop computer to search a remote information base on the spot. Note how the laptop uses a chorded keyboard.

In the database, Julie finds several relevant articles that explain the reason for the disappointing sales of the previous car. Her computer automatically searches further.

Julie interrupts Mike and explains that his assumptions were wrong. To bolster her claims, she brings information over from her laptop to the big multimedia screen where it can be seen by everybody.

In the news archives, Julie's laptop has found a newspaper story that explained the disappointing sales of the previous car: It had been released just before a major earthquake that caused people to temporarily stop buying cars.

Boardroom Meeting

Click here for the *soundtrack.*

The Plot

Julie is giving a multimedia presentation to the Board of Directors (where some of the members are attending remotely). She is proposing that the company start manufacturing a car designed by her division. Her rival, Mike, springs a surprise during the meeting and claims that Julie's car will not sell well since a previous attempt at a similar car failed. Julie uses her laptop computer to search a remote information base on the spot and discovers that an earthquake was the reason for the disappointing sales of the previous car.

www.sun.com

(Facing page) A much better comic-strip design for the same video clip. Here, smaller images download faster and take up less space, allowing for two images per row. The resulting design can be seen without scrolling on a large monitor. Also note the option to play the audio track that goes with the images. Many users get as much benefit from seeing
the comic strip and hearing the audio as they would from playing the full video.

Animation

Moving images have an overpowering effect on human peripheral vision. This is a survival instinct from the time when it was of supreme importance to be aware of any saber-toothed tigers before they could sneak up on you.

These days, tiger-avoidance is less of an issue, but anything that moves in your peripheral vision still dominates your awareness: It is extremely hard to concentrate on reading text in the middle of a page if there is a spinning logo up in the corner. Animations do have their place in web design, and appropriate use of animation is discussed later in this section, but in general, it is best to minimize the use of animation. Ask yourself whether your point would be communicated as well by a non-animated graphic. If the answer is yes, kill the animation. Also, never make animations loop infinitely; have them run a few times and then stop.

A few users do say that they think animations are cool or indicate that a lot of work has gone into the design of a site. Animations may thus be serving a function similar to that of marble columns in banks: to visibly demonstrate status and affluence. Most users, though, say that they are annoyed by the animations. In particular, almost all users hate moving text and scrolling marquees.

One of our test users said, "I have stopped reading crawling text because experience has shown me that it never has any useful information." In fact, moving text had better not have any important information because it is difficult to read and because part of the text is typically off the screen at any given time. Stock tickers are an interaction technique that was necessitated by technological limitations of the early telegraph: The only thing they could do was spit out a stream of tape.

Animation is good for seven purposes, each of which is discussed in more depth on the following pages:

- Showing continuity in transitions
- Indicating dimensionality in transitions
- Illustrating change over time
- Multiplexing the display
- Enriching graphical representations
- Visualizing three-dimensional structures
- Attracting attention

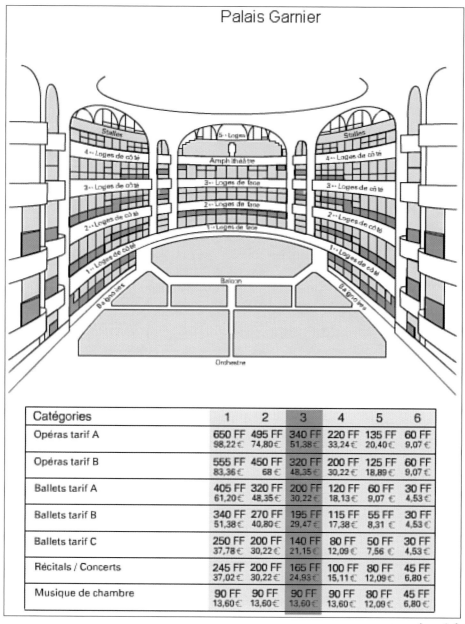

Palais Garnier

Catégories	1	2	3	4	5	6
Opéras tarif A	650 FF 98,22€	495 FF 74,80€	340 FF 51,38€	220 FF 33,24€	135 FF 20,40€	60 FF 9,07 €
Opéras tarif B	555 FF 83,36€	450 FF 68 €	320 FF 48,35€	200 FF 30,22€	125 FF 18,89€	60 FF 9,07€
Ballets tarif A	405 FF 61,20€	320 FF 48,35€	200 FF 30,22€	120 FF 18,13€	60 FF 9,07 €	30 FF 4,53€
Ballets tarif B	340 FF 51,38€	270 FF 40,80€	195 FF 29,47€	115 FF 17,38€	55 FF 8,31 €	30 FF 4,53€
Ballets tarif C	250 FF 37,78€	200 FF 30,22€	140 FF 21,15€	80 FF 12,09€	50 FF 7,56 €	30 FF 4,53€
Récitals / Concerts	245 FF 37,02€	200 FF 30,22€	165 FF 24,93€	100 FF 15,11€	80 FF 12,09€	45 FF 6,80€
Musique de chambre	90 FF 13,60€	90 FF 13,60€	90 FF 13,60€	90 FF 13,60€	80 FF 12,09€	45 FF 6,80€

www.opera-de-paris.fr

A rare case of useful JavaScript rollovers. As
the user moves the cursor over the list of prices,
the corresponding seats light up in the diagram
of the theater. A simple animation effect that
visually indicates the connection between what's
happening in the two parts of the screen.

Showing Continuity in Transitions

When something has two or more states, changes between states will be much easier for users to understand if the transitions are animated instead of being instantaneous. An animated transition allows the user to track the mapping between different subparts through the perceptual system instead of having to involve the cognitive system to deduce the mappings. A great example is the winner of the first Java programming contest: proving the Pythagorean theorem by animating the movement of various squares and triangles as they move around to demonstrate that two areas are the same size.

Indicating Dimensionality in Transitions

Sometimes, opposite animated transitions can be used to indicate movement back and forth along some navigational dimension. For example, paging through a series of objects can be shown by an animated sweep from the right to the left for turning the page forward (if using a language where readers start on the left). Turning back to a previous page can then be shown by the opposite animation (sweeping from the left to the right). If users move orthogonally to the sequence of pages, other animated effects can be used to visualize the transition. For example, following a hypertext link to a footnote might be shown by a "down" animation, and tunneling through hyperspace to a different set of objects might be shown by an "iris open" animation.

One example used in several user interfaces is zooming to indicate that a new object is "grown" from a previous one (e.g., a detailed view or property list opened by clicking on an icon) or that an object is closed or minimized to a smaller representation. Zooming out from the small object to the enlargement is a navigational dimension and zooming in again as the enlargement is closed down is the opposite direction along that dimension.

Illustrating Change over Time

Because an animation is a time-varying display, it provides a one-to-one mapping to phenomena that change over time. For example, deforestation of the rain forest can be illustrated by showing a map with an animation of the covered area changing over time.

Multiplexing the Display

Animation can also be used to show multiple information objects in the same space. A typical example is a client-side imagemap with explanations that pop up as the user moves the cursor over the various hypertext anchors. It is also possible to indicate the active areas by having them shimmer or by surrounding them with a marquee of "marching ants." As always, objects should only move when appropriate, for example, when the cursor is over the image.

Enriching Graphical Representations

Some types of information are easier to visualize with movement than with still pictures. In icon design, it is always easier to illustrate objects (a box) than operations (removing pixels), but animation provides the perfect support for illustrating any kind of change operation. In one particular experiment, Ron Baecker and colleagues increased the comprehension of a set of icons from 62 percent to 100 percent by animating them. Of course, an icon should animate only when the user indicates a special interest in it (for example, by placing the mouse cursor over it or by looking at it for more than a second if eye-tracking is available). It would be highly distracting if all icons were to animate at all times.

Visualizing Three-Dimensional Structures

Because the computer screen is two-dimensional, users can never get a full understanding of a three-dimensional structure by a single illustration, no matter how well designed. Animation can be used to emphasize the three-dimensional nature of objects and make it easier for users to visualize their spatial structure. The animation need not necessarily spin the object in a full circle; just slowly turning it back and forth a little will often be sufficient. The movement should be slow to allow the user to focus on the structure of the object.

Three-dimensional objects may be moved under user control, but often it is better if the designer determines in advance how to best animate a movement that provides optimal understanding of the object. This predetermined animation can then be activated by the user simply by placing the cursor over the object, whereas user-controlled

Animation Backfires

Before advertising banners go down in flaming defeat, they will have delivered a deadly strike against an otherwise useful design technique. In an attempt to overcome ever-declining click-through rates, advertisers use highly animated graphics that blink, flash, and move around incessantly. Such animation has no usability benefits for the user but is simply being used to try to attract attention to something that is irrelevant and that users don't want to look at. Users have realized this and are now avoiding design elements that move in the belief that they are probably useless. Sad but true. Often, people will look *less* at a design element the more it animates. Also, it is becoming a firm design guideline never to include any interface element that looks like an advertising banner because users will ignore it.

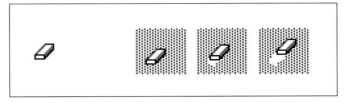

Two different ways of visualizing the tool used to remove pixels in a graphics application. The canonical icon is an eraser as shown on the left, but in user testing I have sometimes found that people think the icon is a tool for drawing three-dimensional boxes. Instead, one can use an animated icon as shown on the right in the figure; when the icon animates, the eraser is moved over the background and pixels are removed, clearly showing the tool's functionality.

movements require the user to understand how to manipulate the object, which is inherently difficult with a two-dimensional control device like the mouse used with most computers. To be honest, 3D is never going to make it big-time in user interfaces until we get a true 3D control device.

Attracting Attention

Finally, there are a few cases where the capability of animation to dominate the user's visual awareness can be turned to an advantage in the interface. If the goal is to draw the user's attention to a single element out of several or to alert the user to updated information, then an animated headline will do the trick. Animated text should be drawn by a one-time animation (for example, text sliding in from the right, growing from the first character, or smoothly becoming larger) and never by a continuous animation because moving text is much harder to read than static text. The user should be drawn to the new text by the initial animation and then left in peace to read the text without further distraction.

At first, it might seem that any animation could be rationalized as appropriate under the goal of "attracting attention." The differentiation between legitimate and spurious attention-getting comes from whether the animation would be of value to a typical user. Analyze the interaction from the average user's perspective to determine whether the user would be helped in a typical or frequent task from having something pointed out. In other words, it is *not* appropriate to have five ads all shouting "Look at me." That would be of value to the advertiser, not the user.

An example of user-derived value would be a personal site with a high-school class photo that had a link to something like "See my high school class photo." If the user followed the link, it would be appropriate to have an animated circle or arrow that pointed to the author in the

www.sun.com

It is a close call as to whether this button is an appropriate use of attention-getting animation, but I initially thought so. Our button design had three lines of text and only the middle line animated, thereby making it possible for users to read the important text in the outer two lines. Our first attempt (top) used a scrolling effect for the middle line, but we had to abandon that idea due to user hostility. About half of our test users had vitriolic reactions to the scrolling text and one user ignored it because he thought it was an advertisement. The second attempt (middle) used much more subtle animation and did not evoke any hatred, but we still ended up with a non-animated button for our final design (bottom).

The goal of the button was to attract users to take a user survey that rotated between various pages on the site. The animation was initially thought necessary because the button was not an integrated part of the page design, nor did it have a logical place on the page because it was present only temporarily. In the final analysis, the animation provoked negative feelings in the users and was not used. We settled on a static button that, while non-moving, still indicated dynamism in its graphic design and user activism in its wording, thus encouraging survey participation.

photo. Another example would be a page with lots of stuff on it, but where one item in the middle is new or for some other reason particularly important. It would then be okay to draw the user's attention to that item by a non-looping animation.

Normally, of course, the page should be designed to put the important content on top—thus, most pages will not need this type of animation—but sometimes the logical structure of the information dictates a certain ordering. Other times, information about user preferences or interests would allow the presumption of importance for information that would not be seen unless the user's attention was drawn to it by an animation.

Video

Due to bandwidth constraints, use of video should currently be minimized on the Web. Eventually, video will be used more widely, but for the next few years, most videos will be short and will use small viewing areas with low image quality and disgustingly slow frame rates. Under these constraints, video has to serve as a supplement to text and images more often than to provide the main content of a website.

Currently, video is good for

- Promoting television shows, films, or other non-computer media that traditionally use trailers in their advertising.
- Giving users an impression of a speaker's personality. Unfortunately, most corporate executives project a lot less personality than, say, Captain Janeway from *Star Trek*, so it is not necessarily a good idea to show a talking head unless the video clip truly adds to the user's experience. When people see a video, they immediately think "television," and anybody who has less screen presence than Tom Brokaw will come across as uninteresting.
- Showing things that move, such as a clip from a ballet. Product demos of physical products, such as a coin counter, are also well suited for video, whereas software demos are often better presented as a series of full-sized screendumps where the potential customer can study the features at length.

A major problem with most videos on the web right now is that their production values are much too low. User studies have found that users expect broadcast-quality production values any time they see a video and that users get very impatient when the quality is not up to these expectations.

A special consideration for video (and spoken audio) is that any narration may lead to difficulty for international users as well as for users with a hearing disability. People may be able to understand written text in a foreign language because they have time to read it at their own speed and because they can look up any unknown words in a dictionary.

Additionally, spoken words are sometimes harder to understand, especially if the speaker is sloppy, has a dialect, speaks over a distracting soundtrack, or simply speaks too quickly. Poor audio quality may contribute to the difficulty of understanding spoken text, so it is recommended that you use professional quality audio equipment and/or lavaliere microphones when recording a narrator. The classic solution to these problems is to use subtitles but, as shown in the figures, subtitles require special attention on the Web.

Streaming Video Versus Downloadable Video

Because of the poor quality of streaming video, it is often best to digitize a higher-quality version of the video and make it available for download. If the video actually has value, users won't mind waiting, say, five minutes to download a one-minute video where they can actually see something.

Linear playbacks are very pacifying; there is nothing to do except sit and watch the video roll through a predetermined sequence of scenes. Such lack of interaction conflicts with the basic web-user experience, which is one of taking control and moving around. As such, most audio and video clips should be kept to less than one minute in length. Sitting still to watch something that takes more than five minutes should be the rare exception on the Web.

For example, instead of putting an entire 30-minute keynote lecture on the Web as streaming audio or video, put up text files with a transcript. If possible, employ an editor to edit the transcript into something that is more

(Facing page)   Traditional subtitles look good on a full-sized videotape (here's a still from Sun's "Starfire" film).

Unfortunately, the subtitles are virtually unreadable when the video is reduced to the size usually transmitted over the Internet (left image). Much better readability is gained from placing the subtitles in a letterbox and sizing them for computer viewing (right image). Doing so does not increase the file size proportionally because the black area compresses very nicely.

Jakob Nielsen: Designing Web Usability

readable than most lectures. Then, supplement the text with a few photos of the speaker and the audience, as well as high-quality versions of any visuals. Finally, you can communicate the speaker's personality and the spirit of the event by linking to a one-minute audio clip of the most exciting sound bytes. Or, use a video clip if the speaker was sufficiently animated.

To preserve the feeling of user control, even when presenting multimedia, try segmenting longer presentations into short chapters that can be chosen from a menu. When converting a television news program to the Web, for example, don't make it into a single, 60-minute streaming video that cannot be controlled by the user. Instead, break the program into one segment for each news story. Then, prepare a standard web page that lists the stories with a short summary and a single thumbnail photo from the most visual ones. Allow users to link to individual stories from this page.

In the future, we will hopefully get the bandwidth for full-sized video. As long as bandwidth is a concern, we can save download time by transmitting the subtitles as ASCII (or Unicode) and have them rendered in the letterbox on the client machine: a perfect job for an applet. It should also be possible to have the user select the language for the subtitles through a preference setting or a pop-up menu.

Jakob Nielsen: Designing Web Usability

The Queen's Speech
The Christmas Broadcast

The Programme | **Royal Watch** | **Links** | **Archive**

The Speech

Bridging the generation gap: the theme of a speech in which the Queen spoke of the inspiration of the young, and the experience and wisdom that can be learned from the old

Watch the whole programme

Headlines

Bridging the generation gap
The Queen acknowledged it was sometimes hard for younger people to understand their elders could have valuable experience worth learning from – and then revealed she drew much day-to-day inspiration from the Queen Mother

Video

Memories of war and sacrifice
The memories of sacrifice and war – poignantly underlined by commemorations this year – were a theme of the Monarch's speech. The Queen also paid tribute to the British forces who saw recent action against Iraq

Video

Prince Charles: a birthday to remember
The Queen spoke of her son's 50th birthday as "a moment of great happiness and pride." She paid tribute to his public work and achievements.

Video

www.itn.co.uk

The Queen's speech is segmented into topics that are easily available from this page on the site of the British ITN network. Viewers are not forced to sit through the entire program like they would have had they been watching television, although the entire speech is still an available option for those who do want everything. Whether it is appropriate to run advertising on top of Her Majesty is a topic for another day.

Audio

The main benefit of audio is that it provides a channel that is separate from that of the display. Speech can be used to offer commentary or help without obscuring information on the screen. Audio can also be used to provide a sense of place or mood, as done to perfection in the game Myst. Mood-setting audio should employ quiet background sounds in order not to compete with the main information for the user's attention.

Music is probably the most obvious use of sound. Whenever you need to inform the user about a certain work of music, it makes much more sense to simply play it than to show the notes or to try to describe it in words. For example, if you are out to sell seats to the "La Scala" opera in Milan, Italy, it is an obvious ploy to allow users to hear a snippet of the opera. In fact, the audio clips are superior to the video clips from the same operas that are too fidgety to impress the user and yet take much too long to download.

Another use of sound includes voice recordings, and these can be used instead of video to provide a sense of the speaker's personality. The benefits include smaller files, easier production, and the fact that people often sound good even if they look dull on television. Speech is also perfect for teaching users the pronunciation of words as done by the French wine site; it used to be the case that you could buy good wine cheaply by going for a Chateau that was hard to pronounce (because nobody dared ask for them in shops or restaurants). No more in the webbed world.

Non-speech sound effects can be used as an extra dimension in the user interface to inform users about background events. For example, the arrival of new information could be signaled by the sound of a newspaper dropping on the floor, and the progress of a file download could be indicated by the sound of water pouring into a glass that gradually fills up. However, these kinds of background sounds must remain quiet and non-intrusive. Also, there always needs to be a user preference setting to turn them off.

Good-quality sound is known to enhance the user experience substantially, so it is well worth investing in professional-quality sound production. The classic example is the video game study where users claimed that the graphics were better when the sound was improved, even though the exact same graphics were used for the poor-quality sound and the good-quality sound experiments. Simple examples from web user interfaces are the use of a low-key clicking sound to emphasize when users click a button and the use of opposing sounds (cheeeek chooook) when moving in different directions through a navigation space.

Enabling Users with Disabilities to Use Multimedia Content

Any time you use any format other than plain text and standard HTML, you risk depriving users with disabilities from being able to use your site. This is one more reason to restrain the use of multimedia to cases where it adds substantial value to a site.

Hearing-impaired users can be supported by the use of captions on videos and transcripts of audio presentations. Such textual alternatives also make the content more accessible to search engines and facilitate translation.

Visually impaired users are more difficult to support. The traditional approach to making images accessible is to provide a textual description that can be read aloud by a talking browser, but doing so for a video can conflict with the audio track. WGBH, a PBS station in Boston, recommends the use of DVS (Descriptive Video Service) with a separate audio narrative that runs between the pauses in the main audio track for users who can't see the pictures. For some videos, this may work. Other times, it may be necessary to provide a completely textual alternative that integrates the information found in the audio and visual tracks of the video.

For those visually impaired users who are not completely blind but instead have reduced vision, it may be possible to simply provide a bigger or cleaner video image (even if it takes longer time to download). Or, you could provide a slide-show presentation with cleaned-up (and possibly simplified) still images as an alternative to a moving-image presentation.

Any time you use any format other than plain text and standard HTML, you risk depriving users with disabilities from being able to use your site.

Three-Dimensional Graphics

It's almost always better to have 2D than 3D because people are not frogs. If we had been frogs with eyes sitting on the sides of our heads, the story might have been different, but we humans have our eyes smack in the front of our faces, looking straight out.

Evolution optimized Homo sapiens for wandering the savanna—moving around a plane—and not swinging through the trees. Today, this evolutionary bias shows in comparing the number of people who drive a car versus the number of helicopter pilots: 2D navigation (on the ground) versus 3D navigation (in the air).

Using 3D on a computer adds a range of difficulties:

- The screen and the mouse are both 2D devices, so we don't get true 3D unless we strap on weird head-gear and buy expensive bats (flying mice).
- It is difficult to control a 3D space with the interaction techniques that are currently in common use because they were designed for 2D manipulation (dragging and scrolling, for example).
- Users need to pay attention to the navigation of the 3D view in addition to the navigation of the underlying model; the extra controls for flying, zooming, and so on, get in the way of the user's primary task.
- Poor screen resolution makes it impossible to render remote objects in sufficient detail to be recognizable; any text in the background is unreadable.
- The software needed for 3D is usually non-standard, crash-prone, and requires an extra download (which users don't want to wait for).

Bad Use of 3D

Most abstract information spaces work poorly in 3D because they are non-physical. If anything, they have at least 100 dimensions, so visualizing an information space in 3D means throwing away 97 dimensions instead of 98: hardly a big enough improvement to justify the added interface complexity.

In particular, navigation through a hyperspace (such as a website) is often confusing in 3D, and users frequently get lost. Three-dimensional navigation may look cool in a

Jakob Nielsen: Designing Web Usability

demo, but that's because you're not flying through the hyperspace yourself. As such, you don't have to remember what's behind you or worry about what remote objects are hidden by nearby objects. (The person giving the demo knows where everything is. The first law of demos: Never try to actually use the system for anything. Instead, simply step through a well-rehearsed script that does not touch anything that might cause a crash.)

Also, avoid virtual reality gimmicks (say, a virtual shopping mall) that emulate the physical world. The goal of web design is to be better than reality. If you ask users to "walk around the mall," you are putting your interface in the way of their goal. In the physical world, you need to schlepp between shops; on the Web, you teleport through cyberspace directly to your destination using a navigational topology that conforms to user needs (assuming good information architecture, of course).

One of the main reasons to take it easy on 3D is the reduced legibility of rotated text. Of course, it doesn't help to use low-contrast colors as done here for the product captions.

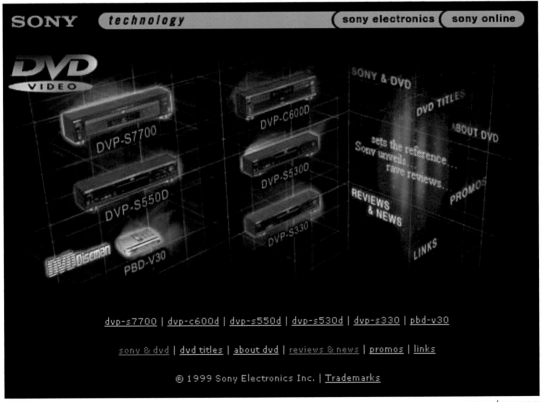

www.sel.sony.com

PlanetOasis global view

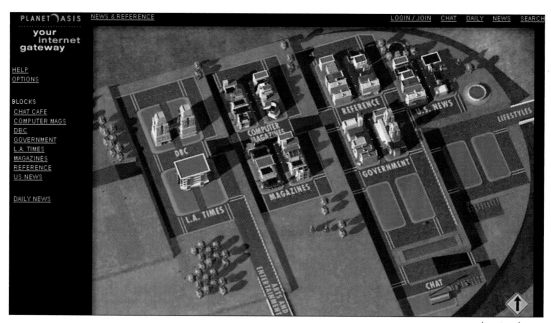

PlanetOasis district view

Jakob Nielsen: Designing Web Usability

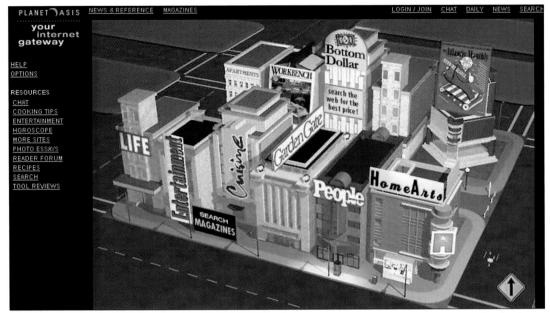

your
internet
gateway

HELP
OPTIONS

RESOURCES
CHAT
COOKING TIPS
ENTERTAINMENT
HOROSCOPE
MORE SITES
PHOTO ESSAYS
READER FORUM
RECIPES
SEARCH
TOOL REVIEWS

www.planetoasis.com

PlanetOasis block view

Moving through PlanetOasis from the view of the entire island (facing page) through a view of a district to a view of an individual block (above). A very slow and awkward way to get to *People* magazine. Pure visual gimmick. Do you really have the feeling that if you turn around, the *Los Angeles Times* will be behind you? More important: Can you remember this?

When to Use 3D

Use of 3D can be appropriate when you need to visualize physical objects that need to be understood in their solid form. Examples might include:

- Surgeons planning where to cut a patient. The body is 3D, and the location of the tumor has a 3D location that is easier to understand from a 3D model than from a 2D x-ray.
- Mechanical engineers designing a widget that needs to fit into a gadget.
- Chemistry researchers trying to understand the shape of a molecule.
- Planning the layout of a trade-show booth.

Sometimes, physical objects work better in 2D. A help system explaining how to replace a hard disk in a computer chassis may be better off with a schematic drawing from exactly the perspective that highlights the correct spot. Or, use a video of a repair tech who removes the old disk and inserts the new one. Video is 2D with respect to the images but uses sound to enhance the understanding of events (e.g., the satisfying snap when the disk is safely docked). Sound provides additional dimensionality without navigational overhead because it's synched to the video.

Abstract data sets that have exactly three attributes are sometimes easier to understand in a 3D visualization. But first, attempt to simplify the problem and experiment with 2D views, including the comic-strip-like layout of multiple charts that Edward Tufte loves so much in his book *The Visual Display of Quantitative Information*.

Finally, entertainment applications and some educational interfaces can benefit from the fun and engaging nature of 3D, as evidenced by countless shoot-'em-up games. Note that 3D works for games because the user doesn't want to accomplish any goals beyond being entertained. It would be trivial to design a better interface than DOOM if the goal was to kill the bad guys as quickly as possible. Give me a 2D map of the area with icons for enemy troops and let me drop bombs on them by clicking the icons? Presto. Game over in a few seconds, and the good guys win every time. That's the design you want if you're the Pentagon, but it makes for a really boring game.

Conclusion

Content is the focus of the web users's attention. It's the reason they go online, and it's the first thing they look at when they load a new page. Quality content is one of the two most important determinants of web usability, the other being whether users can find the page they want (which is the topic of the next chapter: site design).

On the Web, "quality content" means something different than in traditional media. Production qualities are relatively less important; well-crafted writing and beautiful pictures are certainly appreciated, but they are no longer the defining characteristics of quality. Instead, the main questions asked by the user when judging content include "What's in it for me?" and "How does this help me solve my problem?"

Because web users are so goal-driven and so impatient, content needs to be much more oriented toward providing fast answers and being useful to the user.

4 Site Design

Page design sometimes gets the most attention. After all, with current web browsers, you see only one page at a time. The site itself is never explicitly represented on the screen. But from a usability perspective, site design is more challenging and usually also more important than page design.

Once users arrive at a page, they can usually figure out what to do there, if only they would take a little time (OK, users *don't* take the time to study pages carefully, which is why we also have many usability problems at the page level). But getting the user to the correct page in the first place is not easy.

In a study by Jared Spool and colleagues, when users were started out at the home page and given a simple problem to solve, they could find the correct page only 42 percent of the time. In a different study by Mark Hurst and myself, the success rate was even lower; only 26 percent of users were capable of accomplishing a slightly more difficult task which, in the case of our study, was to find a job opening and apply for it (averaged across six representative corporate sites with job listings).

(Facing page)   I thought the dreaded "under construction" signs (complete with little animated construction worker digging away) had died sometime in 1995 after it became clear that all websites are *always* under construction. But unfortunately, they keep springing up, albeit in more sophisticated forms.

Don't tell users what you don't have; that's only frustrating. Don't release a partially finished website; keep it under wraps until it has enough utility that it will make sense to users. It is fine to have a small article that talks about future plans or upcoming attractions, but the main entry to the site should focus on what a user can do here and now.

As an aside, what do you think the big question mark does? Never use such cryptic interface elements. The only reasonable interpretation of a question mark would be a help feature because it is somewhat standardized to use a question mark icon to access help. But the Saturn question mark leads to the search engine: Nobody will expect this, so nobody will find it.

The reason for the lower success rate in our study relative to Jared Spool's study was not because we had picked particularly poorly designed sites; on the contrary, we were looking at sites from fairly large and well-respected companies. The difference in success rates was due to differences in the task complexity. The 42 percent success rate was the average outcome across a range of tasks where users were asked to find the answers to specific questions on a website—in other words, the exact task the Web is best for. In contrast, the 26 percent success rate was the average when users had to carry out a sequence of steps in order to complete the task of finding and applying for a job. If a user was prevented from progressing through any one of the individual steps, then he or she would not be able to perform the task. After all, you can't apply for a job if you can't find it. But it also does you no good to find a job posting if the application form is too difficult.

The problem is that web usability suffers dramatically as soon as we take users off the home page and start them navigating or problem solving. The Web was designed as an environment for reading papers, and its usability has not improved in step with the ever-higher levels of complexity users are asked to cope with. Therefore, site design must be aimed at simplicity above all else, with as few distractions as possible and with a very clear information architecture and matching navigation tools.

Jakob Nielsen: Designing Web Usability

Hi. Welcome to our (partially) redesigned Web site. Over the next few weeks, we'll be updating every section of the site to look and work just like the one you see here. And since these new sections will be coming online almost daily, please be sure to come back every so often. Until then, please pardon our cyber dust. And thanks for stopping in.

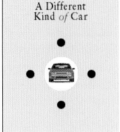

A Different
Kind *of* Car

www.saturn.com

 Think different.

The Apple Store

The Apple Store is closed for the holidays while the computer-making elves work diligently to make the online Apple Store better than ever. Please come back again January 5 to place your order through the Apple Store.

If you don't want to wait, you still have time to start the new year off right by visiting a local Apple reseller who can supply you with all you need to get started.

If you've already placed your order and want to check on the status,
call 1-800-795-1000.

store.apple.com

The Home Page

The home page is the flagship of the site and should therefore be designed differently from the remaining pages. Of course, home pages and interior pages should share the same style, but there are differences. For example, the home page should not have a *Home* button, because it is very annoying to click on a button that links right back to the current page. Also, the home page should typically have a larger logo and a more prominent placement of the company name or site name. The first immediate goal of any home page is to answer the questions "Where am I?" and "What does this site do?"—both of which require a straightforward and large version of the name. The answers should not be in the form of the dreaded mission statements sometimes seen on overly bureaucratic sites. Rather, it should be obvious from the design what purpose the site would serve for a first-time user.

For the first-time visitor, answering the question "What does this site do?" may be the most important function of the home page, but for most other users, the most important function of a home page is to serve as the entry point

What does this company do? Simplicity is good, but a home page needs *some* info.

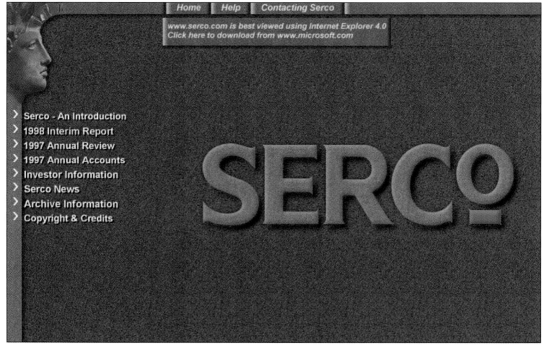

www.serco.com

Jakob Nielsen: Designing Web Usability

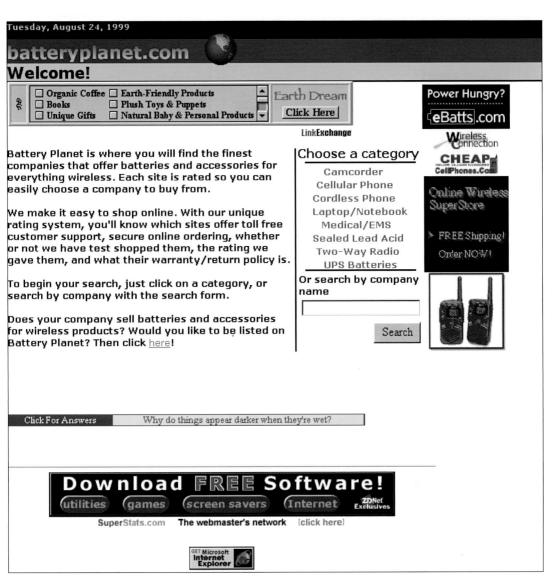

batteryplanet.com

Welcome!

☐ Organic Coffee ☐ Earth-Friendly Products
☐ Books ☐ Plush Toys & Puppets
☐ Unique Gifts ☐ Natural Baby & Personal Products

Earth Dream
Click Here
LinkExchange

Power Hungry?
....
eBatts.com

Wireless Connection

CHEAP CellPhones.Com

Online Wireless SuperStore

► FREE Shipping!
Order NOW!

Battery Planet is where you will find the finest companies that offer batteries and accessories for everything wireless. Each site is rated so you can easily choose a company to buy from.

We make it easy to shop online. With our unique rating system, you'll know which sites offer toll free customer support, secure online ordering, whether or not we have test shopped them, the rating we gave them, and what their warranty/return policy is.

To begin your search, just click on a category, or search by company with the search form.

Does your company sell batteries and accessories for wireless products? Would you like to be listed on Battery Planet? Then click here!

Choose a category

Camcorder
Cellular Phone
Cordless Phone
Laptop/Notebook
Medical/EMS
Sealed Lead Acid
Two-Way Radio
UPS Batteries

Or search by company name

Search

Click For Answers | Why do things appear darker when they're wet?

Download FREE Software!
(utilities) (games) (screen savers) (Internet) ZDNet Exclusives

SuperStats.com   **The webmaster's network**   [click here]

GET Microsoft
Internet
Explorer

www.batteryplanet.com

The first impression from this home page is that this might be a place to buy coffee or get free software when, in fact, it's a place to buy batteries. But there is not a single picture of a battery on the home page, nor is the word highlighted anywhere. The site name is nice and prominent and does imply a battery-oriented site, so the design is not a total loss. Also, the navigation categories are easy to find and fairly logical. But why waste space on a colored stripe across the top with today's date? For a sporadically updated site, there might be some benefits from a footer that mentions the date of the latest update, but the current date will never be used by anybody.

(Facing page) There is too much junk on this home page, especially considering that we are seeing only the top half here. But the page still works because most users will be drawn immediately to the interactive part of the page where they can enter their trip information and go immediately to a list of available flights.

to the site's navigation scheme. Often, this will take the form of a list of the top levels of a hierarchical directory, but depending on the information architecture, different forms of top-level entry aides may make sense.

For example, people visiting a travel site will often want to make an airline reservation, so a way to enter the departure and arrival cities for a trip can often be a good top-level entry point into such a site.

The home page is also the place to feature any news or special promotions you want to bring to the attention of all visitors. But remember that most people come to your site in order to accomplish something specific. Only rarely are they interested in simply checking out what might be happening in your company or what products you feel like putting on sale. Therefore, the news area should be relatively restrained and leave a large part of the page available for navigation—the exception to this rule obviously being sites that focus on news. For such sites, the user's goal in visiting will often be to "see what's up" without having any specific stories in mind in advance. Even for news sites, it is still important to remember that some users will visit in order to research specific stories or current events and that people will also often want to find old articles that have long ago been pushed off the home page. Navigation remains a priority in any case.

Most home pages need a prominent search feature because many users are search-dominant and don't want to bother navigating to their destination link-by-link. For sites where search is a primary access mechanism, it makes sense to include an actual search box right on top of the home page. For other sites, a simple (but still prominent) link to the search page may suffice.

In summary, a home page should offer three features: a directory of the site's main content areas (navigation), a summary of the most important news or promotions, and a search feature. If done well, directory and news will help answer the first-time user's need to find out what the site is about in the first place. Even so, always look at the home page with an eye to asking, "What can this site do for me?" And remember the name and logo.

Expedia.com™

FREE shipping!
Click Here.

eBags
Get Carried Away!

| Home Page | My Travel | Deals | Places to Go | Interests & Activities | Maps | Find | Help |

go to msn.com

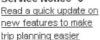
Fare Sale!
Save
up to 30%

Service Notice ⚠
Read a quick update on
new features to make
trip planning easier

Customer Support
- Privacy and security
- Credit Card Guarantee
- Join now. It's free!
- Agents on call 24 hrs.
- New on the site!

Non-U.S. residents
Use our sites in Australia,
Canada, Germany, UK,
Other.

eBags
Need a bag?

Get the dirt on
buying a home
with your honey!

Book a flight   **Reserve a room**   **Rent a car**

Try our fast Roundtrip Fare Finder: New? Register first

Leaving from	Departing (MM/DD/YY) Time
	9/19/99 evening ▼
Going to	Returning (MM/DD/YY) Time
	9/21/99 evening ▼

1 adult ▼   More search options...   Go

This search is limited to adult roundtrip coach fares.

**Shop for
vacations**

**Shop for
cruises**

Special Deals
Resorts
Accommodations
Sports & Adventure
Casino Destinations
Family Vacations
Travel Merchandise

Fare Compare: Are you getting the most for your money? Check out the airfares
that other customers are finding on our most popular routes.

IN MY TRAVEL

🗂 **My Itineraries**

View or update your purchased, reserved, or
planned trips.

- Flight Info: See up-to-the-minute status on flight arrivals and departures.
- Fare Tracker: Receive a free weekly update on low fares to your favorite cities.
- MileageMiner: Track your frequent flyer accounts and maximize your miles.

🔒 **My Profile**

Update your travel preferences
and account information.

FEATURED DESTINATION

Florence, Italy: A 360° tour of Firenze, the art-
filled city along the Arno

Find the latest info on hundreds of
other great travel destinations

Select a region ▼

CURRENT HIGHLIGHTS

- Up to 30 percent off flights worldwide
- One-way fares for $99 and up
- Been there, done that? Send a trip tip
- More headlines...

TRAVEL READ
Plan your next summer road trip
with the most popular guidebooks
at barnesandnoble.com.

www.expedia.com

(Facing page)   What website are we on here? Very clear that it's NetFlix. Second, what is the purpose of this site? Reasonably clear that this is a place to rent DVDs. But if you overlook the top of the page and glance directly at the middle of the page (as done by many users), you might also have thought that this was a site with movie reviews. The most prominent individual design element is probably the text entry box marked "Redeem" which is only useful for users with a special coupon. The entire coupon process takes up too much space on the home page: It would have been simpler to provide a link to a special page that could have explained the process better. Also, the search field slightly vanishes into the background of the navigation bar even though it is more important to most users than the coupon. A bigger problem with this home page, however, is the small amount of space allocated to the content directory relative to the current specials. The true depth of the site (3,700 products) is not well represented. The design does get a bonus point for the "1-2-3" area: simple and scannable content that summarizes the process of doing business with the site.

(Following pages)   These two airline sites show different approaches to home page design. United Airlines focuses on easy access to the many features on its site, whereas American Airlines focuses on easy access to two important features: logging in to your frequent flyer account and finding a flight between two cities. United Airlines' approach works best if use is fairly evenly distributed across multiple features. The home page makes it clear what one can do on this site, even though the "shortcuts" are too indistinct and fail to emphasize the site's most important features. The use of two levels of categories frees users from having to scan through all the features. I would have preferred to use three top-level categories instead of two: I think that "Reservations" and "Mileage Plus" (the frequent flyer program) should be combined into a single top-level category, because they both relate to the individual user's specific data and trips. The two remaining categories contain generic information about air travel and the corporation, respectively.

American Airlines' approach reduces the vast majority of site features to a set of pull-down menus that are difficult to navigate: Users can never see the full set of features (like they can at United) because they can pop up only a single menu at a time. And many of the menus are so long that they require scrolling, meaning that users can't even view the entire list of options in a menu in a single glance. Thus, American Airlines' approach works only if the two highlighted features, in fact, account for almost all use of the site.

For both sites, note how they have successfully combined traditional corporate information with e-commerce capabilities. There is no conflict between having a site that serves both functions as long as users quickly can find the links to buying stuff. United Airlines fails slightly here, even though it does make "Reservations" the first (and thus most prominent) category in its navigation scheme.

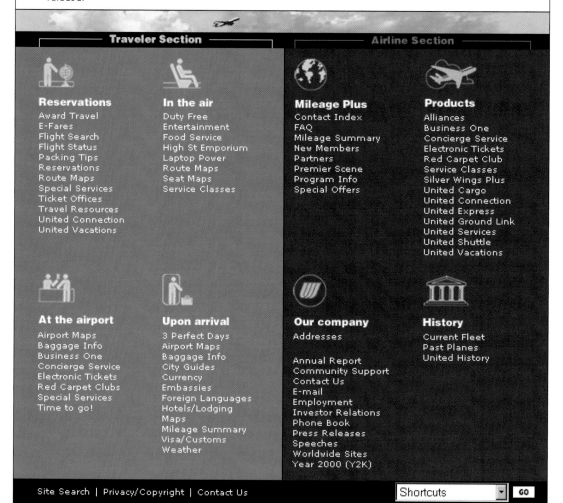

UNITED

United Worldwide Sites [▾] [GO]

Shortcuts   Award Travel | E-Fares | Flight Status | Mileage Summary | Reservations

New UAL.COM Features and Registration Information
Award Travel Redemption is here, along with faster updates to your Mileage Plus account! Learn how to register under our new feature release.

Earn 4,000 Bonus Miles!
Purchase your first roundtrip flight at ual.com and receive 4,000 Mileage Plus miles when you complete your travel on United, United Express or United Shuttle.

United E-Fare Specials for Hawaii
Aloha! Special discounts for travel to and from Honolulu, Maui and Kona are available until September 12. Click on the link for more details.

— Traveler Section —   **— Airline Section —**

Reservations
Award Travel
E-Fares
Flight Search
Flight Status
Packing Tips
Reservations
Route Maps
Special Services
Ticket Offices
Travel Resources
United Connection
United Vacations

In the air
Duty Free
Entertainment
Food Service
High St Emporium
Laptop Power
Route Maps
Seat Maps
Service Classes

Mileage Plus
Contact Index
FAQ
Mileage Summary
New Members
Partners
Premier Scene
Program Info
Special Offers

Products
Alliances
Business One
Concierge Service
Electronic Tickets
Red Carpet Club
Service Classes
Silver Wings Plus
United Cargo
United Connection
United Express
United Ground Link
United Services
United Shuttle
United Vacations

At the airport
Airport Maps
Baggage Info
Business One
Concierge Service
Electronic Tickets
Red Carpet Clubs
Special Services
Time to go!

Upon arrival
3 Perfect Days
Airport Maps
Baggage Info
City Guides
Currency
Embassies
Foreign Languages
Hotels/Lodging
Maps
Mileage Summary
Visa/Customs
Weather

Our company
Addresses

Annual Report
Community Support
Contact Us
E-mail
Employment
Investor Relations
Phone Book
Press Releases
Speeches
Worldwide Sites
Year 2000 (Y2K)

History
Current Fleet
Past Planes
United History

Site Search | Privacy/Copyright | Contact Us   Shortcuts [▾] [GO]

www.ual.com

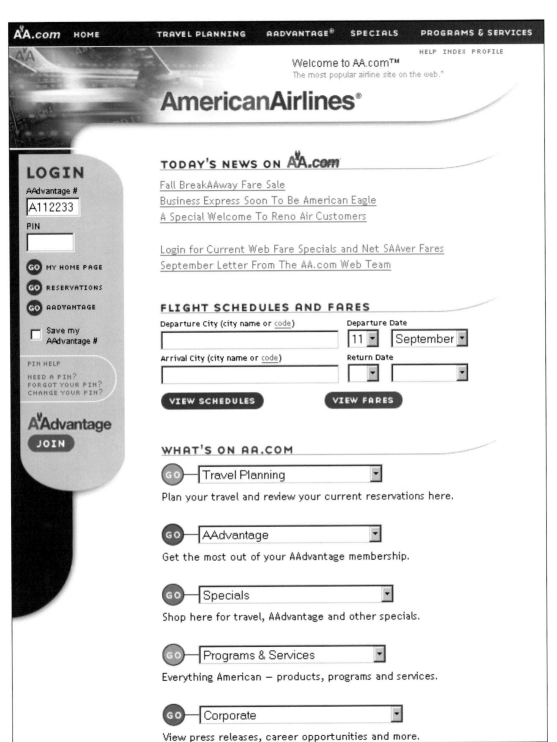

How Wide Should the Page Be?

The most-frequently asked question in all my web seminars is "What width screen should I design for?" People usually want to know whether 640 pixels or 800 pixels is the goal. My standard answer is that you shouldn't design for *any* standard width; it is far better to create page layouts that will work across a range of window sizes. Not only do users have varying monitor sizes set to a variety of resolutions, but they may not always have their windows maximized to take up the entire screen.

Those users who have small screens should not be required to scroll horizontally to use your home page (vertical scrolling is bad enough), and users who have large screens should be allowed to benefit from their investment. Even so, many home page designs do take up a specific size, and if you choose this approach, you are advised to stay under 600 pixels in width unless you are designing for an intranet where the users are known to have large monitors. The use of 600 pixels instead of 640 is important because on all screens, several pixels are gobbled up by the browser's window borders—the page content, therefore, cannot use the full width of the monitor.

Home Page Width

During the first years of the Web, home pages tended to get bigger and bigger as designers threw in options and used ever-more bloated graphics. At various times, I surveyed the early Web and calculated the average width of the home pages I found:

April 1995:	525 pixels
January 1996:	568 pixels
August 1996:	598 pixels
May 1997:	586 pixels

In 1998 and 1999, some home pages ballooned to 775 pixels (to fit an 800-pixel monitor), but most stayed at 600 pixels.

It is now rare to see narrow home pages (say, 300 pixels wide), although some sites use "liquid" designs that don't have any specific width. In principle, it is best to design this type of resolution-independent home page, which can adapt to various screen sizes. If this is not possible, then the standard advice is to assume that many users will still be using 640 pixels for several years to come.

Newsweek.com

Tuesday, August 24, 1999

Photo Gallery
This Week: Turkey's Tragedy

(Corbis-Sygma)

(Gary Moss)

Holbrooke: Mission Difficult
The new U.N. ambassador is headed for the Balkans. He has his work cut out for him.

Oklahoma City Syndrome
Mental health experts find a high incidence of postdisaster psychiatric disorder among victims of the 1995 bombing.

Behind the Myth
Changes: the view from Bill Gates's head. Submit Questions Now for a live talk with Steven Levy, Wednesday at noon E.D.T.

Unsafe Cybersex
Did online chat sessions lead to an outbreak of venereal disease?

Cars: Hot Wheels
America discovers a new generation of sleek, supercharged sports cars. They're sure not for kids.

Top News
washingtonpost.com
Last updated: 9:14 p.m. EDT
Fed Raises Rates 0.25 Percent

Prosecutor: Sheinbein Pleading Guilty to Murder

Whistleblower Already in Private-Sector Job

Technology ▶ A Web service takes the pain, and the paper, out of bill payments

Stock Watch Dow 11,283.30 −16.46 Nasdaq • **Your Portfolio**
2,752.37 +32.80 • **Market Update**

Photo Op

Ray Lustig - The Washington Post

Fed Raises Rates: *Federal Reserve Chairman Alan Greenspan and his policymakers today raised short-term interest rates a quarter-point.*

MY TURN
Family Heroes
Every family has its story...
Tell yours here.

Perspectives

"I wouldn't be surprised; I know we used to have money."
—**Imelda Marcos,** *widow of former Philippine leader Ferdinand Marcos, answering questions about a secret Swiss*

Today's Features

Television | *Turmoil at ABC*
Jamie Tarses wins an 11th-hour reprieve. But for how long?

Law | *The Cocaine Question*
A legal expert explains why it's time to debate drug-use penalties

Politics | *'The Gift of Fame'*
Warren Beatty's new script calls for the star to highlight

Judge Blocks Ohio School

www.newsweek.com

Newsweek attempts to satisfy both common screen sizes with this home page: At 800 pixels wide, you see everything (as depicted here), and at 640, you still see the main part of the page and only miss the rightmost column with secondary news. Even the page logo is designed to work at both screen sizes. This is admittedly a clever design, but I ultimately recommend against this approach. Users with 640-pixel screens will want to know what they are missing and will often be forced into horizontal scrolling—one of the most hated interaction techniques in a web browser. Also, users with any other size screen will be in trouble, for example, when using WebTV (smaller than 640) or when using a big PC monitor with several windows that are sized to, say, a width of 700 pixels (which would cut right down the middle of the rightmost column of this home page).

Splash Screens Must Die

I have discussed the home page as if it were the first thing a new user would see upon entering a site. And that's how it *should* be. Unfortunately, some sites employ totally wasteful and useless splash screens, which simply slow down the user as he or she is attempting to reach the home page.

The theory behind splash screens is that they can set the stage for the home page by showing some kind of welcome message or possibly simply the name or logo in isolation without the distractions of the navigation elements on the home page proper.

One of the few appropriate uses of splash screens is for sites that need to filter users and warn certain visitors against the content that will be found on the actual home page.

In reality, splash screens are annoying and users click off them as fast as they can. It is much better to design a single home page that unifies the situational identity message with a display of some useful news and directory information. Content itself can be used to tell users where they are and what the site is about.

XXX-banners specializes in the production of adult site banners.
The following sample material contains adult content .
If you are offended by nudity, are not of appropriate age to view adult content or live in an area where such viewing is illegal please exit now.

If you are a surfer looking for a good sex site **Click Here**.

EXIT   ENTER

XXX-Banners is listed in the following webmaster resources:

www.xxx-banners.com

What possible benefit is derived from forcing the user to look at the splash screen first? Some users may just give up in desperation. Very few people are interested in having their every click turn into a "mystery of the Internet," where they have to ponder what might be next instead of simply being told where they have arrived.

www.tigerlily.com

The Home Page Versus Interior Pages

The most prominent design element on the home page should be the name of the company or the site. The name does not necessarily have to be the *biggest* design element, but at least it should be in the upper-left corner of the screen or some other place where it is easy to spot. Additionally, the site name should be repeated on *all* interior pages because users may enter the site at any page, not just the home page. People who come from search engines or who follow links from other sites need a clear and simple way to tell at what site they have arrived. At the same time, interior pages need to focus more on specific content and less on providing a general welcome statement or an overview of the site. These two goals should be reserved for the home page.

There is a conflict between the need to accommodate people who may enter at any page and the need to restrain general information and top-level navigation aides to the home page. The resolution to this problem depends on how often you expect people to enter the site on low-level pages, and on how distinct and famous your site is. If the site is instantly recognizable to most users, then don't bother putting a lot of general jazz on the interior pages. Simply have a single, consistent link to the home page from every page. I recommend placing this link in the upper-left corner of the page, which is also the preferred placement of the site name and/or logo. Of course, sites in languages that are read right-to-left should use the upper-*right* corner of the page for this purpose.

The important point is to make the home page into a landmark that is accessible in one click from any interior pages on the site, no matter how people entered. On all interior pages, the logo should be clickable and linked to the home page. Unfortunately, not all users understand the use of the logo as a link to the home page, and it will take a while until this convention is fully established. So for the next few years, it will also be necessary to have an explicit link named "home" on every page.

Sites that are less recognizable may need to provide a small amount of additional identification on every page. They should also make their name or logo larger than needed on more famous sites.

Deep Linking

It is an erroneous strategy to force users to enter the site on the home page. So-called *deep linking* enables other sites to point users to the exact spot on your site that is of interest to those users. A website is like a house with a thousand doors: lots of ways to enter. A very welcoming place, indeed.

With a single front door and all other entry points locked, users will be dumped at the home page without really understanding how your site relates to their goals or their departure point. This is true because the home page can never be as specific or helpful to a particular problem as the actual page that describes the product or answers the question. One point against you. Then, you force users to learn your navigation system and the quirks and conventions of your site before they can get to the place they want to go. Second point against you. Any new customers left at this point? Probably not.

Much better to allow deep links. In fact, you should *encourage* deep links, which is what the affiliates programs in e-commerce are about.

Affiliates Programs

An affiliates program is a way to pay for inbound traffic. If Site A links to Site B, then B will pay a small referral fee for those users who follow the link. Most current affiliates programs pay commissions only for users who end up buying something on the destination site, but in principle it would be possible to have a layered commission structure and pay more for users who actually purchase and less for users who simply visit but don't buy anything (under the theory that they may return later and buy something).

Metaphor

Metaphor is sometimes over-used in web design. Maybe the greatest weakness of metaphors is that they seem to entice designers to be overly clever and push the site in directions that seem fun and appropriate within the metaphor but leave users' real goals behind. Users don't live in the metaphor world; they live in the real world.

That being the case, it is usually better to be very literal and describe each interface element for what it is and what it does rather than trying to make everything fit into a single metaphor.

This said, metaphor can be useful for two reasons. First, metaphor can provide a unifying framework for the design that will make it feel like more than a collection of individual items. Second, metaphor can facilitate learning by allowing users to draw upon the knowledge they already have about the reference system.

For example, using a "shopping cart" metaphor for e-commerce immediately makes users understand the basic functionality. You can place products in the shopping cart where they are kept ready for purchase but have not been bought. You can place multiple products in the same shopping cart. You can remove items from the shopping cart as long as you have not yet paid. And you can take the shopping cart to the checkout line.

Shopping carts also highlight the weaknesses of metaphor. Knowledge of the reference system would indicate to users that the way to buy five copies of something is to repeat the action of placing a single item in the cart five times over. Also, the way to remove objects from the shopping cart would be to place them back on the shelf. In contrast, most e-commerce shopping carts allow users to edit the number of an item they want to buy and to remove an item by buying zero copies. This latter action is a well-known usability problem and is often done wrong.

(Facing page) A television channel metaphor used for navigation is cute but useless. Instead of showing static when the user first approaches the page, it would be better to show a summary of what can be done here. And although the use of numbered channels for choosing options may be metaphorical, it has very low usability. It is impossible to predict what a given number will correspond to, and it is hard to remember where to go back for information you have already seen. Channel numbers are bad on television as well and work only because stations have spent huge amounts of money in an attempt to brand something as impersonal as the number Four.

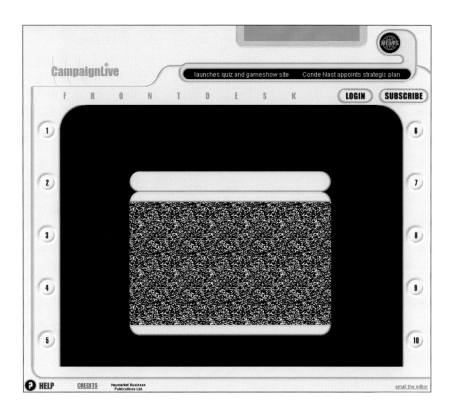

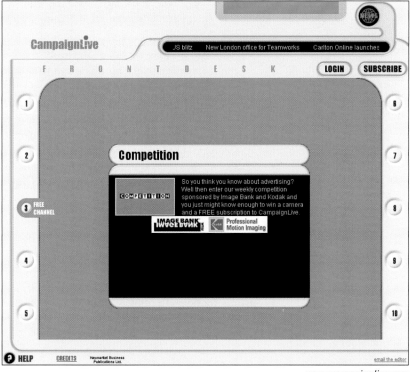

www.iflyswa.com

The 1995 design for Southwest Airlines was highly metaphorical and survived until about mid-1999, at which time it was replaced by a much more literal design. Even though the old design tried to give the feeling of an airport check-in counter, the new design looks more like an airline site. And from a usability perspective, trying to actually do anything is much easier in the new design. The old design clearly highlights one of the main downsides of metaphor: that it often does not extend well enough to cover all the necessary features of a system. In this case, the designers wanted to include a message from the Chairman (often a bad idea, but let's accept it for now) and had to accommodate this link by hanging his picture on the wall. True Chinese Embassy design.

SOUTHWEST AIRLINES
A SYMBOL OF FREEDOM®

Now $99 or less will take you anywhere Southwest flies from Las Vegas, Phoenix, Chicago, St. Louis, and Houston.

WHAT'S NEW

- Click 'n Save℠ Internet Specials

- Southwest offers $30 fares for 30 days between St. Louis and eleven destinations.

- Earn double Rapid Rewards credit when you plan and purchase Ticketless Travel Online and fly by December 31, 1999.

- Visit the Site Index for help navigating our newly remodeled site.

www.iflyswa.com

WELCOME TO THE BEMARNET TRADE FAIR GROUNDS

BemarNet ... Makes Business Easier

[Français | Español | Deutsch]

BemarNet Fast Find

BemarNet Sites ▾

THE MOST INNOVATIVE BUSINESS SITE ON THE NET

Thank you for visiting our website ... the future of exhibition technology. You are entering the BemarNet Virtual Wholesale Trade Fair, and admission is free.

With Flash 2.0

BemarNet Management is inaugurating a completely new concept in the use of the internet for international trade, blending the virtual with real-time services through the use of real-time offices in each country that has been licensed to a responsible Country Partner.

This network of Country Partners gives businesses around the world the power to do business in real-time with manufacturers, shippers, customers and collaborators from a single platform.

We have taken the technology of the internet to the next level, by adding the human intervention so necessary for international commerce. BemarNet solves this problems by having human representatives in every country where it does business, giving businesses what they need most ... world - class technology and a human face.

www.bemarnet.es

Geographical metaphors are almost always bad, except when dealing with geography. Here, we have the virtual fairground and the virtual business center high-rise. On the facing page, we have moved to the third floor of the business center (where the transport companies have their offices).

← Second Floor | **THIRD FLOOR** | Fourth Floor →

demasiado [ ] Buscar

Seleccione país ▾

▷ **Transnatur, S.A.**
International transport by road, air and sea. Fair services all over the world. Customs agent. Service door to door. Storage, "picking and distribution". Insurance agent.

▷ **Indigo Online**
INTERNATIONAL: measures/weights. SHIPPING: abbreviations

▷ **The Chartering Handbook**

▷ **FSU Freight (HK) Limited**

▷ **Everything about Shipping**

▷ **Cargolaw**
Cargolaw is full of useful Links for the Cargo-Community!

▷ **Transena**
International transport (Spain). Trucking (including ADR). Sea - and Airfreight. Storage and Logistic. Custom clearance.

▷ **Cempaka S.L.**
International Transport Services

▷ **Arnedo Medina Valencia, S.A. "ARMESA"**
International and national transports. Frigo-trailers and frigo-tilts. Complete cargo or partial cargo. Specialists in distribution and logistics of delicate goods: fruits, vegetables, frozen food, meat, ... , to all of Europe. Storage en freeze stores or deep freeze stores. 24h at your service.

▷ **Aduana USA**
Servicios de aduana en Estados Unidos

▷ **WCO Home Page**
World Customs Organisation

consigue dos altavoces para tu euipo multimedia **GRATIS** ????

Enter your e-mail address if you want to be notified when new companies are added to this page

E-mail: [ ] Submit e-mail

IF YOU WANT TO BE A BEMARNET PARTNER IN YOUR COUNTRY
>> CLICK HERE <<

www.bemarnet.es

The navigation system includes links to the second floor and the fourth floor, but try to guess what might be there. These floors host business services and software companies, respectively, but why these firms should be placed closer to transport companies than, say, telecommunications companies (17th floor) is anybody's guess. And moving from software to telecommunications is pure hardship: "walking" up from the fourth floor to the 17th floor. At least the exercise will be good for you.

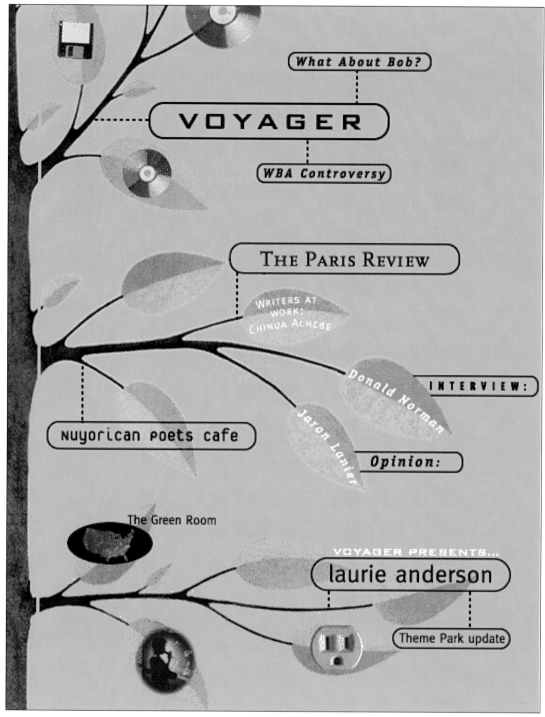

In 1995, the CD-ROM company Voyager used a tree metaphor to structure its navigation interface. Although somewhat cute and possibly acceptable given its artistic ambitions and "green" leanings, this is neither an informative way of utilizing the available screen space nor a helpful structure for the information. Why are certain things on the same branch? You are left to guess.

monster.com

SEARCH JOBS | STORE RESUME | RESEARCH COMPANIES | MY MONSTER | VISIT OUR ZONES | JOIN CHAT | FOR EMPLOYERS

QuickSearch

Enter Keyword:

go

August 26

JOB SEARCH UPDATE:

Search our **240,379** job opportunities now!

POST A JOB

Reach millions of job prospects now!

New Beetle® trademark used with permission of Volkswagen of America, Inc.

DECLARE YOUR INDEPENDENCE

Monster Talent Market℠

Visit The World's First Online Talent Auction

Personalize

With a personalized My Monster page, you can track jobs, store your resume and cover letters, and connect with our growing career community.

Career Zones

The career advice you need to succeed:

Campus
Mid-Career
Executive
Independent
Professional

International **NEW!**
Technology
Healthcare
HR

Headlines

This Week's Poll

Does a personal home page help a job search?

○ Yes - I have one and it gets results.
○ Yes - but it has to be specifically built for the job search.
○ No - I have one and it doesn't help.
○ I don't have a personal home page but I think I need one.
○ I don't need a personal home page.

Results

Previous Poll Results

Chats & Boards

Chat Schedule
Click here to chat

Sponsored by:
Olsten Staffing Services

Free Newsletter

Enter your email address

Subscribe

Newsletter archive
Specialty newsletters

www.monster.com

Just imagine the potential for metaphor run amok on The Monster Board: the Monster's Lair (secrets of job search), Left-Over Bones (jobs that have been on the system some time), Haunted House (employers in trouble), and Loch Ness Monster (overseas jobs). Given the name, the site exercises remarkable restraint and limits itself to a funny drawing that gives the site some personality. One can always argue whether a name like "Monster" works for a site that's not about monsters, but it definitely is memorable and makes the site stand out in a crowded field of names such as CareerPath, CareerWeb, Career Central, Career Connector, Career Exposure, Career Avenue, CareerMart, CareerSite, CareerExposure, CareerExchange, CareerCity, Career Shop, and so on.

Shopping Carts as Interface Standard

Shopping carts are now so common on e-commerce sites that they have morphed from metaphor to interface standard. When users encounter a web shopping cart these days, they don't think of a physical supermarket as the reference system. Instead, they think of all the other websites where they have seen shopping carts. Once something becomes sufficiently widely used, it becomes an interface convention and people simply know what to expect.

The standardization of shopping carts is good and bad. The benefits come from consistency, which is even stronger than metaphor as a learning tool. In fact, the user doesn't have to learn *anything* as long as an interface element behaves exactly like the user is accustomed to. At the same time, shopping carts are an inappropriate interface for many applications, and yet designs are forced to use a shopping cart because that is what users expect.

Navigation

The Web is a navigational system: The basic user interaction is to click on hypertext links in order to move around a huge information space with hundreds of millions of pages. Because the space is so vast, navigation is difficult, and it becomes necessary to provide users with navigational support beyond the simple "go-to" hyperlinks.

Navigation interfaces need to help users answer the three fundamental questions of navigation:

- Where am I?
- Where have I been?
- Where can I go?

Where Am I?

The most important navigation question is probably "Where am I?" because users will never stand a chance of understanding the site's structure if they don't understand where they are. If you don't know where you are, then you also don't have the ability to interpret the meaning of the link you just followed.

The user's current location needs to be shown at two different levels:

- Relative to the Web as a whole
- Relative to the site's structure

You need to identify your site on all of your pages because they form a subset of the Web as a whole. All web pages are much the same from the user's perspective; they share interaction techniques, they are downloaded (slowly) from the Internet, and they have relatively similar layouts. These similarities are in fact good because they allow users a measure of transfer of skill from one site to the next. My usability studies show that users complain bitterly when a site tries to use navigation interfaces that are drastically different from the ones they have come to expect from the majority of other sites.

The Web as a whole dominates the user experience because users tend to view no more than four to five pages at a time at any individual site. The potential downside is that users will not know what site they are on unless you tell them. Thus, navigation rule number one is to include your logo (or other site identifier) on every page. The logo should have consistent placement (preferably the upper-left corner if the page is in a language that

Navigation Support in Browsers

At a minimum, web browsers need to have better support for structural navigation. They should have features for moving up one or more levels in the information architecture from the current page as well as features for visualizing the relationship among the pages visited by the user. Special features should be available for moving to the next and to the previous elements in a sequence of objects (which is different from the Back button found in browsers, which doesn't move to the neighboring object but instead to the previously seen object). Also, links should differ, depending on whether they stay within the current site or point to another part of the Internet.

It would also be helpful to have integration between the client-side knowledge of what the user is doing and the server-side knowledge of the site's structure. An active sitemap might highlight the user's current location as well as visualize his or her trail through the site. And, of course, the search could be integrated with this sitemap and show the main areas of the sites that match the user's current query.

Internet-wide search engines should be integrated with the browser to permit searches that are limited either to sites that the user likes or to specific pages that the user has already seen. How often do you attempt to find something that you *know* you've seen on the Web? Well, if you could only tell the search engine this, the search problem would be drastically simplified (any individual user will typically have seen no less than a few thousand and, at most, a million pages out of the billions that are available).

"To satisfy the **global messaging** needs of our customers."

"A mutual commitment for increased sales and profit."

AT&T Global Alliance Marketing Program – Domestic

AT&T Global Alliance Member Program – International

Calendar   Comments   Documentation   GAM   Web Sites   EasyLink   Search   EasyCommerce   AT&T

[Calendar | Comments | Documentation | GAM | Web Site Services | EasyLink | Search | EasyCommerce]

AT&T   · (AT&T HOME) · · (HELP · SEARCH) · · (WRITE TO US) · · (AT&T SERVICES) ·

www.att.com

(Facing page) This page does a good job of letting users know where they are at three levels:

- They are on the AT&T site, as indicated by the logo in the upper-left corner, which doubles as a link to AT&T's home page. (I would have eliminated the duplicate icon in the lower-right corner, especially because it's the wrong color.)

- Within AT&T, they are in the section about EasyCommerce Services.

- Within EasyCommerce, they are on a page about Global Alliance Marketing.

The natural flow of the user's eye from the top supports an understanding of the hierarchical relation between these three levels of location.

Unfortunately, the icon bar toward the end of the page does not highlight the user's current location. The "GAM" icon should have been drawn larger, rendered in a different color, made to pop from the background, or in some other visual way indicate that it represents the current choice from the list.

It is also confusing that there are two search buttons (actually, there are three search buttons if we count the textual copy of the icon bar, but most users will be used to seeing the icon list and the textual list as being identical).

reads left to right) and should be made into a hypertext link to the home page so that users can get to your home page from any other page.

Location relative to the site's structure is usually given by showing parts of the site structure and highlighting the area where the current page is located. It is also important to have a clear main headline for the page that states its name or main content in a glance. Finally, the page title in the HTML header definition should be used to generate a meaningful name for each individual page so that users can locate it easily in their bookmark list if they bookmark the page.

Where Have I Been?

Because standard web technology is state-less, it may be hard for page designs to directly address the "Where have I been" question, because the site doesn't know without resorting to cookies or other user-tracking measures. Luckily, some of the few useful navigation mechanisms in current web browsers provide some assistance with this question. The Back button takes the user directly to the previous page, the history list includes a list of recently visited pages, and hypertext links are shown in a different color if they point to previously visited pages.

I recommend not changing the standard link colors because users will only understand the meaning of the link colors if they are kept the same. I tested many sites with non-standard link colors where the users ended up not understanding what links they had already followed.

Knowing what links lead to previously visited pages is useful for two reasons: It helps users learn the structure of the site, and it prevents them from wasting time going to the same page many times.

Where Can I Go?

This question is answered by the visible navigation options and any other links on the page. In addition, assuming that the user has acquired some understanding of the site's structure, the user may have a general idea of other, currently invisible, places to go. Because it is impossible to show all possible destinations on all pages, it is obvious that a good site structure is a major benefit in helping users answer the "Where can I go" question.

What do you call a design team that calls the Internet its LAN?

Our company was founded in Kansas City, but our design team logs in from around the world: from Dublin, Ireland to a dairy farm in Vermont.

We collaborate and communicate on the Internet better than many companies might in a single office complex.

Living on the Net has taught us what it takes to communicate ideas with little more than a modem and a dream. Isn't that what you're hoping to do?

Staff

staff   process   web 101   musings   media lab   contact

www.neuromedia.com

(Above)   Overly subtle indication of the user's current location. The navigation bar itself should highlight the current section, but instead, a cute icon (a fish) serves this function.

(Facing page)   Here's a nice example of highlighting the user's current location on the site. Note how the use of standard link colors for the links to neighboring pages makes it very easy for the user to see where he or she has been already. In this example, the user has already visited the "introduction" page as well as the "portfolio" section of the site.

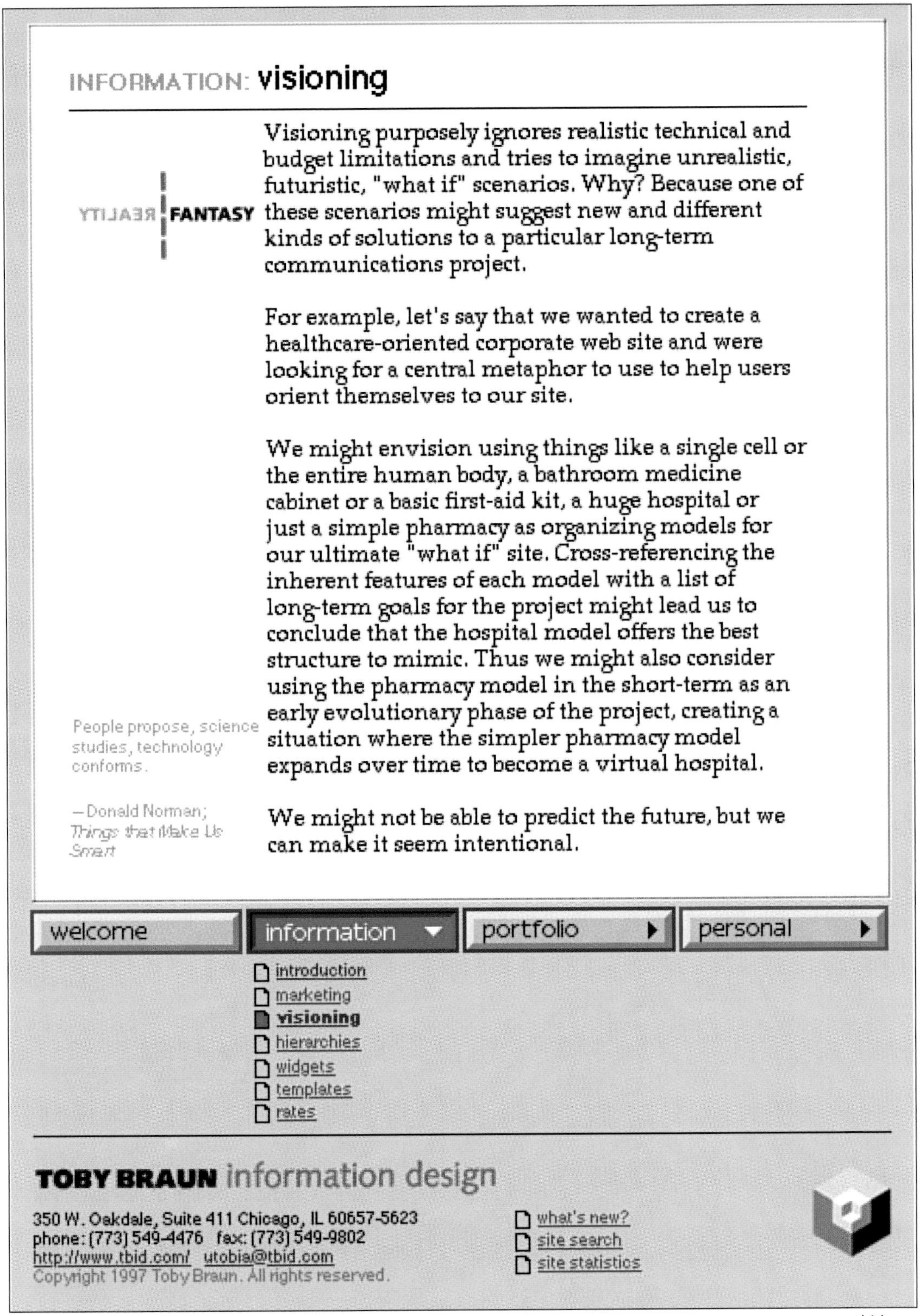

INFORMATION: visioning
REALITY
FANTASY
Visioning purposely ignores realistic technical and budget limitations and tries to imagine unrealistic, futuristic, "what if" scenarios. Why? Because one of these scenarios might suggest new and different kinds of solutions to a particular long-term communications project.
For example, let's say that we wanted to create a healthcare-oriented corporate web site and were looking for a central metaphor to use to help users orient themselves to our site.
We might envision using things like a single cell or the entire human body, a bathroom medicine cabinet or a basic first-aid kit, a huge hospital or just a simple pharmacy as organizing models for our ultimate "what if" site. Cross-referencing the inherent features of each model with a list of long-term goals for the project might lead us to conclude that the hospital model offers the best structure to mimic. Thus we might also consider using the pharmacy model in the short-term as an early evolutionary phase of the project, creating a situation where the simpler pharmacy model expands over time to become a virtual hospital.
We might not be able to predict the future, but we can make it seem intentional.
People propose, science studies, technology conforms.
– Donald Norman; Things that Make Us Smart
welcome
information
portfolio
personal
introduction
marketing
visioning
hierarchies
widgets
templates
rates
TOBY BRAUN information design
350 W. Oakdale, Suite 411 Chicago, IL 60657-5623
phone: (773) 549-4476 fax: (773) 549-9802
http://www.tbid.com/ utobia@tbid.com
Copyright 1997 Toby Braun. All rights reserved.
what's new?
site search
site statistics

www.tbid.com

Xerox WorkCentre XD100 Digital Copier / Laser Printer

P | C | S | S

Overview

Less than (US)	$550.00
Print Resolution	600 x 600 dpi,
Print Speed	8 ppm black,
Max. Paper Size	8.50 X 14.00
Print Technology	Laser
Networkable	N/A
Collation Type	N/A

HOW TO BUY

Product Overview

Everything you want in a copier, including a printer

Key Features and Benefits

- Superior Digital Laser Quality
- Digital Copying
- 8 ppm Printing
- 10 Copies per Minute
- 250-Sheet Paper Capacity
- Printer Cable Included
- 3 Year Warranty

Quick Compare

These products have a price that is identical or close to the price for the product you are viewing.

Xerox WorkCentre XE82 Digital Copier / Laser Printer $450.00

Xerox WorkCentre XD102 Digital Copier / Laser Printer $530.00

Xerox WorkCentre XD100 Digital Copier / Laser Printer $550.00

Xerox DocuPrint P12 $600.00

Xerox WorkCentre 385 Laser All-in-One $600.00

All Desktop Printing

Related Links

Subscribe
Receive product information via E-Mail

Warranty Registration
Register your warranty online

www.xerox.com

(Left) Pull-down menus like the one called "site navigation" in this screen cause many usability problems because users can't see the full set of choices without having to take explicit action. I prefer having a small enough set of global navigation options that they can be shown at all times. Another problem with this site is the very small and non-standard placement of the company name.

This product page provides an interesting example of local navigation in the form of see-also links to similar products under the heading "Quick Compare." Too frequently, web navigation operates on the assumption that users will go directly to the exact destination they need. In fact, users will often arrive at something that is approximately right, but not exactly right. Without local navigation to similar products, users then have no choice but to start all over again and hope for better results next time.

The Quick Compare feature in this example could have been improved with an indication of the underlying navigation dimensions that cause the products to be different. In other words, help users understand *why* and under *what conditions* they might be interested in the various other products. Listing the price provides one such dimension (if you can't afford the current product, then it's easy to find a cheaper one), but it is not clear what the other main differences are among the products. I could imagine that one printer might be the one to click on if you need color and another might be the choice if you print a lot of copies every day, but with the current design, users don't know—nor get any help in deciding—what direction to move in if they want to leave the current page.

There are three kinds of hypertext links that can be used on a page:

- *Embedded links* are the traditional underlined text that indicates that "more stuff" is available about some topic that is discussed in the body text.
- *Structural links* are links that systematically point to other levels of the site structure as well as to siblings or children in a hierarchy. It is important to have the same structural links on all pages so that the user will understand what structural navigation options to expect. Of course, the exact destinations pointed to by the structural links will be different from page to page. Therefore, it is often better to use link anchors that name the specific destinations in addition to giving the generic structural relationship between the current page and the destination page. For example, it is better to have a link that reads "Up to Widget Product Family" than a link that simply reads "One Level Up."
- *Associative links* are used to give users "see also" hints about pages that may be of interest to them because they are similar or related to the current page.

It is usually best to represent links as underlined text, keeping the standard link colors of blue for links to unvisited pages and purple for links to pages the user has seen before. Everybody learns the meaning of this convention the first day they are on the Web, and there is simply no doubt that underlined text means "click here." Because underlining now has a strong perceived clickability affordance, it is best not to underline any text that cannot be clicked.

Usability problems are also associated with links that have any form other than simple, underlined text. Pull-down menus and graphics should be used for navigation only with great care because they don't behave in the standard manner of underlined text. In particular, they don't turn purple if they link to places the user has already seen.

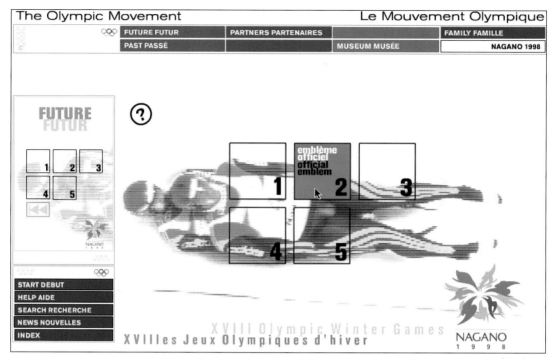

www.olympic.org

One of the most useless navigation aids I have seen on the Web. The user clearly has five different possibilities, but there is no way to know what the possibilities are without rolling the mouse over each of the buttons. Maybe the Olympic Committee wants to ensure that the nerds get some minimal exercise by moving their mouse around. (Wow, I feel my right bicep bulging already.)

A navigation interface needs to show all the available alternatives at the same time so that users can make an informed decision as to which option will satisfy their needs best. Not only is it annoying to have to move the mouse around to see the options, it is outright user-hostile to require users to keep the previously seen options in their short-term memory while they consider additional choices.

The final touch of death in the Olympic navigation design comes from the panel on the left part of the screen. This panel supposedly allows users fast access to the main navigation options on later screens, but only if they happen to remember that a blue square stands for "official emblem." Not exactly a particularly natural color association, so users would be forced to study this website for hours to commit the color scheme to long-term memory if they were ever to use it efficiently. And one thing we really know about the Web is that nobody is sufficiently devoted to a site to go through a special training class to use it.

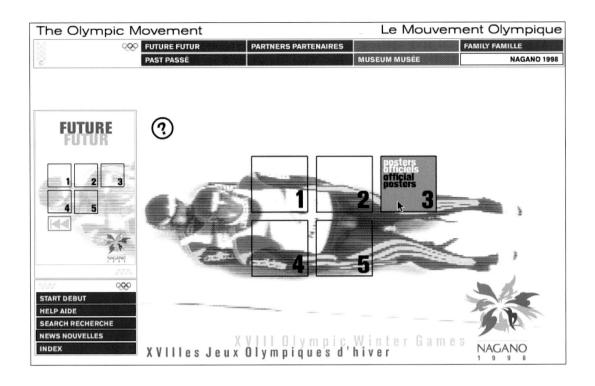

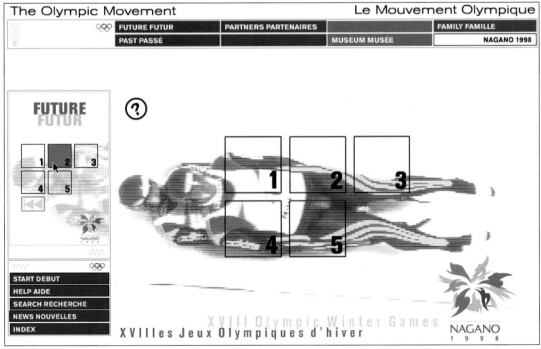

Site Structure

No matter what navigation design you pick for your site, there is one common theme to all navigation: All it does is visualize the user's current location and alternative movements relative to the structure of the underlying information space. If the structure is a mess, then no navigation design can rescue it. Poor information architecture will always lead to poor usability.

Most sites have a hierarchical structure with progressively more detailed levels of information. Other sites have a tabular structure in which pages are classified relative to a number of attributes or parameters. For example, the 1996 Olympic Games site classified events pages relative to their sport, their data, and their location, so users could, if they wanted, see all pages related to soccer or all pages related to events in a certain city. A linear structure makes sense for Web-enabled applications that are a progression of steps.

The two most important rules about site structure are to have one and to make it reflect the users' view of the site and its information or services. It may seem obvious to have a site structure, but many sites evolve without any planned structure and end up in total chaos as a collection of random directories without any systematic relations among different parts of the site. A second common mistake is to have the site structure mirror your organizational charts instead of reflecting the user's view. Users should not have to care how your company is organized, so they should not be able to deduce your organizational structure from the structure of your website. Admittedly, it is easiest to distribute responsibility for the site to divisions and departments according to already established chains of command and budget categories, but doing so results in an internally centered site rather than a customer-focused site.

The site structure should be determined by the tasks users want to perform on your site, even if that means having a single page for information from two very different departments. It is often necessary to distribute information from a single department across two or more parts of the site, and many subsites will have to be managed in collaboration between multiple departments.

The Vice-Presidential Button

A classic sign of a mismanaged website is when the home page has a button for each of the senior vice presidents in the company. Remember, you don't design for your VPs; you design for the users. Therefore, it will be quite common that you can't tell VPs where "their" button is on the home page.

Browse for: ** *Rentals* **

NEW! Released in the Past 15 Days   PRE! Upcoming Releases   RENT Also In Rental

753 Titles In Current Category
1-50 | 51-100 | 101-150 | 151-200 | 201-250 | 251-300 | 301-350 | 351-400 | 401-450 | 451-500 | 501-550 | 551-600 | 601-650 | 651-700 | 701-750 | 751-753

Buy It	Title	Rating	Price
Order	**10,** 'Rental'	R	$3.00
Order	**101 Dalmatians,** 'Rental'	G	$3.00
Order	**12 Monkeys** 'Rental'	R	$3.00
Order	**1941** 'Rental'	PG13	$3.00
Order	**2 Days in the Valley** 'Rental'	R	$3.00
Order	**2010: The Year We Make Contact** 'Rental'	PG	$3.00
Order	**9 1/2 Weeks** 'Rental'	UN	$3.00
Order	**About Last Night...** 'Rental'	R	$3.00
Order	**Above the Law** 'Rental'	R	$3.00
Order	**Absence of Malice** 'Rental'	PG	$3.00
Order	**Absolute Power** 'Rental'	R	$3.00
Order	**Ace Ventura: Pet Detective,** 'Rental'	PG13	$3.00
Order	**Ace Ventura: When Nature Calls** 'Rental'	PG13	$3.00
Order	**Action Jackson** 'Rental'	R	$3.00
Order	**Addicted to Love** 'Rental'	R	$3.00
Order	**Affliction** 'Rental'	R	$3.00
Order	**After Dark, My Sweet** 'Rental'	R	$3.00
Order	**Air America** 'Rental'	R	$3.00
Order	**Air Bud,** 'Rental'	PG	$3.00
Order	**Air Force One** 'Rental'	R	$3.00
Order	**ALICE IN WONDERLAND** 'Rental'	NR	$3.00
Order	**Alien** 'Rental'	R	$3.00
Order	**Alien 3** 'Rental'	R	$3.00

Home | Search | Support | News | Shopping Cart | Affiliates | Order Tracking

DVD WAVE

Search: [   ] Go!

Browse: [Please Select One ▾] Go!

Saturday, Jul 24, 1999

? 🛒   Check Out
Shipping Info
Log In   Billing Info

Free USPS Shipping!
Now, you receive free USPS shipping on every order! And when you order 7 titles or more, you receive a free Priority USPS Upgrade!

Low Price Guarantee!
We guarantee we have the lowest prices available for purchasing DVD. Read more about it in our 6 Point Guarantee, or fill out this form.

Gift Certificates Are Here!
Our Gift certificates make a great holiday or birthday gift. Now you can give the gift of DVD without having to know what kind of movies your friend/family member likes!

Earn Store Credit!
Our Frequent Buyer Program gives store credit to our frequently buying customers!

Six Point GUARANTEE

www.dvdwave.com

A linear information structure is often a warning sign for bad usability because the Web is inherently non-linear in nature. Users don't want to have to step through all the site elements one at a time. In this example, it is hard to imagine a user scanning through a list of 753 films in alphabetical order. It would be better to have a set of alternative structuring principles available, including a way to sort by quality (review) rating and a way to filter out certain types of films. Even if an alphabetical listing is the best that can be done, at least abandon the numeric links to jump around the list. It makes sense to jump to films starting with the letter G, but not to jump to film number 451.

(Facing page)   In April 1998 *The Christian Science Monitor* experimented with a site structure and navigation interface that mirrored its printed newspaper. Users would page through reduced pictures of actual pages from the daily paper and could click on the image of an article to get the full text displayed in the right half of the window.

The main problem with the design is that it is extremely slow to navigate. Each of the page miniatures is about 60 KB, taking about 20 seconds to download over a 28.8 modem. We know that 10 seconds is the absolute maximum response time for getting web pages before users rebel; optimal navigation requires even shorter response times.

Navigating between pages is done through a pop-up menu that lists nothing but page numbers. Because users do not know what articles are on what page, they are left guessing and are relegated to jumping to pages at random. It would have been better to provide a menu of section titles or main headlines. For example, it would be more meaningful to go to "Food Section" than "Page 14", assuming that the food articles were on page 14. Page numbers make sense in print, where users flip through a physical product, but on the Web, everything is equally far away (one mouseclick). Thus, a site structure should rarely be linear.

Furthermore, the *Monitor* design did not allow users to get a quick overview of the current news or focus their attention on parts of the paper that were of particular interest to them. It was a purely linear navigation system that was made almost useless by the slow speed of "turning the page." While viewing a page, it was not possible to read subheads, decks, bylines, or any of the other short but important components of a story design that help people decide what to read.

After a user did manage to find an article of interest, then the design failed again because only half of the window was available to display the actual article, thus necessitating more scrolling than usual and making the text harder to scan. Also, the use of frames made it difficult to bookmark articles of interest or to email URLs of recommended stories to friends and family (otherwise, a great way for a website to grow usage through social interaction).

Jakob Nielsen: Designing Web Usability

Page 13 ◆ page page ▶ ▤ page Last 2 weeks' editions

The Trick of Predicting the Random

BOSTON - THURSDAY, APRIL 2, 1998

Computers for the rest of us

As CD-ROM Books Mature, They Become Full Teaching Tools

Laurent Belsie

The information explosion happens here not with a new breakthrough but another bell and whistle.

I'm talking about those computerized encyclopedias.

Long packed with text, sound, and pictures, the latest crop has expanded onto two or even three CD-ROM disks. More sound and video. More special features. And, surprisingly, more uniformity.

COMPUTERS
FOR THE REST
OF US

Laurent Belsie

As CD-ROM encyclopedias mature, they're getting to look more alike. All four programs reviewed here sport various search mechanisms and links to thousands of Internet sites. Even stodgy Encyclopedia Britannica has seen the writing on the multimedia wall, revamped its interface, and become more visually oriented.

www.csmonitor.com

Ironically, even though I would not recommend this design for any newspaper, it may be particularly ill suited to the *Monitor*. Most of its pages contain no more than one or two articles. Thus, the page layout gives very few cues as to the relation between articles or particular attributes of stories. Other newspapers have more intricate layouts where the relative placement of stories on the page carries more information.

As an example of hierarchical structure, a corporate site may be divided into high-level categories such as product information, employment information, and information for investors. Because the home page is the top level of the hierarchy, these main categories form the second level of the structure. The product information might again be divided into different product families (the third level of structure), and each product family would be divided into information for the individual products (the fourth level of structure). Finally, each product may have pages for specifications, pricing and configuration options, customer case stories, and service information (the fifth level of structure).

Consider a page with pricing and configuration options for the SuperWidget product. This page belongs to five levels of the site structural hierarchy:

1. The company's website (as opposed to being at some other site)
2. The "products" category (as opposed to, say, employment info)
3. The Widgets product family
4. The SuperWidgets product
5. Pricing and configuration

Importance of User-Centered Structure

In one e-commerce project I worked on, the draft home page had three ways of getting to the products: one search function and two navigation schemes, both of which were presented as simple lists of choices. One navigation scheme was structured according to the way most users think about the domain; the other scheme was structured according to the way many of the manufacturer's own staff members thought about their product lines.

Results from usability testing showed that the success rate was 80 percent when people used the navigation scheme structured according to most users' mental model and only 9 percent when using the navigation scheme structured according to the company's internal thinking.

Conclusion: The second navigation scheme was dropped from the design, even though this pained some of the project members. The second scheme had its advantages for those people who used it correctly, but it led most users into trouble, so it did more harm than good.

Comparison of the two success rates of 80 percent and 9 percent leads to the conclusion that user-centered information architecture had about nine times as high usability as internally oriented information architecture. Of course, the exact difference between the two approaches will vary from project to project, but the difference is often large. We're not just talking a few percentage points here; we're talking about the difference between success and failure for anybody trying to sell anything on the Web.

My preference is to show all five levels in the navigation user interface because they are all useful in trying to understand the user's current location. Even better is a design that also shows alternative choices at one or more of the levels; such alternatives make it clear to users not just what they are seeing but also how it should be interpreted in relation to the other options on the site. Also, of course, listing alternatives makes it easy for users to go directly to one of the alternatives if it should prove a better match with the user's needs.

In my example, listing the alternative choices on the fourth level of the site structure would show the user that the Widget product family contained MiniWidgets and WidgetClassic in addition to the SuperWidget. If the user wanted a MiniWidget, he or she could then go directly to the relevant product page and navigate from there to the relevant pricing and configuration page.

Breadth Versus Depth

Currently, the most common navigation design is to list all the top levels of the site, often in a stripe down the left side of the page as was done in the original design of news.com. The benefit of this breadth-emphasizing design is that users are constantly reminded of the full scope of services available on the site. This is particularly useful for users who do not enter at the home page but go directly to a page deep within the site. Although this is a benefit, I do find it excessive to dedicate 20 percent of an interior page to a listing of top-level options, all of which can be accessed from the home page at the cost of a single additional click.

The colored stripe serves a dual purpose as a site branding mechanism, which makes it easy for users to recognize that they are on this particular site. Thus, the stripe doubles as a kind of logo to help users identify their location relative to the Web as a whole.

Whereas news.com had a breadth-emphasizing navigation design, the useit.com navigation bar is completely depth-emphasizing. It shows the full hierarchical path from the home page down through all the levels to the current page. Thus, users get a full sense of their current location relative to the site structure, and they can jump up to any

The navigational apparatus in the original design of news.com included three elements: a list of top-level destinations down the left side, a list of current news stories down the right side, and a list of related stories at the bottom. These latter cross-references are very helpful and enable users to find stories they might have overlooked originally. I am less pleased with the extensive space used to provide links to unrelated current news. I would have preferred to list the related stories at the top of the right column because that would maximize the likelihood that users will see these links. If a user was sufficiently interested in the topic of the current article to have chosen it from the table of contents, then it is very likely that the user would also be interested in reading some of the related stories. This is true even for users who find out that they are not sufficiently interested in the details of this specific story and therefore never scroll to the end of the page.

www.news.com

Jakob Nielsen: Designing Web Usability

The revised 1999 design for news.com is better than the original design in many ways. In particular, the "yellow fever" stripe has vanished, meaning that a larger percentage of the space is allocated to the story. At the very bottom of the article is an innovative navigation aide: "See Story in Context," which links to related stories. Even better, if reading an old story, the context link includes listings of newer articles that describe what happened later.

desired higher-level page in a single click. This navigation support scheme is often called *breadcrumbs* after the *Hansel and Gretel* fairy tale.

A breadcrumb navigation list has the benefit of being extremely simple and taking up minimal space on the page, leaving most of the precious pixels for content. After all, content is king, and my usability studies show that users tend to ignore navigation options and look directly at the page body when they go to a new page. Breadcrumbs are useful only for hierarchical information architectures because they require nested levels of progressively smaller subsites. But for such structures, the list of all the higher levels truly shows the context of the current page and helps users understand it, and it also helps users quickly move away from the page if it was not the right one.

The navigation bar from my own site shows the user's current location relative to a hierarchical structuring of the site's content. Note how much easier it is to read the human-authored hierarchy outline in the breadcrumb trail than having to decode a URL and its directory names in the browser's location field.

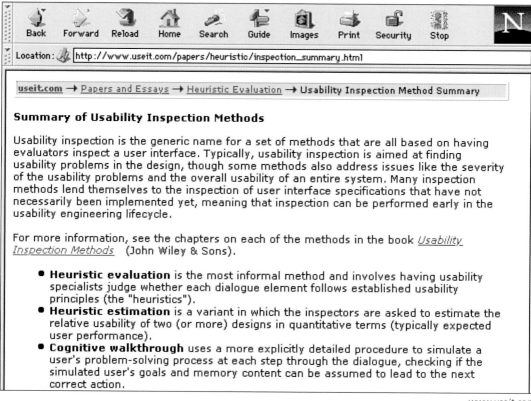

www.useit.com

Jakob Nielsen: Designing Web Usability

The LookSmart design combines depth and breadth by showing many levels of navigational hierarchy (depth) and listing all the alternative options for each level (breadth). The main downside of this approach is that it takes up a lot of space on the screen. Thus, a combined depth-breadth display is probably more suited for a dynamic presentation that abandons simple HTML. Dynamic HTML can be used to combine permanent visibility of all the levels (depth) with a temporary pop-up of the alternatives (breadth) on any given level when the pointer is over that level's name.

A final example is Sun Microsystem's page template, which provides navigational breadth at both the highest and lowest levels of the site structure. Top-level breadth is shown across the top of the page which lists all the high-level categories on the site. Low-level breadth is shown down the left side with links to all the content at the level of the current page, including a few associative links to "see also" material. Finally, the design provides a small amount of depth by indicating the names of some (but not all) of the levels of structure above the current page.

I would recommend use of this elaborate set of navigation mechanisms only for very large sites with highly heterogeneous content. (Currently, I would classify sites with more than 10,000 pages as "very large.") Sites with fewer pages will be easier to use with a simpler navigation design. Even the largest sites will be better off with simpler navigation if their content is so homogeneous that users can easily understand the structure of the information. For example, a site with the collected financial filings of all public companies in the United States could have a very simple structure to support navigation in hundreds of thousands of documents because they all had similar attributes.

Unfortunately, some sites combine quite disparate material—and lots of it—and so end up with a complex structure that needs a lot of navigation support. This is often the case for large companies with multiple product lines that address different customers.

(Following page) **Two different implementations of breadcrumbs from Looksmart (the 1997 and 1999 designs, respectively). Neither is perfect. The old design is cleaner and makes it very clear how the various elements in the breadcrumb trail are related. Placing a > mark between each name implies a hierarchy or sequence between the elements. In contrast, the elements are separated by a — mark in the newer design. This character does not have nearly the same connotation of hierarchy. On the contrary, the breadcrumb trail looks too much like a simple listing of alternatives that do not have a structure. Unfortunately, the old design did not list all the navigation levels and elided the upper levels, which were accessible by clicking on the somewhat obscure triangle glyph. The new design has the advantage of listing all the levels in the navigation hierarchy that are above the current location, from the very top (World) to the name of the current page (Usability). Of course, it is a mistake to make the name of the current page into a hypertext link; never have a link that is a no-op and points right back to the place the user already is.**

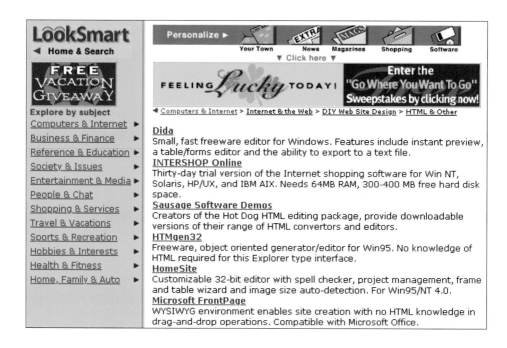

◄ Computers & Internet > Internet & the Web > DIY Web Site Design > HTML & Other

Dida
Small, fast freeware editor for Windows. Features include instant preview, a table/forms editor and the ability to export to a text file.
INTERSHOP Online
Thirty-day trial version of the Internet shopping software for Win NT, Solaris, HP/UX, and IBM AIX. Needs 64MB RAM, 300-400 MB free hard disk space.
Sausage Software Demos
Creators of the Hot Dog HTML editing package, provide downloadable versions of their range of HTML convertors and editors.
HTMgen32
Freeware, object oriented generator/editor for Win95. No knowledge of HTML required for this Explorer type interface.
HomeSite
Customizable 32-bit editor with spell checker, project management, frame and table wizard and image size auto-detection. For Win95/NT 4.0.
Microsoft FrontPage
WYSIWYG environment enables site creation with no HTML knowledge in drag-and-drop operations. Compatible with Microsoft Office.

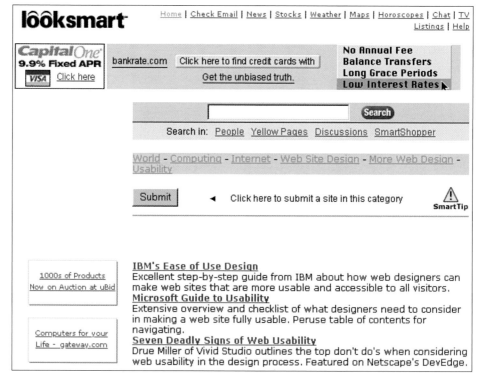

IBM's Ease of Use Design
Excellent step-by-step guide from IBM about how web designers can make web sites that are more usable and accessible to all visitors.
Microsoft Guide to Usability
Extensive overview and checklist of what designers need to consider in making a web site fully usable. Peruse table of contents for navigating.
Seven Deadly Signs of Web Usability
Drue Miller of Vivid Studio outlines the top don't do's when considering web usability in the design process. Featured on Netscape's DevEdge.

www.looksmart.com

Fisheye view of four levels of site content from the 1997
LookSmart design. A fisheye presentation provides progressively
more detail at levels closer to the user's current focus of interest.
In this example, I was interested in HTML
tools for web design, and a click on that option would give me
a list of the tools. But the display provides additional breadth
by also showing me the other types of web design tools
discussed on the site. Stepping up one level takes us further
from the user's current interest, so less breadth is provided. The
third column indicates that more information is available about
other Internet-related issues, but these topics are not described
in as much detail as the web design tools. Going one step far-
ther up, the second column lists other computer-oriented topics,
but this level is described at a very course level of granularity.

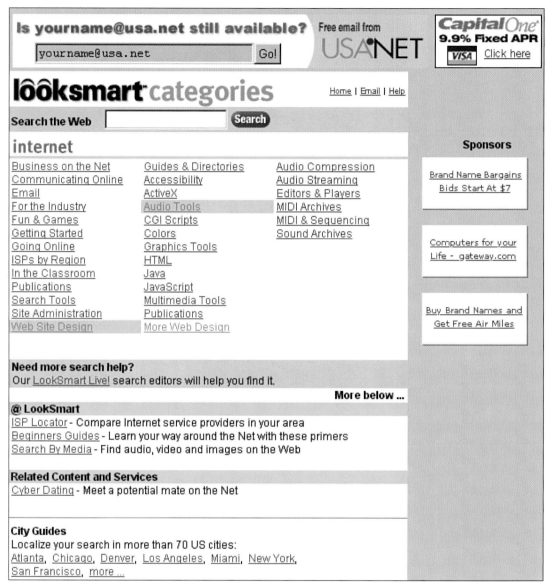

www.looksmart.com

The 1999 LookSmart design provides only a fisheye view of three levels of content. The very top level is not shown at all, and the second level is shown only by the headline "Internet." There is no way to find out that the current top-level category is "Computing" or what the other second-level categories might be within Computing. I prefer the 1997 design over this one. (As an aside, why would anybody run an advertisement for "brand-name bargains starting at $7" without telling us what brands or what types of products are being sold? I can't imagine many people being attracted by the promise that some unknown thing can be had for $7.)

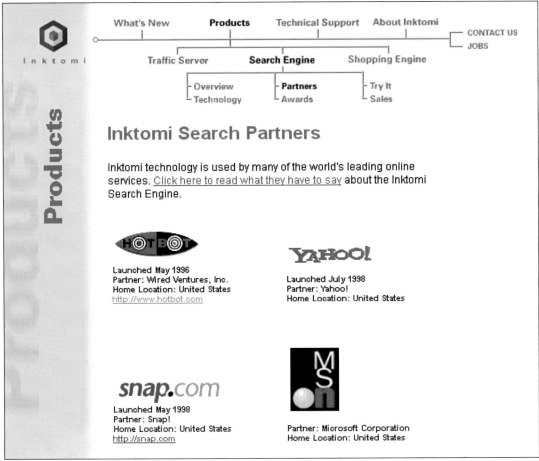

Fisheye navigation support at Inktomi. The graphic at the top of the page clearly shows that we are looking at its search engine product (and that the other products are the traffic server and the shopping engine). Within this set of product pages, we are currently looking at the partner, and there is a simple way to jump to the other five pages about this product.

HOME • BUY

Java
Computing

Products
& Solutions

Support, Education
& Consulting

Technology
& Research

For
Developers

Corporate
Information

Hardware And Networking

Desktop Family

SEARCH SUN

Search Tips • [Search]

CONTENTS OF
PRODUCTS & SOLUTIONS

Sun™ Ultra™ 4000 Creator3D Workstation

Product Overview

Sun Ultra 4000 Creator 3D workstation provides unbeatable price/performance for high-end visual computing.

- Multiple processors.
- Multiple monitors.
- On-chip multimedia technologies.
- High-speed interconnects.
- Accelerated graphics.
- High-bandwidth networking.

Add it all up and you get super computer performance for simulation, modeling, analysis, design automation, medical imaging, animation, and more.

Visualize Affordable High-Performance

We call this merger of advanced technologies UltraComputing™, and these workstations take it to a new level of power and capacity. Ultra 4000 workstations offer fast, realistic graphics at a price that is equally realistic.

www.sun.com

Sun's standard page design is embedded within an L-shaped navigation template with elaborate navigation support. It is instructive to look at the two different ways the navigation features are supported in two different versions of the design.

The 1998 design of the navigation system provided several levels of hierarchy. The choices on the highest level were listed across the top, the current location is stated with two levels of nesting in the second horizontal bar, and choices at lower levels are given down the side. The search box is shown immediately below the logo: a prominent location, but one that turned out to be used relatively rarely by other sites as they started to add search boxes to their pages later in 1998 and 1999.

Sun microsystems

SELECT A TOPIC ▾ [Go]   [Search]

Home › Products & Solutions › Hardware › Information Appliances › Sun Ray 1 Enterprise Appliance

▾ Sun Ray 1 Enterprise
   Appliance
  - Hot Desk
    Architecture
  - Features & Benefits
  - Specifications
  - Enterprise Server
    Software
  - Interconnect
  - Technical
    Information
  - ISV Solutions

Related:
- White Papers

SUN RAY™ 1 ENTERPRISE APPLIANCE

🎥 Event Rebroadcast

The ideal appliance solution for enterprise workgroups.

- Easy to use, easy to administer, easy to like
- Your work is always there -- when you want it, where you want it
- Your data is safe
- Improved productivity and lower costs go hand-in-hand.

Are you looking for centralized administration and a rich user experience? Look no further. The "plug-and-work" Sun Ray™ 1 enterprise appliance requires no client administration or upgrades while at the same time putting the power of the server on your desktop. On top of that, you get the unique capability of "hot desking" -- the ability to instantly access your computing session from any appliance in your workgroup -- exactly where you left off.

The Sun Ray 1 enterprise architecture is made up of the appliance itself, Sun Ray enterprise server software, and Hot Desk technology. The first true appliance for the Service Driven Network, the Sun Ray 1 enterprise appliance is ideal for your enterprise workgroup environment's business-critical applications -- including customer management, call centers, training and education, government, financial services, and ERP -- and never needs upgrading.

Easy to use, easy to administer, easy to like.

With Sun Ray 1 enterprise appliances, you get a greatly simplified environment that offers the benefits of client-server computing without the costs of maintaining fat clients. So you can gain greater control over your desktop -- significantly reducing purchase, service, and support costs, while still securely accessing your favorite applications. In fact, you can access applications on

www.sun.com

The 1999 design is much simplified from a graphics perspective and with respect to download time. The top-level choices are mainly relegated to a drop-down menu, although the most important ones are still shown across the top. The current location is now shown in a breadcrumb trail, which has the advantage of showing all the levels (partic-ularly good for a deeply nested article like the one in the figure) but has the disadvantage of not showing the neighboring alternatives. Finally, the lower-level choices continue to be shown down the side. The search box has been moved to the upper right: a location that started to become a conven-tion during 1999.

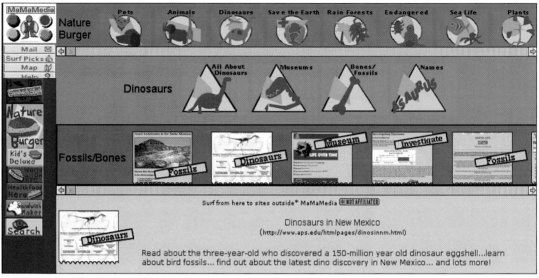

Fisheye view from the children's site
MaMaMedia.

www.mamamedia.com

The User Controls Navigation

In traditional user interface design, the *designer* can control
where the user can go when. You can gray out menu
options that are not applicable in the current state, and
you can throw up a modal dialog box that takes over the
computer until the user has answered the question. On the
Web, however, the *user* fundamentally controls his or her
navigation through the pages. Users can take paths that
were never intended by the designer. For example, they
can jump straight into the guts of a site from a search
engine without ever going through the home page. Users
also control their own bookmark menu and can use it to
create a customized interface to a site.

Web designers need to accommodate and support user-
controlled navigation. Sometimes you can force users
through set paths and prevent them from linking to certain pages, but sites that do so feel harsh and dominating.
It is better to design for freedom of movement and flexible navigation that supports many different ways of moving through a site. Get over it. The user holds the mouse,
and there is nothing you can do about it.

Desktop Printing

Xerox desktop printers and multifunction systems are designed to meet the needs of individual users or a small group of users in a shared environment.

How to Use

Use this table to view and compare these products based on their functions and key features. The table currently displays key features based on the primary function of these products (e.g. printing). To see key features of these products based on their additional functions, click one of the four function tabs below. To compare products according to one of these features (e.g. price), click a feature and the table will re-sort. Select an individual product for more detail.

Printing Copying Scanning Faxing

Product	Price $	Print Resolution (dpi)	Print Speed	Max. Paper Size	Print Technology	Networkable	Collation Type
Xerox DocuPrint XJ6C P C S F	$130.00	600 x 600 dpi B/W 600 x 600 dpi Color	5 ppm B/W 2 ppm Color	8.00 X 14.00	Xerox Color Inkjet	N/A	N/A
Xerox DocuPrint XJ8C P C S F	$200.00	1200 x 1200 dpi B/W 1200 x 1200 dpi Color	8 ppm B/W 4 ppm Color	8.50 X 14.00	Xerox Color Inkjet	N/A	N/A
Xerox DocuPrint P8 P C S F	$300.00	1800 x 600 with image enhancement, True 600 x 600 dpi B/W only	8 ppm B/W only	8.50 X 14.00	Laser	N/A	N/A
Xerox WorkCentre 450cp All-in-One P C S F	$300.00	600 x 600 dpi B/W 600 x 600 dpi Color	7 ppm B/W 2 ppm Color	8.50 X 14.00	Inkjet	N/A	N/A
Xerox DocuPrint P8e P C S F	$349.00	600 x 600 dpi B/W only	8 ppm B/W only	N/A	Laser	Not Available	N/A
Xerox WorkCentre XE80 Digital Copier / Laser Printer P C S F	$450.00	600 x 600 dpi B/W only	8 ppm B/W only	8.50 X 14.00	Laser	N/A	N/A
Xerox WorkCentre XE82 Digital Copier / Laser Printer P C S F	$450.00	600 x 600 dpi B/W only	8 ppm B/W only	8.50 X 14.00	Laser	N/A	N/A

www.xerox.com

Users always request easy ways of comparing products or other items discussed on a site. As long as information is restricted to individual product pages, it is hard for users to form an overview of the space and to understand where they should go. A comparison table is a nice way to reduce the amount of navigation and allow users to go straight to the one or two products they are really interested in.

AutoTrader.com
Your car is waiting.

Decision Guide

- **Find Your Car Now**
- **Sell Your Car Free**
- **New Car Info**
- **Finance And Insurance**
- **Reviews & Info**
- **Find A Dealer**
- Decision Guide ■
- **Help**
- **Home**

Compare Cars

Remove   Remove

Choose Another Car

1999 Mercedes-Benz E430 4-Door Sedan 4.3   **2000 BMW 540 i 4-Door Sedan 4.4**

This color highlights information you might find important.

General Information

Model Year	1999	2000
Car Type	Sedan	Sedan
Number of Doors	4-doors	4-doors
Seating Capacity	5	5
Model	E430	540i
Manufacturer	Mercedes-Benz	BMW
Country of Manufacturer	Germany	Germany
Origin of Assembly	Germany	Germany

Price

MSRP	$51,300	$51,100
Dealer Invoice	$44630	$46150
Destination Charge	$595	$570

Fuel Economy

 The 1999 Mercedes-Benz E430 4-Door Sedan 4.3 gets at least 10 percent more overall miles per gallon than the 2000 BMW 540 i 4-Door Sedan 4.4.

City Mileage	19 mpg	18 mpg
Highway Mileage	26 mpg	24 mpg
Fuel Tank Capacity	21.1 gallons	18.5 gallons

Safety

Safety Features

Anti-Lock Brakes	Yes	Yes
Driver-Side Airbag	Yes	Yes
Passenger-Side Airbag	Yes	Yes

 These cars come with passenger-side airbags. Children in rear-facing car seats should not be placed in the passenger side unless the airbag can be disabled.

Traction Control	Yes	No

 This electronic control system prevents drive wheels from spinning on a low-traction surface by automatically applying brakes or reducing engine power.

Child Safety Locks	No	Yes
Integrated Child Seat	No	No
Child Seat Anchors	Yes	Yes

Also, a traditional application is an enclosed user interface experience. Although window systems allow application-switching and make multiple applications visible simultaneously, the user is fundamentally "in" a single application at any given time, and only that application's commands and interaction conventions are active. Users spend relatively long periods of time in each application and become familiar with its features and design.

On the Web, users move between sites at a rapid pace, and the borders between different designs (sites) are fluid. It is rare for users to spend more than a few minutes at a time at any given site, and users' navigation frequently takes them from site to site to site as they follow the hyperlinks. Because of this rapid movement, users feel that they are using the Web as a whole rather than any specific site. Users don't want to read any manuals or help information for individual sites, but they do demand the ability to use a site on the basis of the web conventions they have picked up as an aggregate of their experience using other sites. In usability studies, users complain bitterly whenever they are exposed to sites with overly divergent ways of doing things. In other words, the Web as a whole has become a genre, and each site is interpreted relative to the rules of the genre.

Traditional GUIs are also part of a whole, of course, and it is advisable to follow the vendor's design style guide because in the balance between individual design and the whole, the scale tips in favor of the whole for web designs. At the same time, we don't have any established web design style guide that can dictate how designers should use their interface vocabulary to build sites that fit this whole. I am a strong proponent of getting an official set of web design conventions; but as long as we don't have one, my advice to web designers is to design to fit in and to acknowledge that your site is not the center of the users' universe. Users are going to move between sites, and we have to make it easy for them to use each new site as they go.

Help Users Manage Large Amounts of Information

Web navigation is a challenge because of the need to manage billions of information objects. Right now, the Web "only" has about a billion pages, but around 2005,

(Facing page)   Dynamic comparison tables are a great way to enhance user control over a large and complex information space. By allowing users to list side by side the exact cars they are thinking of buying, the site can even highlight the most important differences or features that a buyer should pay attention to when contemplating these cars. I don't think I would have highlighted passenger-side airbags when comparing two cars that both have this feature.

there will be 10 billion pages online that can be reached from any Internet-connected device. Current user interfaces are simply not well suited to deal with such huge amounts of information. Virtually every current user interface is more or less a clone of the Macintosh user interface from 1984 (which again was a close copy of research at Xerox PARC in the late 1970s and early 1980s). The Mac was optimized to handle the few documents that an individual user would create and store on his or her disk. Even the PARC research was mostly aimed at office automation where the main goal was to support a workgroup and a few thousand documents. The Web, in contrast, is a shared information environment for millions of users (soon to be hundreds of millions of users) with incredibly many more documents.

Web browsers are applications in the style of the currently dominant UI paradigm, so they are inherently ill suited for the task of browsing the Web. Consider, for example, how a pull-down menu (even with pull-right submenus) is an extraordinarily weak way of organizing a user's bookmarks. Calling the menu "favorites" instead of "bookmarks" does not change its fundamental limitations.

Current software is extremely weak at addressing the Web's navigation problems, meaning that the designers of web *content* have to help solve the problem. Actually, the problems in navigating an information space as large as the Web are probably so hard to solve that we will need all the help we can get, both from better software *and* from better-designed content.

The Web's early days were dominated by simplistic hypertext links: Everybody pointed to everybody else in a very unstructured manner. In fact, it was quite common to have *very* long lists of recommended links without much in the way of explaining *why* the links would be of interest to a user. The assumption was that the Web was so interesting and the users so curious, that they would check out all the links and be grateful the more links they got.

Long hotlists have certainly become less prevalent. Now, there is a renewed appreciation of the value of *selective linking*, where links have added value because they have been carefully chosen by an author to be the best or most relevant to that author's audience.

Design Creationism Versus Design Darwinism

With traditional GUIs we had the luxury of an initial phase of slow research and development at leading companies. Many years passed between the invention of ideas such as windows, menus, and icons, and the introduction of mass-market products. Much in-house experimentation was done by responsible user interface experts like the many researchers at Xerox PARC and Bruce Tognazzini at Apple. As a result, bad ideas were rejected, and good ideas were codified into guidelines before any GUIs were inflicted upon the average computer user. A GUI style guide was a carefully coordinated creation where the best ideas reinforced each other to form a pleasing and usable whole. In contrast, the Web is developing as we speak, and experiments happen on the open Internet with us all as test subjects—not in a videotaped usability lab. The result is a much harsher Design Darwinism, where ideas crash and burn in public. Eventually, the best design ideas will survive and bad ones will decline because users will abandon poorly designed sites.

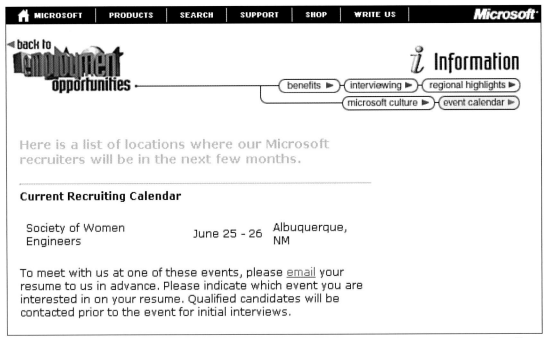

The top row of black buttons is standardized across the site and provides a clear sense of site-identification relative to the rest of the Web as well as an easy way of getting to the home page and to the search page. I would have preferred a more prominent placement of the search button, which seems somewhat lost between a series of less-important buttons. The real problem with this page is the highly confusing, second-level navigation bar. The layout of the five options under "Information" makes it look as if the local information space has two tracks, each with its logical sequence of pages. The current page is highlighted (good), but it's strange that it's the successor to "Microsoft culture" and not to "interviewing" because it concerns the scheduling of interviews. In general, a flow chart layout should be used only when the information space is in fact structured as an ordered sequence.

The "back to" link is a valuable navigation aid that allows user to easily move up a level, but the key phrase "employment opportunities" is rendered as a typographic mess that is inconsistent with the rest of the site, making it difficult to read the second-most-important word on the page, "employment." (The most important word on the page is obviously the site name, although there is no need to clutter up the navigation bar by listing it twice.) The page wastes an opportunity to serve its audience better: A link to the home page for the Society of Women Engineers event would have been very helpful to a potential recruit who was thinking of showing up to meet with the Microsoft recruiters.

One final issue is that I snapped this screenshot three days *after* the end of the Society of Women Engineers conference. Sites need to have procedures in place to remove outdated information immediately.

Jesse Berst's
AnchorDesk
Get Ahead. Stay Ahead.

NEXT
STORY ▶

Get your daily technology fix

enter email

Subscribe Now
See a sample issue

Briefing Centers
Companies
Products
KillerDownloads
Shopping
Top 10 Stories
Search
Week in Review

Community
TalkBack
Help
Home

Click Here!
WIN
color printer
each issue
in the month
of August

Free Email!
hotmail.

Berst Alert

FRIDAY, AUGUST 27, 1999

Just-Add-Water Web Stores

Jesse Berst, Editorial Director
ZDNet AnchorDesk

Go to Page 2 >
Web Store Resources

My boss is coming to town next week. First time he's actually graced our doorstep. And in a lot of ways that's a good thing. Nothing like being 3,000 miles from corporate headquarters.

There are millions of small businesses and Web entrepreneurs who think the same way. They like their independence. They don't mind being 'small' -- long as they're in control of their destiny.

But you know what I think? I think they dream of the day the CEO of Amazon.com or CDnow acknowledges their presence. The day they're no longer just a niche site with a small but loyal following. New technologies and new product offerings make it easier than ever to be a cyberstore. Some companies will even do all the work for you -- and put your name on it. I'm not here to give you an exhaustive list -- I've linked more resources on Page 2. But here are ways the just-add-water storefront trend is shaping up:

All-in-one-kits: Affinia.com just launched a service enabling any Web site to quickly and easily create a customized shopping portal with products relevant to their audience -- for free. Site owners go to the Affinia site, choose products they want to promote from a database of over 1,000 merchants, pick a site design template they like -- then wait for their portion of the sale proceeds to arrive. The transaction processing, shipping and customer service chores are all handled by the merchants. Click for more.

●Find more stories like this
●Email this story to a friend
●Print this story
●Post TalkBack to this story
●ACROMANIA (What's that?)

BRIEFING CENTER:
* Ecommerce

READ MORE:
Storefront Software Market
Consolidation Continues -
PC Week

Microsoft Targets Web
Hosting Outfits - *Smart
Reseller*

Open an Online Store: It's
Easy - *ZDTV*

Rule the Web Through
Affiliate Marketing - *ZDTV*

SUBSCRIBE:
Get AnchorDesk's Email
Summary in Your Inbox! -
ZDNet AnchorDesk

DISCUSS:
Jesse's Berst Alerts

**TODAY ON
ANCHORDESK:**
Just-Add-Water Web Stores

A Leaner, Meaner PointCast
Debuts

www.anchordesk.com

(Facing page) Jesse Berst's AnchorDesk places links to related, longer stories in the right margin. The left rail is dedicated to site-wide navigation, following a fairly common convention. Users will often overlook the left column completely (except if they deliberately want to locate a different part of the site). But the links on the right are a great way for Berst to recommend additional articles that are relevant to his current topic.

Sitemaps are becoming somewhat of a cliche. All users say they want sitemaps, and we even know from hypertext research that overview diagrams help users find information faster, so I am not opposed to sitemaps. But current sitemaps do not seem to help users much. For example, they lack the one feature that any mall-goer knows to be essential for a map: the "you are here" indicator. Many sites seem to design their sitemaps as a simple list of all their stuff. A better solution would be a dynamic sitemap that indicates the page from which it was accessed and that has ways of highlighting information of interest to specific user populations.

Reducing Navigational Clutter

We obviously cannot represent every single information object in a navigation UI (given that there are so many). Instead, designs must employ a variety of methods to reduce the clutter. Some useful methods are:

- Aggregation (showing a single unit that represents a collection of smaller ones). This can be done quite easily within a site (indeed, the very notion of a "site" is one useful level of aggregation, as are various levels of subsites), but it may be harder to aggregate across sites.
- Summarization (ways of representing a large amount of data by a smaller amount). Examples include the use of smaller images to represent larger ones and the use of abstracts to represent full documents. We need ways of summarizing large collections of information objects.
- Filtering (eliminating entire wads of stuff we don't care about). Collaborative filtering and quality-based filters are particularly useful (for example, only show stuff that other people have found to be valuable).
- Truncation. Cut off everything except the first initial parts of the information and let users click a "More…" link for the rest.
- Example-based representations. Instead of showing everything, show some representative examples and say something like "3 million more objects."

Future Navigation

We need to stop thinking of navigation as being the responsibility of either the browser or the server in isolation. Instead, it needs to become a shared responsibility of the client, the server, and shared resources such as proxy servers.

So, for example, I would expect the server to send a sitemap definition in XML to the client so that the browser can integrate it with maps of other regions of the Web frequented by the user and then generate a customized navigation map for that individual user. This map could then be annotated with quality ratings downloaded from a proxy server that kept track of what pages and/or sites the user's colleagues had found useful in the past. You could imagine a map of places to go that had been color-coded according to how many other users had found each area useful.

Every few months, the trade press reports a new technology to navigate websites in three dimensions. In particular, we see a lot of designs where users have to fly through a three-dimensional space in order to navigate. Most of these systems hurt users more than they help, for several reasons:

- Navigating a 3D space is in fact unnatural for us humans. It is much easier to learn to move on a surface than in a volume.

- Input and output devices are both 2D (typically a mouse and a screen), so the so-called 3D interfaces are in fact *projections* rather than true 3D, meaning that movements and manipulations are indirect and awkward.

- Information space is n-dimensional, where *n* is a very big number, so there is no inherent reason why a mapping to 3D should be any more natural than a mapping to 2D.

- Much of the information is hidden when the user has to fly through a 3D space, so it may in fact be harder to get an overview (which is the primary purpose of a navigation aid).

- None of these 3D interfaces have been subjected to user interface evaluations to measure whether users can perform any typical navigation tasks any faster than with a simpler 2D design. These designs may make for cool demos, but they never seem to actually help any real users perform any real tasks.

The bottom line is that 3D is no magic bullet that makes the navigation problem go away. Even if somebody makes a 3D interface that works, we still have the fundamental problems of structuring the information in a way that makes sense to the users and matches what they want to do.

Subsites

Web users need structure to make sense of the many and varied information spaces they navigate. The fundamental nature of the Web does not support any structure beyond the individual page, which is the only recognized unit of information.

Single pages are obviously not sufficient as a structuring mechanism, and from the early days of the Web, I have advocated an emphasis on the site as an additional fundamental structuring unit. Because a single click can take the user to the other end of the world, every page needs to provide users with a sense of place and tell them where they have landed.

Explicit recognition of the site as a structuring mechanism is important for web usability, but most websites are much too large for the site level to provide the only structure. Much information can be hierarchically organized, and so an explicit representation of the hierarchy can be added to the top of the page to provide additional context and navigation options. For example, the intranet for the hypothetical BigCo company might have the following list of the nested hierarchy leading to the home page for the Stockholm office:

BigCoWeb -> Sales -> European Region -> Sweden -> Stockholm Office

Each of the elements in the hierarchy list should be made a hyperlink to the appropriate top page for that level of the hierarchy. Note that the name of the lowest level of the hierarchy (here, Stockholm Office) should not be a link when displayed on the top page for that level. However, even the lowest-level name should be made active when displayed on a leaf page on that top level.

For information spaces that cannot easily be hierarchically structured, the subsite can be used as a helpful additional structuring mechanism. Subsites can also be used in hierarchical information spaces to give particular prominence to a certain level of the hierarchy, which is used as the subsite designator.

By *subsite*, I simply mean a collection of web pages within a larger site that have been given a common style and a shared navigation mechanism. This collection of pages can be a flat space, or it can have some internal structure, but in any case it should probably have a single page that can be designated the home page of the subsite. Each of the pages within the subsite should have a link pointing back to the subsite home page as well as a link to the home page for the entire site. Also, the subsite should have global navigation options (for example, to the site home page and to a site-wide search) in addition to its local navigation.

Subsites are a way of handling the complexity of large websites with thousands or even hundreds of thousands of pages. By giving a more local structure to a corner of the information space, a subsite can help users feel welcome in the part of a site that is of most importance to them. Also, a large site will often contain heterogeneous information that cannot all be squeezed into a single standard structure, so the capability to have subsites with somewhat different look-and-feel can provide an improved user experience. A subsite is a home environment for a specific class of users or a specific type of usage within a larger and more general site.

There is a tension between the desire of the subsite designer to optimize fully for the specific needs of local information versus the need for consistency across the entire site. Subsites should definitely not aspire to become independent sites with no relation to the parent site of which they are part and which should provide them with context and richness.

A good example of a subsite done right is ZDNet's AnchorDesk. AnchorDesk provides a platform for the respected computer industry commentator Jesse Berst to discuss current events in computing and pull together recommended links to additional information from across the rest of the Ziff-Davis site. The AnchorDesk subsite uses human editing as a guide to an otherwise overwhelming information space and has value-added use of hyperlinks to provide the foundation for the commentary.

Search Capabilities

My usability studies show that slightly more than half of all users are search-dominant, about a fifth of the users are link-dominant, and the rest exhibit mixed behavior. The *search-dominant users* will usually go straight for the search button when they enter a website. They are not interested in looking around the site; they are task-focused and want to find specific information as fast as possible. In contrast, the *link-dominant users* prefer to follow the links around a site. Even when they want to find specific information, they will initially try to get to it by following promising links from the home page. Only when they get hopelessly lost will link-dominant users admit defeat and use a search command. *Mixed-behavior users* switch between search and link-following, depending on what seems most promising to them at any given time, but they do not have an inherent preference.

Despite the primacy of search, web design still needs to be grounded in a strong sense of structure and navigation support. All pages must make it clear where they fit in the larger scheme of the site. First, there is obviously a need to support those users who don't like search or who belong to the mixed-behavior group. Second, users who do use

Don't Search the Web

For unknown reasons, many websites feel compelled to offer a search-engine feature that allows users to choose whether to search the current site or the entire Internet. This is a bad idea. People know where to find a web-wide search engine; these sites are the most used services on the Web. There is no need to clutter up your interface with one more option that has so little utility.

Micro-Navigation

In addition to moving across the expanse of the site, users also need to move around inside a local region of the site. They even need to be able to move between the pages that constitute a single "package," such as an article with sidebars or a product page.

search to get to a page still need structure to understand the nature of the page relative to the rest of the site. They also need navigation to move around the site in the neighborhood of the page they found by searching. It is a rare case that a single page holds all the answers, so normally users also want to see related pages.

Search should be easily available from every single page on the site. Search-dominant users will often click on a search button right on the home page, but other users may move around until they become lost. Once that happens, you don't want them to have to search for the search, so it should be right there on the page. This means *any* page because you can't predict when users will give up navigating and look for the search button.

Sometimes, special areas of a site are sufficiently coherent and distinct from the rest of the site that it makes sense to offer a scoped search that is restricted to only search that subsite. In general, I warn against scoped search because our observations have shown that users often don't understand the structure of sites. It is quite common for users to believe that the answer is in the wrong subsite, meaning that they will never find it in a scoped search. Other times, users don't realize where they are and what scope they are searching, so they may think that they are searching the entire site or a different subsite than the one they are actually in.

In contemplating a scoped search option, designers should have a strong bias in favor of avoiding scoping. If the site in fact has subsites that necessitate scoped search, then all scoped search pages must do two things:

- Explicitly state what scope is being searched. This should be indicated at the top of both the query page and the results page.

- Include a link to the page that searches the entire site. Again, this link needs to be on both the query page and the results page. On the results page it should be encoded as a link saying something like "Didn't find what you were looking for? Try to extend your search to the entire Foo.com site." Following this latter link should activate the global search with the same query as used for the scoped search, and it should take the user directly to the results page for the expanded search.

At first sight it may seem strange to consider Bill Gates' speeches and columns to be a subsite, but considering his many fans (and opponents) it is actually quite likely that many users will be interested in finding Bill-quotes. This subsite search is well-designed in most ways: It is clear that it is searching a subsite, and the subsite is well-defined. I doubt any users will try to use this page when searching for a workaround to the latest Excel bug.

I only have two problems with this page. There should be an explicit link to searching the full Microsoft site, and the type-in box should be wider to encourage users to enter more terms. The top navigation bar does include a button for global search, but considering the many occurrences of the word "search" on this page, I would have preferred an explicit link located in the content of the page. Very few users will look above the colored "Bill Gates" bar.

Advanced Search

Boolean search should be avoided because all experience shows that users cannot use it correctly. We have studied many groups of users who have been given tasks like this:

You have the following pets:

- cats
- dogs

Find information about your pets.

Almost all users will enter the following query:

cats AND dogs

In our studies, users typically do not find anything with this query, because our test site does not include any pages that mention both animals. Upon encountering a "no hits found" message, the vast majority of users conclude that there is no information available about these pets. Even experienced programmers will normally use the erroneous query. The main difference is that when the geeks get the null result, they typically say, "Oh, yes, I should have used an OR instead of the AND."

Unfortunately, most users have not been taught debugging, so they are very poor at query reformulation. This is why I recommend minimal use of scoped search and no use of Boolean search in the primary search interface. Advanced search is fine if offered on a page *different* from the simple search. The advanced search page can provide a variety of fancy options, including Boolean, scopes, and various parametric searches (e.g., only find pages added or changed after a certain date). It is important to use an intimidating name like "advanced search" to scare off novice users from getting into the page and hurting themselves. Search is one of the few cases where I do recommend shaping the user's behavior by intimidation.

In general, computers are good at looking at long lists of stuff and remembering whether any alternative words exist that should be searched for. Users are notoriously bad at this exact same task, so it is pretty clear what a well-designed search system should do. The system should perform spelling checks (both for user queries and for document terms), and it should offer synonym expansion.

Search ||install AND printer
◉ Personal Library ○ Complete Library Tips

Results of search across personal library for: install AND printer

 Solaris 2.6 Software Developer AnswerBook Vol 2

 Solaris X Window System Developer's Guide

○ Installing and Managing Fonts

To improve your search results:

- Try different words
- Try the same words, but select **Complete Library**
- Try a more advanced search... Tips

Search ||install AND printer
◉ Personal Library ○ Complete Library Tips

docs.sun.com

(Above) Sun's *AnswerBook2* web-based documentation interface uses scoped search: Each user can set up a so-called personal library with a list of those parts of the large information space that normally is of interest to them. By default, the search uses this personal library as the search scope. In this example, only one, and not very promising, hit was found for the user's search.

Below the list of search hits are suggestions for how to improve the search. We tried many different placements for these instructions, and the one just below the search hits proved to be the best. When users get to this part of the page, they're motivated to read about ways to improve their search. Without the instructions, many users overlooked the option to search the complete library and so never found any information that was not within their initial search scope.

(Facing page) To get this page, the *AnswerBook2* user has repeated the search, but this time with the search scope set to the complete library. Many more hits were found, including many good ones in the System Administrator collection. Apparently, the problem the user wanted to read about (installing printers) was considered a system administration task by the designers of the documentation. Because the set of online documentation is a structured information space, the search results list can present the search hits in context, which makes it obvious to the user that most of the promising hits are in the System Administrator collection.

The use of book icons (and indeed the very name of the online documentation) indicates a book metaphor that is emphasized by terms such as "personal library." In general, book metaphors are probably not the best for hypertext, but it is a good match for this particular information space, which is highly structured with all information about a certain domain made into a "book."

Jakob Nielsen: Designing Web Usability

Search | install AND printer

○ Personal Library ● Complete Library Tips

Results of search across complete library for: install AND printer

Solaris 2.6 System Administrator Collection Vol 1

System Administration Guide

- ● Managing Printing Services
- ● Managing Fonts
- ● Planning for Printer Setup
- ○ Adding a Network Printer
- ○ Setting Up a Print Server

Font Administrator User's Guide

- ○ To Install Fonts

Solaris 1.x to 2.x Transition Guide

- ○ Preface
- ○ How This Guide Is Organized
- ○ Transition Information for Users and System Administrators
- ○ Printing

Help

Accessing Online Documentation

- ○ Printing
- ○ Changing Printing Options
- ○ Installing Document Server Software

Solaris 2.6 Software Developer AnswerBook Vol 2

Solaris X Window System Developer's Guide

- ○ Installing and Managing Fonts

Solaris 2.6 on Sun Hardware AnswerBook

SunVTS 2.1 Test Reference Manual

- ○ spdtest Error Messages

docs.sun.com

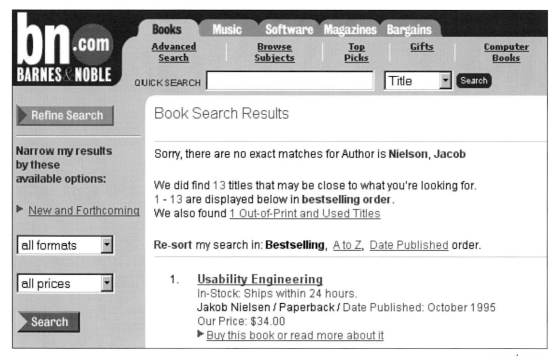

www.bn.com

Barnes & Noble's search engine conducts a spelling check on the user's query terms when it doesn't find any matches. In this case, the user could misspell my name (which is done very frequently) and still find my books. As an interesting aside, note that this spelling correction also handles cases where the user spelled the name correctly but the site had a spelling error in its database.

The Search Results Page

The search results page should have a sorted list of hits with the best hits at the top. Some search engines list search scores next to the hits, but because users don't understand how these scores are computed they are essentially meaningless. As long as the best hits are at the top, users can easily start scanning the list from the top and will automatically see the most important hits first without wasting time trying to interpret search scores.

The search results list should eliminate duplicate occurrences of the same page. In particular, it is quite common to see the default page in a directory listed multiple times with slightly varying URLs. On many servers, the following three URLs will point to the same page:

http://www.foo.com/bar
http://www.foo.com/bar/
http://www.foo.com/bar/index.html

Even though these URLs are distinct in principle (that is, they *could* point to different pages under certain conditions), they should be unified and listed only once in the search results listing. It is very confusing for users if they click on different links and get the same result.

Search systems should also explicitly recognize quality in addition to relevance when prioritizing search hits. For example, if the site has a FAQ about the user's query term, then the FAQ page should be listed on the top of the results page even if other pages have higher relevance scores. After all, it is likely that a FAQ is of higher quality with respect to answering the user's questions. It would also be possible to build up a database of quality ratings for each of the pages on the site relative to each of the more popular search terms. For example, every time users follow a link from a results list to a page, they are asked how well that page satisfies their search, and the ratings are then saved and used to prioritize the results list for future searches.

Traditionally, the chunking unit for web search has been the page. In other words, the search output is a list of pages that match the user's query. Unfortunately, most of these lists of pages have no indication of the relation between the pages that were found. It would be better to structure the search results relative to the structure of the site. For example, if many pages were found within a single subsite, then it might be better to cluster all these hits into a single entry on the search results page. Sometimes, it may even make sense to chunk the search by larger units than the pages. For example, an advanced search of a site with many distinct subsites could initially use the subsites as the chunks and list those subsites that, taken as a whole, were good matches for the user's query. The user could then search these subsites further.

Page Descriptions and Keywords

Some of the Internet-wide search engines show the author's abstract of the page instead of trying to generate their own summary text. In general, I favor this approach because humans are still better than computers at deciding what a page is really about and at writing readable text. The page abstract is contained in a META tag with the

(Following page) MaMaMedia integrates a structural overview into its search results pages. When doing a search on the term "bird," the user retrieves pages both about birds as animals and about birds as pets (as well as pages about dinosaurs). The difference in emphasis between the different pages is made clear while the child is still on the search results lists, thus eliminating the need to spend time going to some pages only to read about the wrong topic.

www.mamamedia.com

name "description" in the page header. The format for these abstracts is

```
<META NAME="description" CONTENT="This is a summary of
the content of this page">
```

Deciding the best length of a page abstract for a search-results listing is a trade-off between providing a good prospective view of the possible destinations and providing an overview of the full set of alternatives; long abstracts are better at allowing users to assess each individual page but make it more difficult for users to compare destinations without excessive scrolling. In almost all cases, some form of abstract is necessary because the page titles alone are not sufficient to allow users to guess what the pages are truly about.

Page abstracts should be kept short. Most search engines display only the first 150 or 200 characters of the description text, so it is best to stay below this limit when writing pages for the open Internet. Even if you are using your own search engine, it is still best to have very short abstracts because users are more likely to scan the abstracts than to read them in full.

In addition to descriptions, it is also common to add a list of keywords in a META tag in the page header. Typically, the keywords are not displayed in research results lists but instead are used only to determine the relative ranking of the retrieved pages: A page is assumed to be mainly about the terms included in its keyword list.

The keywords list should include both simple terms (e.g., "bus") and compound terms (e.g., "double-decker bus") because users search surprisingly frequently for multi-word terms. In pre–Web search studies, we used to find that users were overwhelmingly most likely to enter single-word queries. For example, in a study of a traditional online documentation system, Meghan Ede and I found that 81 percent of the users' queries consisted of a single word. Maybe the overwhelming amount of information on the Web has forced users to be more precise in their queries. Whatever the reason, single-word queries are not quite as common as they used to be. In 1997, I analyzed 2,261 queries from WebCrawler and 24,743 queries from www.sun.com. In both cases, I found substantially more two-word queries as well as longer queries.

Use a Wide Search Box

Most search engines provide more precise results when the user enters more words in the query. And yet users are notorious for entering very short queries. Maybe the search engine design shares part of the blame. Jussi Karlgren and Kristofer Franzén from Stockholm University conducted a small experiment where they had students use the same website with two different text entry boxes for the search engine. On average, the students entered 2.8 words per query when using the version of the site with a small text box, but when using a design with a much larger text entry box, the students entered 3.4 words on average.

This result makes sense from a usability perspective for two reasons. First, users don't like to enter something they can't see, so they will be reluctant to type any more than the number of characters that are visible at any given time in the text field. So, even if the entry field scrolls, people will often not type longer queries than it can hold. Second, the very size of the query box sets some expectations regarding the probable size of the query string.

Sites are an important unit of hierarchy on the Web, so clustering search hits by the site they belong to is a great way of making users see the forest for the trees of pages in their search results. In this example, I would probably have sorted www.world-ready.com above www.useit.com because it would seem to be more important to have 50 percent more pages about the query than to have whether the highest scoring page on the site scores 83 or 82.

Jakob Nielsen: Designing Web Usability

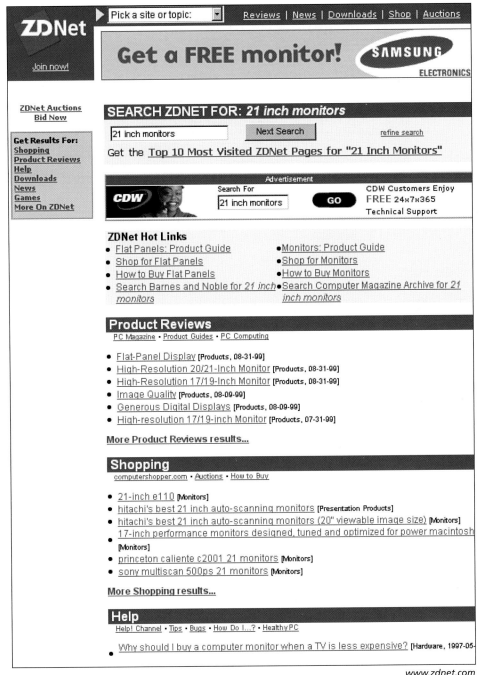

Clustering also works for searches within a single website, although the structuring mechanism obviously needs to be different. For example, results could be structured by subsite or by category as done in this example from ZDNet. Also note the use of shortcut links to the most important areas of the site of interest to the user's query. I am less enamored with the advertising search box: Even though it is clearly marked as an ad, it intrudes too much on the user.

● **news center**
World
Business
Technology
Sports

● **smart info**
People & Business
Stocks/Companies
Street Maps
Shareware/Chat
Desk Reference
Infoseek Investor

● **big yellow**
Find Businesses
Find People
Find E-mail
Global Directories

Related Topics
User interface
Computer science institutes in Georgia

Sites 1 - 10 of 23,981   Hide Summaries   next 10

Usability Laboratories Survey
useit.com Papers and Essays Usability Labs Survey Usability Laboratories: A 1994 Survey.
by Jakob Nielsen Affiliation at time of writing: Bellcore (Bell Communications Research) ..
66% http://www.useit.com/papers/uselabs.html (Size 28.9K)

Discount Usability for the Web
Discount usability engineering is the only solution for the Web's hypergrowth (designing 100
billion intranet pages in four years) to avoid productivity losses of $50 billion per year
65% http://www.useit.com/papers/web_discount_usability.html (Size 6.9K)

Microsoft Usability FAQ
About Microsoft Home Page Usability Home Page Search Microsoft Microsoft Home Page
Frequently Asked Questions What is the Microsoft Usability Group? The usability group was
created in ..
65% http://microsoft.com/usability/faq.htm   (Size 8.9K)

Practical Education for Improving Software Usability
John Karat and Tom Dayton IBM T. J. Watson Research Center 30 Saw Mill River Road
Hawthorne, NY 10532 USA +1-914-784-7612 jkarat@watson.ibm.com Bellcore 444 Hoes
Lane, RRC 4A-1112 ...
65% http://www.acm.org/sigchi/chi95/proceedings/papers/jk_bdy.htm (Size 48.3K)

An Example of Formal Usability Inspections in Practice at Hewlett-Packard
Company CHI '95 ProceedingsTopIndexes PostersTOC An Example of Formal Usability
Inspections in Practice at Hewlett-Packard Company Cathy Gunn Usability Engineer
Hewlett-Packard ...
65% http://www.acm.org/sigchi/chi95/proceedings/intpost/cg_bdy.htm (Size 9.7K)

Digital Library Design for Organizational Usability Rob Kling and Margaret
Elliott Computing, Organizations, Policy and Society (CORPS) Department of Information
and Computer Science and Center for Research on Information Technology in Organizations

www.infoseek.com

Note how pages that provide human-written descriptions make it much easier for the user to determine whether the page is of interest. Compare, for example, the first and second hits on this page: The first hit is represented by Infoseek's automatically generated summary of the page, and the second page is represented by a real abstract. Also note on this page how the search engine tries to identify a few alternative phrases that might be used for query reformulation. I searched on "usability," so the suggestion to search for "user interface" would most likely be helpful and would find pages that were missed by the original search. Obviously, the system's capability to find relevant alternatives is limited, as shown by its second suggestion, "Computer science institutes in Georgia." (Even though there is one such institute that does usability research, there are much better alternative queries.)

Distribution of the number of terms used in search queries in a traditional, pre-Web system and in two web search engines.

	Pre-Web Search	Webcrawler	www.sun.com
1 word	81%	43%	46%
2 words	14%	35%	32%
3 words	4%	13%	15%
4 words	1%	6%	5%
5 words or more	0%	3%	2%

Even though the profusion of material on the Web has encouraged longer queries, it is still true that the vast majority of queries are one or two words. Such ultra-short queries made up more than three quarters of the searches in my sample. The lesson for web designers is the need to use focused and highly descriptive keywords in your META tags, because keyword searches are the way most users will find you. Also, you need to add keywords for all the main synonyms for your topic. In particular, add alternative keywords for any terms used by your competitors to refer to the kind of product you are selling. For example, a page about hard disks should have the acronym DASD as a keyword because many traditional IBM customers will be used to calling disks DASD (direct-access storage devices).

It is unfortunate that people tend to use short searches because search engines are better at finding relevant pages the more information they have about the user's needs. Typically, the way to provide more information about your needs involves specifying additional search terms, including synonyms or alternate phrases. Doing so is hard, and people are notoriously bad at thinking of synonyms. Also, of course, natural laziness encourages users to type as little as possible. Because of these problems with traditional keyword search, search engines need to take on more of the responsibility for allowing users to enhance their searches.

See What People Search For

Several of the major Internet search engines have a service where you can view random samples of the queries entered by other users. It is quite interesting to spend a few moments to look at the ways people phrase queries and try to estimate what they might be trying to find. Searches provide first-hand insights into users' wants.

(The Webcrawler service I used to collect the statistics discussed in this chapter is at http://webcrawler.com/cgi-bin/SearchTicker.)

In addition to looking at people who search the open Internet, you should also study the search logs from your own site search. Any terms that occur frequently in your search logs obviously represent information that many users want to get but have trouble finding on your site.

Search Destination Design

When the user follows a link from a search results listing, the destination page should be presented in context of the user's search. Doing so requires use of a document management system that can construct dynamic pages that change presentation depending on the user's specific search. In principle, destination pages should adapt to the user's search in all cases, but in practice, it is normally only feasible to do so for searches from the site's own search engine. Users who arrive from Internet-wide search engines like Infoseek will probably get static pages because of lack of integration between the site and the search engine.

The most common way to enhance a search destination page is to highlight all occurrences of the user's search terms. By doing so, users can more rapidly scan the page to pick out those parts of the page that describe the topic of interest. Helping users find their search terms on your page also makes it faster for them to assess why the search engine included the page in the results listing and whether the use of the search terms on the page is relevant to their needs.

(Facing page)   In my opinion, Infoseek has the easiest interface for expanding the user's search with related terms. The search engine selects a small number of related terms, meaning that the user will often take the time to read them and consider whether they would be useful search alternatives. Also, repeating the search with a new term is a simple matter of clicking the desired term. Unfortunately, the desire to highlight the advertisement has led to a large distance and a visually intrusive interruption between the user's search term (here "web usability") and the suggested related topics. Many users are probably going to overlook the related topics because they tend to disappear in the clutter in the upper and left parts of the page.

Integrating Sites and Search Engines

It would be pretty easy to integrate sites more closely with search engines. If search engines would agree on a standardized method for encoding the user's query terms, then many sites would probably make the effort to serve programmatically defined pages that highlighted occurrences of the query term.

It should also be possible for search engines to present search results in a more structured manner if they download sitemap definition files and use them to derive the structure of each site's information space. If, for example, a given site has five pages with hits for a given query, and four of these hits are in one closely related set of pages, then the search results list should probably list two hits for the site. The group of four pages should be represented by a single reference to the center, or most important, of the pages (with an icon indicating that the hit represents a cluster of pages).

infoseek®

You searched for **Web usability**

Sites 1 - 10 of 4,661,025

 news center

Intergraph Announces
Solid Edge Version 3.5;
Sheet Metal Design
Tools Deliver
Unprecedented Usa

smart info
  People & Business
  Stocks/Companies
  Street Maps
  Shareware/Chat
  Desk Reference
  Infoseek Investor

company capsules:

E&D Web, Inc.

Continental Web
Press, Inc.

Instant Web, Inc.

big yellow
  Find Businesses
  Find People
  Find E-mail
  Global Directories

Related Topics
Effective web site design
Server logs & marketing
User interface

_____ (seek) Tips

◉ Search **only** these results   ○ Search **the whole Web**

Sites 1 - 10 of 4,661,025   Hide Summaries   next 10

webhci List Archive: ideas for Web usability symposium at CHI 97
ACM List Archives webhci List Archive ideas for Web usability symposium
at CHI 97 Keith Instone (instone@cs.bgsu.edu) Thu, 16 May 1996
14:01:17 -0400 Messages sorted by: [date][...
100% http://www.acm.org/archives/webhci/0009.html (Size 10.3K)

Report on the "Missing Link" Web Usability Symposium
An earlier version of this is published as: The Missing Link: Hypermedia
Usability Research & The Web. Buckingham Shum, S. (1996). Interfaces,
British HCI Group Magazine, Summer, ...
100% http://kmi.open.ac.uk/~simonb/missing-link/ml-report.html (Size 47.4K)

"Missing Link" Web Usability Symposium
HCI Grp logo A Symposium in Association with The British HCI Group &
Special Issue of the International Journal of Human-Computer Studies
The Missing Link: Hypermedia Usability ...
100% http://kmi.open.ac.uk/~simonb/missing-link/ (Size 6.0K)

Alertbox: Jakob Nielsen's Column on Web Usability
useit.com Alertbox The Alertbox: Current Issues in Web Usability.
Semi-monthly column by Jakob Nielsen, SunSoft Distinguished Engineer
How you can subscribe and get update ...
100% http://www.useit.com/alertbox/ (Size 5.5K)

www.infoseek.com

TIP: queries with two or more words match documents containing **ANY** of the words. You might get better results by using a more focused query, e.g., <u>Web +usability</u> or <u>"Web usability"</u>.

```
Web usability
```
[Submit]
[Reset]

Include/exclude <u>a few words</u> out of the following topics to refine your query: <u>Usability</u>, <u>Functionality</u>, <u>Interfaces</u>, <u>Usable</u>, <u>Users</u>, <u>Interaction</u>, <u>Testing</u>, <u>Software</u>, <u>Developers</u>, <u>Windows</u>, <u>Environments</u>, <u>Enhancements</u>, <u>Intuitive</u>, <u>Prototype</u>, <u>Ease</u>, <u>Multimedia</u>, <u>Evaluation</u>, <u>Designers</u>, <u>Platforms</u>, <u>Client</u>.

✗✓ Usability	✗✓ Functionality	✗✓ Interfaces	✗✓ Usable
☐☐ usability ☐☐ user ☐☐ design ☐☐ interface ☐☐ designing	☐☐ functionality ☐☐ application ☐☐ robust	☐☐ interfaces ☐☐ graphical ☐☐ gui ☐☐ guis	☐☐ usable ☐☐ prototyping ☐☐ centered

✗✓ Users	✗✓ Interaction	✗✓ Testing	✗✓ Software
☐☐ users ☐☐ tasks ☐☐ task	☐☐ interaction ☐☐ hci ☐☐ cognitive ☐☐ human ☐☐ factors ☐☐ ergonomics ☐☐ computer ☐☐ ergonomic	☐☐ testing ☐☐ test ☐☐ tests	☐☐ software ☐☐ engineering ☐☐ reliability ☐☐ metrics ☐☐ maintainability

✗✓ Developers	✗✓ Windows	✗✓ Environments	✗✓ Enhancements
☐☐ developers ☐☐ developer ☐☐ methodology ☐☐ methodologies ☐☐ development	☐☐ windows ☐☐ applications ☐☐ desktop ☐☐ compatibility ☐☐ microsoft ☐☐ operating ☐☐ dos	☐☐ environments ☐☐ visualization ☐☐ gvu ☐☐ virtual ☐☐ environment ☐☐ surveys ☐☐ reality	☐☐ enhancements ☐☐ enhanced ☐☐ improved ☐☐ upgrade ☐☐ version ☐☐ release ☐☐ versions ☐☐ upgrades

✗✓ Intuitive	✗✓ Prototype	✗✓ Ease	✗✓ Multimedia
☐☐ intuitive ☐☐ compliant ☐☐ easier	☐☐ prototype ☐☐ prototypes ☐☐ iterative	☐☐ ease ☐☐ product ☐☐ flexibility	☐☐ multimedia ☐☐ authoring ☐☐ interactive ☐☐ interactivity

✗✓ Evaluation	✗✓ Designers	✗✓ Platforms	✗✓ Client
☐☐ evaluation ☐☐ evaluating ☐☐ evaluations ☐☐ nielsen ☐☐ heuristic ☐☐ jakob ☐☐ evaluators	☐☐ designers ☐☐ programmers ☐☐ designer	☐☐ platforms ☐☐ platform ☐☐ unix	☐☐ client ☐☐ relational ☐☐ server ☐☐ databases ☐☐ database ☐☐ servers ☐☐ sql ☐☐ odbc

www.altavista.com

AltaVista seems to overwhelm the user with too many options and alternative terms. Some expert users may appreciate this extensive listing of alternative search terms, but most users are likely to be scared away from the otherwise very useful ability to rephrase their queries. I would have preferred a design with a smaller number of options that were linked to this huge table as an "expert search."

| cascading style sheet | | **Search** | Search Tips Power Search |

Select words to add to your search..
☐ css   ☐ stylesheets   ☐ sheet   ☐ hotmetal   ☐ raggett
☐ wdvl   ☐ dsssl   ☐ winmosaic   ☐ thalia   ☐ stylesheet

·Top **10** of **1011064** matches.   **View Titles only** **View by Web Site**

89% **SoftQuad: Products: HoTMetaL PRO** [More Like This]
URL: http://www.sq.com/products/hotmetal/hmp-org.htm
Summary: ..In my gigantic October 1995 column I recommended version 2.0 of this product. . If you're planning on linking to us from your site, please link to this page (http://www.

87% **HyperText Markup Language (HTML): Workin...** [More Like This]
URL: http://www.w3.org/pub/WWW/MarkUp/MarkUp.html
Summary: When a user clicks on a link, the URL of the page containing the link is passed to the server along with the requested URL. The W3C HTML 3.2 Recommendation defines conformance of HTML documents (web pages) and certain aspects of HTML user agents (web browsers).

87% **Cascading Style Sheets** [More Like This]
URL: http://jaring.nmhu.edu/NOTES/cascade.htm
Summary: Cascading Style Sheets (CSS) is a mechanism for allowing web authors and readers to attach styles including fonts, colors, etc. Authors can attach styles to their HTML documents whild readers may have their own personal style sheets.

87% **Guide to Cascading Style Sheets** [More Like This]
URL: http://www.htmlhelp.com/reference/css/
Summary: . Change the appearance of hundreds of Web pages by changing just one file. An introduction to the various kinds of selectors, pseudo-classes, pseudo-elements, and cascading order.

87% **Cascading Style Sheets** [More Like This]
URL: http://jedi.dmu.ac.uk/JEDI/d3/node24.html
Summary: <HTML> <HEAD> <TITLE>title</TITLE$> <LINK REL=STYLESHEET TYPE="text/css" HREF="http://style.

Click on **"More Like This"** when you want a list of documents similar to a document you really like.

87% **CGI.pm - a Perl5 CGI Library** [More Like This]
URL: http://www-genome.wi.mit.edu/ftp/pub/software/WWW/cgi_docs.html
Summary: $query->param('foo','an','array','of','values'); -or- $query->param(-name=>'foo',-values=>['an','array','of','values']); This sets the value for the named parameter 'foo' to one or more values.

www.excite.com

Excite also provides a way to add synonyms. In this example, it would be useful to search for "css" if the user was interested in "cascading style sheets." More important, each search hit has a "more like this" link that performs relevance feedback and searches for pages that are similar to the one the user liked. In principle, it would be better to have a "find more like this" button on the actual destination pages, but doing so would require integration between the site and the search engine. In this figure, a reasonably subtle background color is used to enclose the available search options and set them apart, leading to a less busy appearance than Infoseek or AltaVista. Putting the hint about the meaning of the "more like this" buttons into the middle of the search results listing is a rather unconventional design, but it does seem to work: The user's eye is caught by the change in background color and layout, and the matching colors lead to a unification of the hint with the main search area at the top of the page.

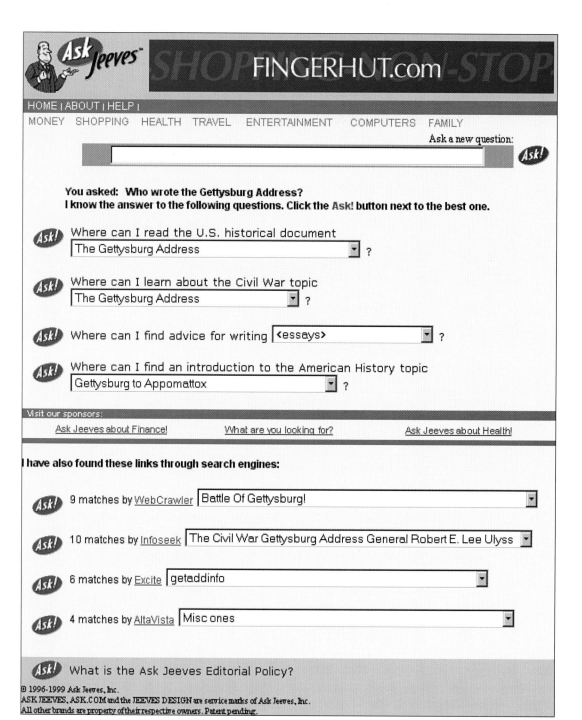

Natural language search engines get much attention but are rarely great for usability. It is extra work for the user to formulate an entire question, and people prefer typing in a small number of keywords. Also, the search engines are not truly capable of understanding human language, so it is misleading to pretend that they do. In this example, asking the natural language question "Who wrote the Gettysburg Address?" on AskJeeves results in many hits that are relevant to the document but not to the authorship. It would almost certainly be possible to find the answer to the question through one of the links, but it is easier to simply type the relevant keywords "Gettysburg Address" into Google because the answer is right on the results page in the title of two of the hits. Google places the full text of the Address as the first hit because it doesn't know that we were interested specifically in authorship.

Search | install AND printer

○ This Book ◉ Personal Library   Tips

Setting Definitions for Printers

Establishing definitions for the printers on your network is an ongoing task that lets you provide a more effective print environment for users. For example, you can assign parameters for all your site's printers to help users find where a printer is located, or you can define a class of printers to provide the fastest turnaround for print requests.

The `lpadmin` command lets you set all of the print definitions, while Admintool lets you set only some of them when you **install** or modify a **printer**. Print Definitions Set With Admintool lists the print definitions and shows whether you can assign the definition with Admintool.

Print Definitions Set With Admintool

Print Definition	Can You Set It With Admintool?
Printer name	Yes
Printer description	Yes
Printer port	Yes
Printer type	Yes
File contents	Yes, but with less functionality than the `lpadmin` command

docs.sun.com

Sun's *AnswerBook2* web-based online documentation highlights the user's query terms (here "install" and "printer") to make it easier for users to scan the rather long pages to find the sections that are of interest to them. The bottom of the page has an outline of related topics in the same region of the information space. Red circles are used to indicate the estimated relevance of each page relative to the user's current search query.

If you have a NEC® printer, look in the **/usr/share/lib/terminfo/n** directory for your NEC printer model.

```
$ cd /usr/share/lib/terminfo/n
$ ls
ncr7900        ncr7901        netty-Tabs     newhpkeyboard
ncr7900-na     nec            netty-vi       nuc
ncr7900i       net            network        nucterm
ncr7900i-na    netronics      netx
ncr7900iv      netty          newhp
$
```

The entry in this directory for NEC is included in the preceding example.

Next Topic

Other topics in System Administration Guide

Complete Table of Contents for book

docs.sun.com

URL Design

Tim Berners-Lee has said that if he had known that the Web would be as popular as it is, then he might have thought harder about finding an alternative to the slash-slash part of the URL, which is particularly annoying when speaking URLs over the telephone. In principle, URLs are machine-readable code and should not have anything to do with user interface design. In practice, it is an unfortunate truth that URLs are exposed to users in many aspects of web usage, so we do have to consider them as a design issue.

Considering the popularity of the Web, there is no need to speak out the "http://" part of a URL when giving it over the telephone or when including it in a television commercial. Most companies simply refer to their website as www.company.com rather than http://www.company.com/ (the syntactically correct

---

Compound Domain Names

How might one make up a domain name to refer to a website that has multiple words in its name? For example, a site for Jakob Nielsen might be called jakobnielsen.com, jakob-nielsen.com, jakob.nielsen.com, jnielsen.com, and many other combinations of the two words. (The underscore character is illegal in domain names, but hyphens are allowed.)

Creating compounds by using dots (e.g., jakob.nielsen.com) only works for a company that owns the primary domain (in this case nielsen.com, which is taken by the Nielsen ratings). And if you have the primary domain, then why make a longer and more complex subdomain for your website? I recommend using the standard "www." as the prefix for websites because people know what it means and because having an address start with "www." is a nice indication that you are talking about a website and not something else (it used to be the case that this goal required the use of a full URL, complete with "http://," but these days, only very meticulous people bother doing so).

Thus, the three reasonable candidates are:
- Run the words together: jakobnielsen.com
- Use an abbreviation: jnielsen.com
- Use a hyphen: jakob-nielsen.com

Current mainstream practice on the Web prefers the first choice; simply run the words together to form a new "Internet word" for the domain name. In usability, the fact that most other people do something is reason enough to follow along because the most common practice is what users expect and find easiest to use.

Abbreviations work as an alternative for three or more words or when the result of running two words together would be very long and/or difficult to spell. My main recommendation is to run the words together if you are dealing with two reasonably short and easy-to-spell words.

Hyphens should be avoided because people often forget them, they can be mistaken for underscores, and they are rare (and thus a usability problem).

Jakob Nielsen: Designing Web Usability

form). Although HTML purists deplore this abbreviated form of stating the name of a website, it seems perfectly acceptable to me, especially because almost all browsers add the missing protocol specification to the front and the missing directory specification to the end. The Web is now so ubiquitous that it is understood that anything starting with www and ending with .com (or .uk, .de, .jp, etc., outside the U.S.) is a website.

I recommend making both company.com and www.company.com aliased machine names for your web server. Currently, most users do include the "www." when typing in URLs, but sometimes they forget. Also, when speaking URLs over the telephone, it is nice to avoid the very awkward-sounding "www."

The most important component of a URL is the domain name (the machine name immediately after the http://). If users can remember your domain name, they can at least get to your home page, from which navigation and search are hopefully sufficient to allow them to find the page they need even if they don't have the rest of the URL. Most companies try to get their company name as their domain name, and I would definitely advise anybody who starts a new company these days to pick a name that is available not simply as a trademark but also as an Internet domain. Having an obscure domain name is going to cost big time in lost customers. Good domain names that are easy to remember and easy to spell are the Internet's equivalent of a Fifth Avenue real estate location in the physical world.

Fully Specify URLs in HTML Code

I do recommended using fully syntactically correct URLs in the hypertext links in actual HTML code. In particular, it is best to include the trailing slash for any URL that points to the default file in a directory. Most web servers can cope with a missing slash, but doing so typically requires the server to redirect the browser's request from the abbreviated version to the correct version, and doing so takes time and adds to the response time delay. Thus, if you want to refer to my Alertbox column in print, you would write the URL as

    http://www.useit.com/alertbox

or even

    www.useit.com/alertbox

If you wanted to include a hypertext link to the column in one of your web pages, the HTML should be coded as

    <A HREF="http://www.useit.com/alertbox/">
    Jakob Nielsen's Alertbox</A>

Our usability studies have shown that users rely on reading URLs when they try to decipher the structure of a site or the possible results of following a hyperlink. It would be preferable if browsers had better ways of making site structures explicit and of previewing the destinations of hyperlinks, but right now they don't, so users read URLs the way the ancients read cracked turtle shells: to divine a hostile environment with no known laws of nature.

Because we know that users try to understand URLs, we have an obligation to *make* them understandable. In particular, all directory names should be human-readable and should be either words or compound words that explain the meaning of the site structure. Also, your site structure should support URL-butchering where users hack off trailing parts of a URL in the hope of getting to an overview page at a higher place in the site hierarchy. Of course, it is better if users can navigate your site structure using your navigation buttons, but we know that a lot of users use URL-butchering as a shortcut: Such users should get reasonable results (typically a table-of-contents-like page listing the information available at the desired level of the hierarchy).

One day browsers, servers, and proxies will all include spelling checkers, but at this time users are doomed if they don't get every single character exactly right when typing a URL. Web designers can reduce the frequency with which users meet the dreaded 404 by making URLs easier to spell. Rules for easy-to-spell URLs are:

- Make the URL as short as possible (the longer the URL, the great the possibilities for making errors).
- Use common natural language words as much as possible because users normally know how to spell these words.
- Use all lowercase characters. If you use MiXeD cAsE, some users are guaranteed to forget some of the caps and get errors (depending on the server). In general, you should never rely on the difference between uppercase and lowercase letters in a user interface because such a distinction is a sure prescription for frequent user errors. Confusing upper- and lowercase characters is a so-called *description error*. Because the two objects are almost the same and because the most

salient part of the description of the two objects (the name of the character) is exactly the same, users are very likely to confuse the two.

- Avoid special characters (anything but letters and digits) as far as possible. If punctuation is necessary, stick to a single character throughout all your URLs. Use all underscores or all hyphens, for example, but not a mix of the two.

Archival URLs

Links from other websites are the third most-common way people find sites (after search engines and email recommendations), so build your site to make it easy to attract inbound links.

Linkrot equals lost business, so make sure all URLs live forever and continue to point to relevant pages. Do not move pages around; instead, keep them at the same URL. It is very annoying for authors of other sites when their links either stop working or turn into pointers to something different because the original page has been moved and replaced by something new.

Content that changes on a regular basis is often stored under temporary URLs. Examples include the current issue of a magazine, today's front page for a newspaper, and the program for the upcoming version of an annual conference. You will often want to publicize virtual URLs that point to the concept of "*CyberTimes* front page," "this week's editorial," "list of keynotes at the next InternetWorld conference," and so on. In fact, users often prefer to bookmark such virtual pointers because they are interested in accessing the most current information whenever they visit.

Often, such topical content may be of long-term interest and should be archived under permanent URLs in addition to the temporary URL, which will be changed to point to new content on a regular basis. For example, I often want to link the readers of my online column to articles in online magazines, but of course I don't want to link to "the current week's editorial" but to "the editorial on overuse of animation." These two concepts may temporarily have the same URL, but it is much easier for me if I can use the permanent URL of the archived version as the link for my own HTML file. It would be a pain to have to update the link at a later date, and many authors forget to do so. Even worse, link-checkers will often not discover the mistake because the old URL continues to be valid. Rather, it simply points to new and irrelevant content.

The preferred way of dealing with virtual URLs is to pre-assign an archival URL to the page and have a method for communicating this permanent URL to authors of other sites who want to link to you. For example, http://www.foo.com/current/editorial.html could be the virtual URL that always points to the current editorial, and http://www.foo.com/990207/editorial.html could be the permanent URL pointing to the editorial for February 7, 1999. The permanent URL should be made active as soon as the page goes up, even if most users will be using the virtual URL to access it in the beginning. The reason to activate the eventual archival URL while the page is still current is that other sites that want to link to the page will get the ability to encode the permanent URL in their links and forget about it.

Basically, there are two ways of communicating archival URLs to other authors. You can list the URL in a footer on the page (e.g., "<SMALL>the permanent location of this page will be http://www.foo.com/990207/editorial.html</SMALL>"), or you can use a simple convention for generating archival URLs. Using a convention frees you from having an extra line on the bottom of your pages (which is good) but places an extra burden on people who want to link to you (which is bad and may cost traffic). Only use a naming convention if it is (a) adhered to consistently, and (b) very easy to guess from seeing one or two examples of older pages and their archival URLs. A good example might be the use of the publication date in the URL for a regular column.

Advertising a URL

To integrate your online presence and your real-world activities, all advertising and marketing collateral should come with appropriate URLs pointing to your website.

> *Whenever you reorganize a site or move files around for other reasons, you have to make sure that the old URLs continue to work. Old URLs should be kept functional for at least half a year, and preferably for two years or more.*

Any physical products should also come with URLs for their corresponding product pages engraved or stamped on the back. Making the URL part of the product ensures that users can easily get service without having to search the site. It also makes it easy for customers to recommend your product to new prospects, and it enhances the probability that they will return to your site when it is time to buy a replacement or make another new purchase.

Supporting Old URLs

Whenever you reorganize a site or move files around for other reasons, you have to make sure that the old URLs continue to work. Old URLs should be kept functional for at least half a year, and preferably for two years or more. In fact, people who have changed site structures long ago still report hits on URLs that are more than two years out of date.

Old URLs have a life of their own, living in users' bookmark lists across the world, in printed documents and email messages, and in other websites' outgoing references. Search engines often take half a year to update their databases and flush out old URLs.

The recommended way of dealing with old URLs is to set up a redirect from your server, which will cause anybody who tries to connect to the old URL to get redirected to the new URL instead. The HTTP protocol specifies two different types of redirect messages: code 301 and code 302. A 301 redirect indicates that the page has moved permanently, and this is the preferred message if this is in fact the case. A decent browser will automatically update its bookmark list if it receives a 301 message upon trying to retrieve a bookmarked page. Similarly, search engines should automatically delete the old URL from their databases and replace it with the new one when they get a 301. The 302 code indicates that the page has moved temporarily and should be used only if you want to revert to the original URL at a later date.

Y2K URL

It is common practice to use two characters for the year when referring to a date in a URL. I am guilty of doing so myself. Such URLs may cause Year 2000 problems and should probably be avoided in sites that use extensive amounts of software on the back end.

The above image is the result of going to http://www.us.pc. ibm.com/ibmhome, as specified in an IBM print ad that ran in the November 1997 issue of *BYTE* magazine. Based on the way the visual leveraged the company's redesigned online identity to achieve integration between print and Web, I would guess that this ad was effective at prodding potential customers into going to the URL mentioned in the ad copy. Unfortunately, the web page the ad pointed to had no relation to the product that was promoted in the print advertisement. Most users probably gave up at this point, resolving never to be tricked by another IBM ad again.

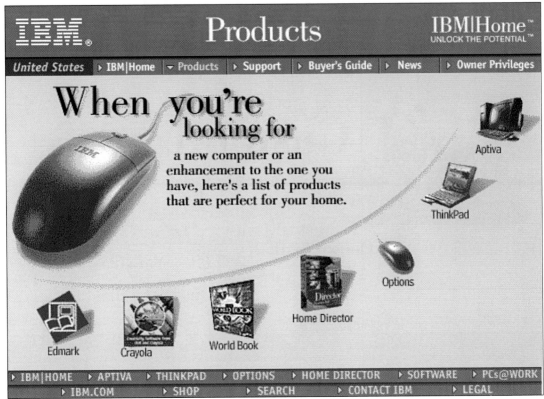

A determined user who is truly interested in the ad's fancy mouse may search onward, guessing that it would be described under the Products button. The above image is the result of clicking on that button. At least we now get to see the mouse, even though there is still no information about it. Clicking on the big mouse photo has no effect: a bad design mistake because many users click on featured objects. Some users may note that the graphic for the "Options" button looks like the large mouse image. In general, "options" is such a general term that it could mean anything, so it's a poor choice for a navigation term.

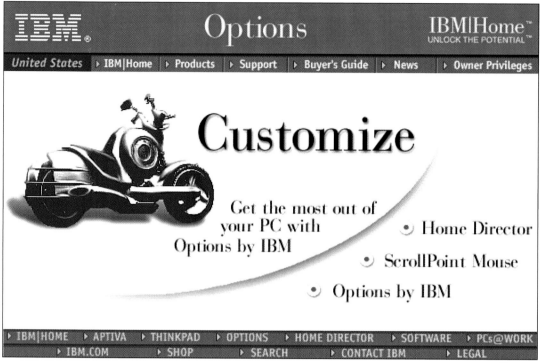

www.us.pc.ibm.com

(Above)   This page has an inconsistent color scheme compared with the previous two, so some users may fear that they had been led astray to an unrelated part of the IBM site. A rushed or superficial user would notice the large bike photo and immediately hit the Back button to return to safe ground. A more careful user would finally notice an option mentioning the mouse and would click on it.

(Facing page)   This page is http://www.us.pc.ibm.com/ibmhome/scrollpoint, which is the URL that should have been printed in the original print ad. A user who typed the actual URL in the ad would not get the desired mouse information until the fourth page. One nice aspect of this page: The center image has an appropriate use of animation to illustrate how one can use the mouse to manipulate a window.

Note, by the way, the inconsistent navigation feedback in this series of screens. In the first two images, the user's current location is indicated by flipping a triangle in the navigation bar and making the button text yellow. In the third image, no feedback is given to let the user know where the current page fits into the navigation space (leaving users stranded like this is the worst option). Finally, in this figure, the current location is indicated by flipping the triangle (a very subtle effect) without changing the color of the button text.

Jakob Nielsen: Designing Web Usability

Power navigation at your fingertip

Scroll Point

Browsing the Web just got EASIER

Presenting the ScrollPoint™ Mouse, with 360° fingertip scrolling that eliminates the hassles of scroll bars.

The ScrollPoint Mouse is a full-function mouse, plus a unique ScrollPoint mini-stick navigator that lets you scroll in <u>any</u> direction without using scroll bars. (Warning: don't try that with a "wheel" mouse).

Scroll web pages, long documents, and spreadsheets without any wasted motion. Find exactly what you want to see - *fast*.

Free yourself from scroll bars using the ScrollPoint mini-stick navigator! Scroll around web pages and large documents with fingertip ease.

Scroll
in any direction without using scroll bars

Browse
web pages and long documents with the touch of your finger

*Zoom**
in and out quickly and easily

Next Page ▷

On sale now at your <u>local computer retailer</u>, or directly from IBM. Call 1-800-426-7235 ext. 5201 or visit our <u>online store</u>.

* Zoom operates in Microsoft Office® 97 compatible applications

IBM and ScrollPoint are trademarks or registered trademarks of International Business machines Corporation. All other company, product and service names may be trademarks or service marks of others.

Download Netscape Now!
This site is best viewed with
Netscape Navigator 3.0

www.us.pc.ibm.com

User-Contributed Content

Some new-media pundits claim that the ability to engage the audience in a discussion with the staff of a website is one of the major benefits of the online medium compared with print and broadcast. Even though user feedback is very valuable for improving the design and direction of a site, I warn against trying to start a dialogue with your users unless you can devote substantial resources to doing so.

A small site that gets a comment or two per day should easily be able to handle a small amount of correspondence with its faithful and eager users. It's quite another matter for larger sites with millions of page views per day and a potential for thousands of messages. The staffs of such large sites could do nothing but correspond with individual users if they were to answer all email.

Instead of encouraging a large amount of two-way communication between your staff and your users, it is possible to invite the users to contribute to discussion groups on the site. User-created content is often quite popular, especially if it is linked off of specific stories or segments of the site. Some sites have general discussion areas, but they tend to degenerate into confusing free-for-alls.

Moderated discussions usually work best of all, but are obviously more expensive to maintain.

Applet Navigation

Whether implemented in Java or other languages, applets are ways of adding advanced functionality to a website by allowing users to interact with a real program and not simply with a bunch of text and links. Applets can be divided into two rough categories:

- Functionality Applets. These are independent mini-applications in their own right, with state transitions and multiple views (e.g., a tabbed dialog). Functionality applets often manipulate "real-world" data that exists separately from the web page, for example, allowing customers to manage their checking accounts, inventory control, and server administration.

(Facing page)   Chat is almost always the worst way to add community to the Web. Even the entertaining visualization of the dialogue in ComicChat cannot disguise the vacuous nature of Internet chat. People simply don't have anything to say. And what they say isn't always appropriate for some audiences.

Jakob Nielsen: Designing Web Usability

WISH YOU WERE HERE
STARRING

 bob

 SpeedFreak

(Image has been edited for content.)

chat.msn.com

- Content Applets. These applets are tightly integrated with the content of a web page. Examples include site navigation controls (an active sitemap or outline flippers to expand and contract a hierarchical listing), active content (a model of an engine that can be rotated, animated, and otherwise manipulated in place), and minor functions (currency converters). Typically, running a content applet has no results other than changing the appearance of the current web pages.

Content applets should be displayed in a browser together with the web page they belong to; functionality applets should display in a new, non–browser window without any web navigation controls.

If functionality applets are displayed in a browser window, then users will invariably confuse applet interactions with browser interactions. Most seriously, users will frequently click the browser's Back button when they want to undo an action in the applet or return to a prior state or view. Of course, going back in the browser takes the user to the previous web page and kills the applet.

The problem is that the hypertext navigation metaphor is too strong as long as the user is within a browser window. Users simply cannot abstract from using the browser's commands to navigate, even when they are "supposed" to navigate within the applet. The only solution is to open the applet in its own window without any browser controls. Once the applet appears in another window, users stop thinking "Web" and start interacting with the applet on its own terms.

In the long term, the solution to this problem is to eliminate browsers and move to a completely integrated navigation system that unifies navigation between system states and information objects, and maintains a single navigation interface for all user actions no matter whether they are on or off the Web. After all, users should not have to care whether they are dealing with HTML or another data type or whether they connect to the Internet, to an intranet, or to local content on their own hard disk.

Functionality applets may include hypertext links back to the Web. Typical examples include help pages and an airline reservation system that enables users to read more about different types of aircraft. Such hypertext links

Double-Click

In principle, applets should follow current user interface standards, so there may unfortunately be cases where double-clicks need to be supported at this time. In the long term, however, double-click must die because it causes novice users great difficulties and because it conflicts with the single-click interaction style of the Web. The main reason for double-click is to allow two operations to be overloaded onto a single-button mouse. Designers of more recent multi-button GUIs have faithfully duplicated a weakness that was made necessary by limitations of an early, single-button GUI. Let's do better in the future. Content applets should be particularly wary of double-click because people will think of them as single-click web content.

should take the user out of the functionality applet and back to the web browser (while the functionality applet remains visible in its separate window).

A functionality applet that spawns its own window(s) should follow traditional GUI design guidelines, whereas a content applet that stays on the page should follow web design guidelines and principles for good information design.

Slow Operations

Applets that communicate back to the server should show a progress indicator while doing so. Progress indicators (often shown as percent-completed bars) are necessary in any user interface for any operation that has slow response times (more than 10 seconds). Applets that connect back to the server will often experience highly variable delays due to the weakness of the Internet. It is thus doubly important for the progress indicator to show the actual progress of the operation and its expected duration. For example, the progress indicator could show the proportion of a database that has been searched or the steps in a sequence that have been completed (while avoiding system-oriented terminology). Such progress indications may require a trickle of info from the server to the applet as it is servicing the request.

Applets also need a cancel button to allow the user to interrupt any slow operations. Interruptability is particularly needed for any server connections.

Conclusion

It is tempting to hope for a technological solution to the problems of site design: a great natural-language search engine that will allow users to find the exact page they want in a single attempt. Or the perfect document management system that will enforce design standards so that all pages have a unified look and feel, no matter what department they are from.

I am hopeful myself that the technology will get better, but the biggest issues in website usability still require manual intervention. A website will not feel like a unified whole unless all the designers and writers agree to actively work for the greater good of one face to the customer.

And no search can find pages that are poorly described or that don't have the information the user is looking for.

Information architecture is getting much lip service, and it is indeed a huge advance that many projects acknowledge that they need to *design* the structure of the navigation space and not simply let it evolve randomly. We still need more sites to base their information architecture on the customers' needs instead of the company's own internal thinking. Once this happens and people become better at writing good links that support navigation and good headlines that work in search engines, there is hope that users will finally be able to navigate the Web.

Today, the dominating web user experience is that *on the average, you are on the wrong page*. Users expect trouble on the Web and they expect to waste time looking at irrelevant pages before they find the one they want. This will hopefully not continue to be true. Once it becomes easier to navigate the best sites, users will revolt against the sites that make them spend most of their time on irrelevant pages.

5 Intranet Design

Designing for an intranet is mostly the same as designing a regular Internet website. The basic human characteristics of users remain the same, and the basic interaction issues in web browsing also remain the same. Thus, the majority of the advice in this book holds just as much for internal sites as it does for external sites.

Even so, intranet design should be treated somewhat differently from Internet design. The most basic reason is that your intranet and your external website are two different information spaces with two different sets of goals, users, and technical constraints. Because the two information spaces are indeed so different, different solutions are necessary to optimize the designs for the two sets of circumstances.

So, on the one hand, intranet designers should follow the basic guidelines for all web design, but on the other hand, they need to take special precautions to ensure that the resulting design is optimized for employee productivity. For external websites "user-centered" design means "customer-centered" design. For intranets, you have to be "employee-centered."

It is best to have different user interface designs for internal and external web information in order to make it easier for employees to understand when they are seeing external information (which is publicly available to the entire world) and when they are seeing internal information (which should be kept confidential). To clarify the distinction between the two information spaces, I recommend using two different visual styles and two different sets of templates for the intranet and the external website. Of course, both styles should comply with the company's overall design language, but they should take this single starting point in two different directions.

The intranet and the external website can, in principle, report into the same management, so long as the department head understands that the two information spaces need to be treated separately. Despite the need for different designs, there is some synergy in having shared management. Many of the same server and authoring technologies can be used to develop the two sites (in fact, a small company may benefit from having the same person serve as webmaster for both internal and external sites). Knowledge about web design and web technology can be more easily shared between staff working on internal and external projects if they are in the same organization. Also, unified management will make it easier to move resources between projects to alleviate the peak workloads that invariably occur in web projects.

Your intranet and your external website are two different information spaces with two different sets of goals, users, and technical constraints.

Differentiating Intranet Design from Internet Design

The most obvious difference between an intranet and the Internet is that your intranet users are your employees, whereas your Internet users are your customers. Internal users will be using the intranet for all the various types of information they need in their worklife, whereas external users go to your site only for a limited range of information related to their dealings with your company.

Because of this difference in user goals, the intranet for any given company typically consists of between 10 and 100 times as many pages as the company's external website. Sun Microsystems, for example, has about 20,000 pages on its external website and about 2 million pages on its intranet. Also, except for extremely small companies, an intranet is typically split across multiple sites, each managed by a different department, whereas an external website hopefully presents a unified face to the customers and feels like a single site.

Intranet designs can assume a less diversified environment than Internet designs. On the open Internet, users have every model of computer ever built, every possible connection speed, and every version of every browser ever shipped. Because a website cannot help the user install an upgrade, it is bad form to require the user to use a specific version of a specific browser just to visit the site. In contrast, it is possible to standardize on platforms and on a single web browser inside a company. Furthermore, it is also usually possible to specify that the browser has to be a specific version or at least that it has to be one of two supported versions. If a user has an outdated browser version, one can require the user to contact a support desk to get upgraded to the supported version. Doing so is acceptable if there is in fact a helpful support staff available to help the user upgrade.

Because of the higher degree of standardization, it is possible to use more advanced browser features in intranet designs a year or more before it becomes feasible to use them on the Internet. It is also often possible to assume that users have certain typefaces installed on their computers, that they have a certain quality of monitor (perhaps everybody has at least a 15-inch screen with 8-bit color), and that they have access to certain standard office applications in a certain version. These assumptions make it possible to design tightly specified interactions that are less cross-platform in nature than is necessary for the Internet.

Most mid-size and large companies will have somebody in the IS department who knows the common system configurations across the company. You should pass the intranet design by this person to make sure that you are in fact compliant with not just the official system standards but also with the reality in various departments. Additionally, it is a good idea for those involved in the intranet project to stay informed about the IS department's plans to upgrade the standard configuration. Often, things that can't currently be done will turn out to be possible after the next upgrade, so you can start planning for them now.

For external websites, I always warn against internally focused designs that expose the company's organization chart to the users. In contrast, intranets usually benefit from an internal focus because the employees do care about their company and because they do know the structure of the organization.

It is also highly appropriate to use major doses of internal terminology and corporate acronyms on an intranet. Doing so on an open site would scare off customers, but employees perform better when more specialized terminology is used; precise language helps them understand exactly what is being discussed. To help new employees, it is always a good idea to provide links to explanations of any such corporate language.

Extranet Design

An extranet is an extension of the intranet designed to incorporate external users with special access permissions to certain subsites. Typically, access may be granted to contractors or consultants who need certain corporate data and product plans, to customers who might enter their own orders or check on the status of pending orders, and to suppliers who want to bid on requests for proposals or monitor inventory levels to plan their own production schedules.

Except for the security needs, extranet design is closer to Internet design than to intranet design. In particular, an extranet should emulate the style of the external website because customers will be switching back and forth between the public site and their private extranet site. The extranet site should have a design twist of some kind to visually emphasize the different status of the two information spaces and to assure extranet users that their information is kept private and not exposed to the public.

The three key differences between extranets and intranets are:

- Lack of control over the extranet users' environment. With a variety of customers and vendors, comes the variety of equipment and software in their companies.
- Slower bandwidth between your server and the extranet users' computers because the Internet is being used as a transport mechanism.
- The fact that your extranet will rarely be the center of the remote users' web experience. Normally, each customer or vendor company will be dealing with many other companies and will be accessing many other extranets besides yours.

Because of these differences, you cannot gain the design benefits of an intranet where you can design for a specific browser, expend bandwidth somewhat freely, and assume that users understand your design because it's the one and only site with company info.

There are also some differences between extranets and traditional websites:

- The extranet will be viewed by people or groups who already have some relationship with the company, so they will know more about you than the average website visitor.
- The extranet will be used for a very specific reason either once (for order tracking, for example) or repeatedly for a few tasks (like tracking multiple orders).
- Extranets have a built-in business model because they serve people with whom you already have a business relationship. Thus, they should not carry advertising banners. They should also not be highly promotional. By the time somebody gets access to an extranet, he or she has already chosen to do business with you. Now, it's time for you to deliver.

Except for the security needs, extranet design is closer to Internet design than to intranet design.

DRIVE(TM) for Your Company

Daily Reporting and Information Via Extranet

Your Company Extranet Home

Shipping

- Searchable tracking information
- Distributor orders
- Submitted problem orders

Inventory and usage

- Daily Inventory
- Latest Month-end inventory report
- Sales Report by month
- Re-Order report

Manufacturing

- Manufacturing order status
- Assembly Instructions
- Submit a new BOM

For comments, suggestions or questions, send mail to Your Account Manager

This is a restricted area with access for Your Company only. Unauthorized access will be denied. Any attempts to gain unauthorized access will be prosecuted to the fullest extent of the law.

www.alom.com

(Above) Demonstration extranet from ALOM Technologies (a fulfillment and back-end manufacturing company). Because extranets almost always contain highly confidential information, prospective new customers cannot access existing extranet pages, and thus, cannot assess this aspect of a company's service.

(Facing page) However, by adding a demonstration area with generic data and a simple password that you can give out freely to all prospects, it is possible to show how the extranet might be used for new projects.

Jakob Nielsen: Designing Web Usability

DRIVE$^{(TM)}$ for Your Company

Daily Reporting and Information Via Extranet

Your Company Extranet Home · **Other shipping reports** · Inventory reports · Manufacturing reports

Other Shipping Reports on DRIVE

- Searchable shipping/tracking reports
- Distributor Orders

SHIPPING AND TRACKING INFORMATION
Shipments on hold

Order #	Recipient Name	Awaiting action from	Remark
56003	Ingram Micro	Test Corp.	Invalid product code
55080	Eric Fromm	Test Corp.	Incomplete shipping address
51007	Fay Cerra	ALOM	Safety stock depleted; building May 20

Tracking				
UPS	FedEx	Airborne	RPS	Roadway

For comments, suggestions or questions, send mail to Your Account Manager

www.alom.com

You do have the option of designing more complex interactions for an extranet than for the Internet because the extranet users will have some motivation to learn your design. After all, they have a business relationship with your company and use your extranet to trade with you or conduct other important business tasks. Also, any given extranet application will typically be used only by a small number of your business partners' employees. For example, your purchasing system will be used by their sales office, and your customer system will be used by their purchasing department. Because most extranet use is specialized in this way, users will have some amount of domain knowledge relative to the topics of those pages they are using.

Improving the Bottom Line Through Employee Productivity

All standard usability engineering methods apply to intranet projects just as well as they apply to Internet projects. In fact, they are even *more* relevant for intranet projects because any improvement in usability is a direct contribution to your company's bottom line.

Some web designers operate on the assumption that you have a license to waste your customers' time. Because you are not paying users, you should aim at keeping them at your site for as long as possible in order to expose them to as many of your pages as possible. I don't subscribe to this theory because I believe that the customers will eventually wise up and notice the contempt with which they are treated. Users will end up going to other sites that have more respect for their time and allow them to get their tasks done more quickly and more efficiently. Nevertheless, the fact remains that whatever time external users spend using your site is on their own dime, not yours.

For public Internet sites, the most important usability attributes are probably learnability and subjective satisfaction. After all, users rarely stay at any given site long enough to become expert users, and their desire to return is often determined mostly by whether they like the site. Web usage is fully discretionary, so users *have* to be kept happy.

(Following pages) **For the 1997 redesign of SunWeb, parallel design was used to produce a large number of alternative styles. These draft designs were put up on the intranet and subjected to a user vote. Normally, majority voting is not a good design method, but there was little reason to believe that the style would have major usability implications. Therefore, we decided to increase the users' level of involvement and their feeling of being part of the design process by letting them vote. The winner was the design with a light purple bar across the top and a light web background pattern.**

Jakob Nielsen: Designing Web Usability

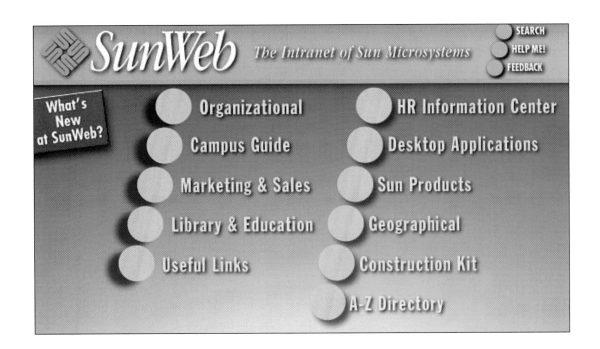

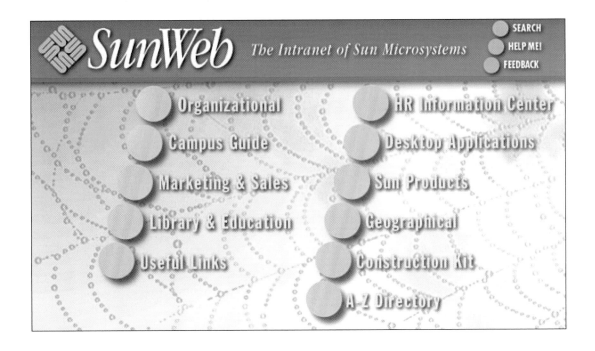

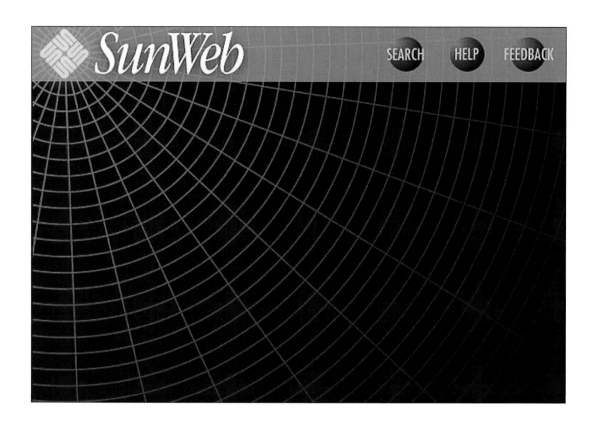

Jakob Nielsen: Designing Web Usability

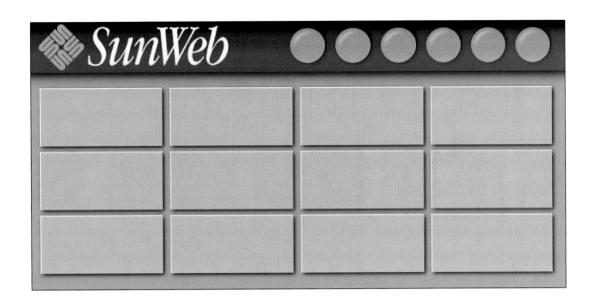

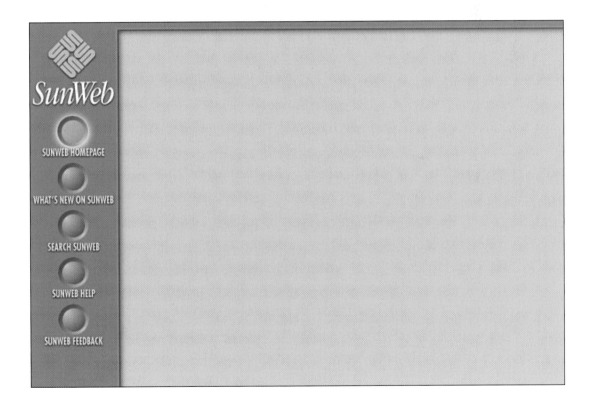

Subjective satisfaction is not as important for intranets as it is for external sites because employees have to use the intranet: It's the only one. Still, it is best to have a pleasing design because the style of the intranet is a prime opportunity for communicating corporate spirit and attitude to all employees. It is important that employees understand that the intranet user interface has been carefully designed because you want to encourage them to comply with your design standards. If people don't like the design, they won't use it for their own pages, and a chaotic and inconsistent intranet will evolve.

For intranet designs, efficiency, memorability, and error reduction become the most important usability attributes. Because employees may use the intranet every day, they soon become experienced users, and the efficiency with which they can navigate the intranet and get their work done will determine their productivity. As more and more job functions move online, the efficiency with which employees can use the intranet becomes a major determinant for the productivity of your corporation.

Because of the productivity impact of intranet design, you can usually justify a rather large investment in usability engineering. As an example, let us consider the value of a redesign that would cut one minute off the average time needed when an employee wants to go to a new part of the intranet. Because employees often spend 10 minutes or more when they try to find new pages on an intranet, an improvement of one minute is a rather modest usability goal and should be achievable with a few days of user tests and redesign attempts.

Let us assume that the company has 1,000 employees and that each employee wants to go to a new part of the intranet once per week. This means that our redesign would save 1,000 employee-minutes per week, or slightly more than two full workdays. Over the period of one year, the redesign would save time corresponding to 42 percent of a full-time worker.

Any usability cost-benefit analysis should value people's time based on their fully loaded cost and not simply on their take-home salary. The fully loaded cost to a company of having a staff member work for an hour is not only that person's hourly rate but also the cost of benefits,

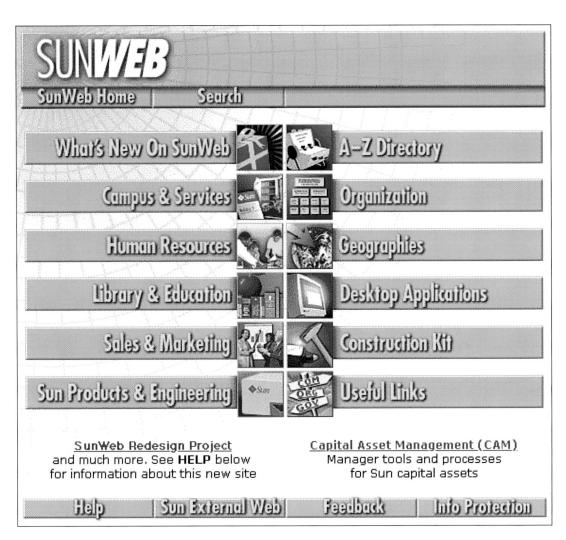

The final home page for the 1997 design of SunWeb. The style was based on the one that won the vote, but the details of the design were evolved through usability testing and iterative design to ensure legibility and easy-to-understand icons. Note how this home page has many more buttons than one would normally recommend for an external home page. On an intranet you can afford to overwhelm novice users in return for better performance for experienced users.

vacation time, facilities costs (office space, heating and cleaning, computers, and so on), and the many other costs associated with having that person employed.

Commonly, the fully loaded cost of an employee is at least twice his or her salary. This is why consultants charge so much more than regular employees. Their billable hours have to cover the many overhead costs that are implicit for your full-time employees. In fact, looking at common consulting rates for the kind of staff you are dealing with is a shortcut for estimating the fully loaded value of your employees' time.

For simplicity, let us assume that the loaded cost of an employee in our sample company is $80,000 per year (corresponding to somewhat less than $40,000 in take-home salary). Realizing the 42 percent savings of $80,000, you come up with $33,600, which would be the annual savings from improving intranet navigation with one minute per new page. My guess is that the usability work necessary to save the $33,600 would cost a few thousand dollars (and certainly less than $10,000), leading to an extremely favorable return on investment.

Intranet Portals: The Corporate Information Infrastructure

Your intranet should be seen as your corporate information infrastructure. It is not simply a way of moving bits around from servers to client computers, and it is not simply a way for employees to browse the cafeteria menu. The intranet can support many real job functions and can become the primary way employees communicate with people in other groups and the way you find the information you need to do your job.

Many large companies have horribly convoluted communications channels, where people sit isolated in their own departments and do not know what happens in other departments. Much effort is duplicated because nobody knows that something has already been done, and other work is wasted because it is directed at a goal different from the one that was really needed (but not communicated). Corporate efficiency goes up dramatically with clearer communication, and the intranet can be the infrastructure for this communication if—and only if—it is designed to make it easy for people to find information when they need it.

The intranet can support top-down communication by making executive decisions, vision statements, and strategy discussions easily available. When a lower-level employee writes a product plan or marketing proposal that builds on a high-level strategy, then he or she can include a hypertext link to the intranet version of the relevant strategy document, thus making it easy for other project participants to familiarize themselves with the strategy as needed. Such links can embed strategic directions much more closely in the organizational fabric than any memo. The intranet allows everybody to connect directly to the original version of the CEO's vision statements in a much more efficient manner than when the CEO makes a presentation to a host of vice presidents who then communicate their understanding of what was said to their staffs, who have to communicate to *their* staffs, and so on.

The main benefit of an intranet as a corporate information infrastructure lies in cross-organizational communication. Because the intranet makes it possible to get information from other organizations without bothering

---

Get Rid of Email

Electronic mail is getting to be an immense productivity sink. In some companies it is a full day's job simply to go through your inbox and reply to that day's email. People have to fight to retain time to do something real outside of email.

Email has become popular because it really does have some benefits in terms of being able to communicate outside the barriers of time and space. It's as fast and easy to send email around the world as it is to send it to your next-door office mate. You can send email whenever you feel like it, 24 hours per day, and it will be ready for the recipient whenever he or she feels like reading it. No more telephone tag.

A small amount of email is good, but a large amount is deadly. One of the main goals of intranets should be to get rid of unnecessary email. This includes most mailing lists and, for sure, any email that goes out to all employees. It is much better to put the information in a properly organized intranet directory and stick a link to it on the home page while it is current.

Information that is stored on the intranet will be indexed and easy to search, and all employees will know how to find it when they need it. In contrast, anything sent out by email shifts the burden of organizing, indexing, and storing the information onto every single employee. What a waste of repeated effort. And because email software is so poor at organizing and retrieving information, employees will often be incapable of managing information they receive by email.

anybody, people are more likely to follow up on hunches and see whether information from other departments might be useful. If the only way to get information is to apply for it in triplicate or to schedule a meeting with at least two-month's notice with an overburdened manager who is not motivated to help you, then you can bet that not much cross-fertilization will happen.

Hypertext links provide great support for finding information within a company. For every employee, I recommend having a personal intranet homepage with links to the department he or she works in, plus links to project pages for all projects he or she works on now or has worked on in the last few years. Much of the knowledge in organizations exists in the form of personal ties and the fact that somebody knows that somebody else might be the person to ask about a certain issue. By going to this latter person's intranet home page, the user will often be able to track down the desired information by following links to the appropriate departments or projects. In addition to the links, personal intranet home pages should have much of the same information as a public home page, including a photo of the person (it is amazing how often you recognize how somebody looks without remembering their name) and an outline of his or her background and experience. This information will help people prepare for meetings and allow for a richer experience in exchanging email and discussion group messages.

All projects should have a home page with links to the personal intranet home pages of everybody working on the project.

Similarly, all projects should have a home page with links to the personal intranet home pages of everybody working on the project. Project pages should obviously also have links to any project plans and reports that are not top secret. Highly sensitive information should preferably also be linked from the page, but with a note stating that access is by prior permission only. Warning people about controlled access prevents them from being disappointed when they try to access information they can't get to. The actual access control can be by password protection or by whatever authentication scheme is available on your corporate network.

Additionally, all organizational units should have a department home page with links to the home pages for the people working in the group (including the boss) as well as links to the appropriate organizational units above and

Jakob Nielsen: Designing Web Usability

below it in the organizational hierarchy. Group and department pages should also have links to the project pages for the major projects they manage. All these cross-reference links serve two purposes: It makes it easier for employees in other departments to find the information they need without knowing the exact way things are structured, and it enhances communications among the department's own employees.

Intranet Maintenance

The many different pages on an intranet need to be maintained. This is as true for individual employee pages as it is for project pages, department pages, and official corporate information pages. If the intranet is allowed to lag behind the actual progress in the projects, people will rapidly stop relying on it, and it will have failed as a corporate information infrastructure. You will be back to the old and inefficient way of communicating by rumor. Intranet maintenance should be seen as a regular part of everybody's job; it's the part of the job that ensures that others can benefit from what you have done.

Intranets typically get very big very fast because all the different departments start putting all their project plans and reports online. Therefore, a high-end search engine is an absolute necessity. Intranet search engines allow people to find things even if they don't have the foggiest idea of who in the organization might be responsible. Just as with the open Internet, hypertext links are great, but not enough. Directories and news are necessary as well.

The Big Three Infrastructure Components: Directory, Search, and News

An intranet portal home page should have three components:

- Most importantly, a directory hierarchy that structures all content on the intranet. This part of an intranet is sometimes called a "Mini-Yahoo." Much can be learned from the design of directory services such as Yahoo and LookSmart because they expend more usability efforts than any intranet project, but it is ultimately necessary to construct the actual topic hierarchy locally because it has to reflect the specific content and concerns of the intranet.

- A search field connecting to a search engine that indexes all pages on the intranet. In contrast to generic Internet searches, an intranet search engine should reflect available knowledge about the relative importance of various areas of the intranet. For example, it could denote official pages with a special icon.
- Current news about the company and employee interests. Typically, the intranet home page can replace traditional employee newsletters and the flood of email announcements and memos that reduce productivity in many companies. Coupling the news listings with an archive and a good search engine ensures that employees can retrieve information as needed and frees them from having to store and manage local copies (tasks that are very expensive considering the poor information management capabilities of current email software).

Intranet Design Standards

Consistency is important for all user interfaces, but it is essential for intranet usability because users will move between a large number of pages every day. If all pages have similar conventions for where to find what information and for how they use links, then your employees will be much more efficient in their intranet use. Navigational structure and presentation is particularly important to standardize in order to speed users on their way and prevent them from getting lost.

Unfortunately, web pages do not become consistent by themselves. Just showing people a great design does not mean that they will emulate it for their own pages. On the contrary, the Web seems to engender a desire to be as drastically different as possible for every page, with disastrous consequences for usability. For intranets to fulfill their potential as a corporate information infrastructure, your company will need to specify a single design standard and promote it heavily with an active evangelism program. Also, of course, any web courses in your company should include instructions in proper use of the intranet design standard.

As mentioned in the beginning of this chapter, the intranet design standard should be different from your external website's design standard. Experience shows that some users have a hard time understanding this distinction, so you should explain it clearly in all presentations and written materials. Do *not* copy design elements from the external site for use on internal pages.

At the minimum, an intranet design standard should specify a navigational structure for your information space. I recommend that every page include an explicit intranet logo to clarify the status of the internal pages as being internal and differentiate them from publicly available information on the Internet. This logo should be made into a link to the main intranet home page. Also, every intranet page should have a search button because search is just as important for intranets as it is for the Web at large.

Additional design elements will depend on the circumstances of each company: Larger companies will need more navigation support than smaller companies. The intranet design standard should also include recommended structure and layout for each of the main types of pages. Typically, this will include personal employee pages, department pages, project pages, and report and memo pages, all of which should be made available as templates. Many companies are likely to have additional types of pages in common use, and conventions and templates for these pages should also be included in the standard.

The standard should obviously be made available on the intranet itself, preferably with a link directly from the main intranet home page. The standard should specify and explain the required, recommended, and optional design elements, giving plenty of examples. Experience shows that users rely more on the examples than on the formal specifications in using such design standards, so be sure to pay detailed attention to all aspects of your examples. Otherwise, you may find thousands of pages that have followed an example from the standard, not just for the point it was supposed to illustrate but also for other, less desirable, attributes.

Guidelines for Standards

To be successful, an interface design standard must

- Be well illustrated with examples because designers go by the examples much more than body text.

It is important to have a central repository for all common page design elements. Not only will they look better if they are designed by skilled web designers, but they will also be consistent with your overall intranet design and will contribute to a professional and coherent look and feel for the various pages. This figure shows the "new" glyph for SunWeb. Note how it ties in well with the other SunWeb design elements shown in this chapter.

- Make sure that the examples fully comply with the standard in all aspects and not just the one they are intended to illustrate (designers may pick up more than one hint from a given example).
- Have extensive and comprehensive checklists as much as possible (designers prefer to scan a list instead of having to read text), for example, a list of all elements that must be on every page or a list of preferred terminology.
- Have a standards expert available both to review new designs in formal standards inspections and for more informal consultations whenever designers are in doubt about the correct interpretation of the standard. (If there is no easy place to turn with questions, then each designer will make up his or her own answer— guaranteed to be different in each case.)
- Be supported by an active evangelism program. It is not enough to wait to be consulted. You must actively seek out projects and visit them to tell them about the standard and to (gently) comment on their designs and how to correct the inevitable deviations.
- Be a living document under the control of a standards manager who updates the standard as new issues emerge.
- Either comply with the most popular other design standards or contain explicit statements highlighting the differences of these other standards.
- Be supported by development tools and templates that make it easier to comply with the standard than to implement a non-standard design.
- Have a good index (if printed) or a good search supplemented with hypertext links to related rules (if online).

Evangelism outreach is especially important for intranet standards because every department will have an inclination to ignore mandates from headquarters. They usually do so with the excuse that "We are different, and the folks at HQ don't know our situation." True, but everybody is special so the total system will be utter chaos if people are allowed to diverge because of special circumstances. Usually, the greater good is indeed greater, and overall usability is increased by consistency. There can be a few cases where circumstances are so special that an inconsistency should be tolerated, but deviations must be limited

 **Human Resources**

| SunWeb Home | Search | What's New | |

> HR > Files > Policies > Sick Leave > Illnesses and Diseases > Colds and Flu >
Other Illnesses Requiring Hospitalization

For the 1997 redesign of SunWeb, we abandoned all hope of controlling the design of the main page content. In principle, an intranet design standard should specify many additional elements, but we restrained ourselves to the header bar. The standard SunWeb header bar consists of three navigation bars. The top bar includes the SunWeb logo, which identifies the page as being an intranet page as opposed to a page from the wild Internet. The logo also doubles as a link back to the SunWeb home page. The top bar also includes a subsite name and icon to identify the part of SunWeb that the user is currently visiting. The name and icon are linked to the subsite's home page.

The middle navigation bar contains a varying set of buttons. The SunWeb Home and Search buttons are mandatory and link to the SunWeb home page and a search page, respectively. The reason for the Home button is that too many people do not understand that the logo is also a link to the home page. The Search button takes the user to the global SunWeb search unless the subsite has a local search, in which case it goes there (and the subsite search page then needs a link to the global SunWeb search page). Depending on the nature of the subsite, optional buttons include a sitemap (not shown) and a What's New button.

Finally, the middle navigation bar may include the page-turning icons shown in this example. Page turning is used to traverse linear content. The third navigation bar is a context indicator and lists the levels of hierarchy between the SunWeb home page and the current page. The names of each of the levels is a hypertext link to that level's home page.

to cases with a very, very good reason (most good reasons are not good enough).

Finally, realize that a standard has its own usability concerns. This is true whether the standard is implemented as an interactive website with hypertext links or whether it is a traditional printed document. Therefore, a proposed design standard should be tested with designers to ensure that they can use it.

Outsourcing Your Intranet Design

If you outsource parts of your intranet design to outside web design shops, then it is important to allow these contractors full access to your intranet design standard and templates. The best way of doing so is to create an extranet where authorized design vendors can log in, read the standard, and download the templates. Alternatively, you can create a printed version of the standard to give to outside designers, but doing so would be considerably less beneficial. The printed version would tend to get out of date, it would typically not have color illustrations, and it would be hard to search (unless you invest the resources to have a professional indexer create a good index).

If you outsource parts of your intranet design to outside web design shops, then it is important to allow these contractors full access to your intranet design standard and templates.

No matter what you do, your contractors will need the ability to download your templates and to upload the resulting pages. This exchange of machine-readable files can be done by email, but works much better if using an extranet. In one of my projects, I used an external graphics artist who had made his primary hard disk available to his clients on an extranet. Throughout the project I was able to look at the latest working versions of all the icons without the delay inherent in shipping email attachments back and forth.

Managing Employees' Web Access

Information systems departments often have the responsibility for supporting the end user's access to the Web. Such support is made considerably easier if it is possible to standardize on a single web browser in a single version. You may be able to negotiate favorable site licensing terms for any software that is not free, and your help desk staff will need less expertise and training. Also, having a single supported browser version makes authoring easier for all contributors of intranet content. All authors will know what version of HTML to use and will be assured that their readers will see pages that look more or less exactly the same as they do on the author's own computer.

Unfortunately, it is not always possible to standardize on a single browser in a single version. Often, the preferred browser version will not be available for all the different platforms in use across a large company, so some users will have to use another browser or at least a different version. Export restrictions may interfere and make it necessary to use different types of encryption and other restricted technology in overseas offices.

Even if all technical or legal concerns can be overcome, there will still be pockets of users with browsers different from the one true version you prefer. Any group that creates content for the external website will have a legitimate reason to download experimental beta releases of new versions long before you feel comfortable having them within your firewall. After all, anybody whose job is to design or plan for the Web needs personal experience with upcoming technology, so they have to run barely breathing software on their own machines and use it to view live web pages off the Internet.

Also, there will always be users with obsolete machines or with oddball devices who want to connect from home or from a handheld PDA while traveling. Many of these users will have no choice but to use a non-standard browser or a several-generations-old version. Therefore, your best standardization plans will still need to incorporate some amount of leniency and ability to allow users to use alternative browsers.

Hardware Standards

In addition to software, there are also benefits from standardizing on some hardware aspects. In particular, if you can guarantee a minimum bandwidth to even the most remote branch office, then you free your intranet designers to create more elaborate and advanced applications and interactions. Also, if you get rid of any tiny monitors and standardize on a reasonably large screen size as the smallest monitors across your company, then intranet designers will have the ability to design larger and probably more useful pages than if they have to be considerate of small-screen users. The added cost for larger monitors will most likely be more than recovered in increased productivity for those employees who used to have substandard screens. You will probably gain an added productivity bonus because a higher-end lowest common denominator allows for better intranet designs that will benefit all employees.

In June 1999, the magazine *PC/Computing* published a usability study of a variety of computer monitors that concluded that 19-inch displays on average provide a 17 percent productivity increase over 17-inch displays. Seeing more information in a single glance speeds up most of the things employees do with computers. The one downside of large displays is that some users have acquired a tendency from working with small displays of maximizing browser windows to take up the full screen. With a big display, this is a very poor strategy; it is much better to use the space for two narrow windows that are placed side-by-side. A single big window will cause text to be displayed on lines that are too long for comfortable reading. Therefore, the IS department should provide employees with a tip to use multiple windows when they are given a big screen. And browser vendors should redefine the meaning of the "maximize" button to make the window a useful size as opposed to full-screen.

Browser Defaults

Ideally, users should adjust their browser preference settings from the defaults to values that make sense for them, given their level of computer expertise and their Internet habits. I do recommend allowing users to change the preference settings from the ones you provide, because different people do have different needs, but I strongly encourage you to provide a good set of default settings to your end users. Unfortunately, much experience shows that many users never adjust the default settings in their web browser. I can't tell you how much email I got with complaints about having "gray pages" before I started specifying a white background color for my own site, even though the gray background was the users' own "fault" for not having changed the (then) browser default color.

Some reflection shows that this user behavior is only to be expected. Remember that the Web is not a way of life for the average user. Most people simply want to click on a few links and read a few pages—they don't want to mess with web technology for its own sake. Browsers have rather intimidating preference dialogs, with many networking, proxy, cookie, and cache settings that are totally obscure to the average user (and which most IS managers would probably prefer that the users didn't touch anyway). As a result, many users never change any of the preference settings, and they will therefore be doomed unless IS helps them. It is an unfortunate fact that browser vendors are motivated to ship default settings that encourage suboptimal user behavior in ways that attract "eyeballs" to the vendor's own services.

The following default preferences should be set:

- The default home page should be set to your intranet home page. John Graham-Cumming from Optimal Networks presented an interesting study regarding home page defaults at the *WWW6* conference (April 1997). In the companies he studied, 13 percent of total Internet bandwidth was consumed by people downloading Netscape's home page every time they started up their browser, because most of the users had not changed their home page settings. Newer browsers may be set for home pages other than Netscape's, but the problem remains the same. The average user does not need to visit a browser vendor's site, because the IS department is supposed to take care of upgrades. Most users will benefit much more from getting regular exposure to their own company's internal home page with its news and announcements for employees.

- Remove any links, bookmarks, buttons, channels, and other distracting references to content provided by the browser vendor or its business partners. You may potentially add a set of links to carefully selected sites of value to your own company, but there is no need for you to waste your employees' time by having the browser prod them to go to sites that are included simply because a content provider paid money to the browser vendor.

- Set up the browser's email preference to use the email program supported by your own IS department. In some companies, it may be reasonable to use the browser vendor's email, but if you recommend another email solution, then it will be very confusing for your users to get zapped into a different email user interface when they click on mailto: links.

- The default web-wide search button should be set to a single search service. If the search on your intranet comes from one of the big Internet search engines, you should set the browser's web search to that engine's public site in order to promote consistency between intranet and Internet searches. If the same search engine is used for internal and external searches, users will be more likely to learn its search syntax and to build effective search skills.

If you do not have an intranet search, or if your intranet search is different from any of the Internet search engines, then simply pick one of the Internet search engines as your default. It is highly recommended to choose a single search engine and stick to it. If you allow a default setting that rotates between search engines, your users will never learn the best way of using any of the engines. Non-technical users typically do not understand that search syntax and search features differ between systems, so they will just randomly combine search ideas picked up from multiple engines, with disastrous results.

Search Engine Defaults

I am not going to recommend an Internet search engine because of the constant change in these engines. Whatever one is best now may very well be surpassed by another engine in a few months. There is a fairly simple way of picking a good search engine, though. Simply select five or so problems that would be typical for people in your industry and phrase short queries (two to three words) for each problem. Enter these queries in each of the leading search engines and inspect the top 10 retrieved links. For each of the top 10 referenced pages, give a rating on a 0–3 scale: 0 for irrelevant, 1 for slightly useful, 2 for somewhat useful, and 3 for very useful (relative to your stated problem). The sum of these 10 ratings across your five problems will be your score for quality of the engine's search performance.

You need to assess four additional attributes beyond sheer search quality:

- Number of seconds from typing in the search engine URL until the first page has finished downloading.
- Prominence of the search type-in field on the search page (some search engines load their pages with junk in an attempt to distract users from their primary task and capture more "eyeball-minutes"—leading to a loss of productivity for your employees).
- Number of seconds from clicking the "search" button until the search result page has finished loading.
- Predictive value of the search results listing (how well does each hit allow you to estimate the quality of the page without following the link).

Combine these five estimates, and you have a good idea of which search engine you should choose. I would probably give 50 percent weight to search quality; 10 percent weight each to initial download time, search field prominence, and search response time; and 20 percent weight to the predictive value of the results listing.

Intranet User Testing

User tests for intranet designs are done in exactly the same way as user tests for external websites. The main rules for user testing remain the same: Get representative users as your test participants and have them perform representative tasks.

User tests for intranet designs are done in exactly the same way as user tests for external websites.

The main difference is that the "representative users" change from being your customers to being your employees. Therefore, the way you recruit test users should change from externally focused methods such as advertising and recruiting agencies to internally focused ones. Fruitful recruiting methods for intranet studies include simply asking people in different departments to recommend participants from their group and posting announcements on the intranet itself or in the cafeteria. Some simpler studies can be done by simply stopping people in the halls and having them comment on a page or an icon, although this method is not recommended for larger studies because it tends to produce a less diversified set of participants.

Often, your human resources department can serve as a source of novice users in the form of new hires who are not yet familiar with your company's structure and special terminology. Even though experienced employees are the main target of intranet design, you should always include some new employees in studies of fundamental issues such as navigation design and home page design. The intranet is one of the main ways for new employees to learn about their new workplace, and you do not want them to be too confused by strange or unfamiliar concepts.

Unfortunately, it is not possible to do competitive testing of intranet designs because other companies' intranets will not be available for use in your tests. As a replacement, you can interview new hires about their experience using intranets in other companies. Even without violating confidentiality agreements, new hires can often provide many ideas about things they liked or didn't like about their previous employer's intranet design and features. You should not press your interviewees to reveal any details that make them uncomfortable or that they feel are trade secrets of their previous employer.

If your company has offices overseas, international usability also becomes an issue, although it is usually less of a concern than it is for external sites because many employees will be accustomed to communicating in the main corporate language. Also, many overseas employees may have visited corporate headquarters and been exposed to the peculiarities of the host country. The two main solutions to international usability for intranets are to create country-specific intranet home pages and to ensure participation of overseas users in the usability studies of the main intranet design. For more information about international usability, see Chapter 7, "International Use: Serving a Global Audience."

Field Studies

Usability can basically be tested in two ways: in the lab or in the field. Both are important, and both are useful for any project, whether intranet-based or external.

For intranet usability, field studies become even more important because many intranet issues relate to supporting specific jobs and employees. To arrive at an intranet

Jakob Nielsen: Designing Web Usability

For the 1997 redesign of SunWeb, we emailed a set of draft icons to randomly selected employees around the world. The users were not told what the icons represented but were instead asked to send return email with their best guess for each icon. The top row shows some of the draft icons we tested, and the bottom row shows the redesigns used in the final SunWeb design.

The leftmost icon was intended to represent "what's new on SunWeb," but most users thought it was a launch icon (except one respondent who said, "It looks, uhm, suggestive."). Clearly, the rocket didn't do the job, so we used a gift-wrapped package in the final design (which also allowed for the nice connotation that the new services are happy enhancements).

The middle icon was supposed to be corporate campus services, but most users thought it represented navigation. Also, users complained that the lettering on the signs was too small and hard to read. As you read in the Content Design chapter, people are getting too metaphorical in their thinking about the Web, so it's hard to have a set of signs simply be signs. Anyway, we used a building to represent "campus" in the final design.

As it turns out, we did need a new navigation icon for the final design because our initial draft, as shown in the rightmost icon, did not work. The home page label for the navigation icon was "useful links," but without the label nobody got the icon right. Not only did the link not look that much like a link, but international users did not necessarily associate the concept of going to useful pages with the concept of a chain. It's always dangerous to use icons that work because of an overlap in words in your own language. Happily, our studies had shown us that we already had a perfect navigation icon at hand, so we modified the discarded campus icon slightly and used it as our final navigation icon. It is rare to be this lucky, though.

design that truly makes these employees productive, you need to understand what they do and design the system to accommodate their task flow. It is not sufficient that the individual design elements are easy to understand if the flow through the pages is awkward, requires many extra steps, or makes it difficult or impossible to do certain things that people need to do.

It is typically much easier to set up a field study in your own company than in other companies, where you are intruding on others' business and have to soothe confidentiality concerns if you want to observe how people work with their proprietary data. Hopefully, you have good contacts within your own company and can easily convince managers that your company's productivity will gain if you can spend a day or two observing their staff.

Intranet field studies essentially work the same way as any other field studies: You go and observe an employee doing his or her job. When conducting an observation, the observer should stay quiet most of the time. The goal is

---

Don't Videotape in the Field

Some usability specialists like to videotape users during field studies, but I warn against doing so for several reasons:

- Most importantly, adding equipment, time, and overhead to a field study will make it even more expensive, which means that you will usually conduct fewer field studies.

- The video camera itself can be intimidating to the user, and also to the user's own customers who come to the user's office for assistance.

- You will invariably spend a lot of time and effort on getting the video equipment set up and adjusted, and you will usually get very low-quality video and audio unless you spend even more time setting up special lighting and special microphones (which intimidate the user even more and make it harder to move the field study to another room if the user suddenly decides to go elsewhere).

- If you are conducting field studies outside your own company (an extranet project, perhaps), it is often difficult to get permission to film on another company's premises without having to involve several levels of security clearance. Because it's hard enough to begin with to get people to welcome snooping usability folks into their office, there is no reason to make it even harder by going up against the security staff.

The one benefit of a videotape is the ability to bring a visual record back to those members of your development team who could not go on the field trip. Most of this benefit can be gained from simple still photos, which are much easier and cheaper to produce. And a traditional snapshot-camera does not intimidate people very much, especially if you use a digital camera and show them the pictures before you leave.

---

to be as unobtrusive as possible so that users will perform their work and use the intranet in the same way they normally do. Every now and then, it may become necessary to interrupt a user to ask for an explanation of some activity that is impossible for the observer to understand, but such questions to the users should be kept to a minimum. It is normally better to make a note of the strange action and see whether you can understand it if it occurs again later. If not, then the user can be questioned during a debriefing session at the end of the visit.

The users will often want to ask you questions about the intranet project, and they may even request help in using some aspects of the design. During the beginning of the visit, you should decline any such requests for assistance, giving the explanation that you are there to observe how the users work when they don't have an expert around. Toward the end of the visit, it may be reasonable to step out of the role and help the users, both to pay them back for participating in the study and to learn more about the things the users want done and why they could not do them themselves.

One advantage of observing users doing their own tasks is that you often find that they use the intranet in unexpected ways that you would (by definition) not have sought to test in a planned laboratory experiment. Such unexpected findings often turn into candidates for the most interesting redesigns that support additional uses of the intranet.

Conclusion

In 1995 and 1996, the perceived wisdom among web pundits was that intranets were much more important than external websites. "Most of the money will be made on intranets," said countless conference speakers. Whether this statement was ever true is doubtful, but the pendulum has swung too far in the opposite direction in recent years.

The extreme over-valuation of Internet stock has led to a focus on external web projects and a distinct underfunding of internal intranet projects. The public Internet is indeed the most important change factor for business these days, but that doesn't mean that internal networks can be neglected. The usability impact of bad intranet designs translates directly to the bottom line of a company because any usability problems mean an immediate loss of employee productivity.

The cost of poor intranet navigation is high: at least 10 million dollars per year in lost employee productivity for a company with 10,000 employees. Worldwide, the cost of bad intranet usability will grow to about $100 billion by the year 2001 unless better navigation systems are built and much stricter internal design standards enforced.

Even huge companies normally run their intranets with a minuscule staff. I know of only one big company that has an active effort to promote a design standard for all pages on the intranet; almost everybody I talk to says that they can't get departments to follow design guidelines. As a result, most intranets are chaotic collections of documents that cannot be navigated. I will be the first to admit that most external websites have usability problems, but at least they usually have some navigation scheme and design standards. These days, it is a rare exception to find an orphan page with no navigation on a big company's website, but such pages are the *rule* on the same companies' intranets.

Considering the cost of lost employee productivity, my recommendations are

- Dedicate substantial staff for intranet content, design, and usability—commensurate with the potential to increase productivity for all white-collar employees by several percent.
- Establish navigation standards for the intranet and a minimal set of design conventions for all intranet content.
- Actively evangelize the need for departments to follow the navigation and design standards.

6 Accessibility for Users with Disabilities

The Americans with Disabilities Act and similar laws and regulations in other countries often mandate equal access to computer systems for users with disabilities. In particular, there will often be a legal obligation to facilitate intranet use by disabled employees who may not be able to do their job if they cannot access their company's internal websites.

Those of us who plan to be around for a few more years also have personal reasons to promote accessibility because as we get older, we will experience more disabilities ourselves. Estimates are that only 14 percent of people who are younger than 65 years have some kind of functional impairment, compared to 50 percent of those older than 65. Fortunately, many of these impairments are either minor or don't interfere much with current web use (for example, reduced hearing). It's definitely worth remembering what awaits us as we get older. Let's design a world that will be good for us.

In addition to regulatory compliance and common human decency, there are hard-nosed business reasons to make web designs accessible for users with disabilities. Often, disabled users become very loyal customers once they find vendors who give them good service and accommodate their special needs. Designing accessible websites is relatively easy, so going after this customer pool, which is going to get bigger and bigger as the population ages, only makes good sense.

The concept of disabilities needs to be defined relatively broadly when it comes to the Web. It is not a matter of whether a person uses a wheelchair; in fact, many wheelchair users need no special considerations at all when browsing the Web. Rather, the question is whether the user has some condition that makes it difficult to use traditional computer input and output devices in the way they were intended. In the U.S. alone, there are more than 30 million people who have some such problem. This is much too large a customer base to ignore.

Making the Web more accessible for users with various disabilities is to a great extent a simple matter of using HTML the way it was intended: to encode *meaning* rather than *appearance*. As long as a page is coded for meaning, it is possible for alternative browsers to present that meaning in ways that are optimized for the abilities of individual users and thus facilitate the use of the Web by disabled users.

Before discussing the difficulties disabled users may have in accessing web information, I want to note that online information provides many benefits compared with printed information. It is easy for people with poor eyesight to increase the font size, and text-to-speech conversion for blind users works much better for online text than for print. Indeed, many disabled users are empowered by computers to perform tasks that would have been difficult for them with traditional technology.

Web Accessibility Initiative

This chapter provides an overview of the issues in accessible web design. For more detail, see the WAI (Web Accessibility Initiative) guidelines released by the World

Wide Web Consortium. These guidelines and much additional information about web accessibility can be found at http://www.w3.org/WAI/.

The WAI standard tells you what *ought* to be done. In practice, it is necessary to prioritize standard-compliance on large sites and plan a staged roll-out of accessibility:

1. The home page and high-traffic pages should be redesigned to follow the most important accessibility rules immediately. The same is true for any pages on the critical path to successful completion of e-commerce purchases or other important transactions.

2. Next, all new pages should follow both high-priority and lower-priority guidelines, and checking for compliance should be made part of the organization's verification procedures for new content.

3. After that, medium-traffic pages should be gradually redesigned to follow the high-priority accessibility rules.

4. As a longer-term goal, high-traffic pages should be redesigned to follow all the accessibility guidelines. Also, new pages should eventually be made to follow all the guidelines. At the same time, the old low-traffic pages may be left alone unless they concern matters of particular interest to users with disabilities.

Assistive Technology

If your company has employees with disabilities or if you have friends or family members with disabilities who want your help getting online, you should check into the possibility of getting them assistive technology to supplement the standard input-output equipment that came with their computer. The assistive technology that will be most helpful for any given user will depend on that person's specific circumstances. Also, the technology changes too quickly for me to make any specific recommendations here. Instead, let me point out that many such solutions are available and that many more are coming to the market all the time. A good source of information about assistive technology is the Trace Center at http://trace.wisc.edu.

In particular, blind users can be helped by screen readers that convert text into speech. For example, many blind users report good results with IBM's Home Page Reader: a talking browser that understands HTML and speaks out web pages. If web browsing will be one of your primary applications you should avoid older screen readers that are not Web-aware and have problems reading poorly designed web pages. If you are only interested in web use, get a speaking browser because the auditory presentation of information can be much improved when the software can assume that it is only dealing with HTML.

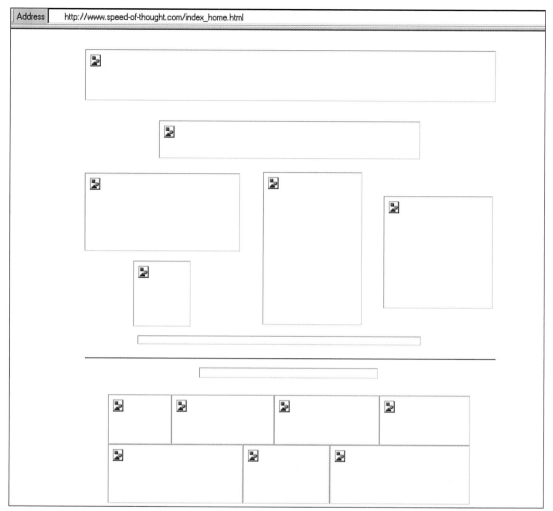

www.speed-of-thought.com

The first release of the website for Bill Gates' book *Business @ the Speed of Thought* was completely inaccessible for users with visual impairments. This image gives an impression of the way the home page would feel to anybody who cannot see the images. After being criticized in *The Los Angeles Times*, the site was redesigned to include proper ALT texts.

The Web Access Symbol from the National Center for Accessible Media. This symbol can be used to signify sites or pages for which an effort has been made to enhance access for disabled users. It can be downloaded in various sizes from http://www.boston.com/wgbh/pages/ncam/symbolwinner.html.

Visual Disabilities

The most serious accessibility problems, given the current state of the Web, relate to blind users and users with other visual disabilities because most web pages are highly visual. For example, it is quite common to see combinations of background and foreground colors that make pages virtually unreadable for colorblind users. At a minimum, you should get feedback on all graphic designs from a red-green colorblind user because that's the most common form of color-deficient sight.

To further enhance accessibility, always ensure high contrast between foreground and background colors, and avoid busy background patterns that interfere with reading. Anything that reduces the legibility of your text is annoying enough for fully sighted users who definitely don't like to be slowed down when they are on the Web, but textured backgrounds or subtle colors may be the last straw that takes your page below the threshold of what a partially sighted user can read at all.

Textual pages are reasonably easy to access for blind or visually impaired users because the text can be fed to a screen reader that will read the text out loud through a synthesizer. Long pages are problematic because it is harder for a blind user to scan for interesting parts than it is for a sighted user. In order to facilitate scanning, it is recommended to emphasize the structure of the page by proper HTML markup: Use <H1> for the highest level heading, <H2> for the main parts of the information within the <H1>, and <H3> and lower levels for even finer divisions of the information. By doing so, the blind user can get an overview of the structure of a page by having the <H1>s and <H2>s read aloud, and can quickly skip an uninteresting section by instructing the screen reader to jump to the next lower-level heading.

In addition to users who are completely blind, there are many users who can see but have reduced eyesight. These users typically need large fonts, which is a standard feature of most web browsers. To support these users, never encode information with absolute font sizes, but use relative sizes instead. For example, when using style sheets, do not set the *font-size* attribute to a specific number of points or pixels; instead, set it to a percentage of the default font size. By doing so, your text will grow or shrink as the user issues "text larger" or "text smaller" commands, and the initial appearance of the page will match the user's preferences.

Full support of users with reduced eyesight would require pages to look equally well at all font sizes. Doing so is often not practical, and it might be acceptable to make pages look slightly worse at huge font sizes as long as the basic page layout will still work. I recommend that you test your pages with the default font set to 10, 12, and 14 points to ensure that the design is optimal for these common font sizes. You should then make additional checks with default fonts of 18 and 24 points to make sure that the design still works at these accessibility-enhancing sizes.

Accessibility for users with visual disabilities is also important for users with perfect eyesight if they are using the Web under conditions that prevent them from using a visual browser. For example, a person using the Web while driving a car would hopefully keep his or her eyes on the road and use an auditory browser.

A final point is to note that search engines are essentially blind users. If you want people to be able to find you, it must be possible for the webcrawlers to navigate your site and for the indexing engines to read your content without seeing the images.

ALT Attributes

In addition to making your text legible, you should also provide an alternative method for "displaying" your images to people who can't see them. The main solution to this problem at this time is to use the ALT attribute. Typical HTML code used to insert an image in a web page might read as follows:

```
<IMG SRC="jakob.jpg" WIDTH="100" HEIGHT="200"
ALT="Photo of Jakob Nielsen">
```

Users who cannot see the photo (whether because they are blind or because they have turned image loading off due to bandwidth concerns) will see or hear the alternative text "Photo of Jakob Nielsen" instead. A sighted user who had turned image loading off could use the text to determine whether it would be worth the wait to request the photo; a visually impaired user would at least know what information was on the page.

[Travelocity Logo]

[TravelReservations]

[Destinations & Interests]

[Points of View]

[TravelMerchandise]

Last Minute Deals

Places To Go, Money To Spend. Don't let the check kill your enthusiasm over summer vacations. We'll give you the scoop on some inexpensive treasures in the latest <u>Spotlight.</u>

(Image)

Go To Great Lengths. This month's <u>contest</u> in Points of View tests your mettle over some of the longest things in the world's best cities. Enter to win a set of cool magnets for your fridge.

<u>**Frequent-Flyer Program Reviews.**</u> Randy Petersen's nonpareil compendium of all the frequent-flyer programs you can imagine.

<u>**Handing Over Hong Kong.**</u> The months before the Union Jack is lowered are turning out to be some of the British colony's most fervent.

(Image)

NWA Cyber Companion Fares

TIP: Call, fax or online--We offer <u>three secure ways</u> to pay for your tickets.

Summer Fare Sale, Take 2. **United States-based airlines again are fighting for your travel dollars in the latest summer fare sale, which lasts through 6/5. <u>Read the details.</u>**

Last Minute Deals are still here and *only* here! Don't miss <u>today's discounts.</u>

"Top News" For Top Travelers. Find out *whassup* around the world daily with <u>Kroll Travel Watch</u> only on Travelocity.

One Eye Open. <u>Our fare-watcher service</u> is your electronic eye on low fares. Ask it to monitor up to five separate round-trips for you.

fare e-mail

Dads 'n' Grads. With Father's Day and graduation ceremonies approaching, PCFlowers and Travelocity offer you <u>two-for-one specials.</u>

Image

Sign Up Today for May! <u>Our newsletter</u> brings you up to date on new site features and promotions.

Flights FYI. Our new <u>Departure / Arrival Information</u> now available from the <u>"Flights"</u> menu in Travel Reservations can give you flight departure and arrival information ... even if you don't know the flight number!

rture/Arriva

Where Are You? If you don't know, or you want to find the shortest distance between two points, use <u>MapIt!</u> from our newest partner, **MapQuest.**

(Image)

www.travelocity.com

(Facing page) The ALT texts make the Travelocity home page understandable even without the images. This figure shows the page as seen by a user who has image loading turned off, but a blind user would also be able to use this page by having a speech synthesizer read each of the ALT texts. Note how lost you feel when encountering an image without an ALT text, here shown as (Image). You have no clue what you might be missing. Also, web browsers currently don't perform a simple thing such as word wrap for ALT texts, so some of the texts are not completely readable in this screenshot, even though they would be read out just fine by a speech synthesizer.

Some accessibility specialists advocate so-called *described images*, where the ALT text is used to verbalize what a sighted user would see. For example, the Web Access Symbol shown earlier in this chapter might be described as "A glowing globe with a keyhole," and the photo of Jakob Nielsen could be described as "Photo of a man in his early 40s with blond hair and glasses, wearing a tasteful red tie." In my opinion, such literal descriptions are fairly useless for web pages unless the user is an art critic. I much prefer utility descriptions that verbalize the *meaning* or role of the image in the dialogue: What is the image intended to communicate and what will happen if it is clicked?

If, for example, the web pages of XYZ Corporation all have the company logo in the upper-left corner, then it would be best to use an ALT text stating "XYZ Corporation." If the logo was linked to the home page, it would also be possible to use ALT="XYZ home page". It would not be a good idea to use ALT="Logo of XYZ Corporation". It would be better to write "XYZ Corporation Logo," putting the most important word first, but it would be even better not to mention that the image is a logo because that information is relatively useless to a person who cannot see the picture.

All imagemaps should be client-side and should use ALT tags for each of the link options so that a user who cannot see the image can have descriptions of the destination read as he or she moves the cursor around. There are still a few browsers that support only server-side imagemaps, but client-side imagemaps are clearly the way to go in the future. Sighted users would also benefit from having ALT tags displayed in the appropriate parts of the picture rectangle if they didn't want to wait for the image file to download, and it is rather obvious that an ALT tag can describe the meaning of the hyperlink destination in much more user-friendly terms than a weird URL. Often, design rules that may have been intended to help users with disabilities end up being of benefit to all users.

Even though the rule of thumb is to provide ALT text for all images, there are in fact some images that are best annotated with the empty string. If an image is purely decorative and has no meaning other than to make the page look better, then there is no reason to slow down blind readers with having to hear an explanation. For example, it is better to use ALT="" than to use ALT="large blue bullet". Meaningless images should have an empty ALT string rather than no ALT text at all because the presence of the empty ALT string is a signal to screen-reading software that it can skip the image. If no ALT text is present in an image tag, most screen readers would feel obliged to inform their user that an unknown image was present because there would be no way of knowing whether the image was important.

An ALT string has to be plain text and cannot contain its own HTML markup, although special characters such as > for > are allowed. ALT texts should be brief and to the point, typically no more than 8 to 10 words.

Some browsers show the ALT text as a tooltip (a small pop-up) when the user rests the cursor over an image. The

ALT texts should obviously be localized to suit the user's language preferences, as shown by this example from The National Palace Museum in Taiwan. Users who prefer English would go to a different version of the text by following the link under the main image. See the next chapter for additional discussion of how to accommodate international users.

most common use of this feature is to name icons, but it can also be used to provide a small amount of supplementary information in the ALT text. For example, the ALT text for a "new" glyph could be ALT="new since May 19" rather than simply ALT="new". It is important to design any such supplementary ALT strings in a way that they still make sense to users who cannot see the image, which is why the text must read "new since May 19" and not "since May 19."

Sometimes, it is desirable to include special information for users who cannot see the images on a page. For example, a page could have a special link to a RealAudio presentation with an extensive description of the images. An interesting trick for doing this is to embed the information as the ALT text for an invisible graphic (that is, a GIF image with all pixels set to be transparent). A user who sees images will "see" the invisible graphic (that is, nothing), whereas users who do not have images will be presented with the ALT text.

ALT text used as tooltip to augment a graphic page element with a small amount of extra information will be of help to both sighted and blind users.

Budgeting for Web-Design Projects NEW

Web & New Media Pricing Guide, by J.P. Frenza and M New since May 19 len Books)
Two valuable components to this book: surveys showing the typical range of salary and hourly fees charged by the different kinds of staff needed for a Web project (from graphic artists to HTML coders) and examples of real projects and their budgets (including comparisons between the projected costs and the actual costs for different line items). The data are from 1996 but are still representative in my experience. The two main deficiencies of the book are that it does not estimate the cost of interaction design and usability engineering (the authors clearly come from an advertising background) and that it does not cover budgeting for site redesigns (as opposed to original designs of new sites). Even so: highly recommended.

Implementation-Oriented Books

HTML Sourcebook: A Complete Guide to HTML 3.2 and HTML Extensions, by Ian S. Graham (John Wiley & Sons)
If you don't know HTML there are a million books to learn from. This one is a favorite of mine. Given the constantly changing nature of the Web, it is particularly nice that this book has its own website with updates. Note, this is the third edition of Graham's book (earlier editions covered earlier versions of HTML and are still useful, though you might as well buy the edition covering HTML 3.2 since this that's the recommended current standard).
How to Write Better HTML With Style Sheets, by Håkon Lie and Bert Bos (Addison Wesley) **Finally Out!**
Cascading style sheets are without a doubt the way to manage presentation design across any medium- or large-size website. For once the blurb on a book cover is right: the authors are indeed "the world authorities" on stylesheets, leading the Web Consortium's stylesheet project, so this is the ultimative reference for HTML stylesheets. Many examples of the slightly obscure features in CSS show how stylesheets can be used to achieve quite refined layouts and page-designs. It would be nice to say that you can pick up CSS from simply looking at examples, but good use actually requires a deeper understanding, as provided by this textbook.

www.useit.com

Auditory Disabilities

Since its beginning, the Web has been a highly visual medium, and we have grown accustomed to these visuals—whether in the form of text or graphics—as the primary method to convey information on the Web. Rare is the situation where sound is necessary for understanding; more often, web sound effects are gratuitous—one of the few benefits of bad design, I guess. The usability of a site almost always stays the same when the sound is turned off, but with the trend toward more multimedia, this is not going to remain the case.

Regardless of whether sound is gratuitous or multimedia requires it, you should design your site with a hearing-impaired audience in mind. In particular, transcripts should be made available of spoken audio clips, and videos should be made available in versions with subtitles. This will benefit users who are not native speakers of the language used in the video as well as users who have computers that are not sound equipped.

Speech Disabilities

At the moment, it does not matter at all whether a web user can speak because all computer input is done with a mouse and a keyboard. It is likely that various forms of voice-activated user interfaces will become more popular in the future for circumstances where keyboard use is awkward or simply to support users who prefer to speak commands rather than type them.

As long as speech input is nothing more than a convenient supplement to keyboard input, it may be acceptable to manage without special support for users who cannot speak. After all, these users can still use the primary interaction methods through the keyboard. For those users who use speech input out of convenience and not necessity, they miss a small convenience, which may be "tough," but no big deal.

It will be much more problematic when we move to interfaces where speech is the primary or only input modality. I expect most chat systems to become speech-based relatively soon because speaking is the natural

Jakob Nielsen: Designing Web Usability

approach to chatting for most people. Any chat system that relies on speech should retain the possibility for non-speaking users to participate in the conversation by typed text. Similarly, Internet telephony products should integrate voice and text to allow each party in the conversation to communicate in the way he or she prefers. In fact, even people who have no problem speaking would sometimes benefit from having a text channel available to supplement a voice conversation: to transmit URLs or other codes, for example, or to give the spelling of their name.

Motor Disabilities

Many users have difficulty with detailed mouse movements, and they may also have problems holding down multiple keyboard keys simultaneously. Most of these issues should be taken care of by improved browser design and should not concern content designers except for the advice not to design imagemaps that require extremely precise mouse positioning. Imagine that you had to move your mouse around with your feet: It simply takes too long to hit a small target.

Client-side imagemaps will work even for users who cannot use a mouse at all: The browser can move through the links under keyboard control.

Any applets that use interaction widgets beyond standard HTML should be implemented to allow mouseless operation. These features are included as standard with both Java and ActiveX, so it is simply a matter of implementing the code correctly according to the official guidelines from Sun Microsystems, Microsoft, and other software tool vendors.

Cognitive Disabilities

In the early years, the Web was accessed only by very intelligent people who were early adopters of advanced technology. But as the Web becomes a more mainstream medium, it will get more average users and also users of below-average intelligence. To accommodate such users, it will be important to increase usability and to make sure that content is comprehensible at a grade-school reading level.

Additionally, it is necessary to support users with cognitive disabilities, who may be highly intelligent but have special concerns. Unfortunately, cognitive disabilities have not been the focus of as much user interface research as physical disabilities, so the guidelines for supporting these users are currently not well established.

People vary in their spatial reasoning skills and in their short-term memory capacity. Programmers and graphic designers tend to get uncommonly high scores on tests of spatial reasoning skills and are therefore good at visualizing the structure of a website. Similarly, young people (including most web designers) certainly have better memories for obscure codes, such as URLs, than older people. It is safe to assume that most users will have significantly greater difficulty navigating a website than its designers have.

Simplified navigation helps *all* users, but it's a required enabler for users at the opposite extreme of the scales. People who have difficulty visualizing the structure of information can be helped if the site designers have produced such a visualization for them in the form of a sitemap. They would be further aided if the browser updated the display of the sitemap with the path of the navigation and the location of the current page.

Search Without Spelling

Many ideas from information retrieval research could be used on the Web to eliminate or at least reduce the need for spelling in search interfaces. Spelling-reduced search will be a major help to dyslexic users but will improve usability for everybody.

Similarity search works by letting the user say "Give me more like *this*" (and possibly also "Give me less like *that*"), while pointing to existing documents. The benefit of similarity is that once you have found one thing of the type you want, you can find more without having to specify any search terms. You do need to find the first instance yourself, but that may be possible to do through navigation.

Parametric search allows users to specify the values of various parameters. For example, a user could search a site for products costing more than $1,000 and having been launched within the last month. If the site supports a sufficiently rich set of parameters, users may be able to narrow their search space without typing a single word. Often, users can specify the desired values by moving sliders so that they won't have to generate any text themselves. Of course, any such sliders should be implemented to allow mouseless operation for users with motor disabilities.

Users with dyslexia may have problems reading long pages and will be helped if the design facilitates scannability by the proper use of headings as noted earlier. Selecting words with high information content as hypertext anchors will help these users, as well as blind users, scan for interesting links (no "click here," please).

Most search user interfaces require the user to type in keywords as search terms. Users with spelling disabilities (and foreign-language users) will obviously often fail to find what they need as long as perfect spellings are required. At the very minimum, search engines should include a spelling checker. One option is to spell check any search terms for which no hits were found and then offer the user the option to click on a list of possible correct spellings to have the search repeated.

Conclusion: Pragmatic Accessibility

I must admit that the websites I personally work on do not always follow every last accessibility guideline. I have a pragmatic approach to usability and sometimes cut corners in order to meet deadlines or satisfy other design trade-offs. There is a great difference between less-than-perfect design and completely reckless design, though. Even if you cannot design a fully accessible site, you have the responsibility to include as many accessibility features as possible. Many are, in fact, quite easy and cheap.

A simple way to check for many accessibility problems is to access your website in a text-only browser such as Lynx. If the site looks good and works well in such a browser, then it will probably be reasonably accessible for many users with disabilities. It is also good to ask a color-blind person to review all graphics or at least to look at them yourself in a grayscale version.

Ultimately, it would be best to conduct usability tests with a range of users with various disabilities, but because there are so many different types of disabilities to accommodate, this is not a very pragmatic piece of advice except for sites that specifically cater to disabled users.

7 International Use: Serving a Global Audience

They don't call it the *World* Wide Web for nothing. A single click can take you to a site on another continent, and a business can attract customers from hundreds of countries without ever going to a Frankfurt trade show where they book you into a hotel two hours down the autobahn.

The unprecedented international exposure afforded by the Web increases the designer's responsibility for ensuring international usability. International use is not a new phenomenon.

Most computer companies have half their sales overseas, and several books have been published with general advice for making user interfaces more international (see "Recommending Readings" at the end of this book).

In 1997 the United States and Canada accounted for around 80 percent of total web user population. By 1999, the proportion of web users in the U.S. and Canada had dropped to 55 percent. It is close to guaranteed that the Web will achieve a 50/50 split between North America and overseas in 2000. The only question is whether this will happen early or late in the year. It is likely that the picture will have been reversed by 2005, with about 80 percent of users overseas and only about 20 percent of users in North America.

Around 2010, I expect the Web to reach a billion users, distributed with about 200 million in North America, 200 million in Europe, 500 million in Asia, and 100 million in the rest of the world. By the way, I hope you caught my use of the word "billion" in the previous sentence as an example of an internationalization issue. In American English, "billion" refers to a thousand million (and that's how I was using the term), but in Continental Europe, it refers to a million million (1,000,000,000,000). Because of this problem, it is recommended to avoid the term "billion" in international user interfaces.

Distribution of web users in 1999.
Source: NUA Internet Surveys.

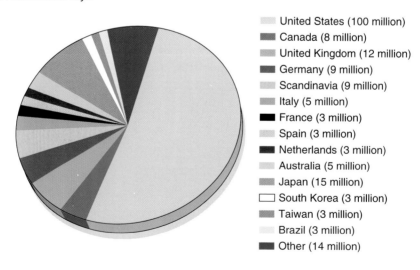

United States (100 million)
Canada (8 million)
United Kingdom (12 million)
Germany (9 million)
Scandinavia (9 million)
Italy (5 million)
France (3 million)
Spain (3 million)
Netherlands (3 million)
Australia (5 million)
Japan (15 million)
South Korea (3 million)
Taiwan (3 million)
Brazil (3 million)
Other (14 million)

This banner ad was clearly not developed with international users in mind. In about half the countries of the world, a light switch that looks like the one in the ad would already *be* on. The fact that there are myriad differences between the many countries and cultures in the world is one of the main reasons for doing international user testing, as discussed later in this chapter. Although many of the worst problems can be avoided by reading a standard guide to software internationalization, smaller things such as the differences between light switches are rarely listed anywhere.

Internationalization Versus Localization

Traditional software development distinguishes between internationalization and localization. *Internationalization* refers to having a single design that can be used worldwide, and *localization* refers to making an adapted version of that design for a specific locale. Internationalization involves the use of simpler language that can be understood by non–native speakers, whereas localization often involves translation. For the Web, it will initially make most sense to internationalize sites rather than localizing them because most countries will not have enough users to make localization worthwhile.

Internationalization is sometimes written I18N because there are 18 letters between the first I and the last N, and because nerds don't like to type. For the same reasons, localization is sometimes referred to as L10N. I don't like these shorthands and will not use them here.

Designing for Internationalization

Most of the internationalization guidelines are the same for the Web as for traditional software design: Don't use icons that give your users the finger (or the foot, or other gestures that are offensive in their culture), don't use visual puns (a picture of a dining table as the icon for a table of numbers), don't use baseball metaphors (except, obviously, at baseball sites), etc., etc. This chapter looks at some of the issues that are specific to the Web.

In two aspects, it is easier to design international user interfaces for the Web than for traditional software. First, HTML has had many international character codes (ü, é, and ø for example) built in from the beginning as part of its heritage of being designed in Geneva, Switzerland.

New **Cool**

Luyendyk wins Indy
NBA - NHL

Rent Net is giving away $10,000
Final Day, Click here!

Tony Awards
Preview

[Search] options

Yellow Pages - People Search - Maps - Classifieds - News - Stock Quotes - Sports Scores

- **Arts and Humanities**
  Architecture, Photography, Literature...

- **Business and Economy** [Xtra!]
  Companies, Investing, Employment...

- **Computers and Internet** [Xtra!]
  Internet, WWW, Software, Multimedia...

- **Education**
  Universities, K-12, College Entrance...

- **Entertainment** [Xtra!]
  Cool Links, Movies, Music, Humor...

- **Government**
  Military, Politics [Xtra!], Law, Taxes...

- **Health** [Xtra!]
  Medicine, Drugs, Diseases, Fitness...

- **News and Media** [Xtra!]
  Current Events, Magazines, TV, Newspapers...

- **Recreation and Sports** [Xtra!]
  Sports, Games, Travel, Autos, Outdoors...

- **Reference**
  Libraries, Dictionaries, Phone Numbers...

- **Regional**
  Countries, Regions, U.S. States...

- **Science**
  CS, Biology, Astronomy, Engineering...

- **Social Science**
  Anthropology, Sociology, Economics...

- **Society and Culture**
  People, Environment, Religion...

My Yahoo! - Yahooligans! for Kids - Beatrice's Web Guide - Yahoo! Internet Life
Weekly Picks - Today's Web Events - **Chat** - Weather Forecasts
Random Yahoo! Link - Yahoo! Shop

National Yahoos Canada - France - Germany - Japan - U.K. & Ireland
Yahoo! Metros Atlanta - Austin - Boston - Chicago - Dallas / Fort Worth - Los Angeles
Get Local Minneapolis / St. Paul - New York - S.F. Bay - Seattle - Washington D.C.

How to Include Your Site - Company Information - Contributors - **Yahoo! to Go**

www.yahoo.com

Localizing Yahoo into German clearly did not require a full redesign of the entire user interface. Even so, the German version is not just a simple word-for-word translation. For example, the sports category has a shortcut to soccer (Fußball) in the German version but not in the American version.

YAHOO! Deutschland

Neu · **Coole Sites** · **EXTRA! Nachrichten** · **Mehr Yahoo**

Heute schon yahoot? **NEU!**

gratis Flash-Upgrade!

Yahoo! auf Ihrer Homepage

[_____] (Suche starten) Optionen

- **Bildung und Ausbildung**
  Hochschulen, Schulen, Sprachen

- **Computer und Internet**
  Internet, WWW, Software, Kommunikation

- **Geistes- und Sozialwissenschaft**
  Philosophie, Geschichte, Sprache

- **Gesellschaft und Kultur** [Ticker!]
  Umwelt, Religion, Cyberkultur

- **Gesundheit und Medizin**
  Medizin, Krankheiten, Ernährung

- **Handel und Wirtschaft** [Ticker!]
  Firmen, Märkte, Beschäftigung

- **Kunst**
  Literatur, Theater, Architektur

- **Nachrichten** [Ticker!]
  Aktuell, Ereignisse, Zeitungen

- **Nachschlagewerke**
  Bibliotheken, Wörterbücher, Postinfos

- **Naturwissenschaft und Technik**
  Ingenieurwesen, Chemie, Bio, Astronomie

- **Sport und Freizeit** [Ticker!]
  Sport, Fußball, Spiele, Kraftfahrzeuge

- **Staat und Politik** [Ticker!]
  Politik, Behörden, Recht

- **Städte und Länder**
  Deutschland, Österreich, Schweiz, Länder

- **Unterhaltung** [Ticker!]
  Fernsehen, Kino, Musik, Zeitschriften

**Yahoo! - Yahoo! UK & Ireland - Yahoo! France - Yahoo! Canada - Yahoo! Japan
My Yahoo! - Yahoo! Internet Life - Yahooligans! - Mehr Yahoos**

Über Yahoo! Deutschland - Hilfe, Fragen und Antworten - Etwas Yahoo! gefällig?
So fügen Sie Ihre Web-Site hinzu - Schreiben für Yahoo! **NEU!**

www.yahoo.com

Second, because web pages do not follow a strict WYSI-WYG layout, but allow for scrolling and the adaptation of each individual page to the user's machine, it becomes easier to translate designs into expansive languages like German. For example, the rule of thumb in GUI design used to be to allow space in dialog boxes for the text to grow by 30 percent in the German translation. On the Web, pages can be translated into other languages, and their layout will automatically adjust to accommodate longer words. The main issue to remember in designing web pages that may be translated is not to overdesign to the extent that the page will not work if some words are pushed around or if some table cells become a little wider.

A new concern for the Web and the Internet relative to traditional software design is that international networking allows real-time interactions. For example, celebrity chat sessions and Olympic or World Cup results can be posted during the events and require user interfaces that allow people from all over the world to participate simultaneously. But be careful. In announcing any real-time event, you cannot simply say that it will happen from 2:30–4:00. First, is it 2:30 in the morning or the afternoon, and, second, what does that translate to in my own time zone anyway? It may be obvious to you that nobody would put on an event at 2:30 in the morning, but if that happens to correspond to 11:30 a.m. in my country, I might not think so.

Any times listed on a web page should—at a minimum—always make it clear whether they are given in the AM/PM system or the 24-hour system (and if AM/PM, then these suffixes should be given) and which time zone they refer to. Time zone abbreviations (e.g, EDT) are not universally understood, so supplement them with an indication of the difference to GMT. Many users don't understand GMT either, so optimal usability would involve translating the time into local times in a few major locations. For example, you could state "The press conference starts 1:00 p.m. in New York (GMT −5), corresponding to 19:00 in Paris and 3:00 the next day in Tokyo."

The date of an event should not be given in a notation like 4/5. Would that be April the fifth or the fourth of May? It is always better to spell out the name of the month in any dates than to use the shorter notation which many of your users will misinterpret.

Other differences include punctuation ($1,000 versus €1.000), the currency symbol or abbreviation, and units of measurement (yards versus meters).

International Inspection

International inspection is a great way of ensuring international usability of a web design. An international inspection simply involves having people from multiple countries look over your design and analyze whether they think it would cause any problems in their country. In contrast to international user testing (discussed at the end of this chapter), international inspection is partly guesswork because it does not involve real users doing real tasks with the system, but at least it results in *educated* guesses.

The inspectors in international inspection should preferably be usability specialists from the various countries in question. Most usability consultants perform usability inspections as part of their everyday practice, and should therefore be experienced in receiving a user interface "in the mail" and returning an evaluation within a few days.

Should Domains End in .com?

The most frequently asked question when I speak overseas is whether it is better to get a domain ending in .com or to use the country's own domain (.uk, .sg., .de, etc.).

Unfortunately, many users have been trained to view ".com" as the standard ending for commercial websites. This is an artifact of the early American dominance on the Web and of the completion algorithm in several popular browsers that automatically add .com to any name. Because of this situation, my advice is

- For a site that uses English and is clearly worldwide in its appeal and user base, get a .com domain.
- For a site that uses any other language, use the appropriate country domain ending.

- For a site that has mainly local appeal, covers mainly local issues, or sells mainly local products, use the country domain, no matter what language is used on the site.

I recommend use of the local domain for local sites because it is misleading to use the "international" domain ending .com for such sites. As e-commerce and other uses of the Web grow around the world, people will start to expect local domains for local sites, and they will not think to type .com for local service. Because the ability to provide great local service is a major selling point, sites are better off by staying with their own country's domain name unless they deliberately want to be seen as disembodied cyberspace entities.

(Facing page) Anybody coming upon this site from a search engine would expect it to be a general travel guide to France. Technically inclined users might inspect the domain name and see that the site lives under .net, which would tend to make it an international or an American site. In fact, this site is based in Australia and is intended to help Australians travel to France. Quite some confusion because of two design flaws: hosting the site under the wrong domain and the lack of a headline such as "French Tourist Bureau in Australia."

In some countries it may be difficult to find usability consultants, but North America, most European countries, and the leading countries in Asia all have plenty of available usability consultants who can be contacted through, for example, postings on the comp.human-factors newsgroup on the Internet or on the jobs bulletin board at major user interface conferences.

If no usability consultants can be found or if you don't have a sufficient budget to hire them, it is also possible to use people without usability expertise from the various countries. Your local sales offices will often serve as a source of available personnel for an international inspection, and you can simply email them the URL of your draft design for comments. When using usability professionals for the international inspection, it will be possible to send out a user interface specification that has not yet reached the design state. Getting international feedback at this early stage increases the likelihood that you will catch any major feature problems while it is still early enough to fix them cheaply. When using non-professional inspectors, it is normally better to have them access a prototype implementation because they may have difficulty in visualizing the user experience from written specs. It is not necessary for all links to work or for all artwork to be final. On the contrary, it is better to have your overseas colleagues inspect an early version of the design.

Typical findings from international inspection might be that inspectors from some countries find that your entire business logic is different from the way customers in their countries want to do business or that certain screens will need to be translated in order to have any hope of success. You want to learn these things before you have invested too much effort on a certain approach to your site and before you have designed it in all details.

Translated and Multilingual Sites

The main way of localizing websites is to translate them into the most commonly used languages. By analyzing your server logs, you can see whether there are any countries with a substantial number of users. Such countries would be candidates for a translation. You cannot rely completely on your logs to guide you in the choice of translations, however, because there are obviously many

Home | Australian Partners | Information | Regions | Activities

Australian Partners
An extensive range of Australian Travel Operators who specialise in travel to France.

Information
Practical information about France and some holiday planning ideas.

Regions
Explore France by region.

Activities
A guide to the extensive range of activities available as you travel around France.

Discover France

France is famous for its beautiful and majestic beaches, scenic mountains, romantic villages, historic museums, fabulous food, exquisite wine, unforgettable rivers, breathtaking gardens and world class sports.

All tastes, styles and budgets are accommodated to make your trip to France a fun, enjoyable, memorable experience, whether in the finest hotels or hostels, by car, bus, boat, train or foot, France has something for everyone.

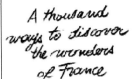

A thousand ways to discover the wonders of France

FOCUS ON FRANCE

Visit Maison de la France's head office in Paris.

HOME | A WEB SITE BY FOX INTERACTIVE MEDIA GROUP

www.franceguide.trav.net

users who are never going to visit your site as long as you don't speak their language. In fact, if your logs tell you that certain countries are *under*-represented relative to their size and number of Internet users, or relative to the size of your customer base in those countries, then you may also have identified a candidate for translation.

In the ideal world, you would translate your entire site into each of the languages important to your audience as well as add local content of interest to your customers in those countries. If you did so, then each translation would essentially be a stand-alone site, and the only special user interface element you would need would be a list of all the other countries on each of the home pages. Most companies do not have the resources for complete translations, however, so they typically apply a hybrid model where some pages are translated and others are left in the original language. This approach results in multilingual sites that do require special interactions to allow users to change between languages.

The site for the 1998 Nagano Olympics made an interesting attempt at overlaying the two official languages on a single home page. Even though the design communicates the excitement and movement of the games, it is ultimately too confusing to intermingle languages the way it was done here. Better to make the users choose and proceed to a unilingual site to their liking.

www.nagano.olympic.org

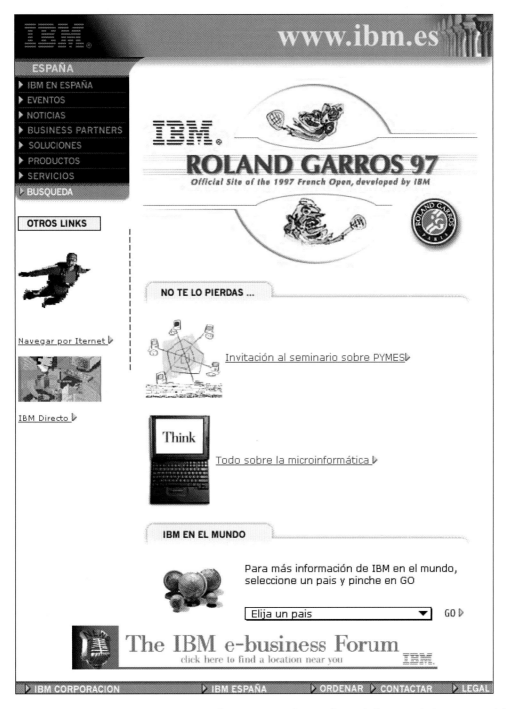

Although much of this site has been translated, the information about the French Open and the e-business Forum apparently have not. It is often sufficient to indicate a link to non-translated information by a simple change of language as done here. An alternative would be to use a small icon to indicate when a link was pointing to material in another language. This would be especially appropriate for hyperlinks that are embedded in text pages where it might seem out of place to suddenly have anchors appear in another language.

Language Choice

In many ways, the ideal international user interface is one that is available in the user's preferred language. Eventually, language choice will be handled by content negotiation between the user's client and your server so that the user will need only specify a list of preferred languages once and for all as a client setting. At the moment, content negotiation is not sufficiently widely used to be a reliable solution, so many websites use manual options for language selection.

The three common ways of implementing language choice are to use a staging page, have a language menu on the home page, or have a language menu on all subsequent pages. My preferred design is to use a staging page only when there is no easy way of deciding on a default language for the home page. After all, if you select a good default language, everybody who prefers that language will

The National Palace Museum in Taiwan employs a staging page where the user has to choose the preferred language before entering the real site. The benefit of this approach is that the language choice is presented clearly, but the price is having to lead all users through this extra page.

Welcome to
The National Palace Museum

Before you enter, please pick your language:

中文 (BIG-5)

English

Crafted by Overseas Connections

be able to use the site without delay. Considering how slow the Web is to navigate, anything that saves users from viewing an extra page is a major usability gain. Another argument in favor of a default language on the home page is that it often allows users who may not prefer that language to still get some idea of what the site is about. They can thus make a more educated decision as to whether they are interested in the site and whether they should wait for a download of the page in their own language.

To choose between a small number of languages, I recommend listing the name of each language as a word, using each language's own name for itself: for example, *English – Français.*

The most frequently used visual symbol for a language is probably a flag, but unfortunately flags represent countries and not languages. The problem with using flags as symbols for language choice is that some languages are spoken in many countries and that some countries have many spoken languages. For example, using an American flag for the English language understandably makes the British upset (they invented the thing, after all) and also irritates Canadians and many others. Of course, using a Canadian flag wouldn't work because many Canadians speak French and/or English.

It is worth some extra effort to ensure that the instructions on the language choice page are properly translated into each of the appropriate languages. If this initial page projects an image of working poorly in one of the languages, then users who prefer that language may never bother entering the site—even if the rest of the site was perfect.

Sommaire

- Le Louvre : palais et musée
- Les travaux du « Grand Louvre »
- Les collections
- Publications et bases de données
- Informations pratiques
- Magazine
- Expositions, Auditorium et Visites-conférences
- Boîte aux lettres

- Français
- English
- Español
- Português
- 日本語

- Questionnaire
- Le serveur

Dernière mise à jour le 12 mai 1997

mistral.culture.fr/louvre

The Louvre Museum defaults to a French home page with clearly listed options to change to English, Spanish, Portuguese, and Japanese. I would have eliminated the option to choose French because that choice is already active and serves only to confuse users and add weight to the interface. Also, it would have been preferable to make the language choice bullets stand out from the other elements on the page. If you assume users cannot read your page, then it does become an unreasonable burden to require them to look through all the choices to find out how they can change language.

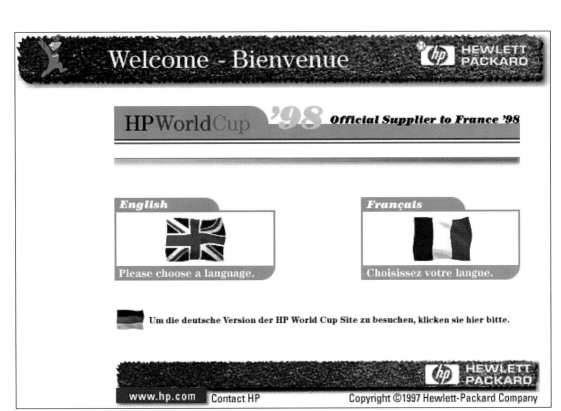

Wonder how German users feel about the relative prominence of the flags on this page? The underlying reason for the design is probably that English and French were the two "official languages" of the World Cup, which is why they are shown more prominently. It might have been better to say so explicitly, with two headings: Official Languages and Other Languages. Finding a link to a German version under the second heading might have made Germans feel good about the additional service they were getting instead of feeling bad about having their flag shown smaller than others.

EUROPA-PARLAMENTET
EUROPÄISCHES PARLAMENT
EYΡΩΠΑΙΚΟ ΚΟΙΝΟΒΟΥΛΙΟ
EUROPEAN PARLIAMENT
PARLAMENTO EUROPEO
PARLEMENT EUROPEEN
PARLAMENTO EUROPEO
EUROPEES PARLEMENT
PARLAMENTO EUROPEU
EUROOPAN PARLAMENTTI
EUROPAPARLAMENTET

EUROPARL
der mehrsprachige Web-Server des Europäischen Parlaments

| Neu ! | Themenverzeichnis |

Fraktionen

Außenbüros des EP

Stand und Entwicklung der Union

- Regierungskonferenz
- Europäisches Parlament und EU-Institutionen...

EP-Dokumente und -Verfahren

- Plenartagungen des Europäischen Parlaments
- Ausschüsse und Delegationen ...

Dokumentation und Studien

- Studien zu Europa
- CERDP - Europäisches Zentrum für parlamentarische Wissenschaft und Dokumentation
- STOA - Scientific and Technical Options Assessment

Presse

- News Report, News Alert
- Info session, EP Aktuell ...

Praktische Informationen

- Termine und Tagesordnungen
- EP-Abgeordnete: Fraktionen, Ausschüsse...

Europa und seine Bürger

- Europäischer Bürgerbeauftragter
- Beziehungen zu den Bürgern
- Auswahlverfahren und Praktika ...

| Ihr Kommentar | unser Angebot im Aufbau | Europa im INTERNET | Webmaster |

© *Europäisches Parlament*
URL: *http://./sg/tree/de/default.htm*

www.europarl.eu.int

The European Parliament employs an unusual menu for language choice. The row of boxes with two-letter abbreviations in the upper right-hand corner of every page leads to all the translated versions that are available for the current page. If a page is not available in a certain language, the code for that language is grayed out. This navigation scheme is certainly not obvious, but makes sense if used consistently.

EUROPARL

Dansk	da
Deutsch	de
Ελληνικά	el
English	en
Español	es
Français	fr
Italiano	it
Nederlands	nl
Português	pt
Suomi	fi
Svenska	sv

EUROPA-PARLAMENTET
EUROPÄISCHES PARLAMENT
ΕΥΡΩΠΑΪΚΟ ΚΟΙΝΟΒΟΥΛΙΟ
EUROPEAN PARLIAMENT
PARLAMENTO EUROPEO
PARLEMENT EUROPEEN
PARLAMENTO EUROPEO
EUROPEES PARLEMENT
PARLAMENTO EUROPEU
EUROOPAN PARLAMENTTI
EUROPAPARLAMENTET

www.europarl.eu.int

The home page for the European Parliament includes a more prominent language choice option than the one used on the interior pages.

Travel Net has one of the most multilingual sites I have seen. The use of the flag of England (as opposed to the United Kingdom) to symbolize the English language may be historically correct, but it's probably not very usable. Also, the word for Portuguese is misspelled. The correct spelling is Português, with a ^. Getting the various accents and special symbols right is mandatory for anybody attempting an international design. I once showed this site in a talk because I wanted to comment on the English flag, but a Portuguese audience member zeroed in on the misspelling of her language. Of course people notice when their language is used incorrectly, and of course it is a design mistake to do so.

Alternative icons playing on national stereotypes are possible and can be fun, but they do risk being offensive (not all Americans wear cowboy hats). Often, it is probably best to avoid icons for languages and simply list them by name.

It is still possible to use flags that match the geographical location of the service and its main intended audience. For example, a tourist site in Continental Europe would use a British flag for English unless it was mostly targeted at American tourists, whereas a tourist site in the Americas would use a U.S. flag unless it was mostly targeted at Europeans. I have seen the English flag (red cross on a white background) used once, but would generally recommend against this seemingly neutral choice because few people outside the U.K. know the regional flags for England, Scotland, and so on.

No matter whether the initial language choice is made on a staging page or on the home page, the user should always be given the option to reconsider the choice of

www.world-travel-net.com

language on subsequent pages. The main reason for doing so is that many users enter a site through lower-level pages and not through the home page (either because they enter from a search engine or because they follow a link from a bookmark or another site). Users may also want to change language in case they are capable of reading multiple languages and they feel that the translation of a certain page into their preferred language is poorly done. In principle, poor translations should obviously be avoided, but in practice users often find that they prefer reading highly technical material in the original language rather than in a translation.

Language choice on lower-level pages could be done with a menu listing all available languages, as was the case with the Europarl site shown earlier. Because users are probably going to change language rarely, it is normally better to simply have an option called something like "change language" and then link it to a page with all the options. Fewer options lead to cleaner and easier-to-use page design, which more than outweighs the need for users to go to an extra page in those exceptional cases where they want to change language.

Multilingual Search

Searching multilingual information spaces presents special usability problems. If all of the information has been replicated in every language, there is no need to search more than one language. In this case, the search interface should know of the user's preferred language and display hits only in that language.

Unfortunately, it is often not possible to translate all documents, so many sites require searches of several languages if the user needs complete coverage of the available information. Currently, multilingual search requires the user to manually enter synonyms of the desired search terms in all the requested languages. This is obviously an unpleasant task, and users often forget to search for translated terms, even if they understand several languages. It would be better to have the computer automatically perform multilingual searches by understanding the meaning of the search terms in several languages. Doing so is easier than the general problem of natural language translation (for example, the term "rock" would not normally refer to music if used

Make Translations Bookmarkable

Different URLs should be used for the different translations of the same content so that users can bookmark the proper entry point and bypass language choice if they visit again.

on a geology site), and there are some research systems that have performed reasonably well on multilingual searches.

Regional Differences

It is often a major problem that websites attract many international customers. "We should all have this problem," you may say, but some companies are not interested in overseas business. Make it clear up front if you are interested in serving only a local market to avoid wasting both parties' time.

Also, many companies have significantly different product offerings across countries, and it can be quite confusing for a customer to access, for example, Mercedes-Benz' main site only to discover that some of the models are not for sale outside Germany. Always make it clear when different models, prices, or procedures apply in different countries.

Some companies use the euphemistically named concept of uplift pricing, which essentially means charging different (usually higher) prices overseas. For a worldwide business tool like the Web it would be preferable to treat all customers the same, no matter where they are located, but it is not always possible to do so. Local regulations may require modified product specs, and existing distributor agreements may dictate pricing.

Regional differences should preferably be dealt with in the same way as language differences. That is, start with a default country and have a list of additional countries on the home page for users to chose from. Furthermore, each page that describes something that differs among countries should have a link to a page allowing users to change to viewing the topic from another country's perspective.

Some websites attempt to hide regional differences by allowing users access only to pages describing the product specs and pricing that are valid for their geography. It is sometimes possible to do so by looking at the user's domain name, so a user browsing the Web from, for example, a machine in the .de domain would be shown only the German prices and not the American ones. My preference is not to prohibit users from seeing specific price lists or other region-specific information. After all, the user

> *Make it clear up front if you are interested in serving only a local market to avoid wasting both parties' time.*

from the .de machine might be working in the headquarters of a German multinational who was in the process of setting up a subsidiary in the U.S. and therefore needed American prices. Also, everybody knows that prices vary around the world, so there is no real need to hide this fact from users.

International User Testing

Because of the myriad issues in international usability, it is recommended to perform international usability testing with users from a few countries in different parts of the world. No guidelines yet published are sufficiently complete to guarantee perfect international usability, so an empirical reality check is always preferred. Luckily, the Web makes international usability testing relatively easy.

As with all user testing, the two fundamentals of international user testing are to involve real users and have them do real tasks without your help. You can usually recruit users through your local branch office in the country in question, but it is important to emphasize that you need users who sit at the keyboard on a day-to-day basis and not necessarily the branch's immediate customer contacts. If you are not explicit about these needs, you may find that unrepresentative test participants have been recruited when you show up for the test. By then it will be too late.

Overcoming the Language Gap

Whether you travel yourself or conduct the test remotely, you will frequently have a language problem. One solution is to recruit users who speak your language, even if they don't speak it fluently. This solution is not perfect, but pragmatically, it is often the easiest to implement. The key issue is to make sure that you don't get unrepresentative users who, for example, have spent years at college in the U.S. and thus have been acclimated to the possible linguistic and cultural peculiarities you hope to smoke out during the test.

Another option is to conduct the test in the local language. This may work if you speak the language reasonably well, but you will often have to rely on an interpreter. Although you can usually understand what is happening on the screen (because you know the product well), the user's comments will normally lose a lot in translation. You should also meet the interpreters beforehand and remind them that they should not help users during the test.

The language problem goes away if you have locals conduct the study. You can either employ a local usability consultant or ask for help from staff from your branch office. You will definitely get the highest quality report from a usability professional, but there are benefits to involving your local staff. Not only is it cheaper, but it brings them into the product-development process, and they will likely learn a great deal from the test itself. As always, additional information is gained from actually carrying out a usability study as opposed to simply reading the report, and this added information might as well benefit people within your company.

When you are not conducting the test yourself, the selection of appropriate test users becomes particularly critical because you will not be able to easily adjust the test on the spot to accommodate users who are different from the ones you expected. To get valid test users, you will have to emphasize the need to recruit representative users in your earliest communications with the people who will be running the test. In spite of the reduced amount of data communicated through a report as opposed to first-hand experience, I have found tests conducted by local representatives to be very useful. Even when the test is conducted by company representatives (normally support engineers or sales staff), there is often much to be learned from reading the reports. As long as it is an infrequent experience for branch office staff to be asked to contribute to product development, they will be highly motivated to do a good job and write thorough test reports.

If the test is conducted by foreign usability consultants, you can assume that they know the basic principles of usability testing, and it will be better in any case to have the foreign experts run the test in the way they are comfortable with. Thus, you should concentrate your discussions with the usability consultants on explaining the goals of the test and the scope of the test tasks. It may be better to have the consultants develop the detailed tasks to make them match the needs of the country in question, even though some billable hours can be saved by providing an initial set of test tasks from your domestic testing. If the test is conducted by staff from your local office, you will have to assume that they know nothing about usability and that your test will be their first user test. Thus, you will have to design the test and the test tasks yourself and then give detailed instructions on how to run the test and what you want to see in the report.

How Many Countries Should You Test?

You must determine how many foreign countries to cover in international usability engineering. The optimal solution is to cover all countries in which you have non-negligible sales (or where you hope to expand). However, doing so is normally unrealistic unless you are a rather small company that exports only to one or two countries. The typical solution is to evaluate international usability in a few countries with at least one country in each of the main areas of the world. If you have the resources to cover only a single foreign country, then you should still do it. There is much to be gained in taking that first step, and the knowledge extends well beyond the benefits you gain in the test country.

Thanking Your Participants

One touchy point regarding international testing is the possibility of offering the user a gift or payment in return for having participated in the study. It is common practice to do so, but both gift-giving and appropriate levels of payment are highly culturally dependent, so you will be wise to discuss these issues in advance with representatives of your local branch office. Consulting advice can also be had from companies that specialize in organizing focus groups or other market research (your advertising agency may have a local contact, or your branch office may have a company on contract already). Sometimes, it is preferable to have a professional recruiting firm find test participants for you, although you will have to be explicit about the user profile you need for your study because these companies often know more about physical products than about testing interactive products.

Methods of Testing

As with normal usability testing, there are several methods available for testing international usability. The five main ways to conduct international user testing include the following:

- Go to the foreign country yourself.
- Run the test remotely.
- Hire a local usability consultant to run the test for you.
- Have staff from your local branch office run the test, even though they are not trained in usability.
- Have the users perform a self-administered test without supervision.

A sixth possibility is open only to the largest companies: Build additional usability groups in your major markets. This last option may be the best, but it is usually beyond the available budget. Also, even if you do have local usability groups in major foreign markets, you may still want to do additional testing in some of the smaller markets—in which case, you face the same problem over again.

Travel Yourself

In many ways, the ideal approach is to go to the country and conduct the test yourself. Visiting local customers in various countries will give you a much stronger impression than simply reading even the most well-written report. There are always many small but important details you will observe if you go there yourself.

Because observing the customers in their own environment is beneficial, I recommend trying to set up the test at the customer's premises, but this is not always possible. You often need special equipment, hard-to-install software, and access to data that is available only on your internal corporate network (which works only inside your branch office). If you do visit customer locations, try to get permission to bring a still camera and take pictures of their installation and working conditions. Pasting several such photos on a wall in your development lab will often be a good way to remind everybody on the project team about the different needs in different countries.

Another possibility that will help you save costs is to conduct informal tests during trips that are planned for other

---

Add a Few Days to Your Stay

If you do travel yourself, be sure to account for jet lag. Conducting users tests is a very intense experience: You have to pay attention to the user, the user interface, the test tasks, your notes, any additional observers, and any video equipment you may be using—all at the same time. Also, the test may be conducted in a foreign language, which can make it even harder to concentrate. I recommend that you spend the first two days after your arrival visiting your branch office and checking equipment and software to make sure that the tests will run smoothly.

purposes because you can pull up a web page any place you can get to a computer. For example, I was at a meeting in Sweden recently while the rest of the team continued working on a new subsite design back in California. Not only could I email back comments on the design as it progressed, but I also took the opportunity to run it by a few locals.

One of the results was that people didn't understand the difference between the Information button and the Documentation button. As shown by the example, international usability testing often reveals problems that could well exist for domestic users also.

Remote User Testing

It is possible to test web designs internationally without ever leaving home, and you can eliminate many travel costs by doing so. Because users can access the Web from almost everywhere, they can access your site without you having to travel to their country to set up the test. One option is to place telephone calls to the users and ask them to think aloud as they navigate your site (or a prototype of the pages) from their own computer. Assuming that you can identify users in other countries who speak your language well enough for a telephone interview, this is a very easy way to conduct international testing.

I prefer using telephone calls instead of a video conference because of the added overhead of getting the user to a video conference facility and getting all the extra technology to work at the same time as you attempt to get the user to access your site on a computer.

The procedure in remote testing is very similar to normal user testing: You ask the users to perform one task at a time while thinking out loud. The tasks can be listed on web pages; the pages should contain one task each so that the user concentrates on that task rather than reading ahead. Each page can end with a link to the next task. An alternative option is to send the users a snail mail letter with test instructions and a set of tasks. If so, the tasks should be contained in a separate envelope and the users should be given instructions not to open this envelope before the test because you don't want them to "practice" how to perform the tasks. Also, the tasks should be clearly numbered ("Task 1," "Task 2," and so on), and the printouts should have line numbers so that any details can be unambiguously referred to over the telephone.

In principle, it should be possible for you to monitor the remote user's access to your web server in real time so that you can track what pages they visit and pull these pages up in your own browser at the same time as the user sees them. I am not aware of software that actually makes it easy to do so at this time. It is much more common to simply ask the user to verbalize exactly what he or she is clicking on the screen and then attempt to duplicate the user's browsing behavior. It is also possible to use utility software, such as NetMeeting, that makes your monitor into a slave of the user's screen. Such utilities are perfect for remote user testing, although they sometimes work better over intranets or local area networks than across the open Internet.

You can communicate with the user over an audio link via telephone or the Internet. Even though international phone calls are expensive, it is currently better to use a good ol' telephone for the audio channel of remote user testing. Internet telephony is currently so primitive that the user will need to spend too much effort on getting the audio channel to work rather than on using your website. Also, many overseas users have such low bandwidth that it would significantly change their experience of using your site if they had to run a phone conversation over the same Internet connection. Considering the expense of overseas calls, it is only reasonable that you cover the cost and place the call, and you should make this clear when contacting the users to set up the test.

The downsides to remote testing are that you have little visual feedback as to what the user is doing and must therefore follow the user's navigation from a purely verbal description. Also, the user must install and operate possibly quite unfamiliar utilities. You also have to be in your office at horrible hours to accommodate the time difference.

Usability Labs for International Testing

Usability tests are sometimes conducted in special usability laboratories. For international usability testing, usability labs will usually not be available because only a handful of the very largest computer companies have usability laboratories in multiple countries. The simplest approach is to do without the usability lab and rely solely on initial impressions, notes, and written reports. Doing so will almost certainly be necessary for tests conducted by your branch office because it will not be reasonable to expect them to set up new equipment and learn how to use it.

There are many difficulties involved in using a usability lab for international user testing, so it is usually best to skip the lab even for tests you conduct yourself. Often, the main usability problems are obvious from simply observing the user, and there is no need to spend time reviewing a videotape anyway. I often prefer using still photographs rather than videotapes; they are much easier to produce, especially with a digital camera that generates image files that can go directly up on your internal site with the rest of your test report. Photographs help make the report more approachable and memorable, especially for those team members who did not get to go.

On the other hand, international user testing has two characteristics that make it desirable to have a formal record of the type generated in a lab. First, the user may be speaking a foreign language, meaning that it may be necessary to replay the tape to understand what the user was saying. Indeed, if it is desired to get a full translation in order to know exactly what happened, then it may be necessary to provide the translator with a recording of the user's comments. Second, financial constraints normally dictate that only a very small number of people actually get to travel to the foreign country to conduct the test. Normally, other team members have the opportunity to sit in on as many or as few tests as they like, thus gaining a good impression of the way users use their product. Because most team members will not have the chance to sit in on the international tests, showing them a video is the next best thing and a much more vivid way of communicating the international user experience than a written report.

If you are having foreign usability consultants conduct the test, they may have their own lab or they may have local contacts that allow them to easily rent a lab. If so, pricing considerations will obviously influence whether you should request use of a lab for the test. If you do decide to pay for a lab, I would advise also paying for the editing of a highlights tape (again, of course, depending on the price). Realistically, you will probably be reluctant to sit and watch many hours of video of users talking in a foreign language when you already have a report that shows the main findings. It is much better to watch selected shorter segments of those events that relate to the key findings. Also, if you are getting a highlights tape, it is normally feasible to have the narrative translated and added as subtitles, meaning that the tape can be shown to management and other members of the project team.

A practical consideration is that the highlights tape may be in a different video format than the one used in your country. The typical problem is PAL (most of Europe) versus NTSC (North America and Japan), but because these two formats are very widely used, you may have a multi-format video player available that can show the tape. If not, it is possible to have a video service bureau convert the tape into your local format for a small fee. It is advisable to use a professional service rather than a cheap corner store because you will want to retain as much of the signal quality as possible to be able to see what is happening on the screen.

If you travel yourself, the two main options besides not using a lab are to rent a local lab or to bring a portable lab. Because usability engineering is becoming an integrated part of the development process in more and more countries, you will often find local companies that have usability labs. These labs may not always be highly sophisticated, but they do have the advantage that somebody else is responsible for the equipment and making sure it works under local conditions. In a few cases, foreign usability labs are advertised for rent in various user interface publications or at major conferences, but it is more common that you have to do the legwork yourself and approach a company that is known (or suspected) to have a lab and ask whether the lab can be rented. In addition to real usability labs, it may also be an option to rent a focus group lab from a market research company, although you will then have to worry about setting up the computer and making sure that the cameras are suited for recording events on the screen. If you are renting a lab in a country with a video format different from your own, then the lab will presumably be equipped to support the local format, and it is probably best to rent its editing equipment if you want to construct the (recommended) highlights video, because you will otherwise have to get a very large pile of tapes converted when you get home.

Self-Administered Tests

Any study that can be completed without the need for an experimenter on hand could be conducted remotely by giving the users the instructions and asking them to report the results. For example, users could be asked to find certain information and report back on whether they were successful and how much time they spent. Users could also be asked to access a draft set of pages and either write free-form comments or rate the design on a set of 1–7 scales for look and feel and ease of navigation. The forms and instructions can be on paper, in email, or on a separate web page.

In general, higher response rates are realized from when the instructions and the report are in the same medium. If the invitation to participate in a study is sent out on paper, for example, it would normally be best to ask users to fill in a paper survey to report on their findings.

If at all possible, the instructions and the response forms should be translated into the users' native language in order to maximize the response rate and reduce the bias inherent if you only get participants with fluency in a foreign language. If you avoid open questions and restrict yourself to rating scales and other closed questions, you can analyze the results without the need for a reverse translation back into your own language. If you follow this approach, it is advisable to be careful in translating the rating scale anchor descriptors: "Very satisfied" or "I felt extremely productive," for example). In order for comparisons to be valid across countries, you need to make sure that people have answered the same questions in the same way. As a matter of fact, cultural differences may preclude any detailed comparisons of subjective ratings between regions of the world. There are many Asian cultures where people would be reluctant to be so impolite as to give too many highly negative ratings, and there are other cultures where hyperbole is discouraged and people might not "fully agree" with a statement that "This design is insanely great." Of course, slang and colloquial terms such as "insanely great" should be avoided in international questionnaires, even if they are not translated.

The best way of getting participants for a self-administered test is to select a random sample of users in the countries you want to study and then send them a personalized request to participate. It is also possible to simply put the test up on the Web and link to it from your main site or from a widely distributed email or paper mailing such as a regular customer newsletter. The downside of this latter approach is that the respondents will be self-selected, which will bias the results toward more experienced and more highly motivated users.

No matter how participants are selected, you will have to determine what countries they are from so that their responses can be coded appropriately. The simplest approach is to study one country at a time by contacting users in a single country for each study. Normally, it is preferred to study many countries at once because that is the only way to gather sufficient data within the available development schedule. In a worldwide study, it is common to include a question asking the users to state their country (or to select their region from a menu). A simple question regarding geographical region should be kept even when you otherwise want to minimize demographic questions in order to reduce the time needed to complete the test or in order to alleviate privacy concerns.

If the study is conducted on the Web or if replies are received by email, you can perform a domain name lookup on the machine from which the user was accessing the Internet. If the domain name ends in .uk, the user is probably British, if the domain name ends in .jp, the user is probably Japanese, and so on. Unfortunately, domain names are not perfectly correlated with users' nationalities. Many overseas users have domains in .com for reasons of cost, access speed, or perceived prestige, or because they work in the local office of a multinational corporation. These users would seem to be Americans if a simple domain name analysis was performed. The recommended way around this problem is to revert to simply asking the

(Facing page) Running an icon intuitiveness test over the Web allows for input from people around the world on an equal basis. In this example, all users were shown the same icons, but it is possible to generate a new page for each user and randomize which icons are shown in order to either make a smaller study or to test multiple alternative designs for each concept. In general, I prefer open-ended intuitiveness studies, but the approach used in this example allows for easier analysis of the data in order to determine whether any region of the world has particular problems with the icons. The descriptions are marked with letters (A, B, and so on) in a slightly too intrusive manner. The letters are useful for users who want to refer to specific functions in the comment box, but because experience shows that few people want to spend the time writing free-form comments, it might have been better to place the letters after the descriptions (where they would have been less prominent) and reduce their font size.

Understandability Test for Web Page Editor Graphics (page 2 of 2)

For each definition in the lower frame, enter the number corresponding to its graphical button. It's ok to leave some blank, and to repeat answers. When you're finished, select the **Submit** button at the very bottom of the frame below. You can give us comments about the graphics (or about anything else) in the **Comments** area, also at the bottom of the frame below.

```
1    2    3    4    5    6    7    8    9    10   11   12   13   14   15   16

     B    B    B    B    B    B    B    B    B    B    B
     17   18   19   20   21   22        23   24   25   26   27   28   29
```

A. Pastes the clipboard contents at the insertion point	B. Cuts the selection and pastes it to the clipboard	C. Centers the paragraph between the margins
D. Redoes the last action that was undone	E. Creates a numbered list	F. Changes color of selection
G. Copies selection to the clipboard	H. Makes the selection appear in typewriter font	I. Undoes the last action
J. Inserts a Java applet at the insertion point	K. Aligns the paragraph to the right margin	L. Makes the selection italic
M. Increases the indent of the paragraph	N. Increases the font size by one unit	O. Saves a document
P. Aligns the paragraph to the left margin	Q. Prints a document	R. Inserts a horizontal line at the insertion point
S. Inserts a link at the insertion point	T. Inserts an image at the insertion point	U. Opens a document
V. Creates a new document	W. Decreases the indent of the paragraph	X. Makes the selection bold
Y. Inserts a table at the insertion point	Z. Creates a bulleted list	AA. Finds the text that you specify
BB. Inserts a target (named anchor) at the insertion point	CC. Decreases the font size by one unit	

Comments:

[Submit]

users if it is important that you have detailed country statistics. Otherwise, the best choice is to acknowledge some weakness in your data and keep in mind that the .com replies are not purely American when interpreting the results. Of course, it can also be the case that a .fr response is from a German who is temporarily working in France, so demographics derived from domain name analysis need to be treated with some caution in any case.

Conclusion

Countries are different, and people from different countries are different. Users from around the world will use your website differently. Those who design their sites solely for a single country will be turning away more than half their customers.

As the Web becomes ever more international, it becomes more and more important to pay attention to international usability. Doing so perfectly is a big job: There are really, really many countries in the world. When faced with the expense of potentially testing and adjusting a site for all the different cultures in the world, it is tempting to just give up.

A key point is: *Don't despair!* Don't over plan. Don't give up because you cannot implement the ideal international usability study the first time. You may have to start with a single country, and you may have to start with self-administered tests. The important thing is to *do* it. There is a huge difference between a site that is designed for domestic users only and a site that knows that the rest of the world exists.

Eventually, international usability will be a requirement for success on the Internet. As usage grows on multiple continents, sites will die if they don't provide high-quality service in multiple countries. For now, though, you will have a big lead over most sites if you do even a small amount of international usability work. But if you never start, you will never learn anything about your international users, and at some point it will be too late. So start now.

8 Future Predictions: The Only Web Constant Is Change

This chapter is mainly about the short-term future of the Web, that is, over the next five years or so. During this time, the Web is expected to increase by a factor of 20, meaning that there will be about 20 times more sites on the Internet (increasing from 10 million sites in 1999 to 200 million sites in 2005). The number of pages will probably increase even more, because existing sites will keep adding pages, even as new sites go online. Thus, I expect the Web to grow from one billion pages in 1999 to 50 billion pages in 2005.

The number of users will increase less rapidly because there are many countries where the infrastructure makes it difficult to get a majority of the population online. From about 200 million web users in the beginning of 2000, I expect we will get about 500 million people online around the year 2005; this number will reach a billion people sometime around the year 2010. Anything beyond a billion will be slow progress. It is completely unprecedented to have a billion users sharing the same computer system, and the Web and the Internet will be dramatically changed when this happens. In fact, they will have to change *before* this can happen because it is currently much too difficult to get on the Internet for most people to even try.

Long-Term Trends

In predicting the effect of technology changes, the two most common mistakes are to over-estimate the short-term changes and to under-estimate the long-term changes. In the short term, many of the changes that

The Internet Is Hard

Using the Internet is like pulling a long chain: If any one link breaks, then the entire venture breaks. Experienced users will know how to look at the various links in the chain, find the broken one, and try various strategies for mending it. Users who don't understand the structure of the chain will simply know that they pulled but didn't get anything. The problem can be the configuration of the user's computer, the modem, busy signals, the ISP, the Internet, the remote website, or unclear or confusing instructions any step of the way. Unless everything works perfectly, the novice user will have little chance of recovery. In the long term, we need to build better self-diagnosing systems that can provide more constructive error messages and easier ways of fixing problems. In the short term, developers of web solutions for novice users will need to polish their user interfaces until every fleck of dust is gone.

A study of home users in Pittsburgh recorded these examples of usability problems for new Internet users:

- "I can't log in." The CAPS LOCK key was active while the user was typing the password. This was not noticed because the characters typed by the user were not echoed.

- "My email freezes." The user had never installed the modem (didn't know that it was part of the computer).

- "Modem won't dial." Someone else was using the telephone.

Each of these problems seems trivial for an experienced user, but it was enough to stop the novice users in the study from getting on the Internet. For more information about the study of Pittsburgh home users, see http://homenet. andrew.cmu.edu/progress.

technology experts would like to see do not happen because of human inertia. It takes a long time to get people to change their ways, and it also takes a long time to send out people in trucks to dig up streets to upgrade the infrastructure.

Many of the more fundamental changes do not happen until a technology has permeated society and has become ubiquitous. For example, the automobile is widely blamed for causing the rise of suburbs, but suburbanization could not happen fully as long as only a small percentage of the population had cars. Back when only a few people had cars, they might use them to go on weekend trips while living in the city, or they might move to suburbs, but they would keep a job in the city. As long as very few people had cars, any important company had to remain in the city, but once most of its employees had cars, it became feasible to move to cheaper and more expansive quarters in the suburbs.

The Internet is a networking technology, and the impact of networks grows by approximately the square of the size of the network because that's the number of possible interconnections and thus the possible uses of the network. This phenomenon is usually called Metcalfe's Law, after Bob Metcalfe, the inventor of Ethernet. As an analogy, let's briefly consider another network technology: the telephone. Having a single telephone in a city is useless, and having two telephones is much more than twice as good: Now you can have a conversation. A typical early use of the telephone was for the owner of a company to have a phone at home and one at the office: Even with only two telephones in town, important conversations could take place.

Some time later, when a hundred company owners had installed telephones in their homes and offices, the use of telephony would have grown by much more than a factor of 100. A city with 200 telephones would see them used not simply for the bosses to call their own offices, but also for the offices to call each other. Because company owners would tend to belong to the same social circles, they might even have started calling each other's houses. Several years later, with many thousands of telephones in the city, use would have expanded to companies exchanging calls with their customers. And finally, once almost everybody had a telephone, the entire structure of business and socialization would change: You don't just call a company, you call a specific person within the company; pizza delivery companies happen; and teenagers spend hours on the phone.

Before turning to the trends for the Web in the next few years, I want to briefly look at some possible long-term implications of the explosion of the Web. Many of these changes may not happen for decades, and some of them may not happen at all. Also, of course, it is likely that unexpected changes will happen and will turn out to have more profound effects than any of my predictions. With these caveats, let's hear it for some possible long-term effects of the Web:

- The real estate market crashes in overpriced areas like Manhattan and Silicon Valley. Because web technology allows people to work from anywhere and collaborate despite distance, nobody wants to pay five times the normal cost of a house to live in a densely populated area. Eighty percent of real estate valuations in the former centers evaporate.
- Big corporations turn into shells of their former selves, mainly concerned with maintaining brand recognition while all real work is done by loosely coupled networks of virtual workgroups spread around the world.
- The only way to react to the incredibly accelerated pace of change enabled by a fully networked economy is to change corporate management from a hierarchical command structure to a networked internal marketplace of ideas, skills, and projects. Annual budgets and vice presidents are out the door. After all, Stalin proved that five-year plans managed by commissars do not work for a country, so why should the same principle be the best way to run a company?
- The concepts of career advancement and full-time employment disappear from the job market, to be replaced by the concepts of skill development and reputation building. The job market itself turns into a minor bump on the economy because less than five percent of the population holds jobs in the traditional sense. The rest of the population consists of independent contractors who are not employed by their

customers. Indeed, they are each others' customers most of the time.

- The Post Office is disbanded because all messages move by email, and all package delivery is done by more flexible private services that are part of the shippers' and the recipients' extranets. The term "going postal" changes meaning to refer to a well-planned winding down of a now-useless industry over a period of a few years while it is still needed to serve legacy customers.

- Government revenues drop to half their current level as a percentage of GNP because most value creation takes place online and is hard to tax (if taxed too harshly, services move to more friendly countries). This turns out not to be a problem, however, because GNP more than doubles due to the efficiency of the network economy.

The Anti-Mac User Interface

The anti-Macintosh user interface is a design concept developed by Don Gentner from Sun Microsystems and myself. All current user interfaces are more or less clones of the human interface guidelines set down for the design of the Macintosh in 1984. These principles were optimized for a small computer (128 K of RAM, tiny black-and-white monitor) with small storage (a floppy disk) and no networking. For example, one of the principles was "perceived stability," which makes perfect sense as long as nothing can change without an explicit command by the user. Another principle was to make all objects and actions visible on the screen: fine as long as your floppy holds no more than a dozen or so files, each of which can get its own icon.

The Internet and modern computers reverse most of the design assumptions of the Mac: We have fast machines, large color screens, huge storage devices (your personal hard disk will hold a terabyte in 10 years), and everything is networked and connected to millions (eventually billions) of other users and sites. Stability and full visibility are definitely out the door. Gentner and I discovered that it made sense to reverse the design principles behind the

Macintosh and do the exact opposite in every case. The resulting design (while currently too expensive to build) is well suited to help users make the most of a fully networked environment. The anti-Mac design principles are

- The central role of language. Users can ask for things by name or by description even if they are not visible.

- A richer internal representation of data objects such as documents and web pages. The system knows a large number of attributes for a large number of objects, including knowledge about the user's history in interacting with the objects.

- A more expressive interface. Detailed visual and auditory representation of objects beyond generic icons that are the same for all documents.

- Expert users. Interaction optimized for people with decades of computer experience who have been online since before they could read.

- Shared control. Proactive computers take responsibility for driving the interface and agents make some actions happen without any human commands.

- The Kingdom of Tonga becomes the world's richest country by hosting many large and successful sites that cater to Asia, North America, and Australia through fiber-optic links.

- New financial instruments and investment options appear. It becomes popular to invest in improving the fecundity of individual rice paddies in developing countries; risk is minimized by new types of micro-derivatives, for example, based on the number of bowls of rice ordered daily by patrons of the *Lai Ching Heen* restaurant in Hong Kong.

- Mutual funds disappear because investors can trade fractional shares and supply micro-venture capital with minimal transaction costs. Portfolios optimized for each individual are constructed by personal expert systems using attribute-rich investment descriptions bought over the Web. One closely monitored attribute will be continuously updated customer satisfaction ratings collected by independent web services every time somebody buys a product or a service. If several people stop liking Diet Coke on the same day, the stock price of the Coca-Cola Company takes a dive.

- Most sales people are replaced by customers who refer other customers to products and services they have liked in return for getting a commission or loyal-customer points. People who give bad recommendations get poor satisfaction ratings and are not listened to in the future.

- Despite having given away all the money he made from software, Bill Gates becomes the world's richest person a second time due to earnings from his online businesses. His entry in *Encarta 2020* refers to him as a media mogul who got his start in the computer business.

- Because of the abundance of portable devices with wireless modems, people will be online at all times and can be reached anywhere. **Privacy becomes precious**. Users will pay extra for screening services that allow them a respite from the world. Being out of touch will be seen as a status symbol.

- Computer companies stop cloning the Macintosh and base user interfaces on information retrieval and other means of managing millions of information objects. The anti-Mac design becomes a reality.

The truth is that we don't know what the long-term effects of a fully-pervasive Web will be. I have listed some relatively dramatic predictions in the hope that they will help you think out of the box with respect to the future of your own business. The only thing that is certain is that it will not be business as usual in the 21st century. The only constant is change.

Most companies are severely deficient when it comes to strategic thinking about the impact of the Internet. Accelerating change means that the future will happen sooner than you think, so you have to start thinking about it now.

Information Appliances

Mobile access will be the third "killer app" for the Internet, after email and web browsing. It will become common to access the Internet from portable devices with wireless modems. Untethered use will lead to many innovative Internet services under the slogan "Anyone, anywhere, anytime: *connected*."

A portable device *has* to be small for users to be willing to carry it around, so web designers have to stop designing for a fixed-size screen. Instead, web pages must scale and work on many different sizes of display. No more will you hear that frequently asked question: "Should I design for 640 or 800 pixels?"

Drawing a Computer

If you want to look at the essence of something, it is a good idea to draw a simple sketch. What are the elements you choose to include in the drawing to cue your viewer into the identity of the object? If we ask people to draw a computer, they will typically draw a big box (the monitor) connected to two smaller boxes (the keyboard and the mouse). Maybe they will also draw a box for the actual computer processing unit, though many people overlook that. These days, the computer is identified with its input-output units and not with its ability to perform calculations. Indeed, the very word "computer" is wrong because the machine is used much more as a *communicator* than a *calculator*.

If we had asked people to draw "a typical computer" back in the 1970s—when I was a student—they would probably have drawn a big monster with several closet-sized cabinets with plenty of spinning magnetic tapes and blinking lights. I mention this to provide historical evidence that it is indeed possible for the concept of "a typical computer" to change quite radically. (As I am predicting that it will again soon.)

If you wanted to draw "a computer," then this is about what you would draw: a box with a keyboard and a mouse. The figure shows a draft of a poster for Xerox PARC drawn by Rich Gold. If anybody deserves to say that they invented the current generation of computing, it is indeed PARC.

computers didn't just come from
outer space. they were invented.

at xerox parc.

www.parc.xerox.com/red/members/richgold/

In the near future, a wide diversity of information appliances will flourish, in particular in the form of small, mobile systems.

WebTV

The Web caused the introduction of one of the first information appliances in the form of WebTV in 1996. Unfortunately, WebTV is not a great product and has been somewhat of a disappointment in terms of sales. Actually, I think WebTV is an insanely great product in terms of usability and design. It truly shows how easy it can be to install a new machine and get on the Internet with a minimum of fuss. But the big downfall of WebTV is the very fact that it uses a television for its monitor.

Televisions have substandard screen quality compared to computers, so it is not pleasant to sit and interact intensely with the Internet on a TV set. I hope we will soon get information appliances that are similar to WebTV in design and usability but that use a flat-panel screen as their display. For intensely engaging interactions like those found on the Web, it is a much more natural usage setting to sit and hold a screen like a magazine than to sit and point a remote control at a TV.

Jakob Nielsen: Designing Web Usability

Home   Hardware   The Opportunity
Feedback   FAQ   In The News
About Qubit   Contents   Search

Qubit represents a monumental shift in the way consumers will share in the information explosion on the Internet. What was once extremely complex becomes very simple. What was once error-plagued becomes solidly reliable. What was once anchored to a table or desktop becomes completely portable. The first information appliance truly worthy of the name.

Qubit delivers the full, rich experience of Internet exploration and electronic communication with none of the technical or convenience barriers associated with personal computers. With Qubit any type of embedded portal or browser like America Online and @Home can be accessed, including Java-based applets, along with basic applications such as e-mail and address/phone books. The Qubit has no moving parts, full multimedia capacity, and a touch-controlled, high-resolution color tablet.

Installation is remarkably simple. Just plug Qubit's cradle into an outlet and a phone or cable jack. Everything else is handled automatically through interaction with a remote service provider/content aggregator. Qubit is already configured to handle all types of Internet connections, including 56K, DSL, and cable modems.

Roughly the size and shape of a magazine, Qubit represents the last word in physical freedom for Internet users at home. Its wireless capability lets people go online anywhere in the house and operate in complete comfort. For applications that require typing, a wireless keyboard with a remote infrared link is provided.

www.qubit.net

Qubit Technology's idea for an information appliance in the form of a portable, flat-panel display.

If you want to design websites that are considerate of WebTV users, then follow these guidelines:

- Do not use large images (more than 544 pixels wide or 376 pixels tall) unless they will still work after WebTV's automatic rescaling to the available viewport area.

- Reserve use of imagemaps for the absolutely necessary cases, such as for selecting a location on a map, and make navigation bars and other sets of buttons into discrete images.

- Do not include text in your images because the characters will be difficult to read on the WebTV screen.

- If you need to include text in an image, use 16-point, bold Verdana or larger (or an equally readable font). The 16-point guideline assumes that the image is small enough that it will not be rescaled.

- Do not use a multi-column layout. The figure shows how poorly the 3-column layout

from news.com works on WebTV (even though it is one of my favorite designs on a regular computer screen).

- If your design requires columns, use at most two columns and make sure that they will work on a 544-pixels-wide screen.

- If you have a page that will scroll more than four WebTV screenfuls, repeat any navigation bar at the bottom of the page.

- Split your information into a rich hypertext space with a larger number of smaller nodes.

- If possible, make each unit small enough to fit on a single WebTV screen to eliminate scrolling. (Interestingly, this advice is a return to the "card shark" model of hypertext as exemplified by HyperCard in 1987. Ultimately, we will need to evolve a new form of HTML to define pop-ups, overlays, partial fades, and the other interaction options that enhance card-based hypertext.)

- Brevity: Write less text.

(Following pages) Screen size really does matter. Viewing websites on a reasonably large monitor allows the user to get a much better overview of the available options than the smaller viewport available on a TV monitor. These screenshots show my own website, useit, on a WebTV with varying preference settings of large to medium to small text fonts. Unless using a high-end television set, the smallest size will not be sufficiently clear to read for most people. Compare with the screenshot from a 20-inch computer monitor: much better impression of the content of the site. Clearly, my site is not well-designed for WebTV users. Even though it is clear and easy to read the individual text elements, you lose sight of the structure of the page.

Jakob Nielsen: Designing Web Usability

useit.com: usable information technology | Search

useit.com: Jakob Nielsen's Website

Permanent Content

Alertbox

Five years' archive of Jakob's bi-weekly column on Web usability, including:
Video and Streaming Media
Metcalfe's Law in Reverse
Web research: Believe the data

News

Current Alertbox (August 22)

Do Interface Standards Stifle Design Creativity? Standards ensure a consistent vocabulary, but don't limit designers' freedom (and responsibility) in deeper design issues. Also:

useit.com: Jakob Nielsen's site (Usable ...

---

useit.com: usable information technology | Search

useit.com: Jakob Nielsen's Website

Permanent Content

Alertbox

Five years' archive of Jakob's bi-weekly column on Web usability, including:
Video and Streaming Media
Metcalfe's Law in Reverse
Web research: Believe the data
Top ten mistakes of Web design
Web project management
Failure of corporate

News

Current Alertbox (August 22)

Do Interface Standards Stifle Design Creativity? Standards ensure a consistent vocabulary, but don't limit designers' freedom (and responsibility) in deeper design issues. Also: Guidelines for writing design standards.

Spotlight

E-commerce case study: trying to buy batteries online: of 45

useit.com: Jakob Nielsen's site (Usable ...

www.useit.com

useit.com: Jakob Nielsen's Website

Permanent Content

Alertbox

Five years' archive of Jakob's bi-weekly column on Web usability, including:
- Video and Streaming Media
- Metcalfe's Law in Reverse
- Web research: Believe the data
- Top ten mistakes of Web design
- Web project management
- Failure of corporate websites
- How people read on the Web

About Jakob Nielsen

News

Current Alertbox (August 22)

Do Interface Standards Stifle Design Creativity? Standards ensure a consistent vocabulary, but don't limit designers' freedom (and responsibility) in deeper design issues. Also: Guidelines for writing design standards.

Spotlight

E-commerce case study: trying to buy batteries online: of 45 sites selling batteries, only 3 carried both the two batteries the user

useit.com: Jakob Nielsen's site (Usable …

www.useit.com

useit.com: Jakob Nielsen's Website

Permanent Content

Alertbox

Five years' archive of Jakob's bi-weekly column on Web usability, including:
- Video and Streaming Media
- Metcalfe's Law in Reverse
- Web research: Believe the data
- Top ten mistakes of Web design
- Web project management
- Failure of corporate websites
- How people read on the Web

About Jakob Nielsen

Biography
Press interviews and public appearances

Papers and essays by Jakob Nielsen, including:
- iCab: browser with structural navigation
- The Anti-Mac
- Usability lab survey
- Guerrilla HCI
- The Death of File Systems
- Study of Web usability in 1994
- Heuristic evaluation and usability inspection
- Learning about Usability

For Hire

Speeches, visioneering, "Rent-a-Guru" consulting, advisory board membership for Internet startups: offered through Nielsen Norman Group

Other Reading

Recommended books about Web design, hypertext, and user interfaces
Recommended hotlist of links about Web design and user interfaces

About This Site

Why this site has almost no graphics
Portal traffic referral statistics

News

Current Alertbox (August 22)

Do Interface Standards Stifle Design Creativity? Standards ensure a consistent vocabulary, but don't limit designers' freedom (and responsibility) in deeper design issues. Also: Guidelines for writing design standards.

Spotlight

E-commerce case study: trying to buy batteries online: of 45 sites selling batteries, only 3 carried both the two batteries the user wanted (or, possibly, it was not possible to find the batteries on the site - there is no difference between these two situations as far as the user is concerned). Lesson 1: Carry a wide product selection and make it easy to navigate. The cheapest site didn't get the order because (a) they had too high shipping fees and (b) one of the products was so weakly described that the customer could not be sure that it was the one needed. Lesson 2: Good and detailed product descriptions are essential when the customer can't see and touch the products before buying. Content design closed the sale.
(August 24)

Usability metric from real life: across six corporate websites, the **measured success rate was only 26%** when prospective job applicants were asked to find a job opening that was suitable for them and apply for it on the site. Is this because HR sub-sites are worse than other parts of big-company sites? I don't think so: most other pages would score as low if users had to complete a **series of steps**. A single mistake any step on the way is enough to doom the user to failure. Mark Hurst and I recently wrote a report on these usability studies as well as an analysis of the usability of e-recruiting that has now been published by "GoodReports". Unfortunately, this is an expensive report series, but at least if you follow the link from my site, you get a discount since

The New York Times
ON THE WEB

NYC
Weather
82° F

FRIDAY, AUGUST 27, 1999 I Site Updated 5:00 PM

QUICK NEWS
PAGE ONE PLUS
International
National/N.Y.
Politics
Business
Technology
Science/Health
Sports
Weather
Opinion
Arts/Living
Automobiles
Books
CareerPath
Diversions
Magazine

Greenspan Says Central Banks Must Focus More on Markets

Federal Reserve Chairman Alan Greenspan said Friday central banks must weigh the prices of stocks and other assets when setting interest rates, signaling a growing focus on the equities market. Go to Article
•ISSUE IN DEPTH: The Federal Reserve
•RELATED ARTICLE: Dow Ends Down More Than 100 Points

Hurricane Dennis Creeping Toward Coast of Bahamas

Hurricane Dennis loomed east of the

(AP)

Defending champion Toms River, N.J., fell to Phenix City, Ala. 3-2 in the U.S. championship game at the Little League World Series on Friday. Go to Article

INTERNATIONAL

The New York Times on the Web

CareerPath
Diversions
Magazine
Real Estate
Travel
ARCHIVES
SITE INDEX
New York Today

The New York Times
ON THE WEB
Learning
Network
FOR STUDENTS,
TEACHERS & PARENTS

Text Version

Archives
Classifieds
Forums
Marketplace
Services
Shortcuts

Help
Site Tour

Toward Coast of Bahamas

Hurricane Dennis loomed east of the Bahamian capital of Nassau on Friday, increasing the peril for Florida and threatening to strike South Carolina as a major storm. Go to Article
•WEB SPECIAL: In the Eye of the Storm

Mir Crew Prepares to Abandon Russia's Aging Space Station

The crew on board Russia's Mir space station got ready to depart the craft on Friday. Mir will be retired if funds are not found to continue operating it. Go to Article
•LIVE COVERAGE: Mir Crew Departs Space Station
(Requires Real G2 Player)

FIND A BOOK AT **BARNES&NOBLE**

Friday. Go to Article

INTERNATIONAL
Hong Kong Eases Out of Recession

NATIONAL
Federal Agencies Opposed Leniency for 16 Militants

SPORTS
Clemens Has Raging Fire in the Belly to Excel

MARKETS   20 Min. Delay
Dow   11090.17 -108.28
Nasdaq 2758.90 15.72

The New York Times on the Web

www.nytimes.com

The New York Times
ON THE WEB

FRIDAY, AUGUST 27, 1999 | Site Updated 5:00 PM

QUICK NEWS
PAGE ONE PLUS
International
National/N.Y.
Politics
Business
Technology
Science/Health
Sports
Weather
Opinion
Arts/Living
Automobiles
Books
CareerPath
Diversions
Magazine
Real Estate
Travel
ARCHIVES
SITE INDEX
New York Today

The New York Times
ON THE WEB
Learning
Network
FOR STUDENTS,
TEACHERS & PARENTS

Text Version

Archives
Classifieds
Forums
Marketplace
Services
Shortcuts

Help
Site Tour

Home Delivery
-Order Online
-Service

Greenspan Says Central Banks Must Focus More on Markets

Federal Reserve Chairman Alan Greenspan said Friday central banks must weigh the prices of stocks and other assets when setting interest rates, signaling a growing focus on the equities market. Go to Article
• ISSUE IN DEPTH: The Federal Reserve
• RELATED ARTICLE: Dow Ends Down More Than 100 Points

Hurricane Dennis Creeping Toward Coast of Bahamas

Hurricane Dennis loomed east of the Bahamian capital of Nassau on Friday, increasing the peril for Florida and threatening to strike South Carolina as a major storm. Go to Article
• WEB SPECIAL: In the Eye of the Storm

Mir Crew Prepares to Abandon Russia's Aging Space Station

The crew on board Russia's Mir space station got ready to depart the craft on Friday. Mir will be retired if funds are not found to continue operating it. Go to Article
• LIVE COVERAGE: Mir Crew Departs Space Station
(Requires Real G2 Player)

(AP)
Defending champion Toms River, N.J., fell to Phenix City, Ala. 3-2 in the U.S. championship game at the Little League World Series on Friday. Go to Article

INTERNATIONAL
Hong Kong Eases Out of Recession

NATIONAL
Federal Agencies Opposed Leniency for 16 Militants

SPORTS
Clemens Has Raging Fire in the Belly to Excel

TRIVIA
QUIZ
▶ GO

MARKETS		20 Min. Delay
Dow	11090.17	-
		108.28▼
Nasdaq	2758.89	-15.73▼
S&P 500	1347.27	-14.74▼
Russell 2000	432.45	-3.57▼
NYSE	625.71	-11.69▼

www.nytimes.com

With a small screen as used on WebTV, users have to scroll more to take in the main news on *The New York Times* home page. But the story summaries are still short enough that the page works reasonably well on this small screen.

Death of Web Browsers

A key element of future computers will be to **get rid of web browsers** as a separate application category. There are two reasons you will want to eliminate the web browser from your system in a few years:

- Fundamentally, it is pretty silly to have a special browser for certain information objects simply because they happen to come from a specific storage location. There is no reason to treat information differently because it comes from the Internet instead of from your hard disk. Just imagine if we treated information differently depending on whether it was stored on a floppy disk (the transport protocol for "Sneakernet") or on your hard disk. You try to read a file but get an error message: Sorry, this file is stored on a floppy disk so you need to start your floppy browser before you can read it!

- Web browsers confuse two feature sets that can be delivered more cleanly if they are separated. Web browsers handle both the presentation of information objects *and* the navigation between information objects. Actually, current web browsers do a lousy job of navigation support, but they do try.

A better design will unify the treatment of all information objects, no matter where they live. Local hard disks, local area networks, corporate intranets, and the Internet will all have the same user interface, and users will move seamlessly between various storage locations. Future operating systems will provide a framework for presentation applets that are optimized for each of the various data types accessed by the user. HTML will obviously be one such data type, and an HTML viewer will definitely be available.

Navigation will become a universal support mechanism that cuts across the presentation software and also across each individual user's multiple machines. For example, a history mechanism will allow users to return to previously seen information objects no matter what presentation software was used to display them and no matter whether the information was accessed from a mobile device, at the office computer, or at the home information appliance.

The history list, bookmark list, and so on, will include Internet objects, email messages, and corporate documents intermixed according to the individual user's information access behavior (each person has a single consciousness leading to a linear user experience that can structure the history of information use). There will also be some kind of universal search feature to allow users to find objects by content, although it currently is not clear how to extend the search from local data to Internet data (most likely, the search will be scoped with billion-object searches reserved for exceptional cases).

Slowly Increasing Bandwidth

For the past 15 years, the speed with which a typical user could access the Internet has increased by about 50 percent per year. Despite the many hopeful predictions for faster growth in Internet bandwidth, I see no reason why this long-term trend should not continue to hold.

Average bandwidth increases slowly for three reasons:

- Telecommunications companies are conservative. They need to dig up streets and install equipment in hundreds of thousands of central offices so they think twice (or thrice) before investing the necessary billions of dollars. Even after they invest, it takes time to update their sprawling physical plant.

- Users are reluctant to spend much money on bandwidth. If you buy twice as fast a computer, your software runs twice as fast; if you buy twice as large a hard disk, you can store twice as many files. But if you buy twice as fast a modem, you don't download web pages twice as fast: The speed of the Internet is a function of both the individual user's connectivity and of the infrastructure. You don't get the full benefits of your own bandwidth upgrades immediately—only gradually as the Internet and the host servers improve.

- The user base is getting broader all the time as mainstream users get online. These new users are more likely to be low-end users than high-end users (all the geeks have been online for years), so the average shifts ever lower.

Of course, there are many technologies to deliver faster bandwidth, and Bell Labs has already demonstrated the capability to shoot a terabit per second down an optical fiber. Unfortunately, these technologies will not deliver huge bandwidth increases to the masses anytime soon. DSL and other technologies will give individual users the speed of a T1 line and better, but this will not happen in large numbers until approximately 2003.

There will always be a few super-users who have advanced equipment that runs really, really fast. Here, I am talking about the more normal high-end user who is willing to pay a premium but still wants well-tested equipment that can be bought in a regular shop.

The vast masses are low-end users who will lag two to three years behind the high-end users. Bandwidth is one of the two most important elements in computing these days (together with screen quality), because computational speeds are almost always more than enough for non-engineering tasks. Unfortunately, I can argue as much as I want. Most users still save on bandwidth and prefer a $20/month ISP over a $30/month one with better service.

Web design needs to cater to the masses. Only rarely can a site be successful if it is aimed at the most advanced 10 percent of users. Thus, even though high-end users may have ISDN or better, web design must aim at optimal usability over a 56 Kbps modem. International users have even slower connections, and response times across the oceans will likely get *worse* over the next few years. All the cable ships are already out there laying cable as fast as they can; unfortunately, this is not fast enough for the growth in Internet use across the world.

For the short-term, the Web will be dominated by users with connections so slow that any reasonable web page will take much longer to download than the response time limits indicated by human factors research.

For the short-term, the Web will be dominated by users with connections so slow that any reasonable web page will take much longer to download than the response time limits indicated by human factors research. Thus, the dominant design criterion must be download speed in all web projects until about the year 2003. Minimalist design rules.

Starting about 2003, high-end users will have speeds corresponding to a personal T1 line. This will allow them to download pages in less than a second, meaning that they will be able to navigate the Web freely. The user experience will become radically more gratifying with subsecond response times.

Of course, low-end users will be on ISDN lines in 2003, so high-end users' megabit access will still not sanction bloated design. Looking even further ahead, I predict that the Web will be 57 times faster in 10 years. At that time, even low-end users will be able to access multimedia designs, and the high-end users will be able to use very advanced sites. The future of the Web holds great promise for much richer designs. It is simply that the current Web is so horribly slow that it will take several years to achieve acceptable response times. Only after 2003 can web design change direction and aim at higher bandwidth.

Metaphors for the Web

Most Internet pundits use television as the dominant metaphor when explaining the Net. Words like "channels," "shows," and "eyeballs" feature prominent in many analyses; ideas such as push technology and ever-increasing multimedia flash are given credence despite being losers in usability terms. Television is used as a metaphor for two reasons. It is indeed the most powerful medium of the past, and it's all most media and advertising executives know how to deal with.

Well, most Internet pundits are wrong.

The Web is not like TV. Most fundamentally, the Web is a user-driven, narrow-casting medium utilizing low bandwidth with high flexibility, whereas television is a broadcast mass-medium utilizing high bandwidth with little flexibility. Because of the lack of flexibility and customization, TV has to rely on production values to capture an audience. The Web will not be able to even remotely emulate these production values for the next many years; the only hope is to play up the strengths of the Web, which are the ways in which it is *different* from TV. The Web can be used to integrate the Internet and television to give added value to TV viewers, but such systems will not realize the true potential of the Web.

The Telephone

I believe that the telephone is a more fruitful metaphor for thinking about the Web. This is not to say that the Web will be like the telephone, and let's hope not, because telephony has horrible usability characteristics. Also, no single metaphor can explain all aspects of a phenomenon as powerful as the Web.

Telephony is fundamentally a *narrowcast* medium: 1-to-1 communication along a rather low–fidelity channel. The fact that telephones are so popular despite their poor

---

Different Media, Different Strengths

Experience with traditional media has shown that even media that are quite similar can have different properties and different things they are good at. Consider television, movies, and theater. All three basically show human actors in costumes who read scripts in front of stage sets. All are very different from comic books, novels, conference panels, or a list of the first one million digits of pi. Even so, the focus of the three media is different:

- Television is about *characters*. TV is shown on a small screen that presents faces and close-ups better than landscapes. Because viewers sit in their living rooms with many distractions, shows tend to be at most one hour long, meaning that they cannot evolve complex plots. Series of TV shows are common because the audience likes the convenience of tuning in every week at the same time and because they can easily do so because the TV set is in their house. Seeing the same characters week after week leads to extensive character development during a season.

- Movies are about *stories*. Viewers have gone to the trouble of driving to the movie theater, so they want more than a half-hour show, although most films are still less than two hours long due to human biology. Because viewers are trapped in a dark room for the duration of the film, the storyline

can be developed further than is possible on TV. On the other hand, because of the expense and bother of going to the movies, people rarely do so on a regular basis, meaning that continued series are rare (except for one or two sequels to popular films). Because of the lack of series, characters are developed less and the film rests more on a strong plot.

- Theater is about *ideas*. The audience sits far away from the stage and cannot see the actors as well as on film. Nor can the stage show as elaborate sets or landscapes. These differences lead to prominence of dialogue over visuals. Also, the added expense of live actors for every performance makes the tickets significantly more expensive than movie tickets and attracts a more elite and intellectual audience. At the same time, the start-up cost of putting on the performance is less than the cost of producing a film, meaning that theater is more suited for experimental expressions.

Furthermore, of course, television has a substantial news and non-fiction component that is not present in movies and theater due to the ability of TV to deliver content in real time.

Given the many ways in which the Web is different from TV, film, and theater, I can only conclude that it will not emulate any of these legacy media too closely.

Jakob Nielsen: Designing Web Usability

audio quality is evidence that content is king, even here. What matters is who you talk to and what they say, not whether they sound exactly the same as if they were in the same room as you. Also, video phones have been failures so far, partly because the higher fidelity is often unwanted (you can place an important business call to a client while you are fresh out of the shower). The Web will also remain cursed with low bandwidth for the foreseeable future, so it would be better if we simply accepted this fact and designed sites that worked because of their content and not their production values.

Being a 1-to-1 medium is a characteristic of the Web and a reason the traditional advertising model will fail on the Web. Mass marketing is inappropriate when you can use customized value-added relationship marketing. Rather than blasting banner ads all over the place, companies should build customer value into their own websites and make it easier and more attractive for people to do business right on the sites. Direct marketing is a much better model than TV commercials: What matters is not how many people see your stuff (the "eyeballs" so beloved by old-media thinkers) but how many react on it (to contact you, to buy, or whatever else you want from them).

Unfortunately, the telephone metaphor also leads to telemarketers who invariably call during dinner with irrelevant offers. The Internet has spam, and the faster we get rid of it, the better. It might be possible to borrow from regulatory ideas in the telephone world (many countries outlaw most types of unsolicited calls), but it could also be that the Internet will pioneer solutions (such as filtering and "you-have-to-pay-me-to-get-through" tokens) that could be brought back to help the telephone world.

Another fundamental property of telephones is that calls are initiated by the user at exactly the time he or she wants to. Obviously, this is true only for the caller, whereas the callee is inconvenienced by getting a call as a "push" medium. Consider which of the two parties is better off, and you will see why pull is better than push. On the Web, of course, the second party to the conversation is a computer, so getting hits at an inconvenient time should not matter (assuming that a sufficiently powerful server is used).

Some people claim that the telephone is an example of perfect usability that should be emulated by software designers. After all, it's easy:

- You pick up the handset.
- You punch in the number.
- You are connected.

If only it were that easy in the real world. Of the three steps, only picking up the handset is truly easy. Turning on the device and "logging in" to your account are both accomplished by the simple action of picking up the handset. There is no "boot time," and the dial tone is always there. Computers (and in particular the Web) can definitely learn something from the uptime requirements of the phone system. The Internet should supply users with "WebTone" at the same level of reliability as the telephone supplies dial tone.

Let me debunk the myth that punching in a number is an easy-to-use user interface that should be emulated. First, these numbers are actually hard to learn and remember. Quick, what's the number of your dentist? Second, phone numbers are hard to type, and there is no forgiveness if you mistype a digit—nothing to do but hang up and start over. To make a long-distance call from a typical office in the United States requires the user to type in 12 digits, which is quite cumbersome and takes a long time to do. International calls are even harder.

The real usability problems of the telephone show up when we do a task analysis. What does the user really want to accomplish? In most cases, you want to talk to a specific person. To do so, you have to find that person in the telephone directory (or another list of phone numbers) and then dial the number. Who wants to talk to a *number*?

It would be better to be able to search a database and click on the person's name or photo to get connected, something a computer interface does well. Furthermore, most people have many telephone numbers: office, home, cellular, fax, secretary, etc. Sometimes, several of these numbers have their own voice mail system attached (each having its own inconsistent set of features and commands). Finding out what number to call should not be a matter of guessing where the person is, nor should you be forced to try all the alternate numbers until one works. A computerized communications system would know where the person is and what device currently is the preferred way of reaching him or her.

An integrated communications device may first try a voice call, but if the person is not available, the fall-back should not be voice mail but the person's email if available. Similarly, when voice mail is used, you shouldn't be forced to access it by sitting through a long, linear recital of recorded messages; scrolling through a visual listing of messages would be more efficient.

Another benefit of an integrated communications system is the opportunity for the recipient to specify when he or she is willing to take calls from whom. Currently, anybody who can find your telephone number has a license to bother you (and many telemarketers do so without shame). It is easy to imagine a communications system where the two parties are represented by software agents that negotiate whether or not the call should be allowed to go through, depending on urgency and the caller's level of prominence. For example, you could give out encrypted tokens to your family and closest colleagues that would allow their calls to go through at all times, whereas other callers might only be allowed at certain times or if they pay you, say, $10. The same system could screen both voice calls and email and faxes, although you might be willing to accept unsolicited email for a lower fee (say, $1) because it is less intrusive than a telephone call.

In general, the telephone is interactive, as is the Web. It's not a matter of giving people a huge, packaged chunk of content (as a TV show). Instead, a telephone call is a back-and-forth exchange between two parties, where each turn depends on the information received from the other end.

A final difference is that everybody is a publisher on the telephone. On TV, of course, only a select few get to go on the air. Even though most interest is focused on the large websites, I think the Web as a whole will derive more value from the combined effect of millions of smaller specialized sites (even though each single one will obviously have smaller revenues than a big site).

In thinking about your website or about new web technologies, I encourage you to think in terms of telephony. Metaphors are dangerous if taken too far, but they are helpful in finding perspectives and analogies that can take us further than the immediate surface characteristics of our work.

Contact Tokens

I believe that email systems will need contact tokens in a few years. A *contact token* is basically an encrypted piece of data that you can give out to other users to allow them priority access to contact you. Contact tokens may be valid for a single contact, or they may retain their power until you explicitly revoke them. When people start receiving thousands of email messages every day, any message that does not include a contact token will be given low priority and may well be discarded unread.

Users can give out contact tokens manually. For example, you may include a one-time contact token with your outgoing email to allow the reply to get through with whatever priority you deem appropriate, and you may give your spouse an unlimited-use, high-priority contact token for use in emergencies as well as an unlimited medium-priority token for use in everyday messages.

It may also be possible for senders to acquire contact tokens on their own. The most likely mechanism is that users will put their contact tokens up for sale: A busy executive might charge $100 for a token to get a message through, but most people will probably charge only a few cents or a dollar.

Finally, a determined sender might earn the rights to a contact token by performing certain prescribed tasks: For example, my agent might donate a low-priority contact token to anybody who reads at least 20 pages from my website and then scores at least 7 on a multiple-choice test with 10 questions about my web design philosophy.

The Television

The following table compares television and traditional computers along a number of dimensions.

It is clear that web access from television sets is a different style of medium than web access from a computer screen. This difference is okay and will serve only to strengthen the Web. As an analogy, it doesn't hurt the paper medium that newspapers and books are different.

The Web on computers is a very information-rich medium that is based on a high degree of user initiative and engagement: Users create their own experience through a steady stream of hypertext-following clicks. Clearly, WebTV is ill-suited to support this kind of user experience.

The Web on television should still be more user-driven and individualized than the fully passive mass medium of broadcast TV, but it needs to move in directions better suited to the device. This is not to say that WebTV users cannot benefit from accessing some parts of the traditional

	Television	Computers
Screen resolution (amount of information displayed)	Relatively poor	Varies from medium-sized screens to potentially very large screens
Input devices	Remote control and optional wireless keyboard that are best for small amounts of input and user actions	Mouse and keyboard sitting on desk in fixed positions leading to fast homing time for hands
Viewing distance	Many feet	A few inches
User posture	Relaxed, reclined	Upright, straight
Room	Living room, bedroom (ambiance and tradition implies relaxation)	Home office (paperwork, tax returns, etc., close by; ambiance implies work)
Integration opportunities with other things on same device	Various broadcast shows	Productivity applications, user's personal data, user's work data
Number of users	Social: Many people can see screen (often, several people will be in the room when the TV is on)	Solitary: Few people can see the screen (user is usually alone while computing)
User engagement	Passive: The viewer receives whatever the network executives decide to put on	Active: User issues commands and the computer obeys

Web. After all, successful films have been made based on Shakespeare's plays, and television networks often broadcast feature films. But as pointed out above, the mainstream directions of the media have turned out to be separate.

The most obvious direction for the Web on television is integration with broadcast TV. Online TV program listings are one example of content that would seem optimal for WebTV users. It would also be quite useful to have hyperlinks to detailed information about each show—which actor is playing this role and what are the statistics for this baseball player—with the point being that the system should know what program the user was watching and have appropriate links for that specific show so that the basic user experience would be driven by the television and not by fully flexible browsing.

When more bandwidth becomes available, it will also be possible to use a television-based Web to assemble more efficient evening news broadcasts optimized for the individual viewer. For example, the show could start by having the anchorperson read the list of the day's headlines. Each family could then indicate what stories they wanted to see, either by having a single person click a button as interesting headlines are read or by letting each family member have his or her own button. This latter solution is more family-friendly. The current WebTV design with a single remote control is a divorce lawyer's delight.

Note how my example of selecting stories for a customized evening news show relies on a fairly passive user interface: Click a button as a fixed set of choices are read. In general, I think that the amount of initiative and activity required of the user will be the major defining difference between TV-based Web and computer-based Web. I don't think that the use of video will be as important a difference because I expect computer-based Web to include more multimedia effects as bandwidth grows and more powerful computers (allowing better compression as well as a cache of at least a terabyte on your local hard disk) become popular.

Restructuring Media Space: Good-Bye, Newspapers

Most current media formats will die and be replaced with an integrated Web medium in five to ten years.

Legacy media cannot survive because the current media landscape is an artifact of the underlying hardware technology. Whenever the user experience is dictated by hardware limitations, it is a sure bet that something better will come along once these limitations are lifted.

Why are traditional media separate? Why do you have to choose among (1), seeing moving images of an event on TV, (2), reading the full story in the newspaper, or (3), reading a reflective analysis of the underlying issues in a magazine?

Why not all three in a single medium? And why not link the coverage to archival information from an encyclopedia, an atlas, biographies of the people involved, historical novels that bring the relevant countries' past to life, and many more books?

The answer is obvious. You can't screen a film clip in print, you can't broadcast a long article on television, the newspaper presses don't wait for weeks' worth of research for the reflective story, and it would be too expensive to send magazine subscribers a small library of books just in case they wanted deeper background information.

In other words, current hardware prevents true media integration. Even so, there have been attempts. Newspapers often include a Sunday magazine, and the better ones assign reporters to work for long periods of time to research and write extensive background articles that go far beyond yesterday's news. Sometimes, books are rushed to print to cash in on public interest in a high-profile event.

The Internet has its own hardware limitations that limit integrated media services:

- Limited bandwidth makes video impossible and reduces the amount of graphics, animation, and other non-text formats that can be used. Also, slow response times reduce the depth and richness of services because users do not follow hypertext links freely unless they get sub-second response times.

- Low-resolution computer monitors make users read 25 percent more slowly from screens than from print, leading to a need for fewer words on the pages.
- Poorly designed web browsers and search engines reduce users' ability to navigate the Web and find the information and services they need. (This last item is a software issue, not a hardware issue, but from a content provider's perspective, all that really matters is that the infrastructure is still insufficient to build advanced Internet services.)

These problems will go away over the next five to ten years. Users get 50 percent faster Internet bandwidth every year. In five years, high-end users will have the required sub-second response times to navigate the Web freely. In ten years, all users will have good bandwidth. Also, in ten years, it will be possible to stream good quality video across the Internet (current postage stamp videos are close to useless).

High-resolution monitors with 300 dpi graphics exist and have the same readability as paper. Monitors probably won't drop in price at the speed of Moore's Law, but I still predict that high-end users will have good screens in five years (maybe 200 dpi) and that all users will have good screens in ten years.

Media Distinctions Caused by Technology

Newspapers are published once a day on low-quality paper and deliver quickly written articles with the previous day's news. They have their own distribution network of newspaper carriers to reach subscribers a few hours after their deadline.

Magazines are published weekly or monthly on high-quality paper and deliver more thoroughly researched and written articles that integrate longer-term trends or events. They usually rely on the postal network and reach subscribers a few days to a few weeks after their deadline.

Books are an archival medium and have publication cycles that may stretch across years, sometimes being republished in new editions.

They use a distribution network of booksellers to reach buyers a few months after the author finishes the manuscript.

Television networks have their own broadcast network that reaches viewers in real time. In contrast to the other media listed here, TV is based on moving images and sound.

There are genuine differences in the type of information contained in each medium, and users need all these types of information. My only complaint is with the packaging: The different types of information are kept separate because of the manufacturing and distribution technologies, even though integration would often provide a better user experience.

This means that around 2008, all computer users will prefer using the Web over reading printed pages. High-end users may make this switch around 2003. Once the Internet is as pleasant to use as old media, it will win if it provides services that take advantage of the interaction and integration offered by the new media.

Distributing high-quality video over the Internet does not mean that television networks will simply go online. There is no reason that *Star Trek* and the evening news should come over the same channel or from the same company. The only reason this is done now is that both shows have to share the same broadcast frequency. It would be a much better solution to integrate video clips of news with text coverage of the same news and to link both to background analysis and educational resources.

Even though I predict the death of legacy media formats, I think that most of the people working in these media have a glorious future.

Most of the video clips in these integrated services will be very brief because users want to retain control of the interaction and set the pace of their information consumption. Current CD-ROM encyclopedias are a good role model. Although they do have more bandwidth than the Web, CD-ROMs usually limit their video clips to 30 seconds. Much longer, and users get bored and want to get back to interacting. Also, the videos have to be tied into the rest of the service and integrated with text, image databases, computer animations under user control, and much more. "Multimedia" means many data types, not simply getting linear television on a computer screen.

In addition to the short, integrated video clips, there will also be longer videos available over the Internet. Movies and one-hour productions will remain popular for fiction, because storytelling often works best in a linear format where the user abandons responsibility and simply absorbs the plot as envisioned by the author. Even these linear productions will be distributed over the Internet. Why should a show start at 9:00 if you're ready for it at 8:50? Video-on-demand will require better user interfaces than currently known (people won't suffer through reading a manual to watch a game show), but we do have at least five years in which to invent these designs before the Internet is fast enough to replace television networks.

Jakob Nielsen: Designing Web Usability

Although integrated video has to wait for higher bandwidth, it is possible to integrate text-only (or text-plus-photos) publishing formats today. Services can integrate the spectrum from immediate news over background analysis to archival information. The *Wall Street Journal's* integration of company handbook information with the ability to retrieve old articles about the same companies results in an online service that is more valuable than either feature alone—and much more valuable than any single day's news.

Even though I predict the death of legacy media formats, I think that most of the people working in these media have a glorious future. There will continue to be a need for writers, editors, photographers, camerapeople, video producers, on-screen talent and actors, and many others. In fact, the demand for talented media specialists may grow if interactive content gets to play a more important role in people's everyday lives. I believe this may easily happen because interactive media are more engaging than passive ones.

Current media workers will need to modify their skills for the interactive age. For example, people read differently online, so writers need to change their writing style. Similarly, a photographer must learn to shoot in ways that allow users to interact with the photo (for example, click on objects to have them explained).

I am less optimistic about the future for current media companies than I am about the future prospects for their staff. In principle, media companies could leverage their current staff, skills, brand, financial resources, and audience relationships into the interactive age. In practice, many of them are tied into their traditional media format and not sufficiently willing to consider it expendable. How many newspaper publishers are willing to treat their print product as a cash cow that is planned to survive no more than 10 years? How many fund their website to become an online service in its own right and not simply a set of repurposed print articles and newswires?

Conclusion

The current Web just scratches the surface relative to what's possible once everybody in the rich world is connected through a single network. The current web browsers are an abomination and have not improved significantly since 1993. I safely predict that the future of the Web will be very different from our current reality.

When the Web grows from 10 million sites to 200 million sites and from 200 million users to one billion users, the result is not just going to be more of the same.

The exact changes are extremely difficult to predict. It is a virtual certainty that the future will turn out to be different from the various predictions I have made in this chapter. The only prediction that is guaranteed to be true is that the only constant is change.

I am hopeful that the Web will be much easier to use in the future. In fact, increased usability is not just a desirable quality, it is a necessary quality because the only way we can get the next 800 million people to come online is by making the Web easier, both in terms of the overall technology and in terms of the design of the individual sites.

9 Conclusion: Simplicity in Web Design

What are the top three reasons users come to your site?

When I ask web executives why users come to their site, they often don't know the answer. But even when they know, they sometimes refuse to design the site to support these main user goals. For example, many so-called portals have been redesigned to make the search field tiny, even though a large number of users come to the site to conduct searches.

Websites should make the main things users want to do very simple. Other actions and advanced features can certainly be possible, but simple things should be simple to do. Ask yourself, do I have too much complexity in my life or too little complexity? If you do think you have too little complexity in your life, you will relish the challenge of a website with a mystery interface that makes you work hard to get any results. But most users would rather have simplicity.

People are extremely goal-driven on the Web. They have something specific they want to do, and they don't tolerate anything standing between them and their goal. So, the guiding principle for web design must be to get out of the way and make users successful as fast as possible.

Home-Run Websites

Some analysts love talking about so-called unique visitors, but that's a bogus statistic. It is extremely easy to get a high count of unique visitors by running a big promotion, but it does the site absolutely no good if these visitors take one look at the home page and turn away in disgust, never to return. The only real success criterion for a website is repeat traffic from loyal users.

There are four main reasons users return to some websites and not to other websites. These four criteria are the foundation of good web design because they are the four things users want the most. They can be summarized by the acronym HOME.

- **H**igh-quality content
- **O**ften updated
- **M**inimal download time
- **E**ase of use

Jakob Nielsen: Designing Web Usability

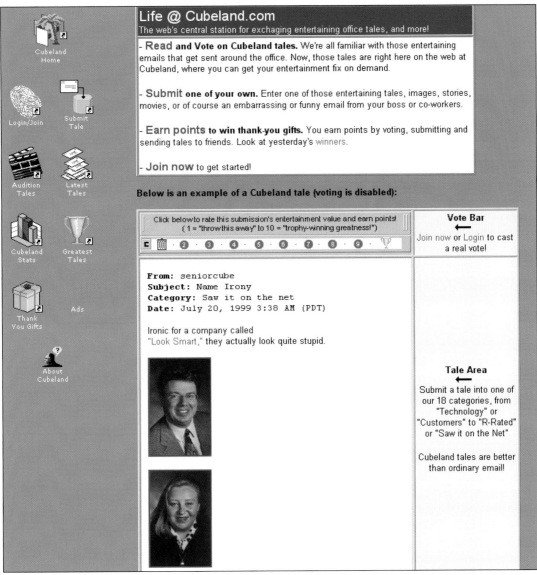

Interesting attempt at transferring the Windows 98 interface style to a home page. Although I do advocate increased integration between desktop computing and Internet computing, I think it's a mistaken approach to make websites emulate Windows, which is much too complex an interface. At least Windows has the advantage that there is only one of it (if you disregard the differences between NT and the consumer versions), so you have to learn only one set of icons and interface conventions. But this advantage does not translate onto the Web where each site has different features and where the interface does not behave like desktop software. Let's aim for simplicity instead of redesigning a complex interface.

If you can provide these four elements, users will be happy and you have a good site. Three of the four letters are fairly self-explanatory, especially after you have read this book. But people often ask me what "often updated" means. There is no simple answer, because the required update frequency depends on the topic and the goals of the site.

Sites that specialize in news or current events need real-time updates and should get fresh content several times per day. A minimal update frequency would be early in the morning and before the end of the working day (both measured in the main target area for the site: If it's a truly world-wide site, updates need to happen 24 hours per day to correspond with the mornings and late afternoons in all major population centers).

Sites that are less grounded in current events need either daily or weekly updates. Monthly updates are possible for sites in very slow-moving fields or where you don't expect users to have a high level of engagement with the site.

Giving users the four HOME qualities will ensure the popularity of your site. But it is not enough to simply give users what they want. You need to go beyond the four basics to have a truly stellar site. To move from a HOME design to a HOME RUN design, add the three extras:

- **R**elevant to users' needs
- **U**nique to the online medium
- **N**et-centric corporate culture

The R in HOME RUN implies that it is not sufficient to provide high-quality content. The content must also be relevant to your users and the specific things they want to do.

Furthermore, the site must provide this relevant high-quality content in a way that's unique to the online medium's special characteristics. If you simply repurpose ideas that work well in the physical world, you will always have an also-ran website.

Finally—and this is the hardest of all—the HOME RUN approach to web design requires the entire company to get behind the website to deliver an optimal customer

User Survey: What Causes Repeat Traffic?

Recognizing the importance of repeat visitors, Forrester Research conducted a survey in which 8,900 users were asked what caused them to return to websites. I am usually reluctant to give much credence to opinion polls as a valid methodology for generating data for web design. After all, what people *say* and what they actually *do* are two very different things. So it is usually worthless to ask users to fill in questionnaires. You will learn little about their actual behavior and how to serve them better.

But in this specific case, there are reasons to believe the study. Basically, it asked people about their opinions and not about what they did on the sites or what caused them to buy certain products. The outcome of the study was that users particularly liked the four site attributes I summarize by the HOME acronym. These four issues were all mentioned by more than half of the respondents. Interestingly, no other trait was mentioned by more than 14% of the respondents.

For more info, check out this site: http://www.webreference.com/new/990125.html#survey.

Jakob Nielsen: Designing Web Usability

experience in the online world. No web team, no matter how good, can create a website that really works if the rest of the company is mired in the physical world and unwilling to put the Internet first in all aspects of virtually all projects.

Many Internet-only start-up companies do have the right attitude and organize their entire corporation around the goal of serving customers online. But it is a hard transition for a legacy company as long as most departments are staffed by people who do not view the Web as a strategic imperative. Therefore, most big-company websites will remain unnecessarily complex for many years to come because they will continue to attempt to paper over an underlying reality that is not Internet-centric.

Better Than Reality

Instead of impoverished facsimiles of reality, design from a basis of strength and go beyond reality to things that were impossible in the physical world. It is painful to use the Web, so reward users by giving them something new and better that they didn't get before.

- Be non-linear. Don't force users to live through a stream of time that they can't control.

- Customize service. Computers can do different things for different people.

- Be asynchronous. A customized link to check the status of an order allows a customer to resume a "conversation" many hours later without spending any time on reestablishing context.

- Support anonymity. If people don't have to reveal who they are, they may be more willing to do certain things.

- Link liberally. Links are the foundation of the Web and can make anything into an extension of your own service.

- Support search and multiple views. Different people have different preferences, and there is no need to be limited to a single way of doing things on the Web.

- Be small and cheap. Because of the efficiency of computers, it is possible to deal in much smaller units than before.

- Be free. It costs very little to offer free samples over the Web, so a book publisher could offer a free chapter and a consultant could offer free advice on some frequently asked questions (while charging for the full product or service, of course).

- Ignore geography. Support users who access your site from home, the office, the car, while away on business trips or vacations, and from anywhere in the world.

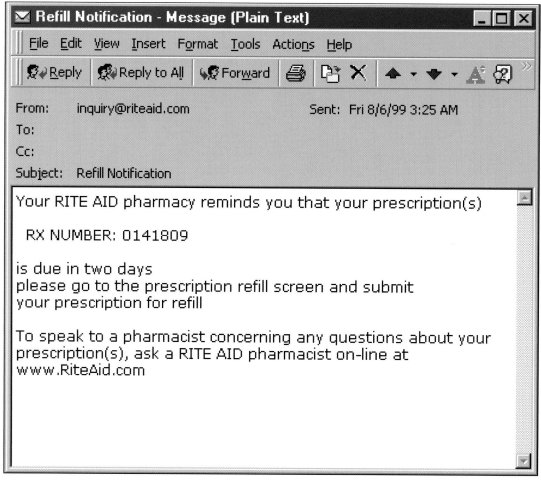

Loyal users who make return visits are key to success on the Web, and email reminders are often a good way to encourage people to return. But an electronic mail message is a user interface in its own right and has to be designed for usability. This message does one thing right (it's short) but gets everything else wrong:

1. The "from" field is from somebody named "inquiry," which is not exactly a name that inspires warm feelings (it made me think of the Spanish Inquisition). In any case, this is a reminder message and not something sent out as a result of a customer question.

2. The "to" field is left empty, making the message look like spam rather than personal service.

3. The "subject" field is internally oriented and does not sufficiently explain what the message is about relative to the context of the user's inbox. There are many types of refills in the world, including filling up your car with gasoline and restocking supplies for your laser printer.

4. The message talks about the "refill screen" without giving its URL. Why punish paying customers by making them do more work than necessary? There is a big risk that they will get lost on the site and that the order will get lost.

5. To add insult to injury, the prescription number is not sufficient information to actually place the order. The website also requires a code number for the user's pharmacy. Of course, the computer knows this code, because this is a reorder reminder, but I guess it would have been too easy to give the customer all the required information right in the email.

- Search
- Email
- Chat
- Boards
- Personalize

First visit? **Join now**

w●men●●m

pick a channel ▼

pick a magazine ▼

Wednesday, September 15

COSM●●LITAN

SEPTEMBER 1999

In Cosmo
This Month

Your bedside
astrologer

*Beauty
Giveaway*

Cosmo
asks you
including Cosmo Confessions

From the editor

*This
week's
tips:*
beauty, fashion, health,
relationships, sex

the Cosmo
Quiz

Ecstasy
& Agony

NEW! SPECIAL EXPANDED
WEB VERSION
Cosmo's
dating diary

NEW! A fearless, fun, female survey telling us about YOU!

(Above, following page)   The Web is not print. And a home page is not a magazine cover. In September 1999, *Cosmopolitan* magazine used a home page that looked exactly like a magazine cover. This is a doomed strategy because the criteria for good design are different in the two media. A magazine cover must be arresting above all. When people scan a burgeoning magazine rack at the newsstand, you want your magazine to jump right at them and say "Buy me." A big picture of a glamorous model in a fancy outfit is a well-proven way of doing so. On the Web, the user is already at the site and has already chosen to do business with the site. There is no need to stand out in the crowd when your home page takes up most of a computer monitor that is a few inches from the user's nose. Instead of convincing people to pick up a magazine, a home page has the goal of convincing them to *do* something on the site. The redesigned home page for the October 1999 issue is better—at least it's starting to look like an interface rather than a magazine cover. Small summaries under the headline go a long way in helping users choose what to click on.

Tomalak's Realm
Daily links to strategic Web design news

TODAY'S LINKS « Edited by Lawrence Lee

Tuesday September 21, 1999
updated at 10:21:24 AM PT

PC Magazine: Content or Connection? I'm convinced that when we buy Net access, we aren't looking at content (the Web itself is literally a world of content, far wider, deeper, and more interesting than anything any ISP can layer atop our Net connection), but rather for fast, reliable, transparent connections to the Net.

- Salon: From January 20, 1999; A corporate game of Internet Monopoly. Scott Rosenberg.

NY Times: A Web-Researched Ford in Microsoft's Future. [Jacques Nasser, Ford Motor Company's president and chief executive] By making information on product availability easily accessible to customers, he went on, the service will put them in charge of the transaction, and will ultimately increase customer satisfaction.

Boston Globe: Database compilers fight for copyright protection. Until lately, this had not seemed unfair: Databases, after all, are generally gatherings of information created by someone else. But the rise of the Internet has prompted heated debate over whether those laws should change.

- Cal Law: From; June 4, 1999; Congress Does a Database Dance

Salon: Domain name dunces. Scott Rosenberg. It's hard not to conclude that the folks who run Network Solutions are utterly ignorant of the most basic social and technical realities of the network they play such a central role in managing.

Search the Today's Links Archives

Search

Past five days of Today's Links

Tomalak's Realm Store

Conferences and Events

Stories

Today's Links Newsletter

Support the site

NEW URL:
www.tomalak.org

Recent Stories
Saturn's Sixty-Four Word Web Strategy (August 23)

Thousands of new bestseller lists for Amazon (August 20)

www.tomalak.org

(Previous page) Tomalak's Realm is a type of publication that is unique to the Web. It's nothing but links. Every day, the editor scours the Web for interesting articles and commentary in a narrow area of interest. The topic happens to be strategic web design, but the same idea would work as well for any special-interest domain that is touched upon in a wide variety of publications and sites.

The user gets three benefits from Tomalak's Realm. First, it offers a single page to go to every day to get an overview of all relevant stories within the topic area. Second, all the stories are presented in a consistent format, freeing the user from being bothered with the obscure navigation formats of the various publications. In particular, Tomalak's Realm summarizes each article in a few lines, which is usually enough to determine whether to go and read the full article. In contrast, many other websites are clueless when it comes to microcontent and the ability to write home pages in a way that gives users a decent preview of the articles. Finally, Tomalak's Realm juxtaposes links to articles from multiple sites, often including links to original or early thinking about topics that later are taken up by other sites. This capability to base a publication on pure linking and to provide editorial comments and background by additional links is a true web-only media form.

Best of Times or Worst of Times?

The classic Charles Dickens quote *"It was the best of times, it was the worst of times,"* seems appropriate to describe the present.

In many ways, it is the *best* of times because we are in the middle of inventing a new economy and a new way of dealing with a large segment of both business and daily life. During the 15-year period from 1993 (when the Web started to take off) to 2008, an unprecedented number of changes will happen, and companies will have to become totally customer-driven to survive. At the time of this writing, we are about halfway through this revolution, but because it follows an exponential growth curve, we have probably seen only one or two percent of the eventual change.

We are the people who are building the new economy: We can make it what we want. The things we are working on right now will be used daily by billions of people in a few years. If that's not the best of times, I don't know what would be.

Usability used to be a suppressed and barely tolerated oddity in the computer industry. Computer companies have always refused to make usability the driving criterion in product development. Instead, features and performance were always the goals, and usability professionals ranked at the bottom of the totem pole, just barely above technical writers.

Usability has grown dramatically in importance for web-based companies because of an inversion in the relationship between user experience and the ability to separate customers from their money. In the old world that is populated by most computer companies, customers would pay for a product first and only later take it home and discover that it was difficult to use. By the time you discover that you need a two-inch-thick book to figure out how to format chapter headings, your check has already been deposited in the Bank of Redmond.

Sure, the computer industry has been paying lip service to usability during the last ten years. To be fair to the many talented usability people at traditional computer and software companies, it is indeed a hard job to retrofit usability

Jakob Nielsen: Designing Web Usability

onto designs that stem from the age of DOS when fear and loathing were part of the basic system architecture. But ultimately, usability was a secondary consideration in the computer industry because customers were not faced with the consequences until *after* they had paid for the product.

The situation is the reverse on the Web. Users experience a site's usability from the very first moment they consider doing business with a company. Users need to navigate a site and find the products *before* they get to the stage where they make a decision to spend money. Usability comes first even if a site is not trying to sell anything. Loyal users are the only true value on the Internet, and users don't return to sites that are too difficult to use. Only if people get a positive user experience on their initial visit will they return and start generating revenues for the site.

So the tables have been turned, and usability has become a core competency that is necessary for business survival in the network economy. Only usable sites get any traffic. If customers can't find a product on an e-commerce site, they are not going to buy it. Most of the new Internet start-ups in Silicon Valley recognize that their new technologies don't stand a chance unless they are incredibly easy to use. It does indeed seem like the best of times for usability people who are breaking the chains of oppression in the computer industry and moving to the Internet industry in record numbers.

But in some ways, we are living in the *worst* of times as well. The present is a unique period in human history in that this is the first time humanity has lost mastery of its tools.

Since the dawn of time, people have been in control of their tools. The stone-age primitive knew the properties of flint and how to turn it into sharp axes. Peasants in the Middle Ages knew how a plow was constructed and how to use it to till their fields. And they sure knew how to master their oxen. In recent history, people used to understand automobiles: Even if they were not trained mechanics, drivers in the 1950s knew much of what was under the hood, knew the meaning of the various sounds their car might make, and knew how to fix the beast if it acted up.

Today, the average computer user lives under a reign of terror where he or she is subjected to loss of data at the whim of a blue screen that appears at unexplainable times. We have lost 2,000 years' of progress in rationalist thinking and reverted to superstitious and animist behavior where users chant magic incantations at their computer without understanding the meaning but hoping that the outcome will be blessed. Look at offices around the world and count the number of yellow sticky-notes at the side of computer monitors and you will know what I mean. Each sticky-note has a magic incantation on it with a number of steps that are followed as an offering to the Great Machine. If step 5 in printing handouts from a slide presentation were to sacrifice a goat, then people would do that just as gladly as they click a checkbox they don't understand.

The computer industry even acknowledges the unknowable and magic nature of their creations by using metaphors like "wizards" when they want to wave the wand over particularly obtuse designs.

We should not accept the oppression of information technology. It is time to rise to the defense of humanity in the age of machines. Users of the Web, unite at the useful sites: You have nothing to lose but your download delays.

We don't have to take it. We are creating our own future right now, and we can decide to respect humans and design to help users regain mastery of their technology, their tools, and their websites. At one level, this book is a prescription for how to increase traffic and sales on your website by increasing customer satisfaction through usable design. But at another level, the book is a manifesto to make the Web atone for the sins of computers and regain a level of simplicity that can put humanity at peace with its tools once again.

Recommended Readings

Much good information about the Web is available on the Web itself. If I gave a lot of specific URLs here, many of them would invariably suffer linkrot and turn out to be a waste of your time. Also, having to type in URLs is a painful exercise that should be avoided as much as possible.

Thus, instead of giving a listing of URLs here, I refer you to my hotlist of recommended sites:

http://www.useit.com/hotlist

Typing in this URL should allow you to proceed to several other good sites at the click of your mouse.

I will mention one more site: Keith Instone's Usable Web database serves as a well-organized and annotated list of many other sites about Web-related human-computer interaction:

http://usableweb.com

Books

As I mentioned in the Preface, there are still good reasons to read printed books when you want to get an in-depth treatment of something. The number of books about web design seems to grow almost as fast as the Web itself, so I cannot give you a full list of books here. Instead, I refer you to my online list of recommended books:

http://www.useit.com/books

Unfortunately, many web design books are directly harmful because they advocate a user-hostile approach to design that leads to slow-loading and confusing (but "cool") pages. It is a bad sign if a book is written by a famous magazine designer, a famous film director, or an art director who is famous for work in the print medium. A second tip-off is if you leaf through the book and see mostly illustrations of gorgeous print designs or mostly screenshots of pages that would take minutes to load over a modem line. Such books only cover the "look" part of the "look-and-feel" equation. The main downside of reading a book as opposed to accessing the Web is that you do not *interact* with the examples; you don't use them for anything, except to look at. Therefore, unless the author is highly attuned to interaction issues, you may well be led down a path that generates designs that work in print but don't work on the Web.

Usability

I have written an entire textbook about user testing and other usability engineering methods. This book, *Usability Engineering* (AP Professional), emphasizes a lifecycle approach to usability and the steps that should be taken at each development phase. The book is also strongly on the side of fast and cheap "discount usability engineering" methodology, which makes it suitable reading for any web designers who are not yet fed up with my writing.

I also want to emphasize the need to consider international users. Even when following user-centered design principles, it is easy to be centered around your local users and their needs and characteristics. Out of sight, out of mind—even though customers halfway around the world may be as important. One of my own books, written with Elisa del Galdo, provides a much-needed international perspective: *International User Interfaces* (John Wiley & Sons). I also used to recommend *Global Interface Design* by Tony Fernandes (AP Professional), but unfortunately this book is now out of print. Buy a used copy if you can find it. The main difference between the two books is that the first highlights differences at the interaction design level, such as different behaviors across cultures and how to conduct in-home or in-office studies of international users, whereas the second highlights differences at the page design level.

Hypertext

The Web is only the latest in a long line of hypertext systems that included Apple's HyperCard, Xerox's NoteCards, and even Vannevar Bush's Memex vision from 1945 (the latter was never built, though). Much inspiration for web design can be gained by looking at the ways in which these earlier systems have approached the fundamental issues of linking and navigating information. There is a very extensive research literature that is summarized in my textbook: *Multimedia and Hypertext: The Internet and Beyond* (AP Professional).

For more about information architecture, I recommend Louis Rosenfeld and Peter Morville's *Information Architecture for the World Wide Web* (O'Reilly).

Web Technology

There must be almost a million books on HTML. My current favorite is linked from my list of recommended books (www.useit.com/books), but it probably doesn't matter much which one you read, as long as it emphasizes the proper way of using HTML for structural markup and does not attempt to teach usability-degrading hacks. A good test is to see how a book recommends readers to code their headlines. Proper HTML uses structural tags such as <H1>, <H2>, and so on, depending on the desired level of heading. In contrast, dangerous HTML uses <B><FONT SIZE=5> and similar presentation-oriented markup.

The best book about style sheets is *Cascading Style Sheets, Second Edition: Designing for the Web* by Håkon Lie and Bert Bos (Addison Wesley). The cover blurb is right: The authors are indeed "the world authorities" on style sheets, being the leaders of the Web Consortium's style sheet project.

The people who are going to produce the images for your website should probably read a book like *<designing web graphics.3> - How to Prepare Images and Media for the Web* by Lynda Weinman (New Riders) if they have been used to working with print images in the past. There are many technical differences in color, resolution, and file size requirements that impact the way graphics designers should use tools like Adobe Photoshop, and the implementation issues for web images are spelled out in great detail in this book.

Finally, for back-end stuff, I recommend Philip and Alex's *Guide to Web Publishing* by Philip Greenspun (Morgan Kaufmann Publishers). A precious sample of geek humor (and still very useful).

Read My Next Book

My final recommendation is that you read my next book. As I discussed in more detail in the Preface, the distinction between these two books is simple. The current volume is the "what" of web usability, that is, the guidelines you guidelines you should follow to make a design easy to use. The second book, tentatively titled *Ensuring Web Usability*, is the "how" of web usability, or the methods and procedures you should follow to learn even more about user behavior and to acquire specific data about your own customers and how they interact with your actual site. For more about the next book, be sure to periodically check out my website: www.useit.com.

Index

Symbols

1998 Nagano Olympics, 322

3D
navigation, 156, 222
poor uses of, 156–157
virtual reality, 157
when to use, 159–160

3D graphics, 156
difficulties with using, 156
legibility of rotated text, 157

A

abstracts, 233
Infoseek, 236

accessibility
cognitive disabilities, 309–310
dyslexia, 311
hearing-impaired users, 308
multimedia, 155
video, 150
helpful technology, 299
multimedia for those with disabilities, 155
speech impaired users, 308–309
spelling disabilities, 311
users with disabilities, 298
users with motor skills problems, 309
visually-impaired users, 302
ALT attributes, 303–307
described images, 305
fonts, 302
multimedia, 155
scannability, 104, 302
search engines, 303
Web Accessibility Initiative, 298–299

accessing the Internet, 348

addresses, websites, 246–247

advertisement banners
animation, 146
links, 77

advertising
banners, Citibank, 81
incoming links, 77
URLs, 250
IBM, 252–254

affiliates programs, 179

aggregation, navigation, 221

aging, 298

ALOM Technologies, extranets, 268

ALT attributes, 303–307

ALT strings, 306

ALT tags, imagemaps, 305

ALT text, tooltips, 306–307

AltaVista
help, 130
searches, alternative terms, 240

alternative terms, keywords, 237, 240

American Airlines, 171

Americans with Disabilities Act, 297

Amundsen, Claire, Proven Edge Inc.
webmaster, 48

anchor text
link titles, 62
links, 55, 58
News.com, 59

AnchorDesk, 51-53
hypertext, 115
links, 221
subsites, 224

animation, 143
attracting attention, 147–149
enriching graphical representations,
146–147
illustrating change over time, 145
indicating dimensionality
in transitions, 145
multiplexing displays, 146
Opera-de-Paris, 144
problems with, 146
showing continuity in transitions, 145
Sun Microsystems, 148
three-dimensional structures,
visualizing, 146

anti-Macintosh user interface, 351

Apple, GUI design, 27

applets, 256
cancel buttons, 259
content applets, 258

CSS (cascading style sheets). *See also*
style sheets
Web Consortium, 84

Cubeland, 381

cultural differences, international
usability, 315

customer feedback, speed (ARUP
Laboratories web site), 47

customer-friendly websites, creating, 383

customized news broadcasts, 371

D

data, life of web data, 43

data ink, 27

Datatrace Inc., 92

dates, internationalization, 318

Davis, Eric, usability studies
(terminology), 188

deep linking home pages, 179

Del Galdo, Elisa, *International User Interfaces*, 395

departure page, links, 66

described images, 305

description errors, 248

designing for WebTV, 356

designs. *See also* web designs
cross-platform design, 25–26
extranet designs, 266, 270
home pages. *See* home pages
internationalization. *See* internationalization
intranet designs. *See* intranet designs
resolution-independent design. *See*
resolution-independent design
style sheets, standardizing, 82–83
URLs. *See* URLs
user interface designs, general principle
for, 22

destination pages
links, 66
scrolling, 115
searches, 238
Sun Microsystems, 244

differences
between extranets and intranets, 267
between extranets and traditional
websites, 267
between intranet design and Internet
design, 265–266
internationalization, regional differences,
332–333

directing marketing, 367

directories, intranets, 279

disabilities
aging, 298
cognitive disabilities, 309–310
dyslexia, 311
hearing-impaired users, 308
multimedia, 155
video, 150
helpful technology, 299
motor skills, 309
multimedia for those with disabilities, 155
obligation to users with, 297–298
speech-impaired users, 308–309
spelling disabilities, 311
visually-impaired users, 302
ALT attributes, 303, 305, 307
described images, 305
fonts, 302
multimedia, 155
scannability, 104,302
search engines, 303
Web Accessibility Initiative, 298–299
web users, 298

disadvantages of remote user testing, 338

DisCopyLabs, 103

display-specific instructions and content,
separating, 38

displaying link titles, browsers, 62

distributing video over Internet, 374

documentation
extranets, 129
guidelines for writing, 131
writing for the Web, 129–131

domain names, 246
choosing, 247

metaphors, 180
   Bemarnet, 184
   Campaign Live, 180
   The Monster Board, 187
   reasons for, 180
   shopping carts, 180
   Southwest Airlines, 182
   Voyager, 186
   for the Web
      telephones, 366–367, 369
      television, 365
   weaknesses of, 180
   writing for the Web, 111

Metcalfe, Bob, 349

Metcalfe's Law, 349

methods of testing, international usability, 336
   remote user testing, 337–338
   traveling to the country yourself, 336–337
   usability labs, 339–340

Microsoft
   navigation, 219
   searches, 226
   Sitebuilder, outbound links, 66, 68, 70

Miller, Robert B., response times (human factors), 42–44

mistakes in web design, 14–15

mixed-behavior users, 224

modems, 49. *See also* Internet connections

downloading, 48

monitors
   future of, 373
   size of, 27
      distribution of monitor size in 1997 and 1999, 27–28
   usability studies, 286
   WebTV, 356

The Monster Board, metaphors, 187

moods, audio, 154

Morkes, John, usability studies (tourism in Nebraska), 104

Morville, Peter, *Information Architecture for the World Wide Web*, 395

Mosaic, 37

motor skills, difficulty with, 309

movies, 366

multilingual searches, 331–332

multilingual sites, 320–322
   Travel Net, 330

multimedia, 131, 134
   animation. *See* animation
   audio, 154–155
   response times, 134
   for those with disabilities, 155
   video, 149
      streaming video versus downloadable video, 150–152

Multimedia and Hypertext: The Internet and Beyond, 395

multiple word queries, 233

multiplexing displays, animation, 146

music, 154

Myst, 154

N

National Center for Accessible Media, 302

National Palace Museum (in Taiwan)

The National Palace Museum
   ALT attributes, 306
   languages, choosing, 324

natural language searches, 243

navigation, 188
   3D, 222
   applets, 256, 258–259
   AT&T, 191
   breadcrumbs, 206
   breadth-emphasizing design, 203
   browsers, 189
   depth and breadth, Looksmart, 207
   fisheye navigation
      Inktomi, 211
      Looksmart, 209–210
   for users with cognitive disabilities, 310
   frames, 86

   future of, 221
   hierarchical structure, 202–203
   home pages, 168
   in 3D, 156

size of monitors, 27
  distribution of monitor size in 1997
    and 1999, 27–28
skimming. *See* scannability
slashes, 50
Slate, scrolling, 116
software
  life of, 43
  navigation problems, 218
  usability, 10
Sony
  graphics, 135
  legibility, 126
sound effects, 154
Southwest Airlines
  error messages, 111
  metaphors, 182
spam, 367
speech-based browsers, 38
speech-impaired users, 308–309
speed, 46. *See also* response times
spell-checking content, 103–104
spelling checkers, URLs, 248–249
spelling disabilities, 311
spelling-reduced searches, 310
splash screens, 176
splitting up hypertext, 112
Spool, Jared, 164
  User Interface Engineering, 64
standardizing style sheets, 82–83
standards
  interface standards, shopping carts, 188
  for intranet designs, 280–281
  intranet designs, guidelines for, 281–282,
    284
Starfire, 137–138, 150
statistics
  home pages, width of, 174
  search queries, 237
  of users on the Web, 348
  of users using the Web by nationality, 314
  users who upgraded versions
    of Netscape, 34

of websites, 347
structural links, 195
structure of websites, navigation, 198,
  202–203
style sheets, 81, 83
  disabled style sheets, 84
  embedded style sheets, 81
  examples for intranets, 83
  guidelines for, 84–85
  implementing, 81
  linked style sheets, 81–83
  standardizing, 82–83
sub-categories, 108
sub-category headers, 108
subjective satisfaction, Internet, 270
subscriptions, incoming links, 76
subsites, 222–224
  AnchorDesk, 224
  searches, 225–226, 228
subtitles, video, 150
  ASCII, 152
suburbs, trends, 348
summarization, navigation, 221
Sun Microsystems
  animation, 148
  destination pages, 244
  international user testing, 342
  intranets, 265
  L-shaped navigation, 207, 212
  Starfire, 137–138, 150
SunWeb
  intranet designs, 282–283
  intranets, testing, 291
super-users for language choice, 325, 330
synthesizers, 302

T

T1 lines, 48, 364
Tbid, navigation, 192
telemarketers, 367
telephones
  trends, 349

usability consultants
  finding, 320, 333
    highlights tapes, 340
    language gaps, 333–334
Usability Engineering, 395
usability labs for international user testing,
  339–340
usability studies
  boolean searches, 227
  content, 100
    humor, 101
  human factors research, 42
  link colors, 64
  modem users, 48
  monitors, 286
  navigation, 189, 202
  navigation options, 206
  queries, 233
  reading large amounts of text, 141
  reading online, 101, 103
  reading URLs, 248
  scannability, 104
  scrolling, 112, 115
  searches, 224
  speeding up downloads, 42
  terminology, 188
  writing for the Web, 104
usability testing. *See* international user testing
Usable Web database, Instone, Keith, 394
user interface designs, general principle for, 22
User Interface Engineering, study on link
  colors, 64
user interface specifications, 28
user-contributed content, 256
user-controlled navigation, 214, 217
  links, 218
  sitemaps, 221
user interface specifications, 28
users
  cognitive disabilities, 309–310
  difficulty with motor skills, 309
  disabilities. *See* disabilities
  distribution of Web users by nationality,
    314
  dyslexia, 311
  font preferences, 29

hearing-impaired users, 308
informing of long multimedia
  downloads, 134
Internet, subjective satisfaction, 270
intranets, testing, 289–290
link-dominant users, 224
mixed-behavior users, 224
navigation, 25
outbound links, informing of, 69
search-dominant users, 224–225
speech-impaired users, 308–309
spelling disabilities, 311
statistics of those who use the Web, 348
visually-impaired, 302
ALT attributes, 303, 305–307
  described images, 305
  fonts, 302
  scannability, 302
  search engines, 303
why they scan, 106

V

video, 149
  audio quality, 150
  distributing over Internet, 374
  special considerations, 150
  streaming video versus downloadable
    video, 150–152
  subtitles, 150
    ASCII, 152
video clips, integrating, 374
videotaping, field studies, 292
virtual reality, 3D, 157
virtual URLs, archival URLs, 250
The Visual Display of Quantitative Information,
  27, 160
visualizing three-dimensional structures,
  animation, 146
visually-impaired users, 302
  ALT attributes, 303, 305, 307
  described images, 305
  fonts, 302
  multimedia, 155
  nested headings, 104
  scannability, 302
  search engines, 303

Colophon

The preliminary design direction for *Designing Web Usability* began as a phone conversation between Indianapolis, Indiana and Ashfield, Massachusetts. The first pass of the design was created in Microsoft Word, and snail-mailed to Indianapolis.

The book was then layed out and produced using Microsoft Word, Adobe Photoshop, Adobe Illustrator, and QuarkXPress on a variety of systems, including a Macintosh G3 in Los Angeles, California. With the exception of the initial design pass, all files used for the final design—both text and images—were transferred via email or ftp.

All of the body text was set in the Bembo family, and all headings, sidebars, and figure captions were set in the Frutiger family. Additionally, Helvetica was used for HTML code, and the Symbol and Zapf Dingbats typefaces were used throughout for special symbols and bullets.

The digital color palette for the interior included the following TruMatch colors: 17-a, 17-e, 32-a, 34-a7, 34-f, 8-a, and 8-f. The cover palette was composed of PMS 1375, 289, and 375.

After more than two years in the making, *Designing Web Usability* was printed on 70# Citation Web Matte, with a trim size of 6.75"×9.5", at R.R. Donnelley & Sons in Roanoke, Virginia. Prepress consisted of PostScript computer-to-plate technology (filmless process).